AGGREGATION, CONSUMPTION AND TRADE

**Advanced Studies in Theoretical and Applied Econometrics**

**Volume 27**

---



*The titles published in this series are listed at the end of this volume.*

# Aggregation, Consumption and Trade

## Essays in Honor of H.S. Houthakker

edited by

Louis Phlips
*European University Institute, Florence, Italy*

and

Lester D. Taylor
*University of Arizona, Tucson, AZ, U.S.A.*

SPRINGER-SCIENCE+BUSINESS MEDIA, B.V.

**Library of Congress Cataloging-in-Publication Data**

Aggregation, consumption and trade : essays in honor of H.S.
Houthakker / edited by Louis Phlips and Lester D. Taylor.
p. cm. -- (Advanced studies in theoretical and applied
econometrics ; v. 27)
ISBN 978-94-010-4790-6 ISBN 978-94-011-1795-1 (eBook)
DOI 10.1007/978-94-011-1795-1
1. Consumption (Economics) 2. Futures market. I. Houthakker,
Hendrik Samuel. II. Phlips, Louis. III. Taylor, Lester D.
IV. Series.
HB801.A35 1992
339.4'7--dc20 92-33114

ISBN 978-94-010-4790-6

*Printed on acid-free paper*

## TABLE OF CONTENTS

| | | |
|---|---|---|
| CONTRIBUTORS | | vii |
| INTRODUCTION | | 1 |
| **Paul A. Samuelson** | The Fitness Maximized by the Classical Canonical Economy: A Theme from Houthakker and R.A. Fisher | 9 |
| **Anton B. Barten** | Income and Price Sensitivity in Consumer Demand Analysis | 21 |
| **Birgit Grodal** and **Werner Hildenbrand** | Cross-Section Engel Curves, Expenditure Distributions and the "Law of Demand" | 37 |
| **John Muellbauer** and **Panos Pashardes** | Tests of Dynamic Specification and Homogeneity in a Demand System | 55 |
| **Robert A. Pollak** and **Terence J. Wales** | Specification and Estimation of Dynamic Demand Systems | 99 |
| **R. Robert Russell** | Remarks on the Power of Non-Parametric Tests of Consumer-Theory Hypotheses | 121 |
| **Lester D. Taylor** | Brain Structure and Consumption Dynamics | 137 |
| **Lester G. Telser** | Corners in Organized Futures Markets | 159 |
| **Peter Møllgaard** and **Louis Phlips** | Oil Futures and Strategic Stocks at Sea | 169 |
| **Stephen P. Magee** | The Effect of Income and Prices on Protection and Rent Seeking in the U.S., 1950 - 1986 | 197 |
| INTRODUCTION: | Four Unpublished Papers by Hendrik S. Houthakker | 217 |
| **H.S. Houthakker** | Are There Laws of Consumption? | 219 |
| **H.S. Houthakker** and **Suresh D. Tendulkar** | The Dynamics of Total Consumption and Savings | 225 |
| **H.S. Houthakker** | On a Class of Dynamic Demand Functions | 247 |
| **H.S. Houthakker** | Proposed Technique for Estimating Demand Functions from Time Series | 255 |
| PUBLICATIONS OF HENDRIK S. HOUTHAKKER | | 257 |

## CONTRIBUTORS

Anton P. Barten
*Professor of Economics*
*Katholicke Universiteit of Leuven and*
*C.O.R.E.*

Birgit Grodal
*Professor of Economics*
*University of Copenhagen*

Werner Hildenbrand
*Professor of Economics*
*University of Bonn*

Hendrik S. Houthakker
*Henry Lee Professor of Economics*
*Harvard University*

Stephen P. Magee
*Professor of Economics*
*and Professor of Finance*
*University of Texas*
*Austin*

Peter Møllgaard
*Research Assistant*
*European University Institute*
*Florence*

John Muellbauer
*Official Fellow in Economics*
*Nuffield College, Oxford*

Panos Pashardes
*Institute for Fiscal Studies*
*London*

Louis Phlips
*Professor of Economics*
*European University Institute*
*Florence*

Robert A. Pollak
*Professor of Economics*
*University of Washington*

R. Robert Russell
*Professor of Economics*
*University of California*
*Riverside*

Paul A. Samuelson
*Institute Professor of Economics Emeritus*
*M.I.T.*

Lester D. Taylor
*Professor of Economics*
*and Professor of Agricultural Economics*
*University of Arizona*

Lester G. Telser
*Professor of Economics*
*University of Chicago*

Suresh D. Tendulkar
*Professor of Economics*
*Delhi School of Economics*

Terence J. Wales
*Professor of Economics*
*University of British Columbia*

## INTRODUCTION

The essays in this volume are dedicated to H.S. Houthakker on the occasion of his 68th birthday. Holland over the years has produced a disproportionate share of the world's great economists -- Jan Tinbergen, Tjalling Koopmans, Henri Theil . . . and Hendrik Samuel Houthakker! Henk Houthakker started young. His first published paper (in english), when he was just 26, was an immediate classic. In the words of Paul Samuelson (*Economica*, 1950, p. 356): "A chapter in the history of utility theory has now been brought to a close by Mr. Houthakker's important discussion of integrability." And there is no slackening of activity or enthusiasm in his 68th year.

During the 42 years since he revealed the importance of the Strong Axiom of Revealed Preference in the integrability of demand functions, his interests have ranged widely in economic theory, applied econometrics, and economic policy, and his scholarship has enriched a large number of fields. While his work in demand theory is what he is justly most famous for, he has made seminal contributions in at least five other fields in economics and operations research: Aggregation (1955), futures markets (1959, 1968), agricultural policy (1967), international trade (with S.P. Magee, 1969), and mathematical programming (1960).[1]

In pure demand theory, the list of Henk's contributions includes: The problem of integrability (1950), the analysis of quality variations [1952 (with S.J. Prais), 1952-53], the structure of preferences (1960, 1965), and the theory of rationing (with J. Tobin, 1950-51, 1952). In applied demand and consumption analysis, his contributions include: The analysis of family budgets [1952, 1955 (with S.J. Prais)], consumption dynamics (with L.D. Taylor, 1966, 1970), tests of the Weak Axiom of Revealed Preference (1963), plus numerous empirical analyses of the demand for particular commodities [1951, 1960 (with J. Haldi), 1973 (with P.K. Verleger and D.V. Sheehan), 1979]. In addition, Henk has been a pioneer in cross-country comparisons of family budgets (1957), saving-income relationships (1961, 1965), demand elasticities (1965), and variations in tastes (1963). He was one of the first to program an electronic computer to estimate empirical demand and consumption functions (with J.A.C. Brown and S.J. Prais, 1953), and he pioneered the use of purchasing-power-parity price indices in analyzing variations in tastes across countries and in testing the Weak Axiom of Revealed Preference (1963).

Henk has won a number of important prizes and honors during his career. He is a member of the National Academy of Sciences and a long-time Fellow of the Econometric Society. He has received the two highest honors conferred by the American Economic Association, the John Bates Clark medal in 1963 and was elected a Distinguished Fellow in 1990.[2] He is a past president of the Econometric Society (1967) and a past vice-president of the American Economic Association (1972). He was a member of the President's Council of Economic Advisers in 1968-70, after having been a senior economist on the CEA staff in 1966-67. He has received honorary doctorates from the University of Amsterdam (where he did his

---

[1] A listing of Henk's publications is given at the end of the volume.

[2] See Pollak (*Journal of Economic Perspectives*,) Spring 1990, pp. 141-156.



*L. Phlips and L.D. Taylor (eds.), Aggregation, Consumption and Trade,* 1–8.

graduate work) and the University of Fribourg, and he is a corresponding member of the Royal Netherlands Academy of Sciences. Finally, he is an Adjunct Scholar of the American Enterprise Institute and a public director of the New York Futures Market.

The eleven papers comprising this volume attest to the tremendous originality and richness of Henk's contributions to economic science. Apart from some very general suggestions regarding topic, the only real instruction given authors was for them to contribute what they thought appropriate. Not surprisingly, six of the papers relate to consumption and demand. Of the other five papers, two are on futures markets and one each on economic growth and international trade and policy. All of the contributions either originate from a remark or result of Henk's, or else explore or extend one of his long-standing interests, such as the structure of preferences, consumption dynamics, futures markets, or international trade and policy. Paul Samuelson's piece on economic growth has perhaps the most unusual point of departure, for it takes its cue in a remark in Henk's paper on speciation and the division of labor (1956), which is probably Henk's least conventional paper in terms of subject matter.

The format of the volume is as follows: The volume leads off with Paul Samuelson's paper on economic growth, followed by the six papers which relate to consumption and demand. These are followed by the Telser and Møllgaard-Phlips papers on futures markets, followed by Stephen Magee's paper on international trade and policy. This brings us to Henk's own section, which includes a listing of Henk's publications, together with four of his previously unpublished papers and notes. The first of the papers, "Are There Laws of Consumption?" was his presidential address to the Econometric Society delivered at the winter meetings of the Econometric Society in Washington, D.C. in December 1967. The second paper, written with Suresh D. Tendulkar (now Professor of Economics at the Delhi School of Economics), "The Dynamics of Total Consumption And Saving," was completed in 1967 shortly after publication of the first edition of **Consumer Demand in the United States** (CDUS, 1966). The two notes, written in the early 1960s, relate to the origins of CDUS.

We now turn to a brief synopsis of each of the papers in the volume. As already noted, Paul Samuelson, in "The Fitness Maximized by the Classical Canonical Economy: A Theme From Houthakker and R.A. Fisher," builds upon a remark in Henk's 1956 biology paper in which he refers to the "fundamental" law of genetics of R.A. Fisher by which a species paradoxically grows in fitness up to the point of extinction. Samuelson's concern in his paper is with the "something" that was implicitly being maximized in the growth models of Smith and Ricardo. Using the *canonical classical growth model* that he developed in a paper in 1978, Samuelson defines a fitness function for a classical economy (*i.e.*, one with subsistence wages and profits) in terms of the system's Virtual Rent (defined as "total product left over after the factors of labor and capital were to be paid their equilibrium subsistence wage and profit rates"). Samuelson shows that the canonical classical economy, when buffeted by an exogenous shock, converges asymptotically to a unique equilibrium state that maximizes the system's Vertual Rent.

We now come to the six papers that relate to consumption and demand. Although the papers range over a variety of topics -- consumption dynamics (Muellbauer & Pashardes, Pollak & Wales, Taylor), non-parametric tests of the Weak Axiom of Revealed Preference (Russell), cross-section Engel curves and the Law of Demand (Grodal & Hildenbrand), structure of preferences (Barten) -- each is on a topic identified by Henk as needful of further research in his authoritative survey of consumption theory published in *Econometrica* in 1961. After a masterful presentation in the first part of his survey of the (then) present state of demand theory, Henk turned to a number of unresolved questions and issues, including the form of the Engel curve, aggregation over consumers with different tastes, the nature of substitution, probabilistic preferences, lexicographical preferences, and the dynamical effects of durable goods and habit formation. Each paper involves a theme from this list.

The paper by Anton P. Barten, "Income and Price Sensitivity in Consumer Demand Analysis," is concerned with the structure of preferences and the interactions between goods. The traditional way of characterizing interaction is in terms of the sign of the compensated cross-price derivative. Two goods are judged to be substitutes if the compensated cross-price derivative is positive, and complements if this derivative is negative. One of the problems with the traditional approach is that it does not handle in a satisfactory way the perfect substitutability of a good for itself, for the negativeness of the compensated own-price derivative implies that a good is a complement to itself rather than a substitute. In place of using Slutsky coefficients to characterize interactions between goods, Barten proposes the use of Allais interaction coefficients. Allais interaction coefficients have the important property that goods are indeed characterized as being substitutes for themselves. Allais coefficients also allow for a more satisfactory characterization of the strength of a consumer's attachment to a good. Barten establishes the links between the Allais coefficients and the parameters of the demand functions. These links are used to study the consequences for income and price sensitivity of deviations from the situation of independence (*i.e.*, no interactions among goods).

The next two papers, "Tests of Dynamic Specification and Homogeneity in a Demand System" by John Muellbauer and Panos Pashardes and "Specification and Estimation of Dynamic Demand Systems" by Robert A. Pollak and Terence J. Wales, entail the specification and estimation of a system of dynamic demand functions. Muellbauer and Pashardes dynamize the Almost-Ideal-Demand-System (AI) of Deaton and Muellbauer (1980), while Pollak and Wales explore dynamizations of the quadratic expenditure system (QES), the generalized translog (GTL), the linear expenditure system (LES), and the basic translog (BTL). The LES and BTL are well-known, frequently estimated demand systems, while the QES was proposed and estimated by Howe, Pollak, and Wales (1979) and the GTL by Pollak and Wales (1980).

There are two basic approaches to the specification of dynamic demand models. The first, which is the approach followed by Houthakker and Taylor (1966, 1970), is through the inclusion of state variables either in the utility function or directly in the demand functions. The state variables affect marginal utilities and in turn are affected by current consumption. The second approach, which is the one pursued by both Muellbauer & Pashardes and Pollak & Wales, is through the inclusion of past consumption in the utility function or the demand functions, so that past consumption affects current consumption directly, rather than through the intermediary of state variables. Since the state variables in the Houthakker-Taylor approach are in general unobservable, the two approaches are operationally very similar, for estimation in both cases usually involves a distributed lag on past consumption. The most important difference between the two approaches relates to interpretation. The second approach sees habit formation as representing endogenous taste change, whereas Houthakker and Taylor view the state variables as simply additional arguments in the utility function.

Although the estimation of dynamic demand systems is common to both papers, each has its own focus. Muellbauer & Pashardes are especially interested in the homogeneity postulate of traditional demand theory and are concerned with showing that the frequent rejection of this postulate in static models reflects misspecification of underlying dynamics. Pollak & Wales, on the other hand, explore two different dynamic structures which allow parameters of the demand system to vary systematically with past consumption. Pollak & Wales also carry out a series of tests which establishes a ranking among the four functional forms considered.

The paper by Birgit Grodal and Werner Hildenbrand, "Cross-Section Engel Curves, Expenditure Distributions and the 'Law of Demand'," involves several of Henk's long standing interests: The analysis of family budgets, aggregation, the form of Engel curves, and the distribution of income. Narrowly, the concern of Grobal & Hildenbrand is showing the roles that the shape of the various cross-section Engel curves and the shape of the expenditure distribution play in determining the Law of Demand for the market demand function in a large consumption sector. More generally, the paper is the latest from an impressive program of research into the fundamental nature of market demand functions that has engaged Hildenbrand and collaborators since the early 1980s.[3]

Over the years, applied demand analysis has played an uneasy game with aggregation. In general, there is no better joining of theory and application in all of economics than in demand analysis, but the theory is a theory of individual behavior, whereas empirical analysis of demand systems nearly invariably uses market data. The analyses of Muellbauer & Pashardes and Pollak & Wales in this volume are obvious cases in point. The standard has been to avoid problems of aggregation by appealing to Marshall's notion of a "representative consumer." But this is changing. Thanks to new approaches to aggregation that have been developed by Stoker (1986) and others, it is now possible to approach market demand functions in a thoroughly rigorous fashion and to investigate how the distribution of tastes and expenditure affects the shape of aggregate Engel curves and price elasticities of demand. In their paper in this volume, Grodal & Hildenbrand assume a population of identical consumers except for income and explore how the shape of Engel curves and the market Law of Demand are affected by the distribution of expenditure.[4]

In "Remarks on the Power of Non-Parametric Tests of Consumer-Theory Hypotheses," R. Robert Russell discusses how non-parametric methods pioneered by Afriat (1967), but clearly anticipated by Henk in his 1963 paper, have been developed into a powerful tool for testing the axiomatic foundations of consumer theory. While he is supportive of the approach, Russell expresses skepticism regarding the power of the non-parametric tests, given the data with which economists have to work. Russell is particularly concerned about the necessary conditions for consistent aggregation across individual preferences. Only by getting these conditions squared away will one be able to interpret rejection of the Weak Axiom of Revealed Preference with aggregate data as evidence pertaining to individual irrationality as opposed to failure of maintained assumptions concerning aggregation.

In "Brain Structure and Consumption Dynamics," Lester D. Taylor explores the topic that has motivated his 30 years of collaboration with Henk, namely, the nature of consumption dynamics. Taylor approaches the origin of consumption dynamics in terms of the organization of the human brain. Drawing on recent advances in the neurosciences, Taylor postulates a tri-level hierarchical brain structure, in which each level can initiate consumption activity. The first- (or lowest) level brain is responsible for maintaining the autonomic processes (breathing, heartbeat, *etc.*) at a satisfactory level and is capable of triggering corrective consumption activity whenever actual states of these processes deviate sufficiently from the levels desired. The second- (or intermediate) level brain is capable of learning from experience and has the capacity to initiate a wide range of consumption activities both on its own account and in

---

[3] See Hildenbrand (1983, 1991), Hildenbrand and Hildenbrand (1986), and Härdle, Hildenbrand, and Jerison (1991).

[4] The analysis is extended to a population with varying tastes as well as incomes in Härdle, Hildenbrand, and Jerison (1991).

response to signals from the first-level brain. Many addicting activities are controlled by this brain. The third- (or highest) level brain is what we ordinarily think of as the human brain. It is capable of abstract reasoning and can also form expectations. It can monitor actions of the lower-level brains and has the capacity (at least on occasion) of countermanding certain of these actions, often through the setting-up of anti-markets of the type studied by Schelling (1978). One of Taylor's principal results is to show that essentially all of the standard dynamical models of consumption (state-and flow-adjustment, error-correction, *etc.*) can emanate from activities of the second-level brain.

Despite the fact that the bulk of Henk's research has related to consumption and demand, it has always seemed that the topics that most stir his interest are futures and oil markets. Accordingly, it is fitting that the next two papers, "Corners in Organized Futures Markets" by Lester G. Telser and "Oil Futures and Strategic Stocks at Sea" by Peter Møllgaard and Louis Phlips, are on these topics. Telser provides a careful statement of the conditions under which profitable corners can occur in an organized futures market. His account is extremely readable and is reminiscent in this regard of Henk's contribution on the scope and limits of futures trading to the Haley Festschrift (1959).

The paper by Møllgaard & Phlips is concerned with the organization of the market for North Sea crude oil. This market consists of a spot market, a futures market, and a 15-day forward market. The three markets are analyzed in a three-stage game in which concentration increases at each stage. In the first stage, the International Petroleum Exchange is modeled as a thick futures market. This market is also used to hedge the uncertain outcome of the 15-day forward market, which is modeled in the second stage. In the 15-day forward market, a small club of traders enter futures contracts knowing that this will affect the storage decision and thereby the spot price profile. The third stage then models the spot market as a two-period duopoly with inventories. A principal conclusion of the authors is that positions taken on the IPE are driven by four motives: speculative, strategic, and hedging motives that also apply to the 15-day forward market, plus an additional speculative motive that is geared to the non-unique outcomes of the 15-day game.

Henk's 1969 paper with Stephen P. Magee remains a standard source for price and income elasticities for international trade. In that paper, Houthakker and Magee found an asymmetry in the income elasticities of demand for U.S. Trade: The income elasticity was larger for U.S. imports than for U.S. exports. This led to the prediction of a secular decline in the U.S. trade balance, and represents one of the most accurate predictions ever to come out of an econometric model. In the final paper in this volume, Stephen Magee, in "The Effect of Income and Prices on Protection and Rent Seeking in the U.S., 1950-1986," uses a politico-economic general equilibrium model of endogenous protection developed by Young and Magee (1986) to explore changes in U.S. tariffs, export subsidies, and simulated levels of lobbying over trade policy between two years, 1950 and 1986. An important implication of Magee's model is that protection can go either up or down in response to an income-induced increase in imports relative to exports depending upon the cause in the growth in income. If labor, the factor benefiting from protection, grows relatively faster than capital, protection would increase. Magee finds, however, that capital grew faster than labor from 1950 to 1986, so that U.S. protection in fact declined because of income growth. The analysis also suggests that protection declined because factor intensities of production got closer together, making protection a more potent redistributive tool. For the economy as a whole, there was a decline in resources devoted to rent seeking over trade policy.

Before turning this volume over to readers, one more of Henk's contributions should be noted. Henk was editor of *The Review of Economics & Statistics* for 21 years. His was a devoted stewardship. He maintained and enhanced the *Review's* tradition of publishing high-quality policy-oriented empirical research. As editor, his instincts as an econometrician were always at the fore: The question had to be relevant, the theory sound, and econometrics state-of-the-art. His years at the helm of the *Review* were clearly costly to his own scholarship, but with the burden of editorship lifted the energy and intellect that made him mature at 26, but young at 68, can once again flourish without constraint.

*Louis Phlips*
*Fiesole, Italy*

*Lester D. Taylor*
*Tucson, Arizona*

*May 1992*

**Acknowledgements**

We are indebted to Gloria Gerrig of Harvard University for skillful file pilferation, and to Judy Engel and Julia Miesle of the University of Arizona for preparation of the manuscript.

## REFERENCES


Deaton, A. and J. Muellbauer (1980), "An Almost Ideal Demand System," *American Economic Review*, Vol. 70, No. 3, June 1980, pp. 312-326.

Härdle, E., Hildenbrand, W. and M. Jerison (1991), "Empirical Evidence on the Law of Demand," *Econometrica*, Vol. 59, No. 6, November 1991, pp. 1525-1550.

Hildenbrand, W. (1983), "On the Law of Demand," *Econometrica*, Vol. 51, No. 4, July 1983, pp. 997-1019.

Hildenbrand, K. and W. Hildenbrand (1986), "On the Mean Income Effect: A Data Analysis of the U.K. Family Expenditure Survey," in *Contributions to Mathematical Economics, in Honor of Gérard Debreu*, ed. by W. Hildenbrand and A. Mas-Colell, North Holland Publishing Co., Amsterdam.

Pollak, R.A. (1990), "Distinguished Fellow: Houthakker's Contributions to Economics," *Journal of Economic Perspectives*, Vol. 4, No. 2, Spring 1990, pp. 141 - 156.

Samuelson, P.A. (1950), "The Problem of Integrability in Utility Theory, *Economica*, N.S. Vol. 17, November 1950, pp. 355-385.

Schelling, T.C. (1978), "Economics and the Art of Self-Management," *American Economic Review*, Vol. 68, No. 2, May 1978, pp. 290-294.

Stoker, T.M. (1986), "Consistent Estimation of Scaled Coefficients," *Econometrica*, Vol. 54, No. 6, November 1986, pp. 1461-1481.

I still remember the day when -- while at Fribourg University, Switzerland -- I came across Henk's paper on "Additive Preferences." It produced a shock. For years, I had been wondering -- and turning in circles -- about how to define an "industry" or a "relevant market" in antitrust cases. Rightly or wrongly, I came to the conclusion that a utility tree might give the answer: If one were able to climb high enough in such a tree, wouldn't the smallest branches correspond to what consumers think of as the relevant market for a commodity? A few months later I turned up in Henk's office in Cambridge and told him bluntly that I wanted to "compute a utility tree." Instead of laughing at me, Henk took me seriously. He had just finished estimating the Houthakker-Taylor dynamic demand functions and said: "Why don't you have a look at the variance-covariance matrix of our residuals? Do you know what principal components are?" (Of course, I didn't.) This was going to be the start of 15 years of happy research on applied demand analysis. The end result was what I think of as my "red" book, a set of variations on a theme by Houthakker and Taylor.

I am proud to have been associated with the preparation of this *Festschrift*. Happy birthday!

*Louis Phlips*

During all the time that Henk and I have spent together since we first met at Harvard in the fall of 1960, the remark of his that most sticks in mind is one that he made to me as I was about to meet my first class in September 1962: "Never be afraid of being wrong in front of a class." Harvard at the time was not noted for preparing its new Ph.D.s for the classroom, and his was the only counsel that I received. Short as it was, the remark reflected the insight and humility of a true scholar and gentleman, and I have never forgotten it.

For 32 years, Henk has been a teacher, mentor, collaborator, and friend, for which I am extremely grateful. Thank you, and *gefeliciteerd met je verjaardag!*

*Lester D. Taylor*

# THE FITNESS MAXIMIZED BY THE CLASSICAL CANONICAL ECONOMY: A THEME FROM HOUTHAKKER AND R.A. FISHER

PAUL A. SAMUELSON
*Massachusetts Institute of Technology*
*77 Massachusetts Avenue, E52-383C*
*Cambridge, Massachusetts 02139*
*U.S.A.*

ABSTRACT. Stimulated by a 1956 biology paper of Hendrik Houthakker that mentions the R.A. Fisher paradox in which allegedly a species ever grows in fitness up to the instant of its extinction, I here define a new fitness function for classical economics, namely the system's Virtual Rent. Using my 1978 Canonical Classical Growth Model (for a subsistence-wage-and-subsistence-profit-rate system), I specify for it a Liapunov function of Virtual Rent that is shown to necessarily increase on each growth trajectory. No paradoxes are entailed, since *exogenous* shocks are permitted to raise or lower Rent.

## 1. Portrait of a Scholar

Originality, depth, and versatility --those are the marks of a master scholar. Hendrik Houthakker started off with a bang: A big bang. Reckoning stages of life in fractions of a century -- as I have come to do -- this young and unknown Dutchman resolved a long-standing challenge before he reached his second quarter century. Houthakker (1950) proved that the Strong Axiom of Revealed Preference -- whereby no chain of situations could occur in which "B was revealed to be worse than A, C revealed to be worse than D,...Z to be worse than Y, and yet A showed itself worse than Z" -- did indeed suffice to rule out non-integrability of preferences.

In England, if you were a Triple First at Oxbridge, no matter if afterwards you remained a curate in remote Devon, your reputation was made for life. So it is for the first scholar to prove the ergodic theorem or, heaven forbid, refute the Riemann hypothesis. Hendrik Houthakker, however, could not stop at the beginning and keep creativity down. Avoiding the well-trodden paths, he has again and again struck out in his chosen directions. I have particularly admired his theoretical and empirical pioneering, with James Tobin, in the analysis of postwar rationing [Houthakker and Tobin (1951, 1952)]. It was his *Econometrica* formulation of duality theory for demand under constraint that reawoke my fascination with that topic [Houthakker (1960), Samuelson (1953, 1960, 1965)]. Even old subjects like Ricardian comparative advantage and Purchasing-Power-Parity reflect with new lights from his pen [Houthakker (1962, 1976; 1978)]. And of course there are his important researches on normal backwardation in commodities futures, on durable-goods demand, and on energy scarcity.



*L. Phlips and L.D. Taylor (eds.), Aggregation, Consumption and Trade,* 9–19.

I peruse hundreds of scientific articles, benefitting from almost all of them -- a remarkable testament to the cleanness of refereeing in economics, and an agreeable contrast with the sad tales about plagiarism and experimental fraud in contemporaneous areas of biological research. But rarely do I consciously envy a paper, wishing that I might have conceived it. Houthakker is one of the narrow circle of writers who especially captures my admiration, which is all the more remarkable in that I am ideologically usually more of a bleeding-heart liberal than he is. An instance is Houthakker (1955), in which he analyzes a production model that involves fixed coefficients at every point in space but whose envelope-integrals reproduce for totals of inputs and output smooth relations of the neoclassical type. [All this is an original development of Ricardo's model of land economics, and is in the same spirit as the paradigm of Bensusan Butt (1960) in macro growth theory.]

No need to go on with unfaint praises. As homage to Houthakker, I want to pick up on a sentence of his that I read in a working paper he gave at a summer Stanford workshop in Tokyo of the 1950s. The paper was on evolution and antedated the post-sociobiology fads among economists. See Houthakker (1956) for what I believe is the final draft of the Japanese working paper.

The words that caught my eye are found in Houthakker (1956, p. 186):

> ...biologists tend to use the word "advantage" quite freely, and usually in the sense of something which promotes survival. This may easily lead to paradoxical results; thus R.A. Fisher [1930] in his *Genetical Theory of Natural Selection* maintains that evolution leads to an increase in fitness, which he defines as the chances of survival, from which it follows, oddly enough, that a species has the best chance of survival just before it becomes extinct.

The last view, attributed to Fisher, did seem to me paradoxical. After 1970, when the Swedish Royal Academy of Sciences bestowed on me the illusion of omniscience and infallibility, I determined to study enough biology to master Fisher's "Fundamental Theorem on Natural Selection," which its founder (1930, p.39) modestly equates with the Second Law of Thermodynamics, each holding "supreme position" (respectively in the biological sciences and among the laws of [physical] nature). I should confess at the beginning that Fisher's exposition is so non-optimal as to leave his interpreters in disagreement as to what he meant by his Fundamental Law. (Indeed, the distinguished geneticist James F. Crow confided to me that, only *before* he understood Fisher, did he regard the theorem as *fundamental.*)

There is no way that I could, in limited space, give economist readers any feel for Fisher's so-called Fundamental theorem. It will suffice if I relegate to a footnote one trivial instance of it,[1] and merely sum up its relevance for the present purpose as follows:

Fisher (1930) and Sewall Wright (1971) sometimes can analyze the differential equations of genetic demography with the help of Liapunov-like functions:

(1a) $$dx_j/dt = f^j(x_1,\ldots,x_n), \quad j = 1,2,\ldots,n,$$

where the $f^j$ functions are such that there exists a non-negative Liapunov $L(x_1,\ldots,x_n)$ function such that

(1b) $$dL(x_1,\ldots,x_n)/dt = \sum_j [\partial L(x_1,\ldots,x_n)/\partial x_j] f^j(x_1,\ldots,x_n) < 0$$

(1c) $L(x_1,\ldots,x_n) = 0$ only for $(x_1^*,\ldots,x_n^*)$, the root of

$$\partial L(x_1,\ldots,x_n)/\partial x_j = 0, \; j = 1,\ldots,n$$

and of

(1d) $$f^j(x_1,\ldots,x_n) = 0,$$

so that

(1e) $$\lim_{t\to\infty}[x_j(t), L(t)] = [x_j^*, 0].$$

Actually, Fisher has not even fabricated a genuine paradox concerning fitness's growing until just before the species goes poof and disappears. If the above system refers to n=6 and ecological equilibrium between the number of genotypes of two diploid species, what destroys the old $x^*$ equilibrium is some new exogenous mutation or some new exogenous change in the environment: After such a perturbation, any possible *old* relation between genetic variance and growth in fitness is impulsively abrogated -- leaving no paradox and only the malaise of an obscurely written treatise.

---

[1] Imagine two subsets of a species, each growing at exponential rates $a_1$ and $a_2$: $a_1 > a_2$, $N(t) = \sum_1^2 (c_j e^{a_j t})$. Then Fisherine "fitness" is defined as $N'(t)/N(t) = m(t) = \sum_1^2 (c_j e^{a_j t}) a_j / N(t)$ = Mean <a's>. By tautological differentiation,

$$m'(t) = \left[\sum_1^3 (c_j e^{a_j t}) a_j^2 / N(t)\right] - \left[\sum_1^2 (c_j e^{a_j t})/N(t)\right]^2$$
$$= \mathrm{Var}\ \langle a's \rangle$$

The equality of the Change in Total Growth Rate to the Variance of the Part's Growth Rates is trivial next to the Second Law of Thermodynamics and, in this form, doesn't even involve biology! See Nagylaki [1991] for more meaningful versions of Fisherine selection.

My present analysis discovers exactly what it is that the classical canonical growth model of Ricardo -- and of Smith, Mill, and Marx -- can be conceived of as maximizing. As these writers dimly glimpsed, some variant of land rent is maximized in such a subsistence-wage-and-subsistence-profit model. Here our mathematics pins down precisely what definition of "rent" is teleologically made a maximum by the classical behavior equations, both (1) *ultimately* after any technical innovation or any change in saving and procreating parameters and (2) *at every time instant* during the transition period to long-run equilibrium.

The novelty is in identifying and specifying the existent Liapunov function for which the canonical classical dynamical paths are gradient climbing motions.

## 2. What the Classical System Maximizes

When Columbia University celebrated its Two-Hundredth birthday in 1954, Sir Dennis Robertson spoke from the text: "What Does the Economist Economize?" Few guessed in advance that the Robertsonian minimand was Love, which being so rare needed to be husbanded so preciously.

Smith and Ricardo were hardheaded sons of the Enlightenment with DNA that runneth not over in sentimentality. Their shared growth paradigm did however act as if to maximize something. One of the virtues of the *canonical classical growth model* (of Samuelson, 1978) was that it encapsulated the core common to Smith, Ricardo, Mill, and Marx [as Samuel Hollander (1980, 1987) has extensively documented]. As a further virtue, the canonical classical model is shown here to identify just how the old notion -- that technological progress and supply adjustments of population and capital act telelogically to maximize "total rent" -- needs to be sharpened to the *maximization in both the longest run* and also *in the transitions to equilibrium* of "Virtual Rent as total product left over after the factors of labor and capital were to be paid their equilibrium real subsistence wage and profit rates." (The *exact* wording is vital.)

It will shorten the exposition if we contemplate classical subsistence-wage of labor and classical subsistence-profit-rate grafted on to a regular 3-factor technology of post-1848 type. Motivated readers can duplicate *all* of the present qualitative features in a discrete-activities technology of the von Neumann and Sraffa type that early writers could handle by numerical examples. (What is special about the present model is its restriction to the axiom that there exists but a *single* producible good that can serve as an input.)

## 3. The Canonical Growth Model

Assume a homogeneous land of fixed positive supply, $\bar{T}$. Assume a homogeneous labor supply of L; the growth rate of population is dL/dt or $\dot{L}$. The supply of the produced good is K, with net investment or capital accumulation of dK/dt or $\dot{K}$.

The totals of the three factors, $(\bar{T},L,K)$ or $(V_0,V_1,V_2)$, produce society's output(s), which includes both a consumption good like corn and net capital formation like $\dot{K}$ or $\dot{V}_2$. In inessential aggregation à la Ramsey [1928], we write

$$\text{consumption + net c.f.} = C + \dot{V}_2 = Q(\bar{V}_0,V_1,V_2). \tag{2}$$

The real return of land is rent, written as R or $w_0$. The real wage of labor is $w_1$. The rate of profit (or of interest, they are the same *sans* uncertainty) is $w_2$. Both a 1776 Smith and a 1900 Wicksell would expect a factor's return of $w_i$ to be depressed when its supply of $V_i$ is higher. How does a change in $V_j$ affect the $w_i$ return of $V_i$? The 1900 answer would be more definite and catholic than the answer of 1776, 1817, 1848, or 1867. By this century economists realize that more $V_0$ of land could possibly *lower* labor's $w_1$ wage if land and labor, instead of being "complementary", were "competing factors"; and so forth for any one i and j pairing of the three factors. Classical writers seem implicitly to assume all three factors to be complements. More labor tilling the same corn acres are supposed to induce higher land rent of $w_0$; when doses of capital and labor have more acres to work on, their composite return goes up; the $w_1$ wage could be forced way down if needed capital is short enough in supply; etc. Actually though, there are plenty of passages in the classic texts where horses and men are strongly competitive in their factor returns, and the same can occur for land and produced goods. Here I therefore admit all feasible patterns of complementarity. See Samuelson (1991) for a modern version of the canonical model.

What is peculiarly *non*-neoclassical is the following subsistence-driven supplies of $V_1$ and $V_2$, with $dV_i/dt = \dot{V}_i$ each being a function of $w_i - \bar{w}_i$ deviations, the differences between market returns and needed subsistence returns specifiable as $(\bar{w}_1, \bar{w}_2)$,

$$\text{(3)} \qquad \dot{V}_i / V_i = g_i f_i[w_i - \bar{w}_i], \quad i = 1,2$$

$$\text{(3a)} \qquad g_i > 0, \ f_i[0] = 0, \ f_i'[0] = 1 \text{ by convention}$$

$$\text{(3b)} \qquad f_i'[x] > 0 \text{ so that } x f_i[x] > 0 \text{ for } x \neq 0.$$

(3b)'s final sign-preservng property for $f_j[x]$ and x is vital for what is to come; $g_1$ and $g_2$ are parameters relevant to speeds of dynamic adjustments.

Adjoining to (2) and (3) a 1900 Wicksellian 3-factor marginal-product paradigm, we write

$$\text{(4a)} \qquad w_i = \partial Q(\bar{V}_0, V_1, V_2)/\partial V_i = Q_i(\bar{V}_0, V_1, V_2), \quad i = 1,2$$

$$\text{(4b)} \qquad w_0 = \left[ Q(\bar{V}_0, V_1, V_2) - \sum_1^2 w_j Q_j(\bar{V}_0, V_1, V_2) \right] / \bar{V}_0.$$

Rent as a classical residual is given in (4b), in the classical Ricardian fashion. Constant returns to scale implies

$$\text{(5a)} \qquad Q(\bar{V}_0, V_1, V_2) \equiv \bar{V}_i Q(1, V_1/V_0, V_2/V_0).$$

I assume $Q(1,V_1,V_2)$ is to be strictly concave in $(V_1,V_2)$, twice differentiable, strictly-monotone-increasing, with $Q_i(1,V_1,V_2) \to \infty$ as $V_i \to 0$, and $Q_i \to 0$ as $V_i \to \infty$. These regularity conditions suffice to make the relations of (4) uniquely invertible in the positive orthant

(5b) $$0 < (V_0\ V_1\ V_2) \longleftrightarrow (w_0\ w_1\ w_2) = 0.$$

Substituting (4) into (3) gives us two differential equations in the two unknowns, $(V_1\ V_2)$.

(6a) $$\dot{V}_i / V_i = g_i f_i [Q_i(\bar{V}_0, V_1, V_2) - \bar{w}_i], \quad i = 1,2.$$

The sole stationary point of this dynamical system must occur at $(V_1^*\ V_2^*)$, the unique vector root of the stationary maximum conditions:

(6b) $$Q_i(\bar{V}_0, V_1, V_2) - \bar{w}_i = 0, \quad i = 1,2.$$

The following global stability property will be proved for (6):

*Theorem:*

**(a)** From any positive initial $(V_1^0\ V_2^0)$, the canonical classical system of (6) will, under our stipulated assumptions, converge asymptotically to the unique equilibrium state that maximizes Virtual Rent,

(7a) $$L(\bar{V}_0, V_1, V_2) = Q(\bar{V}_0, V_1, V_2) - \sum_1^2 \bar{w}_j V_j.$$

Thus

(7b) $$\lim_{t\to\infty} [L\ V_1\ V_2\ w_1\ w_2\ w_0] = [\mathrm{Max}L\ V_1^*\ V_2^*\ \bar{w}_1\ \bar{w}_2\ w_0^*],$$

where

$$\underset{V_1,V_2}{\mathrm{Max}}\,L = \underset{V_1,V_2}{\mathrm{Max}}[Q(\bar{V}_0, V_1, V_2) - \sum_1^2 \bar{w}_j V_j],$$

(7c) $$= Q(\bar{V}_0, V_1^*, V_2^*) - \sum_1^2 \bar{w}_j V_j^*,$$

where $(V_1^*\ V_2^*)$ is the unique vector root of

(7d) $$\partial Q(\bar{V}_0, V_1, V_2)/\partial V_i = \bar{w}_i, \quad i = 1,2$$

and

$$w_0^* = \left[Q(\bar{V}_0, V_1^*, V_2^*) - \sum_1^2 \bar{w}_j V_j^*\right] / \bar{V}_0$$

(7e) $$= [\mathrm{Max}L] / \bar{V}_0.$$

**(b)** A technological innovation that is mandatorily viable in the long run must, in the canonical subsistence model, create a higher Long-run Rent, $L^* = \text{MaxL}$ than in the status quo ante. The viable innovation may raise or lower total real wages, raise or lower total real profits, raise or lower output $Q^*$, raise or lower long-run $V_1^*$ or $V_2^*$. [Ricardo was right in asserting that new machinery could depress $Q^*$ and depress Labor$^*$, even though his neoclassical critics, egged on by Wicksell, denied this prior to 1988! See Samuelson (1988, 1989).]

**(c)** Along the transitional path to the new $(V_1^*\ V_2^*)$ rendezvous called for by any once-and-for-all innovation, Virtual Rent (but not necessarily *actual* short-term Rent) is constantly rising. (In this sense, Virtual Rent is so to speak a measure of Darwinian "fitness" that Darwinian competition ever maximizes in the canonical model -- a subtlety apparently not hitherto noticed. Once the Darwinian adjustment has been fully realized, a new technological shock will without paradox' lead to a new climbing path toward a new MaxL.)

Lest any reader suppose this theorem to be a mere tautology not requiring proof, or to be an obvious banality, one must realize that modifying the classical hypothesis about a subsistence wage rate in the direction of *neoclassical exogeneity of the population supply* would demote Rent from its classical primacy and would permit a viable innovation to raise or lower rent and lower real returns of any subset of factors. With ingenuity new Darwinian fitnesses might be formulated for neoclassical models of generality, but the worth of the whole game depends on whether the contrived description has a natural simplicity that improves our description and understanding of the specified system.

That a unique long-run equilibrium obtains for $(V_1^*\ V_2^*)$ follows from (5)'s strong curvature properties specified for the production function Q. That $L^*$ is indeed Maximized (long-run) Rent follows from (4)'s marginal-product interpretation of competitive pricing. (In a discrete technology, the proof is more intricate.)

To prove the long-run comparative dynamics of **(b)**, I can cite the basic factor-price-tradeoff theorem of Samuelson (1975), which asserts that, in the absence of joint products, a time-phased competitive system will have for each profit rate a *convex* trade-off relation between all real factor returns of primary factors (land, labor,..), whatever be the good used as *numeraire*:

$$(8) \qquad T(w_1, w_2 \ldots, w_n) + w_0 = 0,$$

where $\partial T/\partial w_i > 0$ and T is a *quasi*-concave function.[2] In the present case of a continuous-time 1-produced good formulation, T by duality theory must more specially be a strongly *concave* function. For n+1=3 and $(w_1\ w_2)$ frozen at their long-run subsistence levels, $(\bar{w}_1\ \bar{w}_2)$,

[2] Morishima (1989, p. 72 *ff.*), gives a non-optimal account of my writings on Marx and on Ricardo, where this theorem is concerned. When Marx deals with competitive models where labor is the only primary factor, I was right to insist that he could not validly have simultaneously a Law of Reclining Rate of Profit and a law of immiserating real wage rate. Where Ricardo deals with *two* primary factors, labor and land, I have been right to assert that any two of $(w_0\ w_1\ w_2)$ could fall in time.

to viably force its way into long-run existence an innovation must shift $T(\bar{w}_1,\bar{w}_2)$ upward, thereby indeed raising $w_0^*$. *QED.*

To prove the novel result of (c), namely that dL/dt is positive on a transitional climb of the canonical fitness hill, we calculate

$$dL/dt = \sum_1^2 [\partial L(\bar{V}_0, V_1, V_2)/\partial V_j]\dot{V}_j$$

$$(9) \qquad = \sum_1^2 [w_j - \bar{w}_j] g_j f_j [w_j - \bar{w}_j] V_j > 0 \text{ by (3b) unless } (w_j) = (\bar{w}_j). \text{ QED.}$$

Figure 1 sketches how the global convergence to equilibrium cannot involve spiral conveyence corresponding to complex characteristic roots of the system's locally-linear approximant. The quasi-circular contours of Virtual Rent define the top of the hill at E. The paths of approach to E must cut those rent contours in a quasi-perpendicular, or quasi-transversal, fashion. Actually, the paths off aEa′ must swerve penultimately toward the "turnpike path" AEA′, defined by the system's least-negative real latent root in the locality of equilibrium.

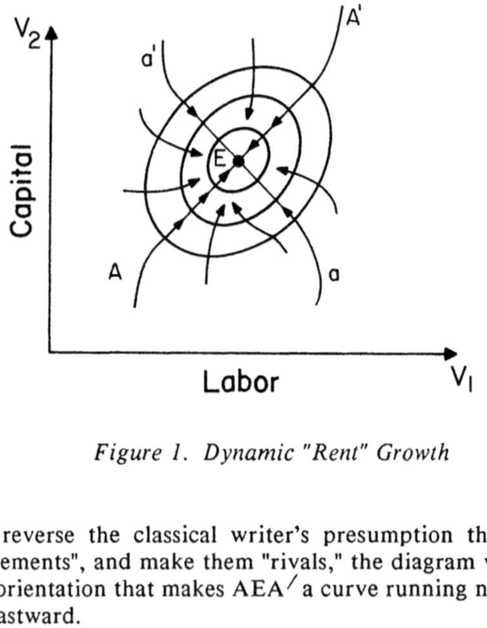


*Figure 1. Dynamic "Rent" Growth*

*Remark:* If we reverse the classical writer's presumption that labor and capital are "complements", and make them "rivals," the diagram will go through a mirror-like reorientation that makes AEA′ a curve running northwestward rather than northeastward.

I must conclude with a warning. Actual rent, $w_0(t)$, can diminish in the short run even though Virtual Rent must always increase. This subtlety eluded the classical writers and, I fear, modern commentators on them.

Here is an example. Let some temporary shock start the system off with a surfeit of both $(V_1\ V_2)$. Then $w_0$ of rent begins above $w_0^*$ equilibrium. As $(V_1\ V_2)$ both fall, $w_0(t)$ falls. QED. (How to reconcile this with an ever-rising Virtual Rent? Rent differs from Virtual Rent by the expression $\sum_1^2 [\bar{w}_j - w_j(t)]V_j(t)$. Since both factors in each of these terms begin as declining, this sum drops more than L rises.) Here is another, similar, example. Science derives an invention that strongly favors land. Rent has immediately risen, while $(w_1\ w_2)$ have immediately fallen. The ensuing drops in both $(V_1\ V_2)$ take away some of the first rise in $w_0$. Warning: new $w_0^*$ cannot end up *below* the prior $w_0^*$. If you plot the new contour of (8)'s $T(w_1,w_2)$, for the old $w_0^*$, it will have shifted outward; when the old $(\bar{w}_1,\bar{w}_2)$ point is reattained, it will now fall on a contour of (new $w_0^*$) that is greater than the (old $w_0^*$). QED.

**Acknowledgments**

For editorial assistance I owe thanks to Janice Murray, and for partial support to my Gordon Y. Billard Post-doctoral Fellowship at the MIT Sloan School of Management.

I have appended to the list of References various relevant citations from earlier writings. It is gratifying that the techniques of more than half a century ago, in *Foundations* (1947, 1983) and elsewhere, should have applied so neatly to the present problem. Also, in Samuelson (1991), there is an elaboration of the comparative statics and dynamics of the classical canonical growth model, a task that would seem overdue in view of the non-optimal state of the classical literature and of the present-day commentaries on it.

## REFERENCES

Butt, D.M. Bensusan (1960), **On Economic Growth: An Essay in Pure Theory**, Oxford University Press, London.

Crow, James F. and Kimura, Motoo (1970), **An Introduction to Population Genetics Theory**, Harper and Row Publishers, New York.

Fisher, R.A. (1930), **Genetical Theory of Natural Selection**, The Clarendon Press, Oxford; see particularly chapter 2.

Hollander, Samuel (1980), 'On Professor Samuelson's Canonical Model of Political Economy', *Journal of Economic Literature*, Vol. 18, 559-74.

Hollander, Samuel (1987), **Classical Economics**, Basil Blackwell, Oxford.

Houthakker, Hendrik (1950), 'Revealed preference and the utility function', *Economica*, New Series, Vol. 17, 159-74.

Houthakker, Hendrik and James Tobin (1951), 'The effects of rationing on demand elasticities', *Review of Economic Studies*, Vol. 18, 140-53.

Houthakker, Hendrik and James Tobin (1952), 'Estimates of the free demand for rationed foodstuff', *Economic Journal*, Vol. 62, 103-18.

Houthakker, Hendrik (1955), 'The Pareto distribution and the Cobb-Douglas production function in activity analysis', *Review of Economic Studies*, Vol. 23, 27-31.

Houthakker, Hendrol (1956), 'Economics and biology: specialization and speciation', *Kyklos*, Vol. 9, 181-87.

Houthakker, Hendrik (1962), 'Exchange Rate Adjustment', *Factors Affecting the United States Balance of Payments*, U.S. Joint Economic Committee, Washington, D.C.

Houthakker, Hendrik (1976), 'The Calculation of Bilateral Trade Patterns in a Ricardian Model with Intermediate Products and Barriers to Trade', *Journal of International Economics*, Vol. 6, 251-88.

Houthakker, Hendrik (1978), 'Purchasing Power Parity as an Approximation to the Equilibrium Exchange Ratio', *Economic Letters*, Vol. 1, 71-75.

Morishima, Michio (1989), **Ricardo's Economics: A General Equilibrium Theory of Distribution and Growth**, Cambridge University Press, Cambridge, U.K.

Nagylaki, Thomas (1991), 'Error bounds for the fundamental and secondary theorems of natural selection', *Proceedings of the National Academy of Science*, 88, 2402-06.

Robertson, Dennis H. (1955), 'What Does the Economist Economize?' in Robert Lekatchman (ed.), **National Policy for Economic Welfare at Home and Abroad**, Doubleday & Co., Garden City, N.J.

Samuelson, Paul A. (1938), 'A note on the pure theory of consumer's behavior', *Economica* New Series Vol. 5, 61-71.

Samuelson, Paul A. (1947, 1983), **Foundations of Economic Analysis**, Harvard University Press, Cambridge, Massachusetts.

Samuelson, Paul A. (1953), 'Prices of Goods and Factors in General Equillibrium', *Review of Economic Studies*, XXI(1), 54, 1-20. Reproduced as Chapter 70 in *The Collected Scientific Papers of Paul A. Samuelson*, Vol. 1, 1966, The MIT Press, Cambridge, Massachusetts.

Samuelson, Paul A. (1960), 'Structure of a Minimum Equilibrium System' in Ralph W. Pfouts, ed., *Essays in Economics and Econometrics: A Volume in Honor of Harold Hotelling*, University of North Carolina Press, Chapel Hill, pp. 1-33. Reproduced as Chapter 44 in *The Collected Scientific Papers of Paul A. Samuelson*, Vol. 1, 1966, The MIT Press, Cambridge, Massachusetts.

Samuelson, Paul A. (1965), 'Using Full Duality to Show that Simultaneously Additive Direct and Indirect Utilities Implies Unitary Price Elasticity of Demand', *Econometrica*, Vol. 33, 4, 781-96. Reproduced as Chapter 134 in *The Collected Scientific Papers of Paul A. Samuelson*, Vol. 3, 1972, The MIT Press, Cambridge, Massachusetts.

Samuelson, Paul A. (1975), 'Trade Pattern Reversals in Time-Phased Ricardian Systems and Intertemporal Efficiency', *Journal of International Economics*, 5, 309-63; see particularly p. 342 *ff*. Reproduced as Chapter 251 in *The Collected Scientific Papers of Paul A. Samuelson*, Vol. 4, 1977, The MIT Press, Cambridge, Massachusetts.

Samuelson, Paul A. (1978), 'The Canonical Classical Model of Political Economy', *Journal of Economic Literature*, 16, 1415-34. Reproduced as Chapter 340 in *The Collected Scientific Papers of Paul A. Samuelson*, Vol. 5, 1986, The MIT Press, Cambridge, Massachusetts.

Samuelson, Paul A. (1980), 'Noise and Signals in Debates Among Classical Economists: A Reply', *Journal of Economic Literature*, 18, 575-78. Reproduced as Chapter 341 in *The Collected Scientific Papers of Paul A. Samuelson*, Vol. 5, 1986, The MIT Press, Cambridge, Massachusetts.

Samuelson, Paul A. (1988), 'Mathematical Vindication of Ricardo on Machinery', *Journal of Political Economy*, Vol. 96, 274-82.

Samuelson, Paul A. (1989), 'Ricardo Was Right', *Scandinavian Journal of Economics*, Vol. 91, 47-62.

Samuelson, Paul A. (1991), 'The Classical Canonical Model in Modern Garb: Comparative Statics and Dynamics', unpublished working paper, Massachusetts Institute of Technology, Cambridge, Massachusetts.

Wright, Sewall (1977), **Evolution and the Genetics of Populations, Volume 3, Experimental Results and Evolutionary Deductions**, The University of Chicago Press, Chicago.

# INCOME AND PRICE SENSITIVITY IN CONSUMER DEMAND ANALYSIS

ANTON P. BARTEN
*Catholic University Leuven*
*and C.O.R.E.*
*34, Voie du Roman Pays*
*1348 Louvain-la-Neuve*
*BELGIUM*

ABSTRACT. Allais interaction coefficients are used to characterize the preferences for goods, including the interactions between goods. The link between the Allais coefficients and the parameters of the demand functions is established and used to study the consequences of deviations from the situation of independence (no interactions) among goods. It appears that the sign and size of income and price sensitivity depends very much on the type and the degree of interaction. Classification of goods as luxuries or necessities is more descriptive than reflecting the intrinsic quality of goods.

## 1. Introduction

Income and price elasticities, or rather simple functions of these, are the usual end product of empirical demand analysis -- see as an example Houthakker (1965a). One frequently finds that the own price elasticity of the demand for a good is in absolute value less, much less often, than the corresponding income elasticity. Is this a "law"? It is not uncommon to classify goods as luxuries and necessities depending on their income elasticity being larger or smaller than unity. Is there a counterpart for price elasticities? Is the price sensitivity of an aggregate of goods always smaller than that of its components?

In what follows we will try to answer these questions and some related ones. They appear to be of some importance. A point estimate is in itself of limited intellectual interest, unless we are able to recognize the structure it reflects. In our discussion this structure will be consciously kept simple in order to make clear statements.

Our approach will be to start off from what Houthakker (1960) calls "additive preferences" and which also plays a role in Houthakker (1961, 1965a and 1965b). We will allow for one deviation from it, which will be either of the complementarity or substitution type. [The analysis of complementarity and substitution "constitutes one of the most cherished achievements of consumption theory," Houthakker (1960)]. The consequences of such a deviation will be studied. To characterize interactions between goods, use will be made of the Allais (1943) coefficients or intensities, which appear to be rather convenient for the purpose at hand.

Before turning to the Allais coefficients some traditional measures of complementarity and substitution are discussed and their defects are pointed out. The Allais coefficients avoid



*L. Phlips and L.D. Taylor (eds.), Aggregation, Consumption and Trade*, 21–36.

these defects. They have rarely been used and are not too well known. For that reason, Section 3 presents them and discusses them at some length. As Section 4 demonstrates, they also provide a convenient starting point for the derivation of a system of demand functions. In the next section, income and price effects under additive preferences are derived to analyze the relation between those effects and the intrinsic desirability of a good, and also to prepare the ground for the following sections which study the implications of a deviation from additivity for the effect of prices (Section 6) and of income (Section 7). The next section turns to the consequences of commodity aggregation for the effect of prices. A numerical example is presented in Section 8 to illustrate the issues of the preceding sections. The last section contains as usual some concluding remarks.

## 2. Traditional Measures of Complementarity and Substitution

The identification of the concept of substitution and complementarity with certain properties of the preference order, or of the utility function, or of the demand functions, is a topic of long standing in economics [see Samuelson (1974)]. The early marginalists like Edgeworth and Pareto considered a pair of goods i,j complements if the marginal utility of i increased with the quantity of j. This criterion amounts to the sign of the second-order derivative of the utility function being positive for complements and negative for substitutes. The case of zero corresponds with that of independence.

On first sight this appears to be a sensible definition. However, it uses a property of the utility function which is not invariant under monotone increasing transformations of the utility function. In other words, it does not correspond with a property of the preference order, and is therefore rather arbitrary. To see this, let u(q) be an (at least) twice differentiable, monotone increasing, strongly quasi-concave utility function, defined on $R_+^n$. Furthermore, let $u_{ij}$ be the first-order derivative, the marginal utility of good i and $u_{ij}$ be the typical second-order derivative. The Edgeworth-Pareto criterion of complementarity and substitution uses the sign of $u_{ij}$. Let v(q) = F(u(q)) be some twice differentiable monotone increasing transformation of u(q). The monotone increasing nature of F guarantees that u(q) and v(q) describe the same preference order. It also means that $F^1$, the first order derivative of F, is positive. The sign of $F^{11}$, the second-order derivative, depends on the as yet unspecified nature of the transformation. Let $v_{ij}$ be the typical second-order derivative of v. As is well known [see Samuelson (1947, p.104)]:

$$v_{ij} = F^1 u_{ij} + F^{11} u_i u_j. \tag{2.1}$$

Here, $F^1 u_{ij}$ will have the same sign as $u_{ij}$, but the sign of $F^{11} u_i u_j$ depends entirely on that of $F^{11}$ which is basically free to choose.

The demand functions only reflect properties of the preference order, not those of a particular utility indicator associated with that order. To interpret empirical demand behavior the Edgeworth-Pareto criterion appears to be useless. Several attempts have been made to propose other criteria which are invariant under monotone increasing transformations of the utility function.

The best-known measure is the Hicks-Allen, which uses the sign of the income compensated or utility constant price derivative $k_{ij} = k_{ji}$ of the demand functions. Note that under the usual properties of the curvature of the indifference surfaces $k_{ii}$ is negative. An increase in the price of i reduces demand for i with utility kept constant. If such a decrease implies an income compensated increase of j, j takes over from i -- *i.e.*, i and j are substitutes. Hence, substitution corresponds with a positive sign of $k_{ji}$. Complementarity is then characterized by a negative sign, while independence has $k_{ji} = 0$.

In footnote 8 of Houthakker (1960), the author draws the attention to a "minor blemish" of this criterion. Indeed, because of the adding-up and homogeneity conditions $\Sigma_j p_j k_{ji} = 0$, where $p_j$ is the positive price of good j, which combined with negative $k_{ii}$ requires a dominance of positive $k_{ij}$, $j \neq i$, *i.e.*, a dominance of substitution. It rules out the possibility of all goods to be mutually independent and *a fortiori* to be all complements. There is another lack of elegance. One would expect a good to be its own best substitute, but the negativity of $k_{ii}$ suggests the opposite. A more fundamental objection against this criterion is that it mixes aspects of consumer "technology" (preferences) with that of the effective budget constraint. Two goods may make each other more attractive, but they compete for the consumer's dollar. Finally, the Hicks-Allen criterion attaches a qualification to a coefficient that is in principle directly observable. It is more descriptive than explanatory.

### 3. Allais Interaction Coefficients

Allais (1943) has proposed a criterion which is invariant both in sign as in size. It is also close to one's intuition about preference interactions among commodities. Samuelson (1974) briefly discusses a similar measure which he attributes to Johnson (1913), but does not mention the work of Allais. A related criterion was proposed by Barten (1971) who also was not aware of the contribution of Allais, which was pointed out by Charette and Bronsard (1975).

Since the Allais approach has hardly penetrated mainstream consumer demand analysis, it is useful to derive it here again. Allais starts with $u_{ij}$, which is divided by $u_i u_j$. The corresponding concept for $v(q) = F(u(q))$ is:

$$\text{(3.1)} \qquad \frac{v_{ij}}{v_i v_j} = \frac{1}{F^1}\left(\frac{u_{ij}}{u_i u_j} + \frac{F^{11}}{F^1}\right).$$

To eliminate the term independent of i and j, he subtracts a similar expression for r and s, a standard point of goods. One then has, on the basis of (3.1),

$$\text{(3.2)} \qquad \frac{v_{ij}}{v_i v_j} - \frac{v_{rs}}{v_r v_s} = \frac{1}{F^1}\left(\frac{u_{ij}}{u_i u_j} - \frac{u_{rs}}{u_r u_s}\right).$$

He next multiplies through by $\Sigma_k v_k q_k = F^1 \Sigma_k u_k q_k$ to remove the $1/F^1$ factor. The result is the Allais coefficient.

$$\text{(3.3)} \qquad a_{ij} = \left(\textstyle\sum_k u_k q_k\right)\left[\frac{u_{ij}}{u_i u_j} - \frac{u_{rs}}{u_r u_s}\right].$$

From the way it has been derived, it is clear that the Allais coefficient is invariant. It is a dimensionless concept like an elasticity. The $a_{ij}$ measure the interaction between i and j in comparison with that between a standard pair of goods r and s. Clearly, $a_{rs} = 0$. It is natural to select for the standard a pair which are mutually independent. According to Allais, this should not be a serious problem. A negative value of $a_{ij}$ reflects substitution, a positive one complementarity.

To see this better, one can start by rewriting (3.3) as:

$$u_{ij} = u_i u_j a_{ij} / \Sigma_k u_k q_k + \alpha\, u_i u_j \,, \tag{3.4}$$

with $\alpha = u_{rs}/u_r u_s$. In equilibrium $u_j = \lambda\, p_j$, with $\lambda$ a positive Lagrange multiplier. Let

$$m = \Sigma_k p_k q_k \tag{3.5}$$

be total expenditure available for consumption, and

$$w_j = p_j q_j / m \tag{3.6}$$

the share of expenditure on good j in this total expenditure. One can then express (3.4) as

$$u_{ij} = u_i a_{ij} w_j / q_j + \alpha\, u_i u_j \,. \tag{3.7}$$

Consider next a change in the marginal utility of good i:

$$\begin{aligned} du_i &= \Sigma_j u_{ij} dq_j \\ &= u_i \Sigma_j a_{ij} w_j\, (dq_j)/q_j + \alpha\, u_i \Sigma_j u_j dq_j \,. \end{aligned} \tag{3.8}$$

With $du = \Sigma_j u_j dq_j$ one can write this in relative terms as:

$$d\ln u_i = \Sigma_j a_{ij} w_j d\ln q_j + \alpha\, du \,. \tag{3.9}$$

The first term on the right-hand side is invariant and specifically involves the i, j interactions. The second term is general, not invariant, and relates to the choice of the utility indicator. If $a_{ij}$ is negative, an increase in $q_j$ will reduce $u_i$, a symptom of substitutability between i and j, by way of the first component, while the effect by way of the second component is not of interest. By selecting as the utility indicator one for which $u_{rs} = 0$ (and hence $\alpha = 0$), the second component vanishes.

It is obvious that the sign and the size of $a_{ij}$ depends on the choice of the standard pair. One can say that a negative $a_{ij}$ means that i and j are more substitutes than r and s, and a positive $a_{ij}$ that i and j complement each other more than r and s. Selecting a standard pair removes a degree of freedom comparable with what happens when selecting a particular utility indicator, except that intuition, or Wittgenstein's schoolboys in Samuelson (1974), can more easily identify preference independence than select a reference utility function.

Let $A = [a_{ij}]$ be the n x n matrix of Allais coefficients. As is shown in Barten (1990), the requirement of strong quasi-concavity of the utility function implies $x'A\,x < 0$ for all $x \neq 0$ such that $\iota' x = 0$ where $\iota$ is the summation vector. Obviously, requiring A to be negative definite is sufficient but not necessary to meet this condition; still, there is no objection against it since it is a testable property of the preference order. It implies that the $a_{ii}$ are all negative. Goods are their own substitute.

Under the condition of negative definite A, one can formulate the Allais interaction intensities as

$$a^*_{ij} = a_{ij} / \sqrt{a_{ii} a_{jj}} \,, \tag{3.10}$$

which are between -1 and +1. Barten and Bettendorf (1989) report values of $a^*_{ij}$ around -0.5 for the interaction between various types of fish. Barten (1990) gives values of $a^*_{ij}$ much closer to zero for the interaction between six broad categories of food.

## 4. The Relation with Demand

It is a straightforward matter to use (3.9) in the derivation of a system of demand functions. We will first reformulate it in matrix-vector notation.

$$\text{(4.1)} \qquad \text{dln } u_q = A\overline{w} \text{ dln } q \, ,$$

where $u_q$ is the vector of marginal utilities $u_i$, q is the vector of quantities $q_i$, while $\overline{w}$ is a diagonal matrix with the budget shares $w_i$ on the diagonal. Here $\alpha$ has been set at zero, without loss of generality. The first-order conditions for a relative maximum of the utility function consist of budget equation (3.5) and Gossen's Second Law: $u_q = \lambda p$, where p is the n-vector of prices $p_i$. Taking log-changes, one has

$$\text{(4.2)} \qquad \text{dln } u_q = \iota \text{ dln } \lambda + \text{dln } p \, .$$

Combining (4.1) and (4.2) and using the nonsingularity of A, one obtains

$$\text{(4.3)} \qquad \overline{w} \text{ dln } q = A^{-1} \iota \text{ dln } \lambda + A^{-1} \text{ dln } p \, .$$

The second component is the specific one. It corresponds with the specific substitution effect of Houthakker (1960).

The first component represents the effect of the change in $\lambda$, the marginal utility of money, or income. It can be eliminated by using the budget equation (3.5) in log-change form, *viz.*

$$\text{(4.4)} \qquad \text{dln } m = w' \text{dln } q + w' \text{dln } q \, ,$$

where w is the vector of budget shares $w_i$. It follows from (4.3) that

$$\text{(4.5)} \qquad w^1 \text{dln } q = \iota^1 A^{-1} \iota \text{ dln } \lambda + \iota^1 A^{-1} \text{dln } p = \text{dln } m - w^1 \text{dln } p$$

or

$$\text{(4.6)} \qquad \text{dln } \lambda = (\iota^1 A^{-1} \iota)^{-1} (\text{dln } m - w^1 \text{ dln } p) - (\iota^1 A^{-1} \iota)^{-1} \iota^1 A^{-1} \text{dln } p \, ,$$

which used in (4.3) leads to the Marshallian demand equations in log-change form:

$$\text{(4.7)} \qquad \overline{w} \text{ dln } q = b \text{ (dln } m - w' \text{ dln } p) + S \text{ dln } p \, ,$$

with

$$\text{(4.8)} \qquad b = A^{-1} \iota (\iota^1 A^{-1} \iota)^{-1} = (1/\varphi) \, A^{-1} \iota \, ,$$

$$\text{(4.9)} \qquad S = A^{-1} - A^{-1} \iota (\iota^1 A^{-1} \iota)^{-1} \iota^1 A^{-1} = A^{-1} - \varphi \, bb^1 \, ,$$

and where

$$\varphi = \iota^1 A^{-1}\iota \,. \tag{4.10}$$

Here, b is the vector of marginal propensities to consume. As is seen from (4.8), $\iota' b = 1$, which is the adding-up condition. S corresponds with the substitution effect or price changes, the $k_{ij}$ of Section 2. $-bw'$ represents the income effect of price changes. $\varphi bb'$ in (4.9) is what Houthakker (1960) names the general substitution effect. It works by way of the change in $\lambda$ and could be neutralized by an appropriate change in m. As is clear from (4.6), $\varphi$ is the reciprocal of the elasticity of $\lambda$ with respect to m, or the money flexibility of Frisch (1959). All these concepts involve the matrix A, which therefore provides a link between them. Knowing b and S is not enough to identify A. Some value for $\varphi$ is needed for that purpose. Actually, we will be interested here in the relation of A to b and S. For details on the reverse relation, see Barten (1990).

Note that the choice of b and S as constants corresponds with the Rotterdam system as formulated by Theil (1965). This choice then implies constant Allais coefficients. Our discussion, however, does not hinge upon the constant nature of these coefficients. So far we have also not assumed any special structure of the A matrix. The next section will be different in this respect.

## 5. Overall Independence

What Frisch (1959) calls *want independence*, or what Houthakker (1960) calls *additive preferences*, corresponds with $\alpha_{ij} = 0$ for all $i \neq j$. For our purpose this situation is not so much of interest for its empirical validity, but more for its convenience as an analytical benchmark.

Diagonality of matrix A means diagonality of its inverse, *i.e.*, absence of specific interaction in demand. Then

$$\varphi = \Sigma_j(1/a_{jj}) \tag{5.1}$$

$$b_i = (1/a_{ii})/(\Sigma_j(1/a_{jj})) \tag{5.2}$$

$$s_{ii} = (1/a_{ii}) - (1/a_{ii})^2/\Sigma_j\,(1/a_{jj}) \,. \tag{5.3}$$

It can be shown -- see *e.g.* Barten and Böhm (1962) -- that the curvature condition on the indifferences locus requires all $b_i$ to be positive, or one of them to be positive and the others to be negative. The second case can be ruled out as empirically without interest. Moreover, our assumption of negative definite A also excludes it. Under additivity our $b_i$ will be positive and $\varphi$ negative.

It is clear from (4.7) that the income, or rather budget elasticity $\eta_i$, equals $b_i/w_i$, while the Slutsky elasticity $\epsilon_{ij}$ is $s_{ij}/w_i$. The overall price elasticity $\epsilon^*_{ij}$ is then $\epsilon_{ij} - \eta_i w_j$. Under preference independence, $s_{ii} = \varphi\,(b_i - b_i^2)$ and

$$\epsilon^*_{ij} = \eta_i\,[\varphi(1-\eta_i w_i)-w_i] \,. \tag{5.4}$$

The term in square brackets is roughly equal to $\varphi$, if n, the number of goods considered, is not too small. Indeed, $w_i$ is of the order of $1/n$ and $\eta$ is of the order of one. There is a near (negative) proportionality between the own price elasticity and the income elasticity. This is what Deaton (1974) calls "Pigou's Law." A similar approximate proportionality holds for the Slutsky and the income elasticities, while it is an exact proportionality for the own specific substitution elasticity and the income elasticity, with $\varphi$ as the factor of proportionality.

In the empirical tradition of demand analysis a good is called a *luxury* if its income elasticity is larger than one, a *necessity* if this elasticity is less than one and an *inferior* good if it has a negative income response. An income elasticity larger than one means that the budget share for the good in question increases with income, the reverse holding when the income elasticity is smaller than one. The case of income elasticity equal to one or constant budget shares is of some theoretical interest -- see *e.g.* Samuelson (1965) and Houthakker (1965b) -- but not of great empirical importance. Associating luxury with increasing budget shares and the opposite with decreasing ones makes good sense. It is a classification which is rather robust in cross-sections. It is simple to check the behavior of budget shares across total expenditures.

In view of the Pigou proportionality, additive preferences associate luxuries with own price elasticities which are relatively high in absolute value, while for necessities these are relatively low. Note that additivity rules out negative income elasticities and hence inferiority of goods. There is no indication about the absolute levels of these price elasticities. Empirical results under additivity -- see *e.g.* Houthakker (1965a) -- usually show rather low (in absolute value) own price elasticities in comparison with the income elasticities. This points to a value of $\varphi$ rather close to zero. Barten (1974) estimates $\varphi$ as a constant for eight European countries. The point estimates range between -0.921 for the Federal Republic of Germany to 0.093 for France. A positive value for $\varphi$ is to be ruled out. The value of -0.921 for Germany is also atypical. The next one in the order is -0.479 for Denmark. These rather low (absolute) values of $\varphi$ correspond with rather high (absolute) values of its reciprocal, the money flexibility of Frisch (1959). They are mostly in a range which Frisch associates with poverty. Perhaps the Frisch intuition that the desirability of money decreases with prosperity is more relevant for a cross-section of consumers than for international comparison of whole economies.

That luxuries have income elasticities larger than one is a tautology. The corollary that under additivity the price elasticities of luxuries are in absolute values larger than those of necessities is more descriptive than illuminating. The deeper cause of relative income and price sensitivity is the value of the own Allais coefficient $a_{ij}$. Its reciprocal determines the relative size of the substitution effect and that of the income response. A low value of $a_{ii}$ means strong responses, a high value relatively weak ones.

One might turn back to (3.9). Under overall independence, it is reduced to

$$\text{(5.5)} \qquad d\ln u_i = a_{ij} w_i d\ln q_i \, .$$

If one prefers to reason in term of the marginal rate of substitution between goods i and j ($MRS_{ij}$), one has

$$\text{(5.6)} \qquad d\ln MRS_{ij} = d\ln u_i - d\ln u_j = a_{ii} w_i d\ln q_i - a_{jj} w_j d\ln q_j \, .$$

Clearly, $a_{ii}w_i$ is the elasticity of $u_i$ or $MRS_{ij}$ with respect to $q_i$. Note that it is negative.

A low (negative) value of $a_{ii}w_i$ means that the (relative) desirability of $q_j$ is not easily reduced by more of $q_j$. Newly available means will be used for the purchase of good i, rather than that of another good with a higher elasticity. The budget share $w_i$ will not easily diminish. This means that the small size of $a_{ii}w_i$ is due to the small (absolute) value of $a_{ii}$.

One can view (5.5) as the expression for the (relative) willingness to pay for $q_i$. For low $a_{ii}w_i$ this willingness goes down only very slowly as $q_i$ increases. If the market price of good i goes up considerably, a very large movement of $q_i$ is needed to bring the willingness to pay down to the level of the market price. Low $a_{ii}w_i$ then means a high price response. With the empirically rather high price elasticity of minus one, the budget share $w_i$ is constant, but its level is not easy to determine *a priori*. Still, a high value of $a_{ii}w_i$ is not easy to reconcile with a low value of $a_{ii}$. One may take indeed the size of $a_{ii}$ as the fundamental determinant of the income and price sensitivity under additive preferences.

The next question is why $a_{ii}$ is smaller in absolute value than for another good. The answer to this question is perhaps better left to psychologist, physiologists, and sociologists. Anyway, given the limits of one's competence, the answer will not be attempted here.

## 6. Price Effects with Interaction

Preference independence is an extreme case. It is an analytically convenient assumption but not very realistic. There is moreover the intuition that with substitution between goods i and j, a price increase for good i will meet with a sharper decrease in the demand for it than without the alternative offered by the substitute. The purpose of this section is to verify this intuition.

To keep matters simple, we allow for a single deviation from independence. We will assume that $a_{12} = a_{21}$ is not zero, but that all other $a_{ij}$, $i \neq j$, are zero. We will write

$$a_{12} = c\,\sqrt{(a_{11} \cdot a_{22})}\,, \tag{6.1}$$

where the positive square root is taken. This means that a positive Allais interaction coefficient c corresponds with complementarity and a negative one with substitution. At this stage of the discussion, the question of the sign of c can be left open.

To trace the effect of this deviation from independence on the price effects, we will concentrate on the matrix of specific substitution effects, *i.e.*, matrix $A^{-1}$. We will indicate this matrix by H for C = 0, and by G for $c \neq 0$. We will assume that the diagonal Allais coefficients are independent of c. Otherwise said, $H^{-1}$ and $G^{-1}$ only differ because of the nonzero nature of $a_{12}$. The purpose is to trace the effect of nonzero c on the difference between G and H.

Let $a_i$ be the positive square root of $-a_{ii}$ and $\overline{a}$ be the diagonal matrix with the $a_i$ on the diagonal. Then one can write on the basis of (6.1)

$$A = -\overline{a}(I - c\, e_1e_2' - c\, e_2e_1')\overline{a}\,, \tag{6.2}$$

with $e_i$ being an n-vector with all elements equal to zero except the i-*th* one, which is one. Next, one has

$$\begin{aligned} A^{-1} &= -\overline{a}^{-1}\left[I + \frac{c}{1-c^2}\left(e_1e_2' + e_2e_1' + c\left(e_1e_1' + e_2e_2'\right)\right)\right]^{1}\overline{a}^{-1} \\ &= H - \frac{c}{1-c^2}\,\overline{a}^{-1}\left[e_1e_2' + e_2e_1' + c\left(e_1e_1' + e_2e_2'\right)\right]\overline{a}^{-1} = G. \end{aligned} \tag{6.3}$$

Concentrating on the own specific price effect, one has

$$g_{11} = e_1' G e_1 = h_{11} - \frac{c}{1-c^2} e_1' \bar{a}^{-1} e_1 \cdot e_1' \bar{a}^{-1} e_1$$

(6.4)
$$= h_{11} + \frac{c}{1-c^2} h_{11} = \frac{1}{1-c^2} h_{11}.$$

A similar result holds for $g_{22}$. The own price sensitivity has indeed increased because $1/(1-c^2) > 1$. Note, however, that this is true independently of the sign of c. It is not just a matter of being able to use more of a substitute.

There is now also a cross specific price effect:

$$g_{12} = e_1' G e_2 = -\frac{c}{1-c^2} e_1' \bar{a}^{-1} e_1 \cdot e_2' \bar{a}^{-1} e_2$$

(6.5)
$$= -\frac{c}{1-c^2} \sqrt{(h_{11} \cdot h_{22})}.$$

This effect is positive if c is negative, *i.e.*, if goods 1 and 2 are substitutes. it is negative if c is positive, if there is complementarity between goods 1 and 2. One can also write (6.5) as

(6.6)
$$g_{12} = -c \sqrt{(g_{11} \cdot g_{22})} ,$$

which is the analogue of (6.1).

It also follows from (6.3) that for k, l = 3, ..., n,

(6.7)
$$g_{kk} = h_{kk} \qquad g_{kl} = h_{kl} = 0,$$

*i.e.*, the specific price effects for the other goods have not changed.

Can one resolve the paradox between the intuition about increased sensitivity of the own price effect because of substitution and the outcome that the own specific price effects increase with interaction but irrespective of its sign?

First of all, one may point out that prices only matter when the budget is effectively constraining (some might refer to Veblenesque effects, but even then one might say that without an effective budget limitation, being more expensive would yield little prestige to a good). To limit the attention to the specific substitution effect without considering the budget limitations and the ensuing indirect effects is misleading.

Turn to (4.3), which under preference independence specializes for good 1 to

(6.8)
$$w_1 d\ln q_1 = h_{11}(d\ln \lambda + d\ln p_1) .$$

An increase in $p_1$ will decrease $\lambda$, which mitigates somewhat the direct substitution effect. The net effect will be negative for demand for good 1. Next rewrite (4.3) for the conditions of this section, setting $d\ln p_2 = 0$:

$$w_1 d\ln q_1 = \left(g_{11} + g_{12}\right) d\ln \lambda + g_{11}\, d\ln p_1$$

$$= \frac{1}{1-c^2} h_{11} \left(d\ln \lambda + d\ln p_1\right) - \frac{c}{1-c^2}\sqrt{\left(h_{11} \cdot h_{22}\right)}\, d\ln \lambda. \tag{6.9}$$

The first term shows a sharper decrease in the demand for good 1 for an increase in its price, assuming that $d\ln \lambda$ does not change too much. However, since the second term has an effect of the same sign as c, substitution ($c < 0$) will work the opposite way. There is a difference in the own price effect depending on the sign of c, but not one in the *specific* own price effect.

In conclusion, one may say that substitution increases own price sensitivity, sometimes substantially. For complementarity the case is not so clear-cut, but an increase is possible there as well. The fact that only one interaction is considered does *a priori* not seem to limit the validity of the qualitative results.

## 7. Income Sensitivity and Interaction

Under preference independence, inferior goods are virtually excluded. Although at the (high) level of aggregation over goods usually considered in empirical work one rarely finds negative income effects, one cannot rule out inferiority. It can only exist under deviations from additivity. Intuitively, one can expect inferiority only if there is a close substitute for the inferior good which draws away purchasing power from the inferior good as income increases. Can one corroborate this intuition formally?

We will employ the same scheme as in the previous section, but concentrate more on the elements of the vector b defined by (4.8) and see how these change when c in (6.2) is not zero.

Under independence (5.2) holds, which we here rewrite as

$$b_1^0 = h_{ii}/\Sigma_j h_{jj} \qquad \text{for all i.} \tag{7.1}$$

Under the conditions of the previous section

$$b_i = \Sigma_j\, g_{ij}/\Sigma_h \Sigma_j g_{hj}\ , \tag{7.2}$$

which specializes to:

$$b_1 = (g_{11}+g_{12})/\text{denom1} \tag{7.3a}$$

$$b_2 = (g_{21}+g_{22})/\text{denom1} \tag{7.3b}$$

$$b_k = h_{kk}/\text{denom1} \qquad k = 3, \ldots, n, \tag{7.3c}$$

where $\text{denom1} = \Sigma_j\, g_{jj} + 2\, g_{12}$ forces the $b_i$ to sum up to one.

To make the impact of c explicit, use the results of the previous section to obtain:

$$b_1 = 1/(1-c^2)\, (h_{11} - c\, \sqrt{(h_{11} \bullet h_{22})})/\text{denom1} \tag{7.4a}$$

$$= (b_1^0\, /(1-c^2))(1 + c\, \sqrt{(b_2^0/b_1^0)})/\text{denom2}$$

(7.4b) $$b_2 = (b_2^0/(1-c^2))(1 + c\sqrt{(b_1^0/b_2^0)})/\text{denom2}$$

(7.4c) $$b_k = b_k^0/\text{denom2} ,$$

where denom2 is guaranteeing the adding up of the $b_i$ to one. One may expect denom2 not to be too much different from one. The difference between $b_i$ and its counterpart under independence then consists of two factors: One, $1/(1-c^2)$, is positive and larger than one. The other, namely,

(7.5) $$1 + c\sqrt{(b_2^0/b_1^0)} ,$$

is positive when c is positive, *i.e.*, under complementarity. Goods 1 and 2 reinforce each other's attraction. If c is negative (substitution) the sign of this factor is not *a priori* clear. If

(7.6) $$c < -\sqrt{(b_1^0/b_2^0)} ,$$

good 1 has become an inferior good. The parameter c is an interaction intensity and therefore in between minus one and plus one. Inferiority of good 1 requires $b_1^0 < b_2^0$. This condition is asymmetric in the two goods. They cannot both be inferior. Note that the requirement $b_2^0 > b_1^0$ seems to correspond with the intuitive notion that the superior good should have greater intensity of purchasing power than the inferior one.

In the case of substitution ($c < 0$), factor (7.5) will be less than one. To what extent this means that the new marginal propensity to consume is less than the old one depends on the size of $1/(1-c^2)$ and the extent denom2 differs from one. The numerical example of Section 9 will make this clear.

This section has shown that complementarity between goods increases the marginal propensities to consume and probably also the income elasticities. To attribute high income sensitivity only to the luxury nature of a good seems unwarranted. Substitution can reduce the income sensitivity. It has not much to do with the intrinsic nature of the goods in question as necessities. Strong substitutability is indeed a condition for inferiority. The classification of goods in luxuries, necessities and inferior goods is not too helpful, since the income sensitivity does not only depend on the nature of the good itself but also on its interactions with other goods.

## 8. Commodity Aggregation and Price Sensitivity

Conventional wisdom maintains that the low absolute values of the own price elasticities, which are so common in empirical research, are due to the highly aggregate level of the commodities considered. At the brand level the price sensitivity could be almost infinite, at the product level the alternatives are already less equivalent in satisfying one's needs, reducing the price effect and so on. In this section we will attempt to analyze the consequences of aggregation over goods on the price sensitivity. Again the approach considers a single deviation from independence, namely between goods 1 and 2 which are the components of an aggregate.

We start again from the situation of full preference independence. Then one has on the basis of (4.3):

(8.1) $$w_1 d\ln q_1 = h_{11} d\ln \lambda + h_{11} d\ln p_1$$

(8.2) $$w_2 d\ln q_2 = h_{22} d\ln \lambda + h_{22} d\ln p_2.$$

The left-hand sides are in a convenient form for commodity aggregation. One may define the composite variable to be explained as

(8.3) $$w_A d\ln q_A = w_1 d\ln q_1 + w_2 d\ln q_2 ,$$

where $d\ln q_A = (w_i/w_A)\, d\ln q_1 + (w_2/w_A)\, d\ln q_2$ and $w_A = w_1+w_2$. We now have from (8.1) and (8.2)

(8.4) $$w_A d\ln q_A = (h_{11}+h_{22}) d\ln \lambda + (h_{11}+h_{22})(r_1^0 d\ln p_1 + r_2^0 d\ln p_2) ,$$

where

(8.5) $$r_1^0 = h_{ii}/(h_{11}+h_{22}) = b_i^0/(b_1^0+b_2^0) \qquad i = 1, 2.$$

Since

(8.6) $$h_{AA} = h_{aa} + h_{22} ,$$

equation (8.4) can be written as

(8.7) $$w_A d\ln q_A = h_{AA} d\ln \lambda + h_{AA}(r_1^0 d\ln p_1 + r_2^0 d\ln p_2) ,$$

where the term in the prices is an aggregate price index using the properly scaled marginal propensities to consume or marginal budget shares as weights.

Following a procedure similar to the one in section 6, we have

(8.8) $$w_A d\ln q_A = g_{AA} d\ln \lambda + g_{AA} (r_1 d\ln p_1 + r_2 d\ln p_2) ,$$

with:

(8.9) $$g_{AA} = g_{11} + g_{22} + g_{12} + g_{21}$$

(8.10a) $$r_1 = (g_{11}+g_{21})/g_{AA} = b_1/(b_1+b_2)$$

(8.10b) $$r_2 = (g_{12}+g_{22})/g_{AA} = b_2/(b_1+b_2).$$

The difference between the price index of (8.8) and that of (8.7) is not of crucial importance. We are interested in the effect of the log-change in the price of the aggregate which may be of the type $d\ln p_A = d\ln p_1 = d\ln p_2$ and which does not differ between (8.7) and (8.8).

We will concentrate our attention on the difference between $g_{AA}$, which incorporates interaction, and $h_{AA}$, which assumes independence. Using again (6.4) and (6.5), we have

(8.11)
$$g_{AA} = \frac{1}{1-c^2}\left(h_{11} + h_{22} - 2c\sqrt{(h_{11}\cdot h_{22})}\right) = \frac{1}{1-c^2}\left(h_{AA} - 2c\sqrt{(h_{11}\cdot h_{22})}\right).$$

There are two components of the difference between $g_{AA}$ and $h_{AA}$. The first is the factor $1/(1-c^2)$, which is larger than one and tends to make $g_{AA}$ in absolute value larger than $h_{AA}$. The second component increases the difference for positive c, *i.e.*, for complements. It decreases the difference for negative c, substitution. In the case of substitution it is not *a priori* clear whether $g_{AA}$ is smaller (in absolute value) than $h_{AA}$.

One can also compare $g_{AA}$ with $g_{11}$. Then

(8.12)
$$g_{AA} = g_{11} + (g_{22}+g_{12}+g_{21}).$$

In the case of complements, $g_{12} = g_{21} < 0$, $g_{AA}$ is more negative than $g_{11}$. In the case of substitution, $g_{12} = g_{21} > 0$, it is possible but not necessary that $g_{AA}$ is less negative than $g_{11}$. Of course, in terms of price elasticities one should compare $g_{AA}/s_A$ with $g_{11}/w_1$. The smaller denominator in the latter case might make this elasticity more negative than for the aggregate. Still, aggregation as the reason of small price elasticities appears to be less evident than conventional wisdom suggests it is.

## 9. A Numerical Example

Some of the conclusions of the preceding sections were ambiguous in the sense that without further information one could not make definite statements. It seems useful to present a numerical example as a kind of illustration of the theoretical discussion of the preceding sections. Of course, neither realism nor generality is claimed.

We will assume locally constant Allais coefficients. We will also assume a structure like (6.2). All the other goods except the first two are separable from the first two, *i.e.*, $a_{ij} = 0$ for $i = 1, 2$ and $j = 3, \ldots, n$. They are merged and form together the third good. We distinguish three cases: i) Complementarity: $c = 0.5$; ii) independence: $c = 0$; and iii) substitution: $c = -0.5$. The diagonal elements of matrix A are kept the same across the three cases. Results for b, S and $\varphi$ are given in Tables 1 through 3.

**TABLE 1 : NUMERICAL EXAMPLE FOR COMPLEMENTARITY**

| A | | | b | S | | |
|---|---|---|---|---|---|---|
| -20.0 | 4.5 | 0.0 | 0.188 | -0.040 | 0.002 | 0.038 |
| 4.5 | -4.0 | 0.0 | 0.545 | 0.002 | -0.111 | 0.109 |
| 0.0 | 0.0 | -5.0 | 0.267 | 0.038 | 0.109 | -0.147 |

$\varphi = -0.75$

TABLE 2 : NUMERICAL EXAMPLE FOR INDEPENDENCE

| A | | | b | S | | |
|---|---|---|---|---|---|---|
| -20.0 | 0.0 | 0.0 | 0.100 | -0.045 | 0.025 | 0.020 |
| 0.0 | -4.0 | 0.0 | 0.500 | 0.025 | -0.125 | 0.100 |
| 0.0 | 0.0 | -5.0 | 0.400 | 0.020 | 0.100 | -0.120 |

$\varphi = -0.50$

TABLE 3 : NUMERICAL EXAMPLE FOR SUBSTITUTION

| A | | | b | S | | |
|---|---|---|---|---|---|---|
| -20.0 | -4.5 | 0.0 | 0.020 | -0.066 | 0.070 | -0.004 |
| -4.5 | -4.0 | 0.0 | 0.575 | 0.070 | -0.185 | 0.115 |
| 0.0 | 0.0 | -5.0 | 0.445 | -0.004 | 0.115 | -0.111 |

$\varphi = -0.45$

As predicted in Section 6, the own price effect becomes much stronger with substitution. The net effect of complementarity amounts in our example to a reduction in price sensitivity in comparison with that under independence. Note that the Allais complementarity has turned into Hicks-Allen substitution. In Table 3, Hicks-Allen complementarity occurs for goods 1 and 3 which are Allais independent.

Complementarity between goods 1 and 2 has increased the $b_1$ and $b_2$ as Section 7 predicted. Substitution has made good 1 into an inferior good. Indeed,

$$\sqrt{(b_1^0/b_2^0)} = \sqrt{(0.1/0.5)} = \sqrt{0.2} = 0.45 \qquad (9.1)$$

and c = 0.5 < -0.45. At the same time $b_2$ has been strengthened. If good 1 has a budget share of 0.15, for example, it is a luxury in Table 1, a necessity in Table 2, and an inferior good in Table 3. The only differences between the three cases is the interaction with good 2. There is also little stability across the tables in the relations between the $b_i$ and the $s_{ii}$.

In the section on the effects of commodity aggregation on price sensitivity, the elements of the leading 2 x 2 block of the matrix $A^{-1}$ were summed. One can do basically the same for the leading 2 x 2 block of the matrix S. One finds for complementarity -0.147, for independence -0.120 and for substitution -0.111. Complementarity increases the sensitivity measured in this way, substitution decreases it. The aggregate effects are all stronger than those of $s_{11}$ and for complementarity also than that of $s_{22}$. Aggregation is in itself not necessarily a cause of reduction in price sensitivity.

## 10. Conclusions

The major thesis of this contribution is that the sensitivity of the demand for a good to changes in income and prices is not only due to the intrinsic qualities of the good in question, but also to its interaction with other goods. Qualifications like luxury or necessity might be misleading.

Allais coefficients have been used as invariant measures of both the intrinsic desirability of a good and of the degree of interaction with other goods. They also serve as a convenient starting point for the derivation of differential demand systems. In this way properties of observable demand can be linked to those of the unobservable preference structure.

To study the impact of interaction, one deviation from overall preference independence has been allowed. The consequences for the demand responses with this deviation have been compared with those under preference independence. Whether the deviation reflects complementarity between two goods or substitution depends on the sign of the relevant Allais coefficient. Using a single deviation only is no doubt not realistic. It is more an analytical device to come to clear-cut statements. It is believed that empirically more interesting widely spread interactions will not change the qualitative conclusions.

Under overall independence, high demand sensitivity corresponds with a low value of the own Allais coefficient. Otherwise said, it reflects a low sensitivity of the marginal utility of a good with respect to its quantity. The resistance of a good's marginal utility to decrease as income increases leads to a large budget share for higher incomes. In this sense it is a luxury, not, as the term would suggest, something which could be easily missed. Under overall independence there is an approximate negative proportionality between income and price effects. Still, the level of the price effects it not *a priori* determined and there is no reason to associate, say, a value of less than -1 for a price elasticity as an indication of a luxury.

Allowing for interaction removes the approximate proportionality between income and price effects. Substitution increases price sensitivity. The effect of complementarity consists of two components of opposite sign, so an *a priori* conclusion is not possible.

Complementarity increases the income sensitivity. The effect of substitution can turn a positive effect of income into a negative one. In general, however, the consequences of substitution on income effects are not *a priori* unambiguous. The income effects depend just as much on the own nature of the good as on its interactions with other goods.

Aggregate goods do not appear to have necessarily smaller price responses than their components. The explanation of the empirically found low values of the price responses cannot be the aggregate nature of the goods used.

The thesis mentioned in the beginning of this section seems to have been substantiated by our analytical results: Interaction matters for the sign and level of income and price effects.

## Acknowledgement

Hendrik Houthakker's contribution to the 1960 Festschrift in honor of Ragnar Frisch, which also appeared as an issue of *Econometrica*, set me on the trail of consumer demand analysis, which has become a dominant research topic for the rest of my life. I am happy to offer in the form of this contribution some of the interest accrued for this intellectual debt, of which the creditor, I presume, is hardly aware.

## REFERENCES

Allais, M. (1943), "Les données génerales de l'économie pure," **Traité d'Economie Pure**, Imprimerie Nationale, Paris.

Barten, A.P. (1971), "Preference and Demand Interactions Between Commodities," *Schaarste en Welvaart*, Opstellen aangeboden aan Prof. dr. P. Hennipman, Stenfert Kroese, Leiden, 1971.

Barten, A.P. (1974), "Complete Systems of Demand Equations: Some Thoughts about Aggregation and Functional Form," *Recherches Economiques de Louvain*, Vol. 40 (1974), pp. 1 - 18.

Barten, A.P. (1960), "Allais characterisation of preference structures and the structure of demand" in **Economic Decision-Making, Games, Econometrics and Optimisation**, J.J. Gabszewicz, J.-F. Richard, and L.A. Wolsey (eds.), Elsevier, Amsterdam, pp. 328 - 349.

Barten, A.P. and L. Bettendorf (1989), "Price Formation of Fish: An Application of an Inverse Demand System," *European Economic Review*, Vol. 33, pp. 1509 - 1525.

Barten, A.P. and V. Bohm (1982), "Consumer Theory," Chapter 9 in **Handbook of Mathematical Economics, Volume II**, K.J. Arrow and M.D. Intriligator (eds.), North-Holland, Amsterdam, pp. 381 - 429.

Charette, L. and C. Bronsard (1975), "Antonelli-Hicks-Allen et Antonelli-Allais-Barten, sur l'utilisation des conditions d'intégrabilité d'Antonelli," *Recherches Economiques de Louvain*, Vol. 41, pp. 25 - 34.

Deaton, A.S. (1974), "A Reconsideration of the Empirical Implications of Additive Preference," *Economic Journal*, Vol. 84, pp. 338 - 348.

Frisch. R. (1959), "A Complete Scheme for Computing All Direct and Cross Demand Elasticities in a Model with Many Sectors," *Econometrica*, Vol. 27, pp. 177 - 196.

Houthakker, H.S. (1960), "Additive Preferences," *Econometrica*, Vol. 28, pp. 244 - 257.

Houthakker, H.S. (1961), "The Present State of Consumption Theory (A Survey Article)," *Econometrica*, Vol. 24, pp. 704 - 740.

Houthakker, H.S. (1965a), "New Evidence on Demand Elasticities," *Econometrica*, Vol. 33, pp. 277 - 288.

Houthakker, H.S. (1965b), "A Note on Self-Dual Preferences," *Econometrica*, Vol. 33, pp. 797 - 801.

Johnson, W.E. (1913), "The Pure Theory of Utility Curves," *The Economic Journal*, Vol. 23, pp. 483 - 513.

Samuelson, P.A. (1947), **Foundations of Economic Analysis**, Harvard University Press, Cambridge, 1983.

Samuelson, P.A. (1974), "Complementarity: An Essay on the 40th Anniversary of the Hicks-Allen Revolution in Demand Theory," *Journal of Economic Literature*, Vol. 12, No. 4, December 1974, pp. 1255 - 1289.

Samuelson, P.A. (1965), "Using Full Duality to Show that Simultaneously Additive Direct and Indirect Utilities Implies Unitary Price Elasticities of Demand," *Econometrica*, Vol. 33, pp. 781 - 796.

Theil, H. (1965), "The Information Approach to Demand Analysis," *Econometrica*, Vol. 33, pp. 67 - 87.

# CROSS-SECTION ENGEL CURVES, EXPENDITURE DISTRIBUTIONS, AND THE "LAW OF DEMAND"

BIRGIT GRODAL, *Copenhagen*[*]
WERNER HILDENBRAND, *Bonn*[*]
*Institut für Gesellschafts- und Wirtschanftswissenschaften'*
*Abteilung Wirtschaftstheorie II*
*Rheinische Friedrich-Wilhelms-Universität Bonn*
*Adenauerallee 24-26*
*D-5300 Bonn 1*
*Germany*

ABSTRACT. In this paper we shall use two traditional concepts of applied demand analysis in order to analyze some fundamental properties of the market demand function of a large consumption sector. These concepts are the cross-section Engel curve and the distribution of households' total expenditure.

We show that the shape of the various cross-section Engel curves as well as the shape of the expenditure distribution plays an important role in deriving the Law of Demand for the market demand function.

## 1. Introduction

In this paper we shall use two traditional concepts of applied demand analysis in order to analyse some fundamental properties of the market demand function of a large consumption sector. These concepts are

- the *cross-section Engel curve*; and
- the *distribution of household total expenditure.*

Both concepts have been used and critically analysed in Hendrick S. Houthakker's theoretical contributions and empirical analysis. See for example Houthakker's monographs (1955), (1966) and the publications (1953), (1957) and (1961).

We shall show in this paper that the *shape* of the various cross-section Engel curves as well as the *shape* of the expenditure distribution plays an important role in deriving the Law of Demand for the market demand function. The shape of a cross-section Engel curve and the expenditure distribution is, of course, an empirical matter. Consequently, an empirical

---

* This research was supported by Deutsche Forschungsgemeinschaft, Sonderforschungsbereich 303 and Gottfried-Wilhelm-Leibniz-Förderpreis.



*L. Phlips and L.D. Taylor (eds.), Aggregation, Consumption and Trade,* 37–53.

analysis of cross-section Family Expenditure Surveys is required. Houthakker made numerous and well-known fundamental contributions to this field of empirical research.

We denote by $\overline{f}_k(p,x)$ the *average demand for commodity* $k \in K$ *of all households in the population with total expenditure* x, given the price system $p \in \mathbb{R}^K_{++}$ We imagine that there are typically many households with total expenditure x. Hence, $\overline{f}_k(p,x)$ is not the demand of an *individual* household, but the *average* demand of many households.

The function

$$x \mapsto \overline{f}_k(p,x)$$

defines the *cross-section Engel curve for commodity k*, given the price system p, of the consumption sector.

We shall assume that the distribution of total expenditure can be described by a density $\rho$ on $\mathbb{R}_+$. Thus, $\rho(x) \geq 0$,

$$\int_{\mathbb{R}_+} \rho(x)dx = 1 ,$$

and mean expenditure

$$\overline{x} := \int_{\mathbb{R}_+} x\rho(x)dx$$

is finite.

The *market demand function* F *for commodity* $k \in K$ is then defined by

$$F_k(p) = \int_{\mathbb{R}_+} \overline{f}_k(p,x)\rho(x)dx .$$

The vector-valued function $F : \mathbb{R}^K_{++} \rightarrow \mathbb{R}^K$, defined by

$$p = \begin{pmatrix} p_1 \\ \vdots \\ p_K \end{pmatrix} \mapsto \begin{pmatrix} F_1(p) \\ \vdots \\ F_K(p) \end{pmatrix} = F(p) ,$$

is called the market demand function of the consumption sector. By definition we have all for all price vectors p,

$$p \cdot F(p) := \sum_{k \in K} p_k F_k(p) = \int_{\mathbb{R}_+} x\rho(x)dx = : \overline{x} .$$

The market demand function F satisfies the *Law of Demand* if for every pair of price vectors p and q the following inequality holds:

$$(p - q) \cdot \left(F(p) - F(q)\right) \leq 0 .$$

That is to say, the vector of price changes and the vector of demand changes point in opposite directions.

Clearly, the Law of Demand implies that all partial market demand curves are downward sloping (more precisely, are nowhere increasing), but it is a much stronger property. Indeed, for a differentiable demand function F, one can show that the Law of Demand is equivalent with the negative semi-definiteness of the Jacobian matrix $\partial_p F(p)$ for every p. That is to say,

$$\sum_{k\in K}\sum_{j\in K} v_k v_j \cdot \partial_{p_k} F_j(p) \leq 0 \ ,$$

for every vector $v \in \mathbb{R}^K$. Thus, all diagonal elements, *i.e.*, $\partial_{p_k}F_k(p)$, are less than or equal to zero. Yet this does not imply the negative semi-definiteness of the Jacobian Matrix $\partial_p F(p)$.

The market demand function F satisfies the *Weak Axiom of Revealed Preference* if for every pair of price vectors p and q

$$q \cdot F(p) \leq \overline{x}$$

implies

$$p \cdot F(q) \geq \overline{x} \ .$$

One easily shows that the Law of Demand implies the Weak Axiom but not the converse. In the case of a differentiable market demand function F, one can again characterize the Weak Axiom in terms of the Jacobian matrix $\partial_p F(p)$. Indeed, the market demand function F satisfies the Weak Axiom if and only if the Jacobian matrix $\partial_p F(p)$ is negative semi-definite on the hyperplane $F(p)^{\perp} = \{y \in \mathbb{R}^K \mid F(p) \cdot y = 0\}$, *i.e.*,

$$\sum_{k\in K}\sum_{j\in K} v_k v_j \cdot \partial_{p_k} F_j(p) \leq 0 \qquad \text{for every } v \in F(p)^{\perp} \ .$$

It is well known that the traditional hypothesis of rational behavior of an individual household does not imply that the market demand function F of a large consumption sector, where the consumers may differ in preferences and total expenditure, satisfies the Law of Demand or the Weak Axiom of Revealed Preference. These properties are however needed if one would like to obtain well-determined market equilibria, which are defined as a solution of equating market demand and market supply.

We now want to come back to our claim that the shape of the cross-section Engel curves and the expenditure distribution play an important role for deriving the Law of Demand or the Weak Axiom of Revealed Preference.

Under suitable assumptions on the consumption sector, one can show (for details see section 2 below and Hildenbrand (1991)) that the Jacobian matrix $\partial_p F(p)$ is the difference of a negative semi-definite matrix and the following matrix $\overline{A}$

$$\overline{A} = \left( \int \left(\partial_x \overline{f}_k(p,x)\right) \overline{f}_j(p,x) \rho(x) dx \right)_{k,j=1,\dots,K} \ .$$

Thus positive semi-definiteness of this matrix would enforce the Law of Demand or positive semi-definiteness on the hyperplane $F(p)^{\perp}$ would enforce the Weak Axiom.

The matrix $\overline{A}$ looks formally like an average (with respect to the density $\rho$) of Slutsky income effect matrices which are derived from the "demand function" $(p,x) \mapsto \overline{f}(p,x)$. Note, however, that the cross-section Engel function $\overline{f}(p,x)$ is, by definition, not an *individual* demand function. The cross-section Engel function $\overline{f}$ is, in general, not compatible with the *hypothesis of utility maximimization*, it does not satisfy the *Weak Axiom of Revealed Preference*, and it is, in general, not even *homogeneous* of degree zero in (p,x). Only under suitable assumptions on the *joint* distribution of individual preferences and expenditure will the function $\overline{f}(\cdot,\cdot)$ have these properties.

There are two ways to analyse the matrix $\overline{A}$, either empirically or theoretically. In the first case, using cross-section data, one can estimate the matrix $\overline{A}$ and then check whether the estimated matrix $\overline{A}$ is positive semi-definite. This approach has been followed in

Hildenbrand, K. and W. Hildenbrand (1986). The non-parametric estimations of the matrix $\overline{A}$, which have been carried out so far at the SFB 303 in Bonn, using the UK Family Expenditure Survey for the years 1969-83, show that the estimated matrices are "approximately" positive definite. More precisely, the matrix $\overline{A}$ is typically ill-conditioned; some eigenvalues (of the symmetrized matrix) are very small in magnitude (positive or negative); however, the larger eigenvalues are always positive. In this paper, we want to give a theoretical argument that makes this empirical finding possible.

We shall argue in the following that the matrix $\overline{A}$ tends to be positive semi-definite if the cross-section Engel curves and the income distributions have the following characteristic features:

(1) *The cross-section Engel curves "bend slowly,"* in the sense that higher derivatives can be neglected. A specific form of this property is, for example, that Engel curves can be approximated on the relevant domain by polynomials of low degree (say less than 5).

(2) *There is sufficient "dispersion"* ("inequality") *in the distribution of total expenditure.*

As an illustration, we state the following example (see Proposition 3): The matrix $\overline{A}$ is positive semi-definite on the hyperplane $F(p)^{\perp}$ if

(i) on the relevant domain, all cross-section Engel curves $\overline{f}_k(p,x)$ are of "Working type," *i.e.*,

$$\overline{f}_k(p,x) = \alpha_1^k(p)x + \alpha_2^k(p)x \log x \ .$$

Furthermore, the matrix $\overline{A}$ is positive semi-definite everywhere if one assumes

(ii) the distribution of total expenditure is lognormal and the coefficient of variation is larger than 0.53

Thus, under the (ad hoc!) assumptions (i) and (ii), which however are often made in applied work [see, *i.e.*, Houthakker (1987)], there is no need to estimate the cross-section Engel curves if one is only interested in the definiteness of the matrix $\overline{A}$, It suffices to estimate the coefficient of variation of the income distribution, which typically is much larger than 0.53! Empirical estimates show that the coefficient of variation is typically about 0.7

Finally, we remark that for arbitrary cross-section Engel curves, the matrix $\overline{A}$ is positive semi-definite if the density $\rho$ is decreasing on $\mathbb{R}_+$ (Hildenbrand 1983). This assumption is however not supported by empirical studies. Chiappori (1985) studied Engel curves which permit replacing, without changing the market demand, an arbitrary density by a decreasing one. His conditions are similar to the ones used in this paper.

## 2. Cross-Section Demand Functions

We shall assume that each household is described by a demand function f and a level of total expenditure x, *i.e.*, the characteristics of a household are a pair (f,x). It is convenient to parametrize the set of all admissible demand functions by a parameter $\alpha \in A$. This is no restriction since the parameter space $A$ can be any separable metric space, for example the space of all admissible demand functions itself.

A consumption sector is then described by a joint distribution of (f,x), hence by a measure $\mu$ on the space $A \times \mathbb{R}_+$ of household characteristics. It should be noticed that in this setup the distribution of total expenditure is, by definition, independent of the price system p.

The *market demand function* $F : \mathbb{R}^K_{++} \to \mathbb{R}^K$ is then defined by

$$F(p) := \int_{A \times \mathbb{R}_+} f^\alpha(p,x) d\mu \ .$$

For the purpose of this paper, it is convenient to rewrite the market demand function by conditioning on the expenditure level. That is to say, we define the *cross-section demand function*

$$\bar{f}(p,x) := \int_A f^\alpha(p,x) d\mu|x$$

where $\mu|x$ is the conditional distribution of demand functions given the expenditure level x. Furthermore, let $\rho$ denote a density of the marginal distribution of expenditure. With this notation, we obtain for the market demand function

$$F(p) = \int_{\mathbb{R}_+} \bar{f}(p,x)\rho(x)\, dx \ .$$

As explained in the introduction, in demand analysis one is interested in properties of the Jacobian matrix $\partial_p F(p)$ of the market demand function. Indeed, the Law of Demand as well as the Weak Axiom of Revealed Preference for the market demand function F can be expressed in terms of the Jacobian matrix. That is to say, one is interested in negative semi-definiteness of $\partial_p F(p)$ for the Law of Demand and negative semi-definiteness on the hyperplane $F(p)^\perp = \{y \in \mathbb{R}^K | y \cdot F(p) = 0\}$ for the Weak Axiom.

Since

$$F(p) = \int_{\mathbb{R}_+} \bar{f}(p,x)\rho(x) dx \ ,$$

we obtain

$$\partial_p F(p) = \int_{\mathbb{R}_+} \partial_p \bar{f}(p,x)\rho(x) dx \ .$$

The Slutsky decomposition of the cross-section demand function $\bar{f}$ leads to

$$\partial_p \bar{f}(p,x) = S\bar{f}(p,x) - \partial_x \bar{f}(p,x)\bar{f}(px)^T \ .$$

Hence we obtain

$$\partial_p F(p) = \int_{\mathbb{R}_+} S\bar{f}(p,x)\rho(x) dx - \int_{\mathbb{R}_+} \left(\partial_x \bar{f}(p,x)\right)\bar{f}(p,x)^T \rho(x) dx \ .$$

The first matrix on the right-hand side is not, in general, negative semi-definite. Indeed, one can show that the Slutsky substitution matrix $S\overline{f}(p,x)$ is negative semi-definite for every p and x if and only if the cross-section demand function $\overline{f}$ satisfies the Weak Axiom of Revealed Preference.

However, it is well known that the Weak Axiom of Revealed Preference for individual demand functions does not imply in general that the cross-section demand function $\overline{f}$ has this property. Hence, we either assume without much justification the Weak Axiom for the cross-section demand function $\overline{f}$, or we rely on results which imply this property for $\overline{f}$ by making additional assumptions on the distribution $\mu$ of consumption characteristics. For details see Hildenbrand (1991). We want to show in this paper under which circumstances the second matrix, *i.e.*,

$$\overline{A} := \int_{\mathbb{R}_+} \left(\partial_x \overline{f}(p,x)\right)\overline{f}(p,x)^T \rho(x)dx \quad ;$$

is positive semi-definite, or at least positive semi-definite on the hyperplane $\overline{F(p)}^{\perp}$. Therefore, we consider the sum of the matrix $\overline{A}$ and its transposed $\overline{A}^T$; we then obtain the symmetric matrix

$$B(\overline{f},\rho) := \int_{\mathbb{R}_+} \partial_x\left(\overline{f}(p,x)\overline{f}(p,x)^T\right)\rho(x)dx \; .$$

Clearly, $\overline{A}$ is positive and semi-definite (respectively, on the hyperplane determined by mean demand) if and only if $B(\overline{f},\rho)$ is positive semi-definite (respectively, on the hyperplane determined by mean demand). In this paper we analyse in detail the matrix $B(\overline{f},\rho)$.

The basic assumption is that *on the relevant domain* (*i.e.*, the support of the expenditure density $\rho$), the cross-section Engel curves are of the form

$$\overline{f}_k(p,x) = \alpha_1^k(p)b_1(p,x) + \ldots + \alpha_S^k(p)b_S(p,x) \; ,$$

where the given "base functions" $b_s(.,.)$ of $\mathbb{R}_{++}^K \times \mathbb{R}_+$ into $\mathbb{R}$, $s = 1, \ldots, S$ depend on the price system $p \in \mathbb{R}_{++}^K$ as well as on the expenditure x, but are independent of the commodity $k \in \{1,\ldots,K\}$, while the coefficients $\alpha_s^k(p)$ depend on p and k, but are independent of the expenditure level x.

Of course, if $S \geq K$, it is no restriction at all to assume that a given cross-section demand function has cross-section Engel curves of the above form, since we can let $b_s(.,.) = \overline{f}_s(.,.)$ for $s \leq K$ and $\alpha_s^k(p) = 1$ if $s = k \leq K$ and $\alpha_s^k(p) = 0$ for all other s,k. However, the idea is that the number of base functions is small compared with the number of commodities (commodity aggregates), and that the base functions are chosen independently of the particular cross-section demand function. We allow the base functions to depend on the price system, but in the examples below we shall use base functions which only depend on the expenditure level x.

Obviously, the acceptability of using few base functions is an empirical question. The restrictiveness of the assumption depends not only on the total number S of base functions, but also on the form of the base functions $b_1,\ldots,b_S$, on the size of the relevant domain, and on the definition of the commodities. For example, the cross-section Engel curve for a commodity aggregate, like "food," seems to be well described by a polynomial of low degree (say 4) on an interval which contains, say, 95% of all individual income data. (See *e.g.* Hildenbrand (1989)).

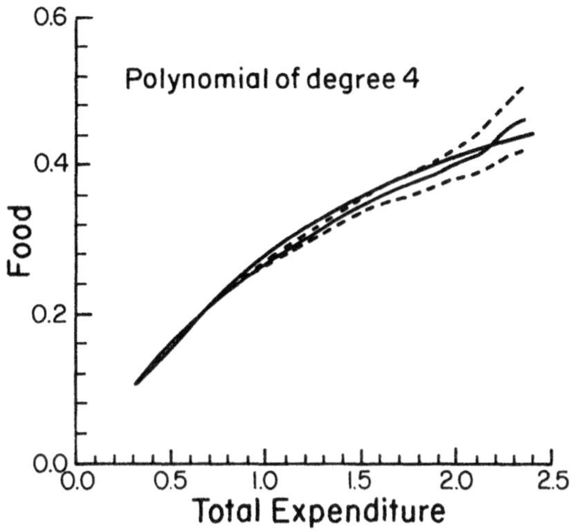


**Figure 1**

Yet even for this statement we have to know how cross-section Engel curves typically look. For this we need *non-parametric* regression analysis of household expenditure data. Economic theory will tell us nothing about the shape of *cross-section* Engel curves, and hence, about the acceptability of our basic assumption. In this paper we shall refer only casually to empirical facts. The purpose here is to show the logical implications of our basic (ad hoc) assumption on the shape of cross-section Engel curves.

Let us now consider a fixed collection of base functions $b_1(.,.),...,b_S(.,.)$ of $\mathbb{R}^K_{++} \times \mathbb{R}_+$ into $\mathbb{R}$. We want to analyse the matrix $B(f,\rho)$ for a fixed price system. Therefore we can drop p as a variable.

Given the collection $b_1,...,b_S$, we denote by $\mathscr{L}(b)$ the linear function space spanned by the functions $b_1,...,b_S$, that is to say the functions $\overline{f}$ of $\mathbb{R}_+$ into $\mathbb{R}^K$ which are of the form

$$\overline{f}(\cdot) = \sum_{s=1}^{S} \alpha_s b_s(\cdot) \text{ , where } \alpha_s \in \mathbb{R}^K .$$

Note that for any function $\overline{f} \in \mathscr{L}(b)$, the image set $\{\overline{f}(x) \in \mathbb{R}^K | x \in \mathbb{R}_+\}$ of $\overline{f}$ is contained in a subspace of dimension less than or equal to S, *i.e.*, the linear subspace spanned by the vectors of coefficients $\alpha_1,...,\alpha_S$.

For every collection of basic functions $b_1,...,b_S$ and every density $\rho$ on $\mathbb{R}_+$ we define

- the S × S matrix $B(b,\rho)$ by

$$\big(B(b,\rho)\big)_{h,j} = \int_{\mathbb{R}_+} \big(b_h(x) b_j(x)\big)' \rho(x) dx$$

and

the vector $a(b,\rho) \in \mathbb{R}^S$ by

$$\left(a(b,\rho)\right)_s = \int_{\mathbb{R}_+} b_s(x)\rho(x)dx \ .$$

Also we define

$$a(\overline{f},\rho) = \int_{\mathbb{R}_+} \overline{f}(p$$

We shall now show that the positive semi-definiteness of $B(\overline{f},\rho)$ is closely related to the positive semi-definiteness of $B(b,\rho)$.

**PROPOSITION 1.** *The rank of the matrix* $B(\overline{f},\rho)$ *is not larger than the number* $S$ *of base functions, and the* $K \times K$ matrix $B(\overline{f},\rho)$ *is positive semi-definite (respectively on* $a(\overline{f},\rho)^{\perp}$*).*

**PROOF.** Consider any function $\overline{f} \in \mathscr{L}(b)$. By definition

$$\overline{f}_k(x) = \sum_{s=1}^{S} \alpha_s^k b_s(x)$$

$k = 1,\dots,K$, for some $\alpha_1,\dots,\alpha_S \in \mathbb{R}^K$. Hence

$$B(\overline{f},\rho)_{h,j} = \int_{\mathbb{R}_+} \left( \left[ \sum_{s=1}^{S} \alpha_s^h b_s(x) \right] \left[ \sum_{s=1}^{S} \alpha_s^j b_s(x) \right] \right)' \rho(x)\, dx$$

$$= \sum_{u=1}^{S} \sum_{v=1}^{S} \alpha_u^h \alpha_v^j \int_{\mathbb{R}_+} \left(b_u(x) b_v(x)\right)' \rho(x)\, dx$$

Let C denote the $S \times K$ matrix of coefficients of $\overline{f}$, and $C^T$ its transpose.

With this notation, we obtain $B(\overline{f},\rho) = C^T B(b,\rho) C$, and moreover, since

$$a(\overline{f},\rho) = \sum_{s=1}^{S} \alpha_s a_s(b,\rho) \ ,$$

we obtain that $u \in a(\overline{f},\rho)^{\perp}$ if and only if $Cu \in a(b,\rho)^{\perp}$. These observations imply the proposition.

**REMARK.** We actually proved a slightly stronger result; let $\overline{f} \in \mathscr{L}(b)$, then the matrix $B(\overline{f},\rho)$ is positive semi-definite (positive definite, respectively) if and only if $B(b,\rho)$ is positive semi-definite on ImC, the image space of C (positive definite on ImC and rank $C = K$); the matrix $B(\overline{f},\rho)$ is positive semi-definite on $a(b,\rho)^{\perp}$ if and only if $B(b,\rho)$ is positive semi-definite on $\mathrm{Im}C \cap a(b,\rho)^{\perp}$.

We also remark that if one uses only few base functions, then the typical situation for an estimated cross-section demand function $\overline{f} \in \mathscr{L}(b)$ will be that rank $C = S < K$.

There are two different ways of looking at Proposition 1. From a theoretical point of view, one may hope to specify collections of base functions which imply that $B(b,\rho)$ is positive semi-definite (or at least positive semi-definite on $a(b,\rho)^{\perp}$) for a reasonably large class of expenditure distribution. We shall pursue this view below.

However, Proposition 1 also shows that, if for a given data set one wants to analyse whether the matrix $B(\overline{f},\rho)$ is positive semi-definite, then one has not to estimate the cross-section demand function, provided one assumes that it is generated by a given collection of base functions. Indeed, one should investigate directly whether the matrix $B(b,\rho)$ is positive semi-definite for the estimated expenditure distribution. Only in the exceptional case where rank $C < S$, $B(\overline{f},\rho)$ can be positive semi-definite without $B(b,\rho)$ having this property.

## 3. Polynomial Cross-section Engel Curves

In this section, we choose particularly simple base functions, namely

$$b_s(x) = x^s, \qquad s = 1,\dots,S .$$

Thus, on the relevant domain, all cross-section Engel curves are assumed to be polynomials of degree S. Clearly, if S is large and if the support of $\rho$ is bounded, then our assumption is not very restrictive. If it is applied to commodity aggregates, then, as we illustrated above for the case of "food," even for small S (say less than 5) the assumption is not very restrictive.

Let $\rho$ be a density such that the moment $m_h = \int x^h \rho(x)\,dx$ exists for $h = 1, \dots, 2S - 1$. The matrix $B(b,\rho)$ in Proposition 1 now becomes the $S \times S$ "matrix of moments"

$$M(S,\rho) = \left((h+j)m_{h+j-1}\right)_{h,j=1,\dots,S} .$$

Correspondingly the vector $a(b,\rho)$ becomes the S-vector of moments

$$m(S,\rho) = \left(m_1,\dots,m_S\right) .$$

Proposition 1 consequently implies the following:

**COROLLARY 1.** *Assume that all cross-section Engel curves* $\overline{f}_k$ *are, on the relevant domain, polynomials of degree* S. *Then a sufficient condition for positive semi-definiteness (respectively, on the hyperplane of* $a(\overline{f},\rho)^{\perp}$*) of the matrix* $B(\overline{f},\rho)$ *is that the "matrix of moments"* $M(S,\rho)$ *is positive semi-definite (respectively, on the hyperplane* $m(S,\rho)^{\perp}$*). This matrix involves only the moments of the income distribution up to order* $2S - 1$.

Our problem thus reduces to the question: For what kind of income distributions $\rho$ is the "matrix of moments,"

$$M(S,\rho) = \left((h+j)m_{h+j-1}\right)_{h,j=1,\dots,S} ,$$

positive semi-definite?

Again we can approach this question empirically or theoretically. Using the UK Family Expenditure Survey for the years 1969 - 83, we estimated the moments of the expenditure distribution (for different household groups) and checked the estimated matrix of moments for positive definiteness.[1] For values of S less than 4, the estimated matrices turned out to

---

[1] These estimations and calculations have been made by H. P. Schmitz, SFB 303, Bonn. We would like to thank him for his help.

be positive definite. For larger values of S, say S = 7, some eigenvalues turned out to be negative but they were all very small.

It is interesting to remark that in the case S = 2 the "matrix of moments" M(2,$\rho$) is positive semi-definite on $(m(2,\rho))^{\perp}$ *for any density* $\rho$.

Indeed, we have that

$$m(2,\rho) = \begin{bmatrix} 2m_1 & 3m_2 \\ 3m_2 & 4m_3 \end{bmatrix} \text{,and}$$

$$m(2,\rho) = \begin{bmatrix} m_1 \\ m_2 \end{bmatrix}.$$

Using the Schwarz inequality, it is easily seen that $y^T M(2,\rho) y \geq 0$ for all $y \in (m(2,\rho))^{\perp}$.

This remark is similar to a result in Freixas and Mas-Colell (1987) since, when S = 2, the image of any function in $\mathscr{L}$(b) is contained in a two-dimensional subspace of the commodity space.

In order to understand which property of the income distribution drives the matrix of moments to become positive definite, we now compute this matrix for a lognormal distribution:

$$\rho(x) = \frac{1}{\sqrt{2\pi\sigma^2}} \cdot \frac{1}{x} \exp\{-\frac{(\ln x - \mu)^2}{2\sigma^2}\}.$$

These calculations should be taken only as illustrations. In fact, our assumption is that the cross-section demand functions on the relevant domain are in the linear span of the base functions. We should therefore also restrict the lognormal distribution to the relevant domain. To simplify the calculations we will not do so.

**PROPOSITION 2.** *Let* $\rho$ *be the density of the lognormal distribution. Then the positive definiteness of the matrix of moments* M(S,$\rho$) *depends only on the parameter* $\sigma$, *and hence on the coefficient of variation of* $\rho$; *for every integer* S *there exists a constant* k(S) *such that a coefficient of variation of* $\rho$ *larger than* k(S) *implies that* M(S,$\rho$) *is positive definite. Specifically,* M(S,$\rho$) *is positive definite if*

S = 2 *and* $\sigma^2 \geq 0.12$ *i.e., the coefficient of variation of* $\rho \geq 0.36$

S = 3 *and* $\sigma^2 \geq 0.22$ *i.e., the coefficient of variation of* $\rho \geq 0.50$

S = 4 *and* $\sigma^2 \geq 0.30$ *i.e., the coefficient of variation of* $\rho \geq 0.59$ .

Moreover, M(S,$\rho$) is positive semi-definite on $m(S,\rho)^{\perp}$ for any coefficient of variation of $\rho$, if S $\leq$ 2, and larger than 0.30 if S = 3.

**PROOF.** The h-th moment $m_h$ for the lognormal density with parameter $\mu$ and $\sigma$ is given by

$$m_h = \exp^{h\mu + (h^2\sigma^2/2)}, \quad h = 1,2,\ldots$$

Let $\alpha = \exp^{\mu}$ and $\beta = \exp^{\frac{\sigma^2}{2}}$. For the matrix of moments $M(S,\rho)$ we then obtain

$$M_{hj} = (h+j)\alpha^{(h+j-1)} \bullet \beta^{(h+j-1)^2}.$$

We now claim that the matrix $M(S,\rho)$ is positive definite if and only if the $S \times S$ matrix $\tilde{M}$, defined by

$$\tilde{M}_{hj} = (h+j)\beta^{2(1+h\bullet j-(h+j))}$$

is positive definite. Since the matrices M and $\tilde{M}$ are symmetric, it suffices to verify that the determinant of every principal minor of $M(S,\rho)$ is positive if and only if the determinant of the corresponding principal minor of $\tilde{M}$ is positive.

To show this, let $1 \le i_1 < i_2 < \ldots < i_N$ and the corresponding principal minors of M and $\tilde{M}$, *i.e.*,

$$M(i_1,\ldots,i_N) = (M_{hj})_{\substack{h=i_1,\ldots,i_N \\ j=i_1,\ldots,i_N}}$$

and

$$\tilde{M}(i_1,\ldots,i_N) = (\tilde{M}_{hj})_{\substack{h=i_1,\ldots,i_N \\ j=i_1,\ldots,i_N}}.$$

By definition of a determinant we have

$$\det M(i_1,\ldots,i_N) = \sum_{\sigma} \mathrm{sign}(\sigma) \bullet \prod_{h=1}^{N} M_{i_h, i_{\sigma(h)}}$$

and

$$\det \tilde{M}(i_1,\ldots,i_N) = \sum_{\sigma} \mathrm{sign}(\sigma) \bullet \prod_{h=1}^{N} \tilde{M}_{i_h, i_{\sigma(h)}}$$

where the summation is over all permutations $\sigma$ of $\{1, \ldots, N\}$. Consider the quotient

$$Q(\sigma) = \frac{\mathrm{sign}(\sigma) \prod_{h=1}^{N} M_{i_h, i_{\sigma(h)}}}{\mathrm{sign}(\sigma) \prod_{h=1}^{N} \tilde{M}_{i_h, i_{\sigma(h)}}}.$$

One then obtains

$$Q(\sigma) = \prod_{h=1}^{N} \alpha^{(i_h + i_{\sigma(h)} - 1)} \bullet \prod_{h=1}^{N} \beta^{((i_h)^2 + (i_{\sigma(h)})^2 - 1)}$$

$$= \alpha^{\left[\sum_{h=1}^{N} 2i_h - N\right]} \bullet \beta^{2\sum_{h=1}^{N} (i_h)^2 - N} > 0.$$

Thus $Q(\sigma)$ is independent of the permutation $\sigma$. Consequently, we showed that

$$\det M(i_1,\dots,i_N) = Q \cdot \det \tilde{M}(i_1,\dots,i_N) .$$

Note that the matrix $\tilde{M}$ depends only on $\beta$, and hence on the parameter $\sigma$. Recall that the coefficient of variation of the lognormal distribution is given by

$$\sqrt{\exp^{\sigma^2} - 1} .$$

For S = 2 we obtain

$$\tilde{M} = \begin{pmatrix} 2 & 3 \\ 3 & 4\beta^2 \end{pmatrix} .$$

The matrix $\tilde{M}$ is positive definite if (and only if) $\beta^2 > 9/8$, and hence, if $\sigma^2 > \ln(9/8) = 0.1178$. For S = 3 we obtain

$$\tilde{M} = \begin{pmatrix} 2 & 3 & 4 \\ 3 & 4\beta^2 & 5\beta^4 \\ 4 & 5\beta^4 & 6\beta^8 \end{pmatrix} .$$

The matrix $\tilde{M}$ is positive definite if $\beta^2 > 9/8$ and $\det \tilde{M} > 0$. Since

$$\det \tilde{M} = 8\beta^2(\beta^2 - 1)^2(6\beta^4 - \beta^2 - 8) ,$$

we obtain $\det \tilde{M} > 0$ if

$$\beta^2 > \frac{1}{12}\left(1 + \sqrt{193}\right) = 1.2410$$

and hence, if

$$\sigma^2 > \ln\left[\frac{1}{12}\left(1 + \sqrt{193}\right)\right] = 0.2159.$$

For S = 4 we obtain

$$\tilde{M} = \begin{pmatrix} 2 & 3 & 4 & 5 \\ 3 & 4\beta^2 & 5\beta^4 & 6\beta^6 \\ 4 & 5\beta^4 & 6\beta^8 & 7\beta^{12} \\ 5 & 6\beta^6 & 7\beta^{12} & 8\beta^{18} \end{pmatrix} .$$

By using the first row and calculating the 4 subdeterminants, one obtains that

$$\det \tilde{M} = u^4(u - 1)^4 C(u) ,$$

where $\quad C(u) = 384u^6 + 312u^5 - 615u^4 - 996u^3 - 374u^2 + 700u + 625, \quad u = \beta^2.$

By evaluating C(u), one sees that $C'(u) > 0$ for every $u \geq 1.35$, and moreover, $C(1.35) > 0$. Consequently for $u \geq 1.35$, we have that $\det(\tilde{M}) > 0$, and combining with S = 2 and S = 3 we obtain that $\tilde{M}$ is positive definite for $u \geq 1.35$, and hence for $\sigma^2 \geq \ln(1.35) = 0.300$.

Moreover, it is seen from the structure of $\tilde{M}$ that, in going from S - 1 to S, we add a new restriction which will be satisfied if $\beta$ is large enough, *i.e.*, if the coefficient of variation of $\rho$ is large enough.

For S = 2 the last part of the proposition follows from the remark above.

For S = 3 we have that $m(3,\rho) = \alpha\beta(1,\alpha\beta^3,\alpha^2\beta^8)$, and therefore that $y \in (m(3,\rho))^{\perp}$ if and only if

$$y^T = \lambda \left(1, \frac{t}{\alpha}, -\frac{1}{\alpha^2\beta^8} - t\frac{1}{\alpha^2\beta^5}\right) \quad \lambda, t \in \mathbb{R} .$$

Calculating $y^T M(3,\rho)y$ for $\lambda = 1$, we obtain

$$y^T M(3,\rho)y = 2\alpha\beta(\beta^2-1)[\beta^8(3\beta^4+3\beta^2-2)t^2 + \beta^3(\beta^2+1)(6\beta^4+1)t+3(\beta^6+\beta^4+\beta^2+1)].$$

Since $\beta^2 > 1.09$, we have that $y^T M(3,\rho)y > 0$ for all $t \in \mathbb{R}$. Therefore, $M(3,\rho)$ is positive semi-definite on $m(3,\rho)^{\perp}$ for any coefficient of variation of $\rho$.

## 4. Cross-section Engel Curves of the Working Type

In this section, we choose the following base functions:

$$b_1(x) = x, \qquad b_2(x) = x \log x, \text{ and } \qquad b_3(x) - x \log^2 x.$$

Engel curves which are spanned by these base functions are called "Working Engel Curves." They are often used in empirical studies [see *e.g.* Houthakker (1987) and Deaton (1981)].

Let $n_i - \int x \log^i(x)\rho(x)dx$ , i = 1,..., 4. One easily verifies that

$$B(b_1,b_2,\rho) - \begin{pmatrix} 2m_1 & m_1+2n_1 \\ m_1+2n_1 & 2n_1+2n_2 \end{pmatrix},$$

$$B(b_1,b_2,b_3,\rho) = \begin{pmatrix} 2m_1 & m_1+2n_1 & 2n_1+2n_2 \\ m_1+2n_1 & 2n_1+2n_2 & 3n_2+2n_3 \\ 2n_1+2n_2 & 3n_2+2n_3 & 4n_3+2n_4 \end{pmatrix},$$

$$a(b_1,b_2,\rho) = (m_1,n_1) ,$$

and

$$a(b_1,b_2,b_3,\rho) = (m_1,n_1,n_2) .$$

Since $m_1 > 0$, the matrix $B(b_1,b_2,\rho)$ is positive definite if and only if $\det(B(b_1,b_2,\rho)) > 0$. Correspondingly, the matrix $B(b_1,b_2,b_3,\rho)$ is positive definite if and only if $\det(B(b_1,b_2,\rho)) > 0$ and $\det(B(b_1,b_2,b_3,\rho)) > 0$. We then obtain the following.

**COROLLARY 2.** *Assume that all cross-section Engel curves $\overline{f}_k$ are, on the relevant domain, of Working type. Then a sufficient condition for positive semi-definiteness of the matrix* $B(\overline{f},\rho)$ *is that*

$$\det(B(b_1,b_2,\rho)) > 0 \qquad \text{and} \qquad \det(B(b_1,b_2,b_3,\rho)) > 0.$$

*Moreover,* $B(\overline{f},\rho)$ *is positive semi-definite on* $a(\overline{f},\rho)^\perp$ *if* $B(b,\rho)$ *is positive semi-definite on* $a(b,\rho)^\perp$.

For all empirical income distributions that we estimated, the condition for $S = 2$ was satisfied.

Just as for the polynomial base, we have for the working base $S = 2$ that $B(b_1,b_2,\rho)$ is positive semi-definite on $a(b_1,b_2,\rho)^\perp$ *for any density* $\rho$. Again, this follows from the Schwarz inequality, since

$$\left(\int x|\log x|\rho\,(x)dx\right)^2 \geq \left(\int x\,\log\,x\rho\,(x)dx\right)^2 .$$

In order to understand which property of the income distribution drives the matrix $B(b,\rho)$ to become positive definite, we also compute the above conditions for a lognormal distribution. For the special case of a lognormal income distribution with parameters $\mu$ and $\sigma$, one obtains

$$\det(B(b_1,b_2,\rho)) = m_1^2(4\sigma^2 - 1)\,,$$

and

$$\det(B(b_1,b_2,b_3,\rho)) = m_1^3\sigma^4(8\sigma^2 - 6).$$

**PROPOSITION 3.** *Let $\rho$ be the density of the lognormal distribution, and let the base functions be of the Working type.*

- $B(b_1,b_2,\rho)$ *is positive definite if and only if $\sigma > \frac{1}{2}$, i.e., if the coefficient of variation of $\rho$* $> 0.53$.

- $B(b_1,b_2,b_3,\rho)$ *is positive definite if and only if $\sigma > \sqrt{0.75}$, i.e., if the coefficient of variation of $\rho > 1.06$.*

- $B(b_1,b_2,\rho)$ *is positive semi-definite on* $a(b_1,b_2,\rho)^\perp$ *for any coefficient of variation of $\rho$.*

- $B(b_1,b_2,b_3,\rho)$ *is positive semi-definite on* $a(b_1,b_2,b_3,\rho)^\perp$ *if $\sigma > \sqrt{0.5}$, i.e., if the coefficient of variation of $\rho > 0.81$.*

**PROOF.** The first part of the proposition follows immediately from the calculations above. For $S = 2$, the last part of the proposition follows from the remark above. In the case $S = 3$, we let

$$y^T = \left(1, -\frac{m_1}{n_1} - \frac{n_2}{n_1}v, v\right), \quad v \in \mathbb{R}.$$

Calculating $y^T B(b_1,b_2,b_3,\rho)y$, we obtain

$$y^T B(b_1,b_2,b_3,\rho)y = 2m_0\frac{\beta}{\alpha^2}\left[v^2\left((\alpha-\beta)^2 + \alpha^2(\alpha^2+2\alpha-1)\right) + v\left(-2\alpha+2\beta-2\alpha^2\right)+1\right],$$

where $\alpha = \sigma^2 + \mu$ and $\beta = \sigma^2$. If $\beta \geq 0.5$, we have

$$(\alpha-\beta)^2 + \alpha^2\left(\alpha^2 + 2\alpha - 1\right) > 0$$

for $\alpha \geq \beta$, and

$$\min_{y} y^T B\left(b_1,b_2,b_3,\rho\right)y = 4\alpha^2(2\beta - 1) \geq 0 .$$

As we mentioned above, empirical estimate of the coefficient of variation of the expenditure distribution is typically about 0.7. Therefore, if one has reason to believe that it is necessary to use the Working class with S ≥ 3 as a base for the cross-section Engel curves, then it is necessary to investigate more closely the other matrices in the decomposition of the Jacobian matrix of market demand, as explained in the introduction.

## 5. Some Further Remarks

A natural requirement of a collection of base functions is that for all expenditures x > 0 and every open neighborhood U of x, the restrictions of the base functions to U are linear independent. This is the case for the polynomial base and the Working base we used in sections 3 and 4. If this requirement is satisfied, then any function $\overline{f} \in \mathscr{L}(b)$ has the property that if U is an open neighborhood of some expenditure x > 0, then the span of $\overline{f}$'s image of U, $\{\overline{f}(x) | x \in U\}$, is equal to the subspace spanned by the coefficients of $\overline{f}$. It is this property which allows us to avoid the obvious counterexamples to the positive semi-definiteness of $B(\overline{f},\rho)$.

To illustrate this, let us consider an arbitrary cross-section demand function $\overline{f}$ such that $\overline{f}(0) = 0$ and a differentiable density with support $\mathbb{R}_+$. By partial integration we get

$$B(\overline{f},\rho) = -\int_{\mathbb{R}_+} \overline{f}(x)\overline{f}(x)^T \rho'(x)dx = B_1(\overline{f},\rho) - B_2(\overline{f},\rho) ,$$

where

$$B_1(\overline{f},\rho) = \int_{\{x|\rho'(x)\leq 0\}} \overline{f}(x)\overline{f}(x)^T \left(-\rho'(x)\right)dx ,$$

and

$$B_2(\overline{f},\rho) = \int_{\{x|\rho'(x)>0\}} \overline{f}(x)\overline{f}(x)^T \rho'(x)dx .$$

For each fixed expenditure, the matrix $\overline{f}(x)\overline{f}(x)^T$ is of course positive semi-definite; indeed, it has rank 1, the only non-zero eigenvalue is $\|\overline{f}(x)\|^2$, and the corresponding eigenvector is generated by the vector $\overline{f}(x)$. Therefore both matrices $B_1(\overline{f},\rho)$ and $B_2(\overline{f},\rho)$ are positive semi-definite. Also, $B(\overline{f},\rho)$ is positive semi-definite if every eigenvalue of $B_1(\overline{f},\rho)$ is larger or equal to every eigenvalue of $B_2(\overline{f},\rho)$.

The decomposition above shows that $B(\overline{f},\rho)$ is indeed positive semi-definite if $\rho$ is a decreasing density (compare Hildenbrand (1983)). However, it also allows us to extend the result in Hildenbrand (1983) slightly; if $\{\overline{f}(x)|\rho'(x) < 0\}$ spans the same space as the image of $\overline{f}$, and the eigenvalues of $B_2(\overline{f},\rho)$ are sufficiently small (*e.g.*, all elements of $B_2(\overline{f},\rho)$ are sufficiently small), then $B(\overline{f},\rho)$ is positive semi-definite.

The decomposition however also shows that $B(\overline{f},\rho)$ cannot be positive semi-definite if $\{\overline{f}(x)|\rho'(x) < 0\}$ is contained in a proper subspace of the space spanned by the image of $\overline{f}$. Such a case occurs if, *e.g.*, $\rho$ is unimodal, and there is a commodity which is only consumed by consumers having expenditure less than the mode. We also see that for any cross-section demand function $\overline{f}$, the image of which does not span $\mathbb{R}^K$, and any not decreasing density $\rho$, one can, by turning $\overline{f}$ slightly for expenditures on the increasing part of the density, obtain a function f which is arbitrary close to $\overline{f}$, and for which $B(f,\rho)$ is not positive semi-definite. In the same way, corresponding to any cross-section demand function $\overline{f}$ for which there is a non-null set U of expenditures such that $\overline{f}$'s image of U is contained in a proper subspace of the space spanned by the image of $\overline{f}$, there exists a density $\rho$, such that $B(\overline{f},\rho)$ is not positive semi-definite. This discussion clearly shows the importance of the definition of a commodity (commodity group).

As mentioned in the beginning of the section, we avoid the "counterexamples" above by considering cross-section demand functions, which are in the linear span of locally independent base functions.

## 6. Conclusion

The motivation for this paper is to show under which circumstances the market demand function does satisfy the Law of Demand, or at least the Weak Axiom of Revealed Preference. For this purpose we decomposed the Jacobian matrix of the market demand function into two matrices $\overline{S}$ and $\overline{A}$. We concentrated the analysis in this paper on the most delicate matrix $\overline{A}$. This is justified if the cross-section demand function satisfies the Weak Axiom of Revealed Preference.

In order to analyse the symmetric matrix $\overline{A} + \overline{A}^T = B(\overline{f},\rho)$, it is crucial to have a precise knowledge of the shape of the various cross-section Engel curves. We formalized the common shape of the cross-section Engel curves by considering "base functions" which generate these Engel curves. For every choice of base functions, the desired properties of the matrix $B(\overline{f},\rho)$ depend only on the expenditure distribution $\rho$, since it is sufficient to consider the matrix $B(b,\rho)$. This last matrix has been analysed by means of some examples. The desired properties of $B(b,\rho)$ can be established if there is sufficient dispersion (inequality) in the distribution of total expenditure.

## REFERENCES

Chiappori, P.A. (1985), "Distributions of Income and the 'Law of Demand,'" *Econometrica*, Vol. 53, pp. 109 - 127.

Deaton, A. (1981), "Three Essays on a Srilankan Household Survey," *Living Standards Measurement Study, W.P. No. 11*, The World Bank.

Freixas, X. and A. Mas-Colell (1987), "Engel Curves leading to the Weak Axiom in the Aggregate," *Econometrica*, Vol. 55, pp. 515 - 531.

Hildenbrand, W. (1983), "On the 'Law of Demand,'" *Econometrica*, Vol. 51, pp. 997 - 1019.

Hildenbrand, W. (1989), "Facts and Ideas in Microeconomic Theory," *European Economic Review*, Vol. 33, pp. 251 - 276.

Hildenbrand, K. and W. Hildenbrand (1986), "On the Mean Income Effect: A Data Analysis of the U.K. Family Expenditure Survey," in Hildenbrand W. and A. Mas-Colell (eds.), *Contributions to Mathematical Economics, in Honor of Gerard Debreu*, North-Holland, Amsterdam, pp. 247 - 268.

Hildenbrand, W. (1991), "Two Essays on Market Demand" (forthcoming).

Houthakker, H.S. (1953), "La Forme des Courbes d'Engel," *Cahiers du seminaire d'Econometrie*, Vol. 2.

Houthakker, H.S. and S. J. Prais (1955, reprinted 1971), **The Analysis of Family Budgets**, Cambridge University Press.

Houthakker, H.S. (1957), "An International Comparison of Household Expenditure Patterns, Commemorating the Centenary of Engel's Law," *Econometrica*, Vol. 25.

Houthakker, H.S. (October 1961), "The Present State of Consumption Theory," *Econometrica*, Vol. 29.

Houthakker, H.S. and L.D. Taylor (1st edition 1966, enlarged edition 1970), **Consumer Demand in the United States**, Harvard University Press.

Houthakker, H.S. (1987), *"Engel Curve,"* in Eatwell, J., Milgate, M. and P. Newman (eds.), **The New Palgrave**, Vol. 2, Macmillan Press, London, pp. 142 - 143.

# TESTS OF DYNAMIC SPECIFICATION AND HOMOGENEITY IN A DEMAND SYSTEM*

JOHN MUELLBAUER
PANOS PASHARDES
*Nuffield College*
*Institute for Fiscal Studies*
*Oxford University*
*Oxford OX1 1NF*
*England*

ABSTRACT. Two common findings in empirical analyses of static demand systems are a rejection of the homogeneity postulate together with significant positive serial correlation in the residuals. The thesis of this paper is that these findings reflect an inadequate dynamic specification of the demand functions. An Almost (AI) Demand System is specified which incorporates habits and durability into the utility function and is applied to British data for the period 1954-1980. A static AI model is also estimated. While the static form strongly contradicts homogeneity and symmetry and suffers from serially correlated residuals, homogeneity and symmetry are easily acceptable in the dynamic form and there is no evidence of serially correlated residuals.

## 1. Introduction

Many empirical studies have been carried out of static demand systems, *i.e.*, systems of Marshallian demand equations based on current prices and current total expenditure [see Deaton and Muellbauer (1980a, ch. 3) for relevant background]. Investigators who estimate such systems in levels typically report that significant positive serial correlation is present among the residuals. And when tests of homogeneity, *i.e.* lack of money illusion, are carried out on an equation-by-equation basis, it is common, though not for every equation, to reject the null hypothesis.[1] Investigators who estimate these systems in first differences typically

---

* The early phase of Muellbauer's contribution to this research was supported by the E.S.R.C. under the Research Programme in Quantitative and Comparative Macroeconomics, grant number HR 6235, and more recently under grant B00220012 for research on "The Roles of Expectational Variables and Feedback Mechanisms in Econometric Models" (with David Hendry). The Institute of Fiscal Studies supported Pashardes's contribution.

[1] It has been noted by Laitinen (1978) and others that systems tests based on asymptotic distribution theory tend to be biased towards rejection and therefore need to be interpreted with some care.



*L. Phlips and L.D. Taylor (eds.), Aggregation, Consumption and Trade*, 55–98.

report evidence of moderate but for some equations significantly negatively serially correlated residuals. Rejection of homogeneity on an equation-by-equation basis is again common, if less pronounced than when the equations are formulated in levels. The estimates reported by Deaton and Muellbauer (1980b) for annual British data for eight commodities for 1954-1974 are quite representative in these respects. Although first differencing apparently 'helps,'it eliminates long run information from the model and has been strongly criticized by Davidson, Hendry, Srba and Yeo (1978), as a general procedure.

It is our working hypothesis that an inadequate dynamic specification may account both for these findings of residual auto correlation and for the findings of money illusion. Some recent evidence by Anderson and Blundell (1983) supports this view. They estimate a dynamized form of the 'Almost Ideal Demand System' of Deaton and Muellbauer (1980b) in which they accept homogeneity (and symmetry) as long-run properties of behavior. However, their dynamization is not consistent with utility theory, which makes it difficult to give an economic interpretation to the observed lags. Also it is expensive in terms of the number of parameters required and so unless further, relatively arbitrary restrictions are imposed, its use is restricted to quite small systems.

The notion that demand functions are dynamic goes back at least as far as Marshall, as Phlips (1983, p.169) points out. Theil (1951) discussed (in Dutch) the role of stocks in consumer theory. A particularly influential paper was Farrell (1952) on irreversible 3 demand functions. Stone's (1954) paper on the Linear Expenditure System (LES) raised the possibility of dynamizing demand systems and the idea was implemented by introducing partial adjustment into a demand system in Stone and Rowe (1958). Cramer (1957) contained the first full treatment of the neoclassical theory of the demand for durable consumer goods while Stone and Rowe (1957) applied a partial adjustment model to the demand for consumer durables.

The introduction of explicit habit and durability effects in an empirical demand system seems to be due to Houthakker and Taylor (1966, 1970) who worked with a quadratic utility function. Pollak and Wales (1969) estimated simple habit effects in the context of the LES, while Taylor and Weiserbs (1972) and Phlips (1972) estimated models with rather more general habits and durability effects. In those papers and in the theoretical treatments by Gorman (1967), Pollak (1970,1976, 1978) and Von Weizsacker (1971), habits were considered to be myopic. In other words, consumers do not take into account in their present decisions the implications for building up future stocks of habits. Phlips (1974) discussed rational habits where consumers do take these implications into account. Until Spinnewyn (1979, 1981), it was generally thought that rational habits were analytically intractable. However, Spinnewyn developed user cost concepts for habits which are analogous to those for durables and which greatly simplify the analysis. Phlips and Spinnewyn (1982) showed that under particular expectational assumptions and preferences, myopic and rational habit formation are observationally equivalent in the demand systems context.

In the next section, we draw on this literature to suggest a model which incorporates habits and durability in the utility function and which is quite parsimonious in parameters. Section 3 uses the Almost Ideal (AI) Demand System to incorporate these effects into the empirical model which is applied to British data. In the empirical application, particular attention is paid to ensuring that over a reasonable range of data variation the empirical model implies non-negative consumption of goods. Tests of homogeneity and symmetry are carried out both for the static and dynamic versions of the model and the dynamic system is compared with a range of simpler dynamic models. A number of other diagnostic statistics are computed to evaluate the performance of the dynamic system. Section 4 puts our hypothesis on why the homogeneity postulate is rejected empirically in the context of alternative explanations, and draws conclusions.

## 2. Durability and Habit Formation

Our model incorporates, in an intertemporal preference ordering, the two fairly standard features of durability and habits, which are common to most of the models in the references listed above. It can be explained as follows.

Behind static demand it is typically assumed lies a utility function which is intertemporally separable and has separability of market goods from leisure and public goods. Thus the utility function has the form

$$u = V[v_t\ (q_{1t},...,q_{nt}),...,v_T(q_{1T},\ ...,\ q_{nT})], \tag{2.1}$$

where $q_{ij}$ is the consumption of the i'th market good in period j. Given the assumptions of a single financial asset and that households can lend or borrow at the same interest rate, it can easily be shown that under point expectations there is a linear present value form of the life cycle budget constraint

$$W_t = \sum_{i=1}^{n} \sum_{j=t}^{T} \hat{p}_{ij}q_{ij} = \sum_{j=t}^{T} e_j\ , \tag{2.2}$$

where $\hat{p}_{ij}$ is the discounted price for good i in period j expected at t. Given weak separability, two-stage budgeting is possible so that at the lower stage $v_t(q_{1t},...,q_{nt})$ is maximized subject to

$$\sum_i p_{it}q_{it} = e_t \tag{2.3}$$

conditional upon current total expenditure $e_t$.

To introduce durability into the model, define the stock

$$S_{ij} = q_{ij} + d_iS_{ij-1}, \tag{2.4}$$

where $d_i$ is the proportion of the stock remaining after one period. It can be shown [see for example Deaton and Muellbauer (1980a, Chaps. 4 and 13)] that the lifetime budget constraint is still linear as in (2.2), but with stocks in place of purchases and 'user cost' price $p^*_{ij}$ in place of $p_{ij}$, where

$$p^*_{ij} = p_{ij} - d_ip_{ij+1}/(1+r_{j+1}) \tag{2.5}$$

and $r_{j+1}$ is the interest rate expected at t to prevail between periods j and j+1. Solving the lower stage maximization problem for period t, a demand system for current stocks can be derived.

We generalize this further by introducing habits as well as durability. We replace $q_{ij}$ in (2.1) by

(2.6) $$z_{ij} = S_{ij} - a_i S_{ij-1} = q_{ij} + (d_i - a_i)S_{ij-1},$$

where $0 \leq a_i < 1$. The effect of habits can be understood as follows. If consumption services (proportional to the stock) were high last period, a higher level of current services is needed to give the same contribution to utility than when last period's consumption services were low. This is precisely the addictive effect implied by habituation. The greater is $a_i$, the greater is the degree of addiction.

Our treatment of habits is similar to that in Pollak and Wales (1969). The habit for good i depends only on last period's consumption flow. In Houthakker and Taylor (1970), Pollak (1970), Phlips (1972, 1974), Spinnewyn (1979, 1981) and Spinnnewyn (1982) there is a stock of habit which depends not only on last period's consumption flow, but is a function, with geometrically declining weights, of all previous consumption flows. Compared with ours, their formulation requires n additional parameters.

Given the linearity of (2.6), the lifetime budget constraint takes a linear, present-value form analogous to that for durables:[2]

(2.7) $$W_t = \sum_i \sum_j \check{p}_{ij} z_{ij} .$$

The definition of the 'user cost' $\check{p}_{ij}$ which allows for habits as well as durability is derived in the Appendix. There it is also shown that if households expect relative prices to be the same in period j, all j, as at t and expect a constant real r*, then

(2.8) $$\check{p}_{ij} = \lambda_i p_{it}$$

and that if the horizon is infinite,

(2.9) $$\lambda_i = \frac{1-d_i+r*}{1-a_i+r*}.$$

Given the separable utility function,

(2.10) $$u = V\left(v_t\,(z_{1t},\ldots,z_{nt}),\ldots,v_T\,(z_{1t},z_{nT})\right),$$

the decision how to allocate

[2] This is the fundamental insight of Spinnewyn (1979, 1981) in an even more general treatment of habituation.

(2.11) $$x_t = \sum_i \lambda_i p_{it} z_{it}$$

to the $z_t$'s can be made separately from the rest of the lifecycle decisions by maximizing $v_t(z_{1t},...,z_{nt})$ subject to

(2.12) $$x_t = \sum_i \lambda_i p_{it} z_{it},$$

giving Marshallian demand functions

(2.13) $$z_{it} = g_i(\lambda p_t, x_t).$$

Hence

(2.14) $$q_{it} = g_i(\lambda p_t, x_t) + (a_i - d_i) S_{it-1},$$

where

(2.15) $$S_{it} = \sum_{s=0}^{\infty} d_i^s \, q_{it-s} .$$

Given the simplified assumptions made about expectations on which (2.8) rests, (2.14) represents forward-looking behavior.

However, there is a myopic optimization problem which results in demand functions which are quite similar to (2.14): Maximize $v_t(z_{1t},...,z_{nt})$ subject to

(2.16) $$e_t = \sum_i p_{it} q_{it} ,$$

where $z_{it} = q_{it} + (d_i - a_i) S_{it-1}$. The budget constraint can be rewritten as

(2.17) $$x_t^* = \sum_{i=1} p_{it} z_{it} ,$$

where

(2.18) $$x_t^* = e_t + \sum_i p_{it}(d_i - a_i)\, S_{it-1}\ .$$

The demand functions are

(2.19) $$z_{it} = g_i(p_t, x_t^*),$$

so that

(2.20) $$q_{it} = g_i(p_t, x_t^*) + (a_i - d_i)S_{it-1}\ .$$

Thus while the 'rational' form (2.14) conditions on $\lambda p_t$ and on

(2.21) $$x_t = \sum_i \lambda_i p_{it} z_{it}\ ,$$

the 'myopic' form (2.20) conditions on $p_t$ and

(2.22) $$x_t^* = \sum_i p_{it} z_{it},$$

but the $g_i$ ( ) functions are the same in both cases. Distinguishing between (2.14) and (2.20) in empirical practice is likely to be difficult: If $g_i$ ( ) is represented by a flexible functional form, both (2.14) and (2.20) are flexible functional forms with differences between them only of the second order. Indeed, Phlips and Spinnewyn (1982) have shown that, in the context of LES, their models which correspond to (2.14) and (2.20) are observationally indistinguishable.[3]

In the empirical application below, we estimate an alternative parameterisation of the rational habits model which, in the context of flexible functional forms, should fit about as well as (2.14) but has some attractive features. The utility function $v_t$ ( ) is defined on

(2.6) $$z_{ij}' = \left(\frac{1-d_i}{1-a_i}\right) z_{it}\ .$$

This has the advantage that in a steady state, $z_{ij} = q_i$. Correspondingly, for an infinite horizon

(2.8) $$\lambda_i' = \left(\frac{1-a_i}{1-d_i}\right)\lambda_i = \left(\frac{1-a_i}{1-d_i}\right)\left(\frac{1-d_i+r*}{1-a_i+r*}\right).$$

---

[3] But not so in the context of the AI demand system; see Pashardes (1986).

Since r* is small, $\lambda_i \simeq 1$, except for goods of a high durability where $1 - d_i$ is small. In this parameterisation there is thus the closest similarity possible between the conventional quantities and prices and the effective quantities, the z's, that enter the utility function, and their corresponding effective prices. The budget constraint is as before, since

$$x_t = \sum_i \lambda_i p_{it} z_{it} \equiv \sum_i \lambda_i' p_{it} z_{it}' . \tag{2.23}$$

Thus

$$q_{it} = \left(\frac{1-a_i}{1-d_i}\right) g_i(\lambda' p_t, x_t) + (a_i - d_i) S_{it-1} , \tag{2.14}$$

where effective total expenditure $x_t$ is identical to that in (2.14).

The above parameterisation also enables one to express elegantly an extended kind of partial adjustment mechanism termed an 'error-correction model' by Hendry. Changes in q respond to changes in z but with a stabilizing feedback to last period's deviation between q and z. This is shown by noting that

$$z_i' = \left(\frac{1-d_i}{1-a_i}\right)(1 - a_i L) S_i \tag{2.24}$$

$$q_i = (1 - d_i L) S_i , \tag{2.25}$$

where L is the lag operator. Hence

$$q_i = \left(\frac{1-a_i}{1-d_i}\right)\left(\frac{1-d_i L}{1-a_i L}\right) z_i' . \tag{2.26}$$

Therefore

$$\begin{aligned} q_{it} - a_i q_{it-1} &\equiv \Delta q_{it} + (1-a_i) q_{it-1} \\ &= \left(\frac{1-a_i}{1-d_i}\right)\left(\Delta z_{it}' + (1-d_i) z_{it-1}'\right) \\ &= \left(\frac{1-a_i}{1-d_i}\right)\Delta z_{it}' + (1-a_i) z_{it-1}' \end{aligned} \tag{2.27}$$

and hence the error-correction model

$$\Delta q_i = \left(\frac{1-a_i}{1-d_i}\right)\Delta z_{it}' + (1-a_i)\left(z_{it-1}' - q_{it-1}\right) . \tag{2.28}$$

The lower is durability, $d_i$, and the higher is habit persistence, $a_i$, the slower is the speed by which purchases adjust to the desired $z'$. This makes it clear that durables may not exhibit a severe volatility of purchases if their consumption is also associated with a habit persistence effect, a point to which we shall return later in the empirical section. Note that, if $d_i = 0$, (2.28) simplifies to a conventional partial adjustment model of $q_{it}$ on $z_{it}$.

The tendency of habit persistence to counteract durability effects implies that (whether the rational form (2.14) or the myopic form (2.20) is regarded as the correct model) two alternative sets of values of the a's and d's give somewhat similar behaviour. Compare, for example, $a_i = 0.5$, $d_i = 0$ with $a_i = 0$, $d_i = -0.5$. The former implies, in the context of (2.14)

$$q_{it} = 0.5q_{it-1} + g_i(\lambda p_t, x_t) \tag{2.29}$$

while the latter implies

$$q_{it} = 0.5q_{it-1} - 0.25q_{it-2} + 0.125q_{it-3} - 0.0625q_{it-4} + \ldots + g_i(\lambda p_t, x_t) \tag{2.30}$$

though $\lambda_t$ and $x_t$ are somewhat different in (2.29) and (2.30). The suspicion that it might be difficult to distinguish between the two tended to be borne out by our empirical finding that there appeared to be two peaks for the likelihood, one at positive values for the a's and one for negative values for most of the d's. However, the former was somewhat higher in practice.

To this empirical problem there corresponds a theoretical interpretation. With $a_i = 0$ and $d_i < 0$, (2.14) gives a negative weight to past purchases relative to current ones which is just the effect of habit formation. When $d_i = 0$, $z_{it} = (q_{it} - a_i q_{it-1})$. Then with $-1 < a_i < 0$ we can think of this as the case of a good durable for one period beyond the one in which it was first purchased and consumed. Thus, to some degree, the $a_i$ and $d_i$ parameters are both capable of capturing alternatively elements of habituation and of durability. This suggests that a specification with only one dynamic parameter per commodity for most commodities might not be a bad one.

In Section 4 we search for a minimal set of $a_i$, $d_i$ different from zero which is statistically acceptable. Then we investigate whether any links can be found between homogeneity failures in the static version of the model and its dynamic mis-specification.

## 3. The Empirical Model

For the Marshallian demand functions we choose the 'Almost Ideal (AI) Demand' system of Deaton and Muellbauer (1980b). In its static version this takes the form

$$p_{it}q_{it} = \left( \alpha_i + \sum_j \gamma_{ij} \ln p_{jt} + \beta_i \ln(e_t/P_t) \right) e_t \tag{3.1}$$

where

$$\ln P_t = \alpha_i + \sum_i \alpha_i \ln p_{it} + \sum_i \sum_j \frac{1}{2} \gamma_{ij} \ln p_{it} \ln p_{jt} \ . \tag{3.2}$$

For this model, $\sum_i \alpha_i = 1$, $\sum_i \gamma_{ij} = 0$, all j, and $\sum_i \beta_i = 0$ are the adding-up conditions, $\sum_j \gamma_{ij} = 0$, all i are the homogeneity restrictions and $\gamma_{ij} = \gamma_{ji}$, all i, j are the symmetry restrictions.

The dynamic version of the AI demand system takes the form

$$\lambda_i' p_{it} z_{it}' = \left( \alpha_i + \sum_j \gamma_{ij} \ln(\lambda_j' p_{jt}) + \beta_i \ln(x_t/\overline{P}_t) \right) x_t \tag{3.3}$$

where

$$\ln \overline{P} = \alpha_0 + \sum_i \alpha_i \ln(\lambda_i' p_{it}) + \sum_i \sum_j \frac{1}{2} \gamma_{ij} \ln(\lambda_i' p_{it}) \ln(\lambda_j' p_{jt}) \,, \tag{3.4}$$

$$x_t = \sum_i \lambda_i' p_{it} z_{it}' \tag{3.5}$$

$$z_{it}' = \left( q_{it} + (d_i - a_i) S_{it-1} \right) \left( (1 - d_i)/(1 - a_i) \right) . \tag{3.6}$$

It was thought to be more likely that the disturbances would be homoscedastic if the dependent variable were expressed as a budget share. Thus the budget share $w_{it} = p_{it} q_{it}/e_t$ is

$$w_{it} = p_{it}(a_i - d_i) S_{it-1}/e_t \tag{3.7}$$

$$+ \left( \alpha_i + \sum_j \lambda_{ij} \ln(\lambda_j' p_{jt}) + \beta_i \ln(x_t/\overline{P}_t) \right) \left( x_t (1 - a_i)/\lambda_i' e_t (1 - d_i) \right) + \eta_{it}$$

where $\eta_{it}$ is a disturbance with mean zero. In common with most studies of demand systems, we assume that $\eta_{it}$ is independent of all $p_{it}$ and $x_t$. Specifically, this entails that demand shocks do not feed back within a year through supply and demand interactions to influence prices. Food is the commodity group where this assumption is perhaps most in doubt. The independence of $\eta_{it}$ from $x_t$ has been justified in the usual static demand systems context by Theil (1975). Though a testable proportion in that context [see Blundell and Smith (1985)], it is not easy to test in the context of (3.7) given that $x_t$ itself depends on parameters estimated in (3.5). Strictly speaking, to estimate (3.7) consistently, we also require the independence of $\eta_{it}$ from $e_t$. From this point of view it might have been preferable to achieve a similar heteroscedasticity correction by deflating the expenditures $p_{it} q_{it}$ by $e_{t-1}$ or by $\sum_i p_{it} q_{it-1}$.[4] However, for comparability with most recent empirical studies which model budget shares, we decided to do likewise. To avoid the problem of an ill-defined likelihood function which can arise with too few observations if a general covariance matrix of errors $\Omega$ is specified, we followed Deaton and Muellbauer (1980b) by assuming $\Omega = \sigma^2$ after deleting one commodity.

---

[4] Some experiments with this formulation gave almost identical parameter estimates.

Previous experience with the AI system (see Deaton and Muellbauer 1980b) suggested that the parameter $\alpha_o$ is quite hard to identify empirically. In the context of the static model, the role played by $\alpha_o$ can be seen at reference prices $p_i = 1$, all i.
Then

$$(3.8) \qquad w_i = \alpha_i + \beta_i(\ln e - \alpha_o).$$

Thus, $\alpha_i$ is the budget share when $\ln e = \alpha_o$, while $\beta_i = (\varsigma_i - 1)$ where $\varsigma_i$ is the budget elasticity of the $i^{th}$ good. We can think of $\alpha_o$ being at or below the lowest point in the plausible range of variations of lne, so $\alpha_o = \ln(e_{min})$ say. In addition, it is desirable for the function to imply non-negative values of budget shares at least at reference prices. Since, as we shall see, relative prices do not vary greatly over our sample period, this requirement gets close to the desirable aim of giving non-negative budget shares for reasonable ranges of data.

Thus, if $\alpha_o = \ln(e_{min})$, we require $\alpha_i > o$, all i, which implies that as lne falls to $\alpha_o$, expenditures on luxuries ($\beta_i > 0$) do not become negative. Similarly, to ensure that expenditures on necessities ($\beta_i < 0$) remain non-negative as total expenditure e rises, at least in a range below $e_{max}$, we want $\alpha_i + \beta_i (\ln e - \alpha_o) \geq 0$. One would not want to restrict $e_{min}$ and $e_{max}$ to be the minimum and maximum values respectively of per capita real total expenditure. Since individual behaviour underlies the aggregate data, see Deaton and Muellbauer (1980b) for a discussion of the aggregation properties of the AI demand system, a substantially wider range of variation is desirable. We suggest $e_{min} \simeq \frac{1}{2}$ minimum per capita real expenditure in the sample and $e_{max} \simeq 3$ maximum per capita real expenditure in the sample, given the skewness of the total expenditure distribution.

In practice, the general model we estimate is a dynamic one, not a static one. Thus we want $\alpha_o = \ln(x_{min})$ where $x = \sum_i \lambda_i z_i$ is effective expenditure at reference prices. This and the inequality restrictions

$$(3.9) \qquad \alpha_i \geq 0$$

$$(3.10) \qquad \alpha_i + \beta_i \ln (x_{max}/x_{min}) \geq 0$$

are designed to make the effective quantities $z_i$ as defined in (2.6) non-negative. However, since in a steady state x and e have a similar order of magnitude, it is adequate to replace $x_{max}$ and $x_{min}$ by $e_{max}$ and $e_{min}$ as defined above. Thus $\alpha_0$ was fixed at the same value exp(3.25) for both static and dynamic systems estimates.

In addition to adding-up symmetry and homogeneity, some authors also impose, in the context of static demand systems, concavity [see Barten and Geyskens (1975), Conrad and Jorgenson (1979)]. However, we have decided to impose on the $\gamma$'s boundary restrictions to ensure only that none of the compensated own price elasticities are positive. This restriction is written at reference prices as

$$(3.11) \qquad \gamma_{ij} \leq (1 - w_{it})w_{it} - \alpha_0\beta_i^2$$

and was imposed in estimation together with the restrictions (3.9)-(3.10) above.

#### 4. Empirical results

The data came from CSO, National Income and Expenditure 1981, and, with the inclusion of durables, are for the same groupings analysed by Deaton and Muellbauer (1980b). They are 1: Food, 2: Clothing, 3: Housing, 4: Fuel and light, 5: Alcoholic drink and tobacco products, 6: Other household goods (*i.e.*, books, newspapers and magazines, chemists goods, miscellaneous recreational goods, other miscellaneous goods), 7: Transport and communications (*i.e.*, running costs of motor vehicles, transport fares, communications services, consumer expenditure abroad), 8: Services (*i.e.*, entertainment and recreational services, domestic service, catering, other services), 9: Durable goods.

The basic characteristics of the data are shown in Chart 1. This is spread over three pages, and for each of the nine commodity groups shows budget shares on the left and relative prices measured by $\ln(p_i/p)$ on the right where $\ln p = \Sigma w_i \ln p_i$. In Chart 2, we show real consumer expenditure measured by $\ln(e/p)$. Many of the features one expects are there. For example, the gradual decline in the food share is interrupted by the mid-1970s recession. The share of fuel and light is positively correlated with the real price of energy which is consistent with a plausibly small price elasticity.

First, we present the results for the static version of the AI demand system with homogeneity and symmetry imposed in Table 1 and relaxed in Table 2. In both cases the inequality restrictions (3.2) and (3.3) are imposed within Angus Deaton's NLFIML programme.[5] The increase in the 2 log-likelihood from relaxing the 36 homogeneity and symmetry restrictions is 137.1. Given that at a 5% significance level, the critical value of chi-square with 36 degrees of freedom is 51, not even a small sample correction can rescue the null hypothesis from rejection.[6] The very considerable worsening of the Durbin-Watson statistics under the null is also a notable feature of Table 1 in comparison with Table 2. This offers support for our hypothesis that there is a connection between the rejection of these restrictions and the dynamic properties of consumer demands.

As Table 1 shows, of the inequality restrictions, that of type (3.9) is binding for fuel and light and for durable goods, and that of type (3.10) is binding for food. In fact, the imposition of these three restrictions reduces the 2 log-likelihood by 12.1, which is significant even with a small sample correction. However, we do not find this too worrying: The unrestricted model which gives rise to negative purchases over what seem to us reasonable ranges of data variation just does not seem interesting.

Table 3 gives the budget elasticities and compensated price elasticities corresponding to Table 1 computed at reference 1975 prices. These seem generally reasonable. However, computing eigenvalues for the substitution matrix at reference prices reveals 2 out of 9 to be positive. Thus even though all the compensated own price effects are negative, there is some non-concavity present in this static version of the model.

Now we turn to the estimates of the dynamic model as defined (2.14). To construct stock estimates for 1953, the expenditure data in constant prices for 1947-1953 were used as

---

[5] More precisely, the inequality constraints (3.9)-(3.11) are checked in every iteration and the parameters $\alpha_i$,$\beta_i$, and $\gamma_{ij}$ are adjusted in the same order.

[6] Sims (1980), for example, suggests correcting the chi-square statistic by (T-k)/T where T is the number of observations and k the number of parameters in the unrestricted model divided by the number of equations. Here T = 27, k = 5.78 so that the correction factor is 0.786 giving a corrected chi-square of 107.9 which is still very significant.

follows: Since $S_i = q_i/1 - d_i$ in a steady state, an estimate for the 1947 stock was given by $S_{i1947} = q_{i1947}/1 - d_i$. Then

$$(4.1) \qquad S_{i1953} = \sum_{j=0}^{5} d_i^j \, q_{i1953} + d_i^6 \, S_{i1947} \, .$$

Given computational costs and the somewhat similar behaviour implied by two alternative sets of a's and d's which was discussed above, it is necessary to proceed cautiously. We began by exploring the (a,d) parameter space by estimating the specifications: (i) $a_i = 0$, $d_i \neq 0$, all i; and (ii) $a_i \neq 0$, $d_i = 0$, all i. r* was assumed to be .02 throughout. The first gave a positive d for durables and negative d's for all other goods. The second gave a small negative a for durables and positive a's for all other goods. According to the interpretation offered in the previous section, this suggested habit formation dominates demand except for durable goods. Since specification (ii) gave a higher log-likelihood, this suggested $a_i > 0$, all goods, and $d_i = 0$ for all goods except durables. This gave quite satisfactory results and was then used to explore non-zero values of $d_i$ for non-durable goods. None of these was found to have a significant $d_i$ parameter so that the specification with $a_i > 0$ for all goods and $d_i = 0$ for all goods other than durables was accepted as the most parsimonious dynamic specification of the AI demand system. The results are shown in Table 4, which imposes homogeneity and symmetry; and in Table 5, which does not. Also imposed are the boundary restrictions (3.9)-(3.11). These results are very reasonable and far superior to those obtained by the static model. Indeed, the difference in the 2 x log-likelihood between the dynamic and static specifications suggests that the static AI demand system is strongly rejected.

Imposing the 36 homogeneity and symmetry restrictions gives a chi-square of 17.31 so that the restrictions are easily accepted even without a small sample correction.[7]

There is thus a striking difference between the static and dynamic models. Symmetry and homogeneity are strongly rejected for the static model and easily accepted for the dynamic model. Moreover, while their imposition on the static model induces positive residual autocorrelation, for the dynamic model their imposition eliminates some symptoms of negative residual autocorrelation to give the extremely satisfactory Durbin Watson statistics reported in Table 4. Since the model contains lagged dependent variables, the Durbin Watson statistics cannot be rigorously applied. However, a kind of Lagrange multiplier test can be constructed by re-estimating the demand system including for each equation the lagged residual as a single additional regressor. None of the coefficients on the lagged residuals were significant.

Table 6 reports the long-run budget elasticities and the compensated price elasticities computed at 1975 reference prices, and the 1975 budget level. There are some quite striking differences compared with those in Table 3 for the static model with homogeneity and symmetry. The most striking is that household durables, which for the static model has the largest budget elasticity of all goods, is seen as a necessity in the dynamic model. This is not very reasonable, and contradicts cross-section estimates relating the ownership of household durables to income.

Another notable difference is the large increase in the (absolute) compensated own price elasticity for miscellaneous services and for transport and communication. These are associated with corresponding increases in the budget elasticities. These results make some

---

[7] A sample correction of the Sims (1980) type reduces the chi-square to 12.9.

sense. The elasticities reported in Table 6 are long run, *i.e.*, they correspond to the effective quantities $z_i'$ rather than purchases $q_i$. Given the generally strong habit effects reported in Table 4, which imply sluggish adjustment, it is not surprising that the static price elasticities given in Table 3 should in many cases be smaller, and indeed, for 7 out of 9 categories, this is true. These results have interesting implications for the dynamics of tax revenue and imply that short-run and long-run incidence of taxes is rather different.

However in another respect, namely the failure of concavity, the results of Tables 4 and 1 are similar. The dynamic model also gives rise to two positive eigenvalues for the substitution matrix. Indeed, the compensated own price effect for food at 1975 reference prices and budget level would have been slightly positive, had it not been restricted. In further work it would be desirable to impose the concavity restrictions. Given the often poorly determined estimates of the $\gamma$'s, it is highly unlikely that concavity would be rejected, and its imposition would improve the precision of the estimates.

Turning now to the estimates of the a's, these are almost all strikingly significant and bear out the importance of dynamic effects, even for such goods as food. Furthermore, note the importance of 'habits' for durables. In this case it makes best sense to interpret habits as adjustment costs. As the equation standard errors show, comparing Tables 1 and 4, an explicit allowance both for durability and adjustment costs vastly improves the fit of the durables equation.

One question worth examining is how this admittedly costly systems approach compares with simpler single equation techniques for modelling demands. Table 7 provides some evidence. The first two rows give the means of $w_i$ and of $\Delta w_i$; then follow the standard deviations of $w_i$ and $\Delta w_i$ which thus correspond to the naive models $w_i$ = constant and $\Delta w_i$ = constant. A rather less naive single equation model follows from applying the kind of flexible distributed lag model recommended by Davidson, Hendry, Srba and Yeo (1978). Here the model takes the form

$$\begin{aligned} \Delta w_{it} &= \beta_{oi} + \beta_{1i} w_{it-1} + \beta_{2i} \ln(e_t/p_t) + \beta_{3i} \ln(p_{it}/p_t) \\ &\quad + \beta_{4i} \ln(e_{t-1}/p_{t-1}) + \beta_{5i} \ln(p_{it-1}/p_{t-1}) + \eta_{it} \,. \end{aligned} \tag{4.2}$$

This includes a partial adjustment share model as a special case. It is also of the form estimated by Anderson and Blundell (1983), but without the cross-price effects and the systems restrictions that follow from adding-up and steady-state homogeneity and symmetry. Row 4 of Table 7 gives the standard errors corresponding to (4.2) while the last two rows give the equation standard errors for the static AI demand system of Table 1 and the dynamic AI demand system of Table 2. To make the adjustment for degrees of freedom comparable to that in the previous three rows, the systems equation standard errors in row 4 have been adjusted by T-k/T where T is the number of observations and k is the average number of parameters per equation.

The results are striking. Despite the superficial appearance of an overparameterized model given by the generally insignificant estimates of the $\gamma$'s in Table 4, the dynamic demand system gives a lower standard error for seven out of nine equations for each of the alternatives and for the other two equations it is only a little higher. In contrast, the static demand system has higher equation standard errors than the single equation flexible dynamic model in 5 out 9 cases. For comparison, the estimates of the $\beta$'s for the single equation flexible dynamic model in (4.2) are in Table 8.

The results thus amply confirm the value of the dynamic systems approach and suggest that there may be a greater information content about substitution effects in the estimated $\gamma$'s than the apparently large estimated standard errors at first sight suggest.

However, we have already noted two symptoms of probable misspecification in the dynamic system reported in Table 4. One was the apparent finding that household durables have a budget elasticity under unity. The second was the apparent failure of the own-price elasticity of food to be negative. There is a third which offers clues as to one probable cause of these problems: This is that drink and tobacco, which one thinks of as conventionally the most addictive of goods, have the lowest value of the habit parameter, $a_i$. It is likely that the problem lies with anti-smoking campaigns which have led to a shift model. The aggregation of the two goods, whose relative prices have changed a good deal over the sample period, may also be problematic. There has certainly been a taste shift reflected in the decline in the proportion of UK adults who smoke from about 56% in the mid-1950's to 34% in 1980. However, the proportion of non-drinkers has also declined. Among the other social changes that have taken place, such as increased female labor force participation, and the fall in average family size, particularly notable has been the shift in housing tenure towards owner-occupation. In 1954 around 34% of households owned their own home, while by 1980 this had increased to 56%. Owner-occupiers typically live in lower density accommodation associated with greater use of fuel and light, and probably of household durables. Thus, one might well expect a demand shift towards those commodities to be associated with the increase in owner-occupation.

Given the large number of parameters we are trying to estimate with a relatively limited number of time series observations, there is little hope of obtaining robust estimates of the effects of such demographic or other social changes. One way out is to use cross-section data to pin down such effects and cross-section parameters on the aggregate time series. We suspect that the integration of such an approach with the dynamic specification we propose in this paper is likely to prove the most useful way forward.

## 5. Conclusions

There is much empirical evidence to suggest that systems of aggregate static demand equations conditioned on current total satisfy the basic postulate of homogeneity, *i.e.*, lack of money illusion. As Deaton and Muellbauer (1980a, Chap. 3) note, once homogeneity is imposed, the rather higher level implication of rational behaviour at an aggregate level, symmetry of substitution effects, can usually be accepted.

At present there is little agreement on the reasons for the failure of the data to be consistent with the homogeneity postulate. Let us list some of the possible explanations. The first, which is the one we favor, is dynamic misspecification. In other words, there are habit and durability effects which are omitted from standard static demand systems and the symptoms of these misspecifications include the failure of homogeneity. The evidence of positively serially correlated residuals which usually accompanies the homogeneity failure is consistent with this hypothesis, though it could also be consistent with some of the other explanations.

A second is bias deriving from aggregation. The theory of the rational consumer can be derived at the individual level and may not hold at the aggregate level. Some of the work on constructive aggregation [see Muellbauer (1976), Gorman (1981), Jorgenson, Lau, and Stoker (1982), and Lau (1982)] suggests specific distributional and demographic effects which are omitted in the representative consumer model usually applied to aggregate data. Indeed, Jorgenson and his associates have combined cross-section and aggregate time series information in an imaginative way to model such effects.

Stoker (1986) favors this hypothesis, but his evidence emphasizes our ignorance, rather than resolving the issue. He estimates a four-good linear expenditure system on annual US data. He includes income distribution variables in the form of four aggregate income shares in each equation. These are jointly significant, but he finds that semi-differencing the equations, replacing each variable $y_{it}$ by $y_{it} - \rho y_{it-1}$ fits about equally well. The latter can be regarded as a crude first approximation to a dynamic model. Stoker concludes that on aggregate data it is hard to discriminate between the two very different explanations of the failure of a static demand system, albeit one with the deficiencies of the LES.

One study of micro-panel data applying the Rotterdam demand system comes to the interesting conclusion that symmetry and homogeneity can be accepted. However, this study by Kiefer (1984) is for six groups of foods, and is conditional on aggregate food expenditure. The panel is for two years only, and variation in prices may therefore be relatively low. Also, first differencing of the data, like quasi-differencing, can be an approximation to a dynamic specification, and we already know that homogeneity and symmetry are less strongly rejected for aggregate data in first differences.

A third possible reason for homogeneity failures is bias stemming from aggregation across goods. Demand systems as above are usually estimated for broad commodity groupings in which prices are typically Laspeyres price indices and quantities are Paasche volume indices, though some sort of chaining of these indices usually takes place. The theoretical literature [see Deaton and Muellbauer (1980a, Chap. 5)] suggests two reasons why grouping of goods may be valid. One is Hicks aggregation: This requires the prices of the detailed goods in the group to move in parallel. The other entails separability restrictions on preferences [see Gorman (1959)]. A simple, stronger-than-necessary example is homothetic separability in which the goods in each group are separable and have identical budget elasticities. If neither of these types of restrictions are valid to a close enough approximation, the resulting misspecification could result in the symptom of failure of homogeneity.

A fourth possible explanation is rational money illusion. Deaton (1977) has put forward such a model in which, during inflation, consumers systematically misperceive relative prices and has used it to explain inflation effects in the consumption function.

A fifth explanation is misspecification caused by omitted conditioning variables, or of indicators of taste change. Static demand systems are based on a separable utility function for the purchases being modelled. But if, for example, leisure and public goods also appear in the utility function but not in the empirical model, their omission might show up in the form of homogeneity failure. Deaton (1981) has estimated a system of demand equations conditional on housing and finds both residual autocorrelation and homogeneity failures considerably reduced in severity.

A sixth explanation, related to the first, is failure of the intertemporal separability assumption. In other words, if preferences are not intertemporally separable in the purchases being modelled, then two-stage budgeting in general fails and static demand systems do not exist. In a sense, habit and durability effects are a simple way of relaxing the intertemporal separability assumption while retaining the main benefits for parsimonious modelling that come from two-stage budgeting.

A seventh explanation of homogeneity failures is simultaneous-equation bias. It may be that prices and total expenditure are so endogenous that the estimated price and budget responses are heavily biased, and this conceivably shows up as a homogeneity failure. Indeed, Attfield (1985) argues that there is a way of formulating a test for exogeneity of total expenditure which is equivalent to a test for homogeneity. Thus he finds that those goods for which Deaton and Muellbauer (1980b) reject homogeneity are just the ones where his test finds a significant correlation between total expenditure and the equation error. However, the test is uninformative on the source of the exogeneity failure. To learn more, one would need to specify a more precise alternative hypothesis, *e.g.*, a specific way in which two-stage budgeting breaks down. As it is, Attfield's result is another way of labelling the failure of static demand systems.

Regarding exogeneity failure of prices, Bronsard and Salvas -- Bronsard (1984) -- provide evidence for annual US data on a very aggregated three group system of demand equations to reject exogeneity of prices. However, in more disaggregated systems of four, five, and seven groups of goods for Canada, they find price exogeneity generally acceptable.

Finally, because of the difficulties in measuring quality and because of inadequacies in the data base from which the national accounts are derived, it may be that the quantity and price data contains systematic errors and these are reflected in homogeneity failure.

There may be truth in some or even all of these possible explanaations. However, we present evidence that the first, dynamic misspecification caused by omitted habit and durability effects is likely to be a large part of the story. We estimate static and dynamic forms of the Almost Ideal Demand System for annual UK data for 1954-80. While the static form strongly contradicts homogeneity and symmetry and suffers from serially correlated residuals, in the dynamic form homogeneity and symmetry are easily acceptable and there is no evidence of serially correlated residuals. Moreover, there is strong evidence of habit effects for almost all goods and that durability matters for at least one. In general, the long-run price elasticities implied by the dynamic model exceed those estimated from the static one, and this too makes good sense given the prevalence of habit effects. Finally, the dynamic system performs well relative to simple single equations with dynamic effects, and that is not true of the static system.

There is more work to be done. There is little doubt that the Economics profession at present regards aggregation bias as the leading alternative contender to habit and durability effects in the explanation of homogeneity failures. We sympathise with this view, and one of the most interesting next steps would be to incorporate aggregation effects in dynamic models of the kind we have estimated. Muellbauer (1976) discusses a relatively simple way of introducing aggregation effects in static demand models. To illustrate in the context of the AI demand system shown in (3.1), replace $e_t$ by $e_{ht}/k_{ht}$ for household h where $k_{ht}$ is a function of household characteristics. $k_{ht}$ introduces household characteristics into the demand functions in a simple way. Then the per capita budget share of good i is a linear function of $\ln(e_t/k_t)$, where $e_t$ = mean total expenditure, and

$$\ln k_t = \frac{\sum_h e_{ht} \ln(k_{ht} e_t / e_{ht})}{\sum_h e_{ht}}, \tag{5.1}$$

which is a generalization of (minus) Theil's entropy measure of dispersion. A similar result holds, via (3.3), for the expenditures on the transformed quantities, the z 's. Even if data from a series of cross-sections are available on the joint distribution of total expenditure and household characteristics, however, they are unlikely to be available for the joint distribution of $x_h$ and household characteristics. This is because $x_h$ is total expenditure on the transformed quantities, the z 's. These depend on purchases in previous periods which are typically not recorded in household surveys. However, as behaviors approaches a steady state, $x_h$ approaches conventional expenditure $e_h$ and it may be that the true value of k is well approximated by that constructed using conventional expenditures $e_h$.

Imposing concavity, which the point estimates of the price responses do not quite satisfy, may improve the precision of these rather poorly determined estimates, and further explorations of simplifying restrictions on the substitution matrix are desirable. Relaxing the rather strong assumption for price expectation on which the empirical work was based would be a further useful step. And one can imagine that there is further useful work to be done in exploring the other possible causes of homogeneity failure and specification error that we have mentioned. However, at this stage the returns to working with disaggregated data rather than aggregated data are great. There are time-series of cross-sections such as in the British Family Expenditure Surveys which, though not panel data, could throw much light on aggregation bias as the source of homogeneity failures.

Blundell *et. al.*, (1989) have studied these data. They condition the demand functions on a wide range of household characteristics including housing tenure and ownership of durables. Given such conditioning, they find no rejections of homogeneity,, though the symmetry restrictions remain a problem. Their data, however, do not permit them to test for any effects of lagged purchases.

Finally, a word on 'habits'. This is a loose expression and could cover a variety of phenomena. These include adjustment costs arising from monetary transactions costs or from time costs and psychic costs of altering arrangements. They could include reference group behaviour that operates with a lag: If individuals pattern their behavious on that of a reference group so that differences in behaviour cause a utility loss, at the aggregate level this could show up as habit formation for the representative consumer. Persistence in behaviour might also represent rules of thumb which could be rational response, given costs of obtaining information and making and implementing decisions. The aggregate time-series data we have been examining are unlikely to shed a great deal of light on which of these interpretations of persistence are correct. But our evidence, like that of a whole tradition of demand studies going back to Stone and Rowe (1958) and Houthakker and Taylor (1966, 1970), is that these persistence effects are powerful and cannot be ignored if successful empirical models of demand are to be otained.

Table 1

Static AI Demand System with Symmetry and Homogeneity

Parameters estimated

| Commodity | $\alpha_i$ | $\beta_i$ | $\gamma_{i1}$ | $\gamma_{i2}$ | $\gamma_{i3}$ |
|---|---|---|---|---|---|
| 1. Food | .305<br>(10.9) | -.127<br>(4.2) | 0.050<br>(1.7) | 0.005<br>(0.3) | -0.030<br>(1.7) |
| 2. Clothing | .059<br>(2.4) | .022<br>(.8) | | 0.050<br>(3.3) | -0.014<br>(0.9) |
| 3. Housing | .096<br>(3.5) | .055<br>(1.7) | | | 0.065<br>(2.9) |
| 4. Fuel-Light | .000<br>(0.0) | .051<br>(2.6) | | | |
| 5. Drink-tob | .164<br>(9.0) | -.051<br>(2.6) | | | |
| 6. Transport & Com/tions | .103<br>(3.3) | .000<br>(0.0) | | | |
| 7. Misc. Goods | .155<br>(6.0) | -.035<br>(1.3) | | | |
| 8. Misc. Services | 0.97<br>(2.7) | .021<br>(.5) | | | |
| 9. Durables | .021<br>(.8) | .070<br>(2.5) | | | |

Terms in brackets are t-ratios.

2 log likelihood: 2020.83

**Table 1**

(continued)

| $\gamma_{i4}$ | $\gamma_{i5}$ | $\gamma_{i6}$ | $\gamma_{i7}$ | $\gamma_{i8}$ | $\gamma_{i9}$ | $R^2$ | SE x100 | DW |
|---|---|---|---|---|---|---|---|---|
| 0.025 | -0.021 | -0.050 | -0.028 | 0.022 | 0.028 | .993 | .276 | .88 |
| (2.1) | (1.5) | (2.1) | (1.3) | (.08) | (1.5) | | | |
| 0.006 | 0.003 | 0.008 | -0.046 | -0.020 | 0.009 | .975 | .171 | 1.04 |
| (0.6) | (.03) | (0.5) | (3.1) | (1.0) | (.07) | | | |
| -0.023 | 0.002 | -0.002 | 0.026 | -0.042 | 0.020 | .978 | .310 | .68 |
| (1.9) | (0.2) | (0.1) | (1.5) | (1.9) | (1.2) | | | |
| 0.039 | 0.013 | -0.002 | -0.016 | -0.025 | -0.018 | .420 | .241 | .86 |
| (3.6) | (1.5) | (0.1) | (1.5) | (1.9) | (1.7) | | | |
| | 0.035 | -0.030 | -0.009 | 0.025 | -0.017 | .927 | .204 | 1.08 |
| | (.27) | (1.8) | (0.8) | (1.6) | (1.4) | | | |
| | | 0.017 | 0.038 | 0.009 | 0.012 | .633 | .166 | 1.44 |
| | | (0.4) | (1.7) | (0.3) | (0.5) | | | |
| | | | 0.078 | 0.020 | -0.063 | .992 | .176 | .96 |
| | | | (3.3) | (0.8) | (3.6) | | | |
| | | | | 0.030 | -0.018 | .782 | .169 | 1.02 |
| | | | | (0.6) | (0.7) | | | |
| | | | | | 0.047 | .649 | .493 | 1.42 |

Table 2

Static AI Demand System without Symmetry and Homogeneity

| Commodity | Parameters estimated $\alpha_i$ | $\beta_i$ | $\gamma_{i1}$ | $\gamma_{i2}$ | $\gamma_{i3}$ |
|---|---|---|---|---|---|
| 1. Food | .304<br>(10.3) | -.127<br>(3.9) | 0.132<br>(3.8) | -0.087<br>(2.8) | -0.024<br>(1.3) |
| 2. Clothing | .051<br>(1.7) | .032<br>(1.0) | -0.037<br>(1.1) | 0.070<br>(2.3) | -0.020<br>(1.1) |
| 3. Housing | .175<br>(6.0) | -.034<br>(1.1) | -0.028<br>(0.8) | -0.006<br>(0.2) | 0.062<br>(3.4) |
| 4. Fuel-Light | .027<br>(.9) | .022<br>(.7) | -0.037<br>(1.1) | 0.004<br>(0.1) | -0.000<br>(0.0) |
| 5. Drink-tob | .118<br>(4.0) | .001<br>(0.0) | -0.054<br>(1.6) | 0.055<br>(1.8) | -0.022<br>(1.2) |
| 6. Transport & Com/tions | .097<br>(3.3) | .005<br>(.2) | -0.033<br>(1.0) | 0.026<br>(0.8) | -0.004<br>(0.2) |
| 7. Misc. Goods | .125<br>(4.3) | -.002<br>(.1) | 0.000<br>(0.0) | -0.059<br>(1.9) | -0.002<br>(0.1) |
| 8. Misc. Services | .104<br>(3.5) | .012<br>(.4) | -0.033<br>(0.9) | 0.060<br>(1.9) | -0.051<br>(2.8) |
| 9. Durables | .000<br>(0.0) | .092<br>(2.9) | 0.092<br>(2.6) | -0.064<br>(2.0) | 0.063<br>(3.4) |

Terms in brackets are t-ratios.

2 log likelihood: 2179.65

**Table 2**

(continued)

| $\gamma_{i4}$ | $\gamma_{i5}$ | $\gamma_{i6}$ | $\gamma_{i7}$ | $\gamma_{i8}$ | $\gamma_{i9}$ | $R^2$ | SE x100 | DW |
|---|---|---|---|---|---|---|---|---|
| 0.027<br>(2.2) | -0.050<br>(3.5) | -0.027<br>(0.8) | -0.015<br>(0.7) | -0.012<br>(0.3) | 0.032<br>(1.4) | .998 | .195 | 1.71 |
| 0.020<br>(1.7) | -0.011<br>(0.8) | 0.013<br>(0.4) | -0.017<br>(0.8) | -0.009<br>(0.2) | 0.017<br>(0.7) | .985 | .150 | 1.44 |
| -0.060<br>(5.0) | 0.035<br>(2.5) | -0.020<br>(0.6) | 0.030<br>(1.4) | 0.020<br>(0.5) | -0.016<br>(0.7) | .995 | .174 | 1.47 |
| 0.033<br>(2.9) | 0.009<br>(0.7) | 0.001<br>(0.0) | 0.021<br>(0.9) | -0.031<br>(0.8) | -0.001<br>(0.0) | .832 | .144 | 1.75 |
| 0.001<br>(0.1) | 0.062<br>(4.5) | -0.059<br>(1.8) | 0.016<br>(0.7) | 0.004<br>(0.1) | 0.007<br>(0.3) | .973 | .138 | 1.97 |
| 0.007<br>(0.6) | -0.025<br>(1.8) | 0.026<br>(0.8) | -0.007<br>(0.3) | 0.020<br>(0.5) | -0.003<br>(0.1) | .787 | .140 | 1.78 |
| -0.023<br>(1.9) | -0.001<br>(0.1) | 0.040<br>(1.2) | 0.084<br>(3.8) | 0.022<br>(0.6) | -0.064<br>(2.8) | .997 | .123 | 1.92 |
| -0.016<br>(1.4) | 0.052<br>(3.7) | -0.017<br>(0.5) | -0.019<br>(0.9) | 0.077<br>(2.1) | -0.030<br>(1.3) | .943 | .097 | 2.03 |
| 0.011<br>(0.9) | -0.072<br>(5.0) | 0.071<br>(2.2) | -0.092<br>(4.1) | -0.091<br>(2.5) | 0.057<br>(2.6) | .767 | .446 | 1.66 |

Table 3

The Compensated Price and Budget Elasticities of the Static AI Demand System
(at 1975 price and budget shares)

| Commodity | Price of Commodity: 1 | 2 | 3 | 4 | 5 | 6 | 7 | 8 | 9 |
|---|---|---|---|---|---|---|---|---|---|
| 1. Food | -0.458 | 0.057 | -0.007 | 0.121 | 0.028 | -0.158 | -0.009 | 0.250 | 0.180 |
| 2. Clothing | 0.133 | -0.350 | 0.000 | 0.137 | 0.097 | 0.256 | -0.393 | -0.069 | 0.177 |
| 3. Housing | -0.009 | 0.000 | -0.410 | -0.074 | 0.124 | 0.069 | 0.266 | -0.212 | 0.251 |
| 4. Fuel-Light | 0.502 | 0.243 | -0.233 | -0.107 | 0.361 | 0.101 | -0.225 | -0.336 | -0.287 |
| 5. Drink & Tobacco | 0.044 | 0.066 | 0.151 | 0.138 | -0.583 | -0.131 | 0.072 | 0.342 | -0.097 |
| 6. Transport & Com/tions | -0.293 | 0.203 | 0.098 | 0.045 | -0.152 | -0.741 | 0.467 | 0.185 | 0.198 |
| 7. Misc. Goods | -0.014 | -0.255 | 0.308 | -0.082 | 0.069 | 0.381 | -0.238 | 0.240 | -0.402 |
| 8. Services | 0.411 | -0.048 | -0.266 | -0.134 | 0.354 | 0.164 | 0.261 | -0.681 | -0.055 |
| 9. Durables | 0.405 | 0.170 | 0.431 | -0.156 | -0.137 | 0.240 | -0.597 | -0.075 | -0.287 |
| Budget elasticities | 0.214 | 1.182 | 1.412 | 1.832 | 0.532 | 1.076 | 0.820 | 1.317 | 1.844 |
| Eigenvalues of k-matrix | -0.175 | -0.153 | -0.093 | -0.056 | -0.033 | -0.015 | 0.000 | 0.018 | 0.052 |

Table 4

Dynamic AI Demand System, with Symmetry and Homogeneity (8 d's restricted to zero)

Parameters estimated

| | $\alpha_i$ | $\beta_i$ | $\gamma_{i1}$ | $\gamma_{i2}$ | $\gamma_{i3}$ | $\gamma_{i4}$ | $\gamma_{i5}$ |
|---|---|---|---|---|---|---|---|
| 1. | .299<br>(8.8) | -.124<br>(3.4) | 0.135<br>(2.4) | -0.015<br>(0.6) | -0.074<br>(2.4) | 0.011<br>(0.6) | -0.023<br>(1.2) |
| 2. | .100<br>(3.4) | -.006<br>(.2) | | 0.035<br>(1.7) | -0.045<br>(2.2) | 0.011<br>(0.8) | 0.000<br>(0.0) |
| 3. | .146<br>(4.5) | -.012<br>(.3) | | | 0.105<br>(3.8) | 0.002<br>(0.1) | -0.010<br>(0.8) |
| 4. | .038<br>(1.5) | .011<br>(.4) | | | | 0.034<br>(1.8) | 0.000<br>(0.0) |
| 5. | .192<br>(11.5) | -.067<br>(4.0) | | | | | 0.025<br>(2.0) |
| 6. | .000<br>(0.0) | .104<br>(2.0) | | | | | |
| 7. | .132<br>(3.7) | -.010<br>(.3) | | | | | |
| 8. | .000<br>(0.0) | .130<br>(2.0) | | | | | |
| 9. | .093<br>(9.0) | -0.26<br>(2.9) | | | | | |

* Commodity groupings and terms in brackets as in Table 1.

2 log likelihood: 2229.49

**Table 4**

(continued)

| $\gamma_{i6}$ | $\gamma_{i7}$ | $\gamma_{i8}$ | $\gamma_{i9}$ | $a_i$ | $d_i$ | $R^2$ | SE x100 | DW |
|---|---|---|---|---|---|---|---|---|
| -0.030 | -0.066 | 0.070 | -0.009 | .685 | - | .997 | .175 | 1.93 |
| (0.7) | (1.7) | (1.2) | (1.0) | (.73) | | | | |
| 0.082 | -0.067 | 0.041 | -0.042 | .642 | - | .978 | .167 | 1.48 |
| (2.3) | (2.8) | (1.0) | (7.4) | (.63) | | | | |
| -0.041 | 0.046 | -0.020 | 0.038 | .765 | - | .993 | .177 | 1.52 |
| (1.1) | (1.7) | (0.5) | (5.7) | (13.0) | | | | |
| -0.036 | -0.025 | 0.011 | -0.008 | .682 | - | .727 | .170 | 2.13 |
| (1.4) | (1.2) | (0.3) | (2.0) | (6.4) | | | | |
| -0.018 | 0.019 | 0.043 | -0.034 | .231 | - | .968 | .139 | 2.11 |
| (0.7) | (1.0) | (1.4) | (6.6) | (2.0) | | | | |
| -0.018 | -0.011 | 0.038 | 0.036 | .815 | - | .671 | .161 | 1.90 |
| (0.2) | (0.2) | (0.5) | (3.6) | (15.3) | | | | |
| | 0.043 | 0.048 | 0.014 | .654 | - | .995 | .154 | 1.96 |
| | (0.7) | (0.9) | (1.8) | (6.0) | | | | |
| | | -0.206 | -0.024 | .826 | - | .898 | .119 | 2.27 |
| | | (1.4) | (2.0) | (12.9) | | | | |
| | | | 0.030 | .757 | .945 | .932 | .224 | 2.22 |
| | | | (4.1) | (21.5) | (77.5) | | | |

Table 5

Dynamic AI Demand System without Symmetry and Homogeneity (8 d's restricted to zero)

Parameters estimated

| | $\alpha_i$ | $\beta_i$ | $\gamma_{i1}$ | $\gamma_{i2}$ | $\gamma_{i3}$ | $\gamma_{i4}$ | $\gamma_{i5}$ |
|---|---|---|---|---|---|---|---|
| 1. | .299 | -.125 | 0.135 | -0.018 | -0.074 | 0.016 | -0.026 |
| | (6.3) | (2.7) | (1.5) | (0.2) | (1.3) | (0.5) | (0.6) |
| 2. | .100 | -.008 | -0.013 | 0.040 | -0.047 | 0.012 | -0.006 |
| | (2.0) | (.2) | (0.2) | (0.6) | (1.0) | (0.4) | (0.2) |
| 3. | .145 | -.009 | -0.074 | -0.043 | 0.105 | -0.006 | -0.002 |
| | (2.1) | (.1) | (0.6) | (0.4) | (1.7) | (0.1) | (0.0) |
| 4. | .039 | .011 | 0.008 | 0.007 | 0.003 | 0.035 | 0.007 |
| | (.9) | (.3) | (01.) | (0.1) | (0.1) | (1.2) | (0.2) |
| 5. | .192 | -.067 | -0.023 | 0.001 | -0.010 | -0.001 | 0.025 |
| | (7.7) | (2.9) | (0.5) | (0.0) | (0.5) | (0.1) | (1.4) |
| 6. | .000 | .104 | -0.028 | 0.085 | -0.041 | -0.035 | -0.023 |
| | (0.0) | (1.3) | (0.2) | (0.7) | (0.6) | (0.7) | (0.4) |
| 7. | .133 | -.010 | -0.066 | -0.069 | 0.046 | -0.027 | 0.021 |
| | (2.2) | (.2) | (0.8) | (1.0) | (1.0) | (0.9) | (0.5) |
| 8. | .000 | .130 | 0.069 | 0.040 | -0.018 | 0.013 | 0.039 |
| | (0.0) | (1.5) | (0.5) | (0.3) | (0.2) | (0.3) | (0.6) |
| 9. | .093 | -.026 | -0.009 | -0.042 | 0.038 | -0.007 | -0.034 |
| | (7.2) | (2.0) | (0.9) | (3.6) | (2.7) | (1.6) | (3.7) |

* Commodity groupings and terms in brackets as in Table 1.

2 log likelihood: 2246.80

Table 5

(continued)

| $\gamma_{i6}$ | $\gamma_{i7}$ | $\gamma_{i8}$ | $\gamma_{i9}$ | $a_i$ | $d_i$ | $R^2$ | SE x100 | DW |
|---|---|---|---|---|---|---|---|---|
| -0.032 | -0.066 | 0.069 | -0.003 | .688 | - | .997 | .188 | 2.09 |
| (0.4) | (1.0) | (0.7) | (0.1) | (5.8) | | | | |
| 0.079 | -0.068 | 0.040 | -0.033 | .638 | - | .983 | .165 | 1.86 |
| (1.0) | (1.2) | (0.5) | (0.7) | (4.5) | | | | |
| -0.040 | 0.048 | -0.020 | 0.028 | .762 | - | .994 | .183 | 1.76 |
| (0.3) | (0.6) | (0.2) | (0.3) | (7.1) | | | | |
| -0.036 | -0.024 | 0.011 | -0.014 | .650 | - | .751 | .181 | 2.32 |
| (0.4) | (0.4) | (0.1) | (0.2) | (3.7) | | | | |
| -0.018 | 0.019 | 0.043 | -0.033 | .238 | - | .969 | .151 | 2.15 |
| (0.5) | (0.6) | (1.0) | (1.3) | (1.7) | | | | |
| -0.018 | -0.014 | 0.039 | 0.037 | .814 | - | .683 | .177 | 1.94 |
| (0.1) | (0.1) | (0.3) | (0.4) | (11.1) | | | | |
| -0.009 | 0.044 | 0.048 | 0.012 | .652 | - | .995 | .169 | 2.00 |
| (0.1) | (0.6) | (0.5) | (0.2) | (4.4) | | | | |
| 0.038 | 0.047 | -0.205 | -0.023 | .828 | - | .901 | .131 | 2.34 |
| (0.3) | (0.4) | (1.1) | (0.3) | (11.5) | | | | |
| 0.036 | 0.014 | -0.024 | 0.030 | .757 | .945 | .933 | .248 | 2.23 |
| (3.2) | (1.6) | (1.4) | (3.5) | (15.6) | (34.4) | | | |

Table 6

The Compensated Price and Budget Elasticities of the Dynamic AI Demand System
(at 1975 price and budget shares)

| Commodity | Price of Commodity: | | | | | | | | |
|---|---|---|---|---|---|---|---|---|---|
| | 1 | 2 | 3 | 4 | 5 | 6 | 7 | 8 | 9 |
| 1. Food | -0.000 | 0.004 | -0.238 | 0.097 | 0.045 | -0.138 | -0.217 | 0.388 | 0.054 |
| 2. Clothing | 0.010 | -0.480 | -0.417 | 0.186 | 0.122 | 1.105 | -0.713 | 0.614 | -0.439 |
| 3. Housing | -0.312 | -0.234 | -0.126 | 0.060 | 0.053 | -0.195 | 0.446 | -0.036 | 0.348 |
| 4. Fuel-Light | 0.401 | 0.329 | 0.190 | -0.208 | 0.100 | -0.672 | -0.439 | 0.394 | -0.089 |
| 5. Drink & Tobacco | 0.071 | 0.083 | 0.064 | 0.038 | -0.624 | -0.120 | 0.291 | 0.389 | -0.186 |
| 6. Transport & Com/tions | -0.255 | 0.876 | -0.276 | -0.301 | -0.140 | -0.949 | 0.007 | 0.642 | 0.404 |
| 7. Misc. Goods | -0.328 | -0.462 | 0.515 | -0.161 | 0.277 | 0.006 | -0.526 | 0.486 | 0.200 |
| 8. Services | 0.637 | 0.432 | -0.045 | 0.157 | 0.403 | 0.570 | 0.528 | -2.514 | -0.159 |
| 9. Durables | 0.121 | -0.423 | 0.597 | -0.048 | -0.263 | 0.490 | 0.296 | -0.217 | -0.548 |
| Budget elasticities | 0.342 | 0.923 | 0.918 | 1.246 | 0.432 | 2.029 | 0.919 | 2.137 | 0.692 |
| Eigenvalues of k-matrix | -0.354 | -0.197 | -0.125 | -0.097 | -0.019 | -0.006 | 0.000 | 0.040 | 0.123 |

Table 7

Means of Budget Shares and their Changes and Various Standard Errors

| | 1 | 2 | 3 | 4 | 5 | 6 | 7 | 8 | 9 |
|---|---|---|---|---|---|---|---|---|---|
| mean of $w_i$ | 0.219 | 0.091 | 0.121 | 0.046 | 0.125 | 0.100 | 0.101 | 0.114 | 0.083 |
| mean of $\Delta w_i$ x 100 | -0.41 | -0.14 | 0.27 | 0.04 | -0.05 | 0.02 | 0.23 | 0.05 | 0.06 |
| s.e. of $w_i$ | 3.100 | 0.036 | 1.974 | 0.283 | 0.657 | 0.312 | 1.928 | 0.370 | 0.734 |
| s.e. of $\Delta w_i$ | 0.350 | 0.214 | 0.331 | 0.252 | 0.302 | 0.213 | 0.323 | 0.243 | 0.609 |
| s.e. of single eq. | 0.165 | 0.132 | 0.185 | 0.170 | 0.233 | 0.191 | 0.233 | 0.201 | 0.467 |
| s.e. of static AI ds | 0.258 | 0.185 | 0.299 | 0.360 | 0.164 | 0.140 | 0.140 | 0.166 | 0.503 |
| s.e. of dynamic AI ds | 0.176 | 0.163 | 0.179 | 0.165 | 0.138 | 0.166 | 0.148 | 0.120 | 0.277 |

All s.e.'s are multiplied by 100

Table 8

OLS Estimates of the Single Equation Flexible Dynamic Model in (3.5)

| | 1 | 2 | 3 | 4 | 5 | 6 | 7 | 8 | 9 |
|---|---|---|---|---|---|---|---|---|---|
| $\beta_0$ | 0.69<br>(1.2) | 0.187<br>(5.0) | -0.052<br>(1.0) | 0.011<br>(1.1) | 0.143<br>(3.1) | 0.023<br>(1.8) | -0.070<br>(1.3) | 0.019<br>(0.4) | 0.107<br>(2.0) |
| $\beta_1$ | -0.802<br>(4.3) | -0.824<br>(5.2) | -0.497<br>(2.3) | -0.507<br>(2.9) | -0.024<br>(3.0) | -0.612<br>(2.9) | -0.358<br>(2.3) | -0.394<br>(2.2) | -0.897<br>(4.4) |
| $\beta_2$ | -0.105<br>(5.3) | 0.027<br>(1.4) | 0.104<br>(4.3) | 0.052<br>(2.6) | -0.033<br>(1.0) | 0.005<br>(0.2) | 0.010<br>(0.4) | -0.005<br>(0.1) | -0.023<br>(0.5) |
| $\beta_3$ | 0.059<br>(1.7) | 0.053<br>(3.4) | 0.023<br>(1.0) | 0.041<br>(3.6) | 0.058<br>(2.2) | 0.016<br>(0.7) | 0.116<br>(2.8) | 0.014<br>(0.3) | 0.122<br>(2.9) |
| $\beta_4$ | -0.035<br>(0.6) | -0.056<br>(2.9) | -0.075<br>(2.5) | -0.045<br>(2.2) | 0.016<br>(0.5) | 0.001<br>(0.2) | 0.017<br>(0.5) | 0.020<br>(0.6) | 0.083<br>(1.4) |
| $\beta_5$ | 0.078<br>(1.6) | -0.032<br>(1.6) | 0.000<br>(0.0) | -0.024<br>(1.9) | 0.029<br>(1.1) | 0.011<br>(0.4) | -0.079<br>(1.9) | -0.036<br>(0.8) | -0.077<br>(2.0) |

Absolute t-rations are given in parenthesis.

## APPENDIX

In this appendix, we derive the form taken by the user-cost prices. In principle, the derivation is the same as Spinnewyn's (1979, 1981) though the details are different. We proceed in two stages. First, we recapitulate the derivation of the conventional user-cost prices in (2.5) for stocks of durables. This is done by using the definition of stocks (2.4) to replace the $q_{ij}$'s in the intertemporal budget constraint (2.2) by $S_{ij}$'s:

$$W_t = \sum_{i=1}^{n} \left(p_{it}(S_{it} - d_i S_{it-1}) + \hat{p}_{it+1}(S_{it+1} - d_i S_{it}) + \ldots \hat{p}_{iT}(S_{iT} - d_i S_{iT-1})\right) .$$

Thus

$$W_t + \sum_{i=1} p_{it} d_i S_{it-1} = \sum_{i=1} \sum_{j=t} \hat{p}^*_{ij} S_{ij} , \tag{A.1}$$

where $p^*_{ij}$ is defined by (2.5) and the ^ indicates discounting to period t by the factor

$$v = \prod_{s=t+1}^{j} (1+r)^s .$$

In the second stage, we use a similar technique to replace the $S_{ij}$'s in (A.1) by $z_{ij}$'s. From the definition (2.6)

$$\begin{aligned} S_{it} &= z_{it} + a_i S_{it-1} \\ S_{it+1} &= (z_{it+1} + a_i z_{it}) + a_i^2 S_{it-1} \\ S_{it+s} &= \sum_{\theta=0}^{s} a_i^{\theta} z_{it+s-\theta} + a_i^{s+1} S_{it-1} \end{aligned} \tag{A.2}$$

for s = 0,...,T -t.

Substituting (A.2) into (A.1) and grouping terms we obtain

$$W_t + \sum_{i=i}^{n} p_{it} d_i S_{it-1} = \sum_{i=1}^{n} \left( \overset{v}{p}_{it} z_{it} + p_{it+1} z_{it+1} + \ldots \overset{v}{p}_{iT} z_{iT} + \overset{v}{p}_{it} a_i S_{it} - 1 \right) , \tag{A.3}$$

where:

$$\begin{aligned} \overset{v}{p}_{it} &= (\hat{p}^*_{it} + a_i \hat{p}^*_{it+1} + \ldots + a_i^{T-t} \hat{p}^*_{iT}) \\ \overset{v}{p}_{it+s} &= (\hat{p}^*_{it+s}) + a_i \hat{p}^*_{it+s+1} + \ldots + a_i^{T-t-s} \hat{p}^*_{iT}) \end{aligned} \tag{A.4}$$

for s = 0,...,T - t.

With the weakly intertemporally separable utility function (10) and the budget constraint (A.3) two-stage budgeting is possible. Thus the Marshallian demand function for $z_{it}$ is given by

(A.5) $$z_{it} = g_i(p_t^v, x_t) ,$$

where $$x_t = \sum_i p_{it}^v z_{it}.$$

Making the simplifying assumptions also made by Phlips and Spinnewyn (1982) that consumers expect relative prices to be the same in all future periods and expect a constant real rate of interest $r^*$, we can obtain an expression for $p_{it}^v$. First, note that then

(A.6) $$\hat{p}^*_{it+1} = (1-d_i + r^*)p_{it}/(1+r^*)^{S+1} .$$

Thus

(A.7) $$p_{it} = \left(\frac{1-3_i + f^*}{1 + r^*}\right) p_{it} \sum_{\theta=0}^{T-1} \left(\frac{a_i}{1+r^*}\right)^{\theta}$$
$$= \lambda_{it} p_{it}.$$

When $T \rightarrow \infty$, $\lambda_i = \left(\frac{1-d_i+r^*}{1-a_i+r^*}\right)$ .

# REFERENCES


Anderson, G. & R. Blundell (1983): "Testing restrictions in a flexible dynamic system: An application to consumers' expenditure in Canada," *Review of Economic Studies*, Vol. 50, 397-410.

Attfield, C. (1985): "Homogeneity and endogeneity in demand systems," *Journal of Econometrics*, Vol. 27, 197-209.

Barten, A. & E. Geyskens (1975): "The negativity condition in consumer demand," *European Economic Review*, Vol. 6, 227-260.

Blundell, R. & R. Smith (1984): "Separability, endogeneity and conditional demand models," Mimeo, University of Manchester, Department of Economics.

Blundell, R., P. Pashardes & G. Weber (1989): "What do we learn about consumer demand patterns from micro-data?" Institute for Fiscal Studies, Micro-to-Macro, Discussion Paper series No. 3.

Bronsard, C. & L. Salvas-Bonsard (1984), "On price endogeneity in complete demand systems," *Journal of Econometrics*, Vol. 24, 235-247.

Conrad, K. & D. Jorgenson (1979): "Testing the integrability of consumer demand functions," *European Economic Review*, Vol. 12, 149-169.

Cramer, J. S. (1957): "A dynamic approach to the theory of consumer demand," *Review of Economic Studies*, Vol. 24, 73-86.

Davidson, J., D. Hendry, F. Srba & S. Yeo (1978): "Econometric modelling of the aggregate relationship between consumers' expenditure and income in the United Kingdom," *Economic Journal*, Vol. 88, 899-910.

Deaton, A. (1977), "Involuntary savings through unanticipated inflation," *American Economic Review*, Vol. 67, 899-910.

Deaton, A. (1981): "Theoretical and empirical approaches to consumer demand under rationing," in A. S. Deaton (ed), *Essays in the Theory and Measurement of Consumer Behaviour in Honour of Sir Richard Stone*, Cambridge University Press.

Deaton, A. & J. Muellbauer (1980b): "An almost ideal demand system," *American Economic Review*, Vol. 70, 312-326.

Farrell, M. (1952): "Irreversible demand functions," *Econometrica*, Vol. 20, 171-186.

Jorgenson, D., L. Lau & T. Stoker (1982): "The Transendental logarithmic model of aggregate consumer behaviour," in R. Basmann & G. Rhodes Jr. (eds.) **Advances in Econometrics**. Vol. 1. Greenwich, JAI Press.

Gorman, W. (1959): "Separable utility and aggregation," *Econometrica*, Vol. 27, 469-481.

Gorman, W. (1967): "Tastes, habits and choices," *International Economic Review*, Vol. 8, 218-222.

Gorman, W. (1981): "Some Engel curves," in A. S. Deaton (ed.), op.cit.

Houthakker, H. S. & L. Taylor (1966, 1970 2nd ed.): **Consumer Demand in the United States 1929-70, Analysis and Projections**, Cambridge, Mass.; Harvard Univeristy Press.

Kiefer, N. (1984): "Microeconometric evidence on the neoclassical model of demand," *Journal of Econometrics*, 25, 285-302.

Laitinen, K. (1978): "Why is demand homogeneity so often rejected?" *Economic Letters*, Vol. 1, 187-191.

Lau, L. (1982): "A note on the fundamental theorem of exact aggregation," *Economic Letters*, Vol. 9, 119-126.

Muellbauer, J. (1976): "Community preferences and the representative consumer," *Econometrica*, Vol. 44, 979-999.

Pashardes, P. (1986): "Myopic and forward looking behaviour in a dynamic demand system," *International Economic Review*, 27, 387-398.

Phlips, L. (1972): "A dynamic version of the linear expenditure model," *Review of Economics and Statistics*, Vol. 54, 450-458.

Phlips, L. (1978): "The demand for leisure and money," *Econometrica*, Vol. 46, 1025-1043.

Phlips, L. (1983): **Applied Demand Analysis**, Amsterdam and Oxford: North Holland.

Phlips, L. & F. Spinnewyn (1982): "Rationality versus myopia in dynamic demand systems," *Advances in Econometrics*, Vol. 1, 3-33, JAI Press.

Pollak, R. A. (1970): "Habit formation and dynamic demand functions," *Journal of Political Economy*, Vol. 78, 745-763.

Pollak, R. A. (1976): "Habit formation and long run utility functions," *Journal of Political Economy*, Vol. 13, 292-297.

Pollak, R. A. (1978): "Endogenous tastes in demand and welfare analysis," *American Economic Review*, Vol. 78 (papers and proc), 374-379.

Pollak, R. A. & R. Wales (1969): Estimation of the linear expenditure system," *Econometrica*, Vol. 37, 611-628.

Sims, A. (1980): "Macroeconomics and reality," *Econometrica*, Vol. 3, 1-48.

Spinnewyn, F. (1979): "The cost of consumption and wealth in a model with habit formation," *Economic Letters*, Vol. 2, 145-148.

Spinnewyn, F. (1981): "Rational habit formation," *European Economic Review*, Vol. 15, 92-109.

Stoker, T. (1986): "Simple tests of distributional effects on macroeconomic equations," *Journal of Political Economy*, Vol. 94, 763-795.

Stone, R. (1954): "Linear expenditure systems and demand analysis: An application to the pattern of British demand," *Economic Journal*, Vol. 64, 511-527.

Stone, R. & G. Croft-Murray (1959): **Social Accounting and Economic Models**, London: Bowes and Bowes.

Stone, R. & D. Rowe (1957): "The market demand for durable goods," *Econometrica*, Vol. 25, 423-443.

Stone, R. & D. Rowe (1958): "Dynamic demand functions: Some econometric results," *Economic Journal*, Vol. 68, 256-270.

Taylor, L. & D. Weiserbs (1972): "On the estimation of dynamic demand functions," *Review of Economics and Statistics*, Vol. 54, 459-465.

Theil, L. (1951): **De invloed van de wooraden op her consumentendrag**, Amsterdam: Poortpers.

Theil, L. (1975): **Theory and Measurement of Consumer Demand**, Amsterdam: North Holland.

Von Weizsacker, C. C. (1971): "Notes on endogenous changes of tastes," *Journal of Economic Theory*, Vol. 3, 345-372.

Weiserbs, D. (1983): "Dynamic demand systems with flexible functional forms," Mimeo, Institut de Recherches Economiques, Université Catholique de Louvain.

**CHART 1: BUDGET SHARES AND RELATIVE PRICES, 1954-80**

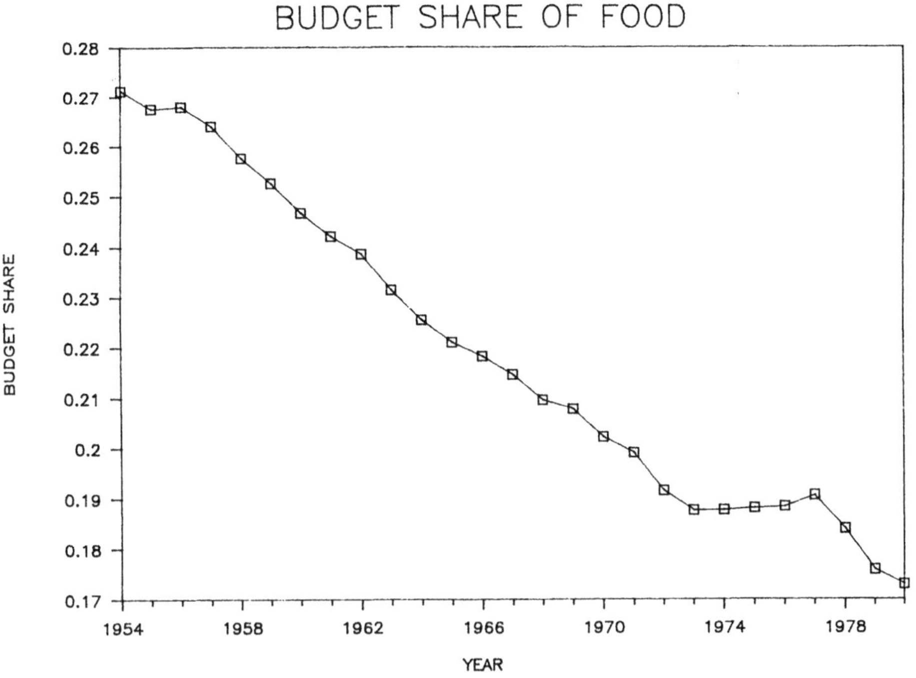


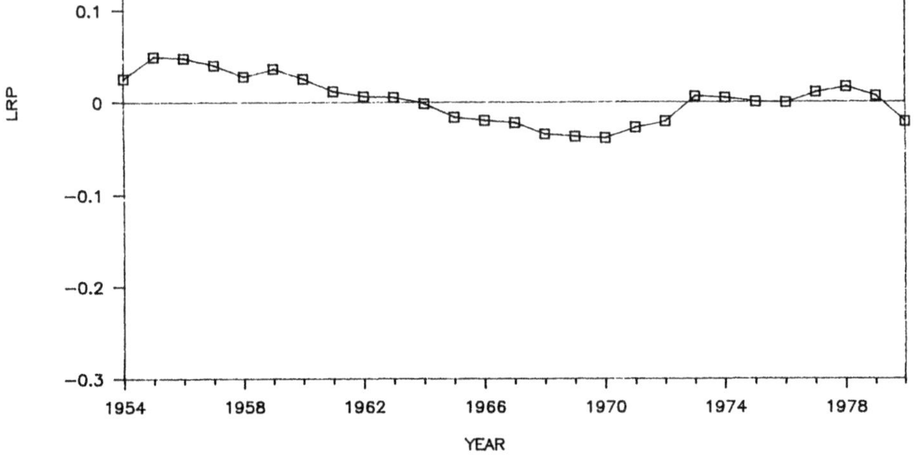

(Chart 1 continued)

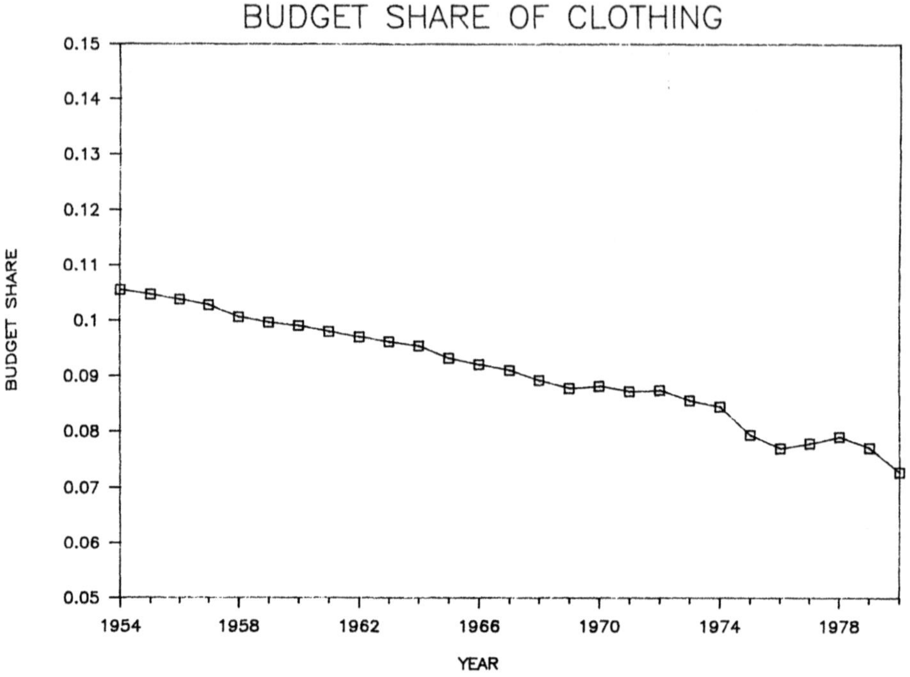


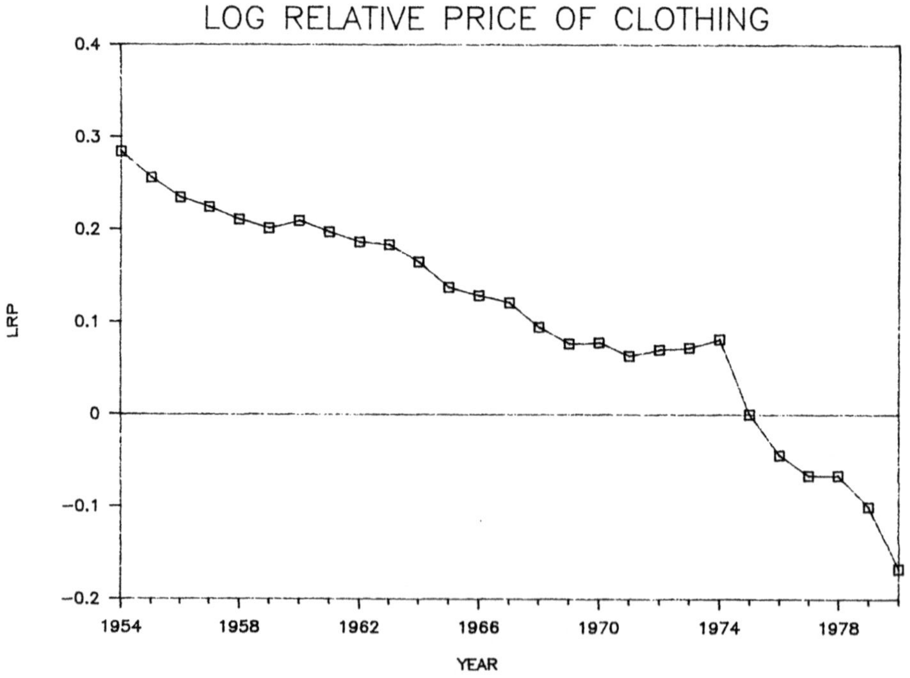

(Chart 1 continued)

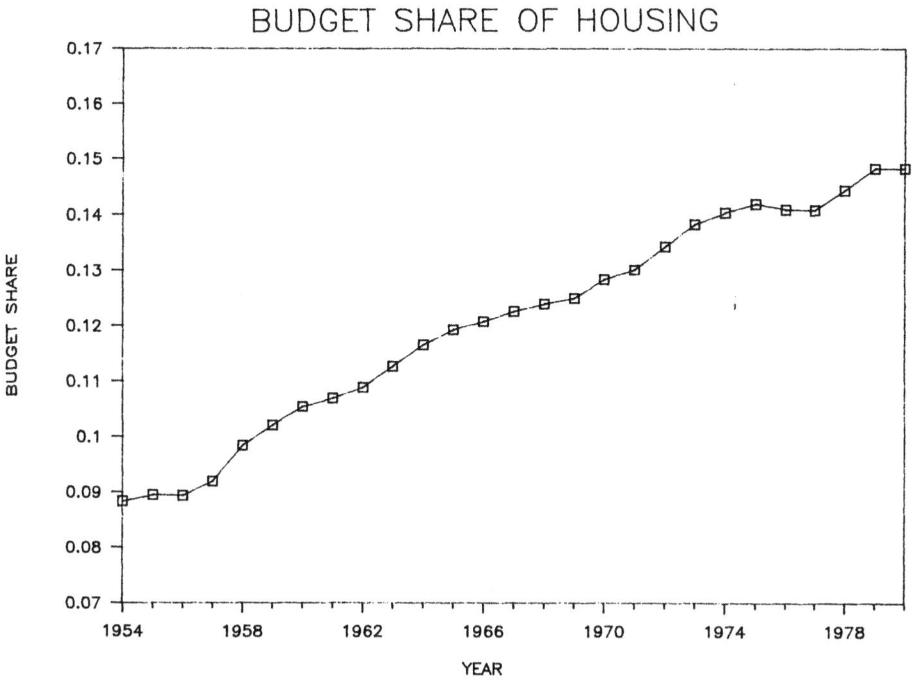


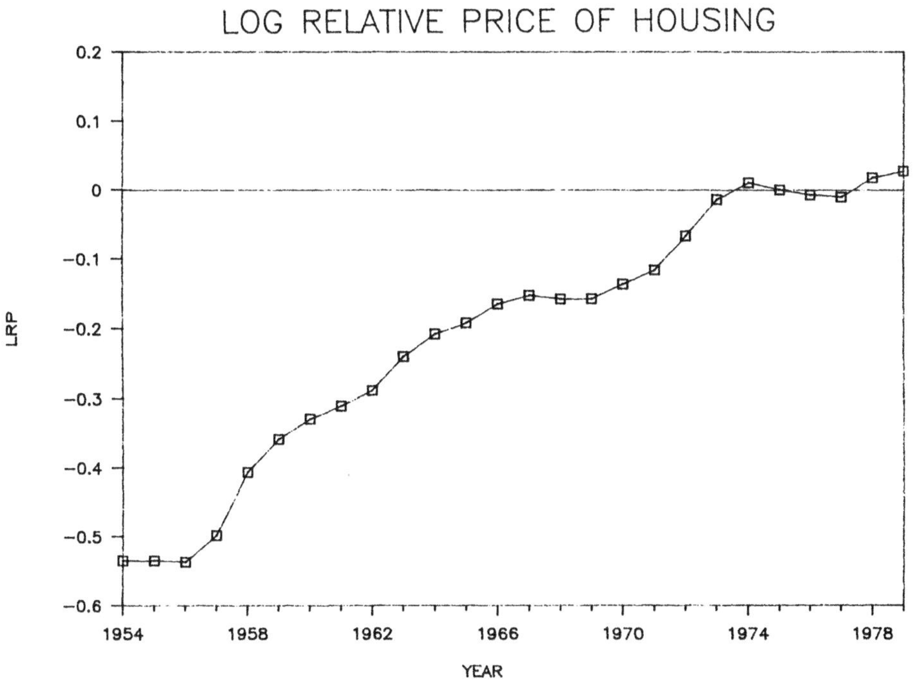

(Chart 1 continued)

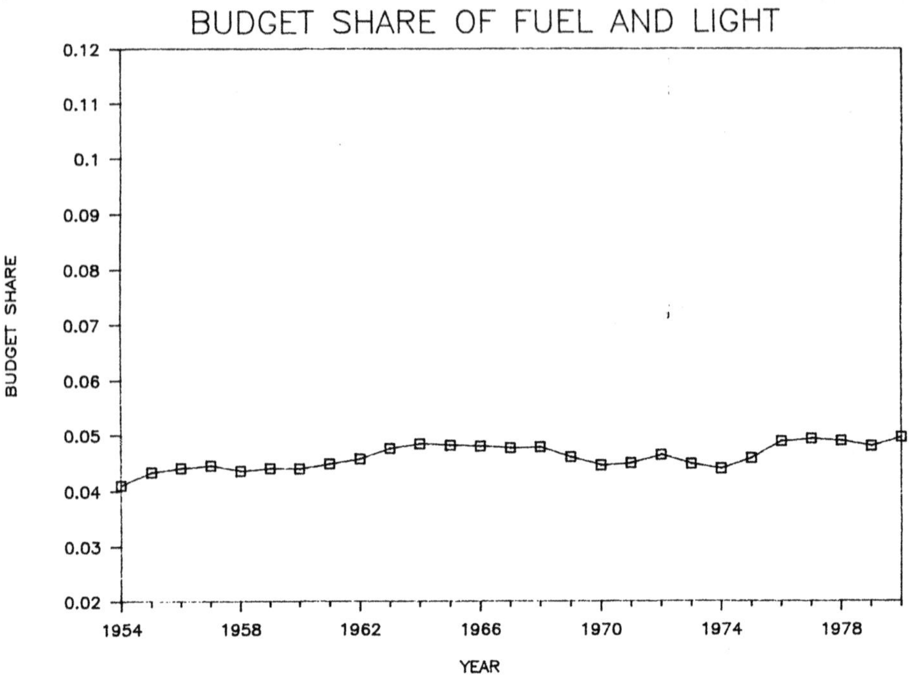


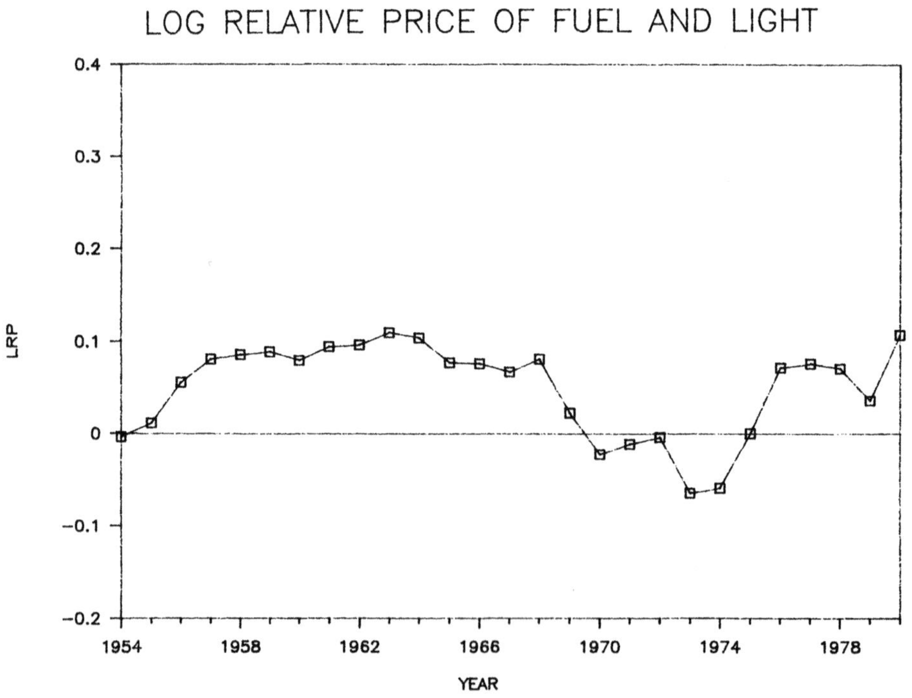

(Chart 1 continued)

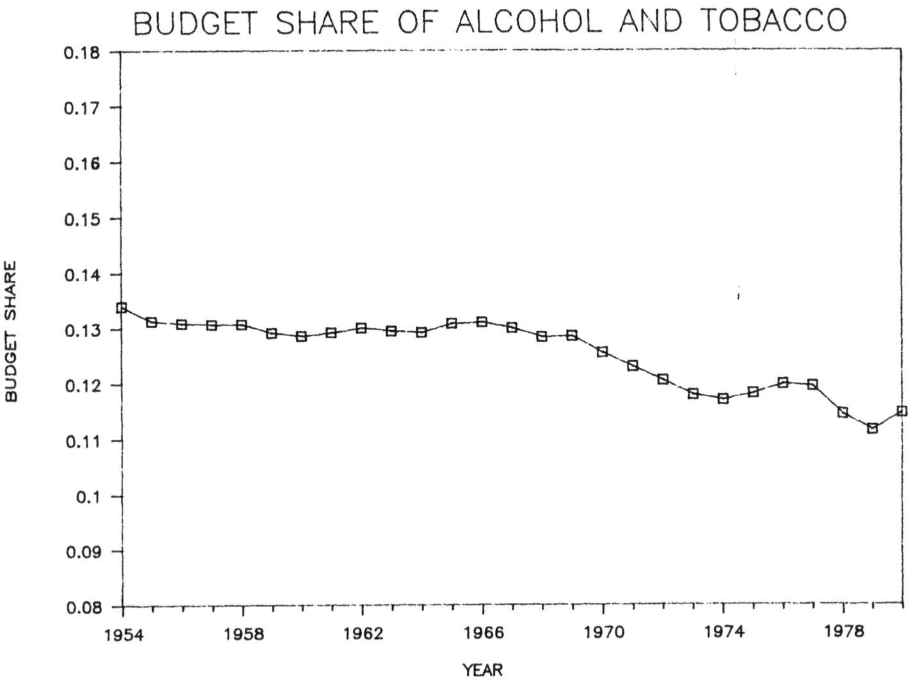


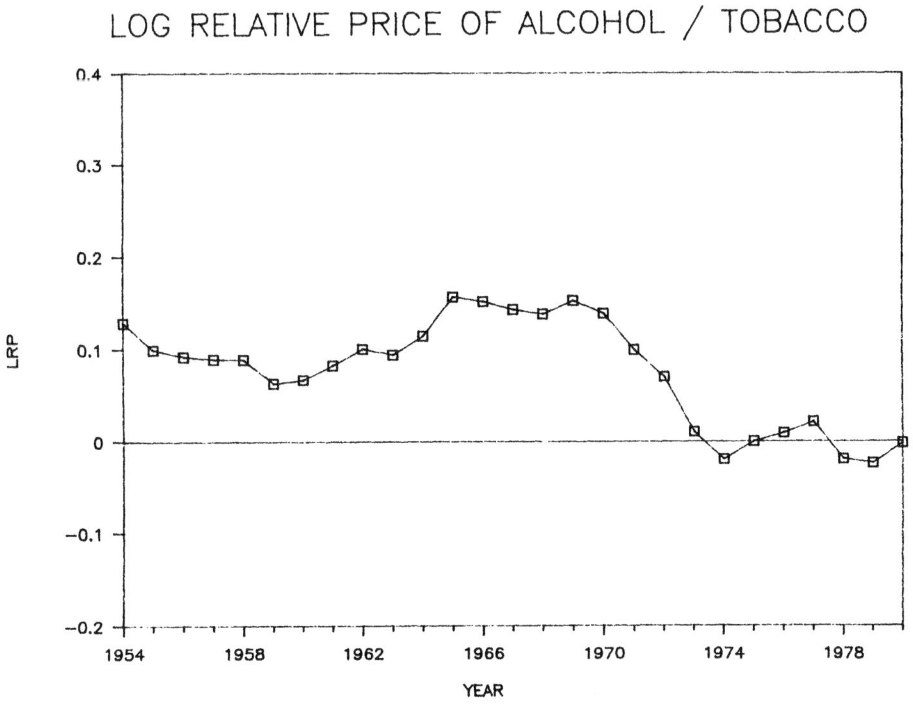

(Chart 1 continued)

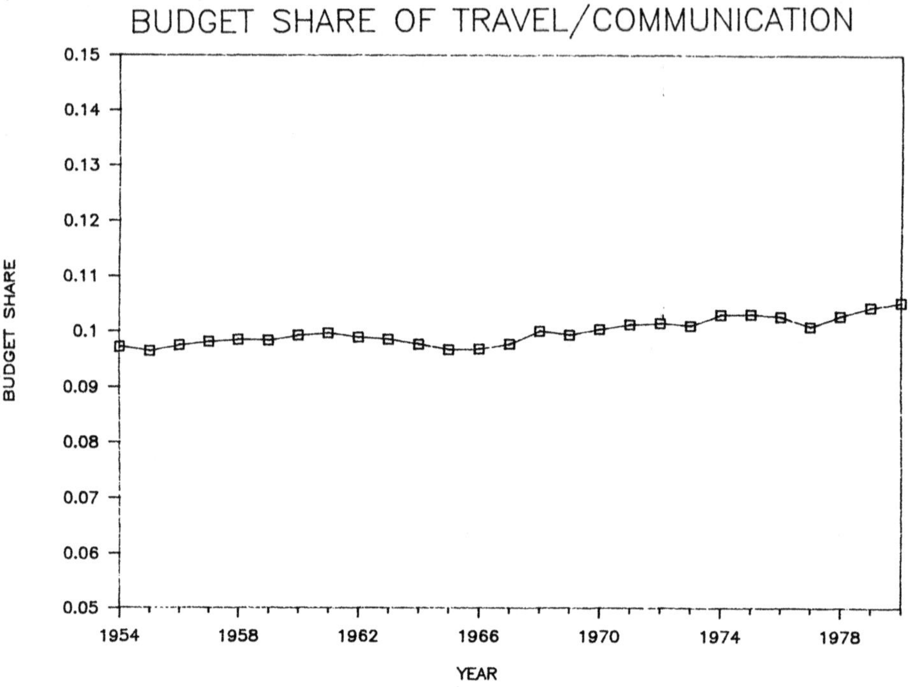


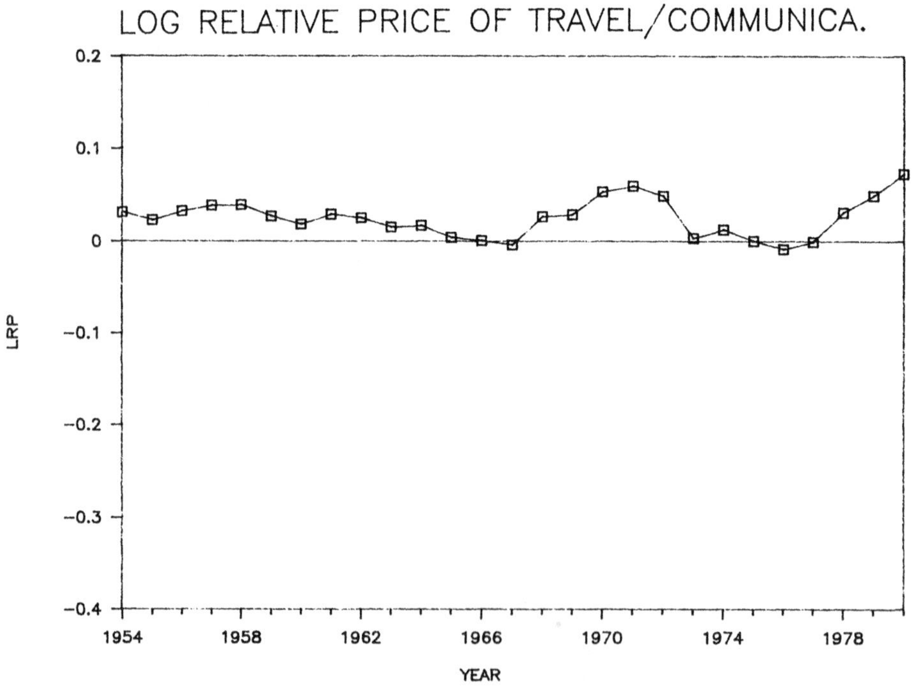

(Chart 1 continued)

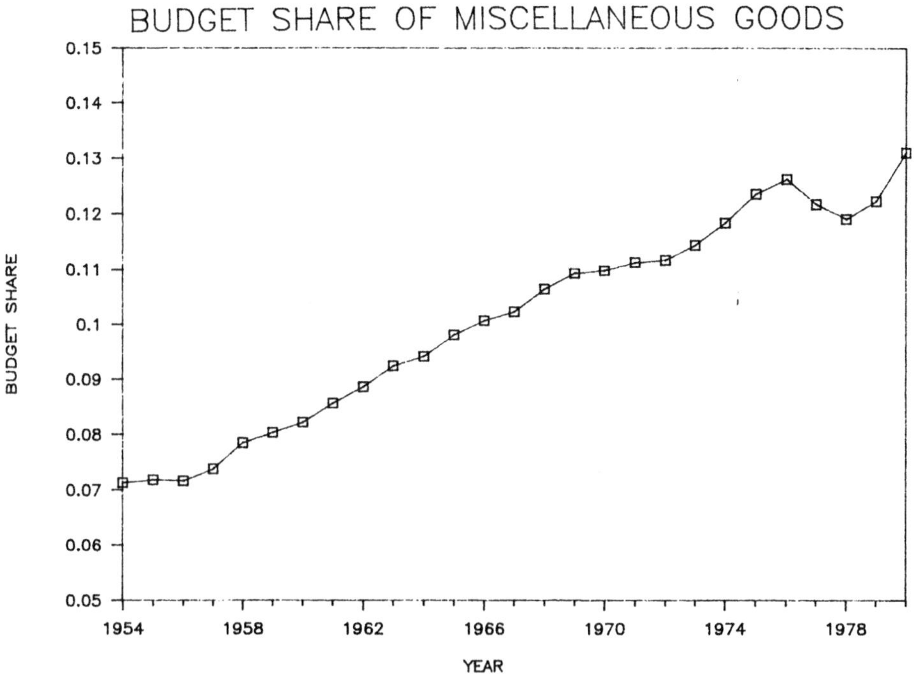


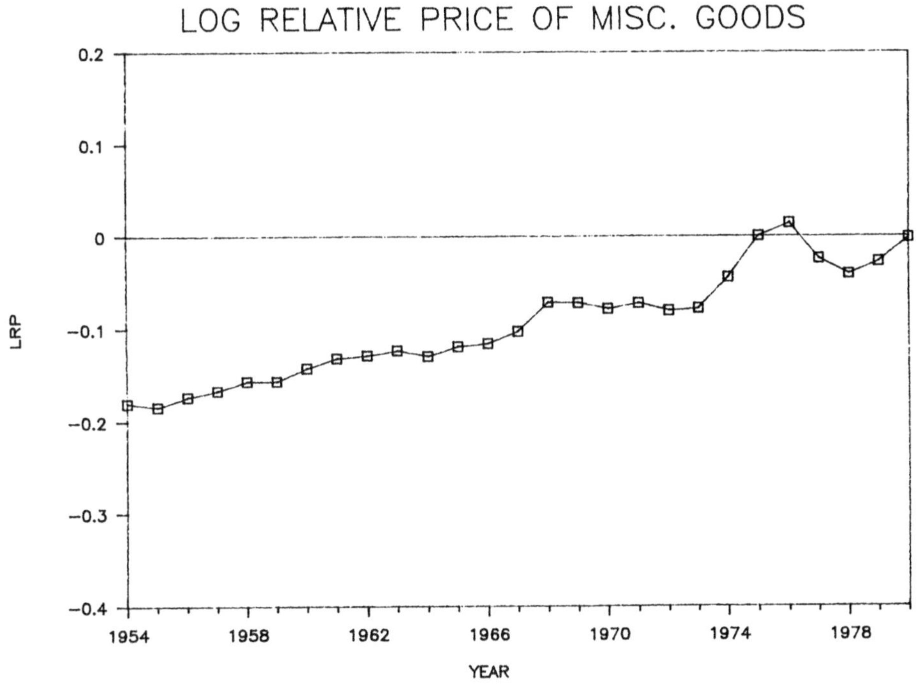

(Chart 1 continued)

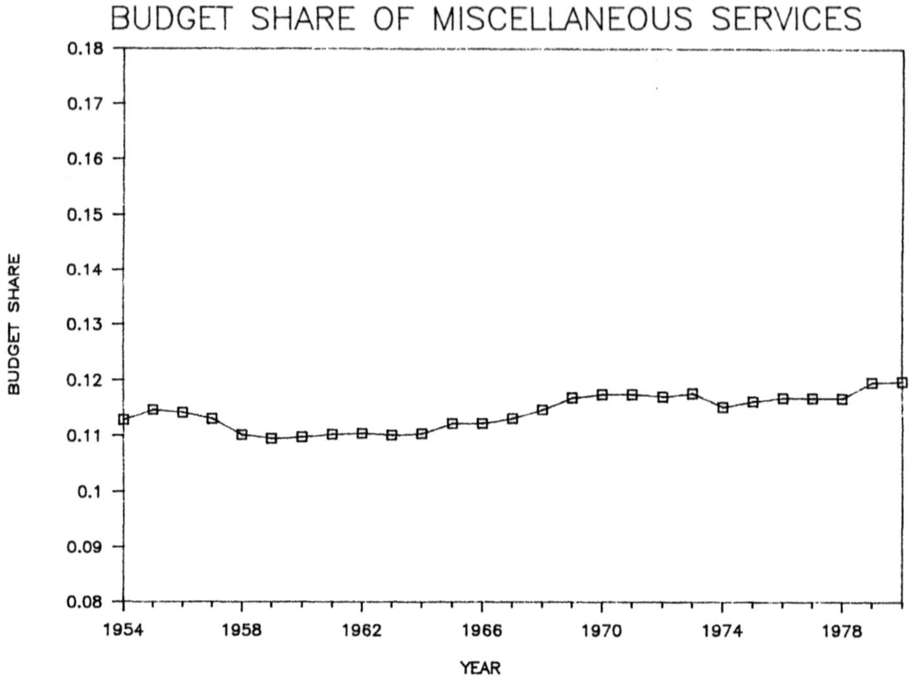


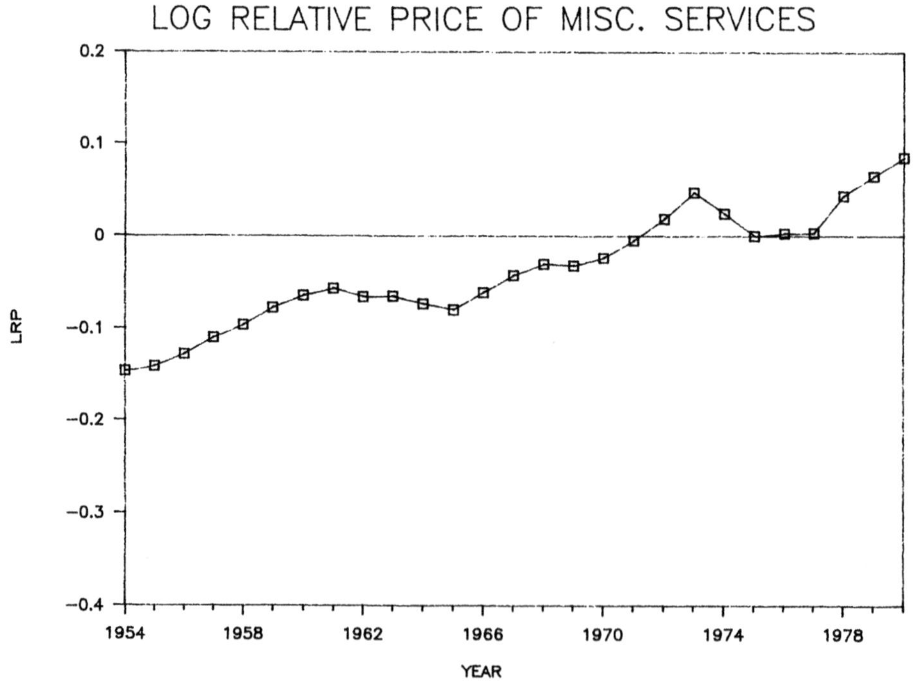

(Chart 1 continued)

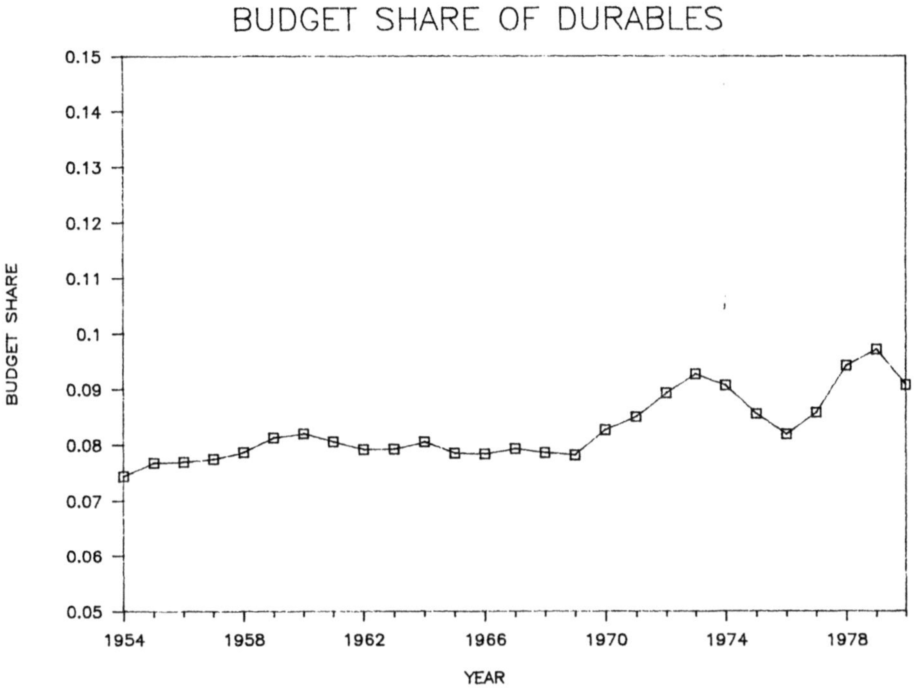


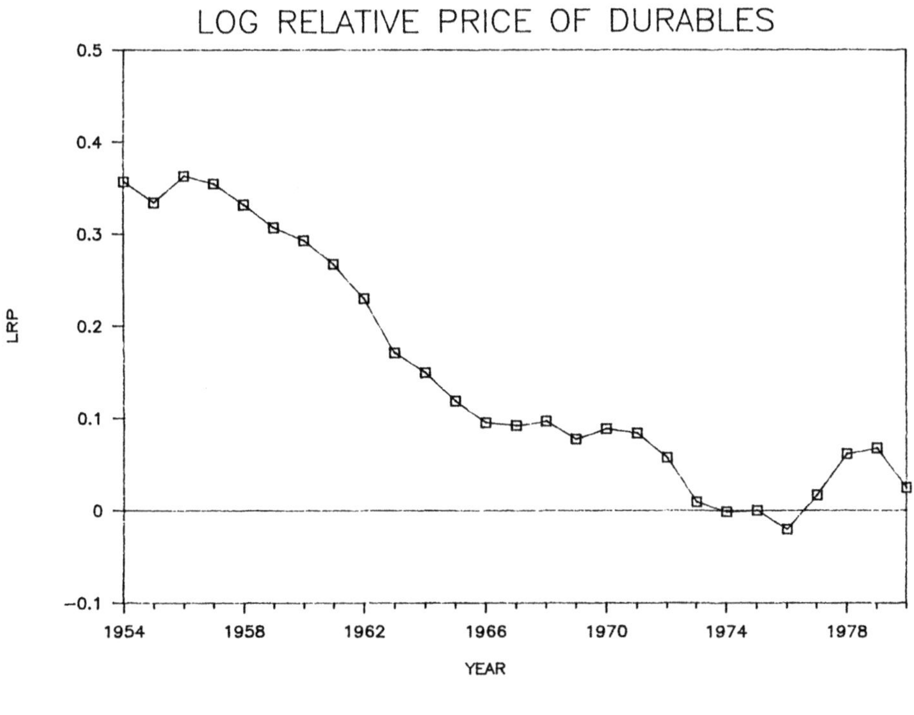

**CHART 2: REAL CONSUMPTION EXPENDITURE 1954-80**

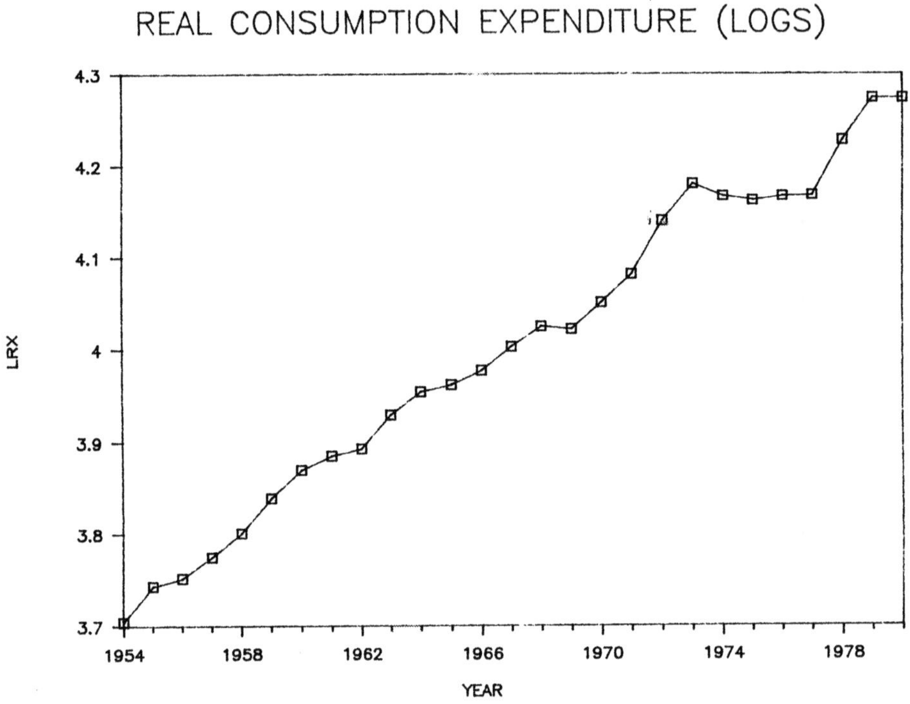

# SPECIFICATION AND ESTIMATION OF DYNAMIC DEMAND SYSTEMS*

ROBERT A. POLLAK
*Department of Economics*
*University of Pennsylvania*
*3718 Locust Walk Circle*
*Philadelphia, PA 19104*

TERENCE J. WALES
*Department of Economics*
*University of British Columbia*
*Vancouver, B.C. V6T 1Y2*

ABSTRACT. This paper focuses on two issues in empirical demand analysis: Alternative specifications of demand systems in terms of functional form, dynamic structure, and stochastic structure; and alternative estimation procedures. Four functional forms and two dynamic structures are considered. Each demand specification is estimated using both a first-difference procedure in which the first observation is included, and a maximum likelihood procedure in which the first observation is excluded. The results show that the treatment of the first observation can have substantial effects on predicted behavior.

## 1. Introduction

In this paper we consider two separate issues in empirical demand analysis. First, we investigate alternative demand system specifications, that is, specifications of functional form, of dynamic structure, and of stochastic structure. Second, we investigate alternative estimation procedures differing in their treatment of the first observation.

The functional forms we consider are the quadratic expenditure system (QES); the generalized translog (GTL); and two special cases, the linear expenditure system (LES) and the basic translog (BTL). The LES and the BTL are familiar, frequently estimated systems. The QES was proposed and estimated by Howe, Pollak, and Wales (1979), and the GTL by Pollak and Wales (1980).

In addition to the usual static specification, in which demand system parameters remain the same throughout the sample period, we consider two dynamic structures -- dynamic translating and dynamic scaling -- which allow such parameters to depend systematically on

* Pollak's research was supported in part by the National Science Foundation. Wales' research was supported in part by the Canada Council and UBC. We are grateful to L.J. Lau and E.O. Olsen for useful discussions, to D. Ryan for research assistance, and to J. Goff for editorial assistance.



*L. Phlips and L.D. Taylor (eds.), Aggregation, Consumption and Trade*, 99–119.

past consumption. Both dynamic translating and dynamic scaling are general procedures in the sense that they do not require the demand system to have a particular functional form, but can be used in conjunction with any complete demand system (*i.e.*, one describing the allocation of expenditure among an exhaustive set of commodity groups).

In addition to the usual "independent" stochastic specification in which disturbances in different periods are unrelated, we consider two specifications permitting first order serial correlation: A "diagonal" specification allowing only one serial correlation parameter for the entire demand system, and a more general "free" specification involving additional serial correlation parameters.

Since the static independent LES often serves as a basis for empirical work, testing this specification against more general ones is useful and important. We carry out a series of such tests, using annual U.S. per capita data for the period 1948-1977. For functional form, for dynamic structure, and for stochastic structure, we consistently reject the most restrictive hypothesis. We find the LES dominated by the QES and the GTL; the static structure rejected in favor of a dynamic one; and the independent stochastic structure rejected in favor of one allowing first order serial correlation.

The second issue we consider is the effect of alternative estimation procedures on the ranking of specifications and on predicted behavior. We estimate each demand specification in two ways: Using a generalized first difference procedure which excludes the first observation; and using a maximum likelihood procedure which includes it. We find that the treatment of the first observation has relatively little effect on the ranking of specifications, but that it can have substantial effects on predicted behavior.

## 2. Specification

Demand system estimation requires specifying a functional form, a dynamic structure, and a stochastic structure. We consider each in turn.

### 2.1 FUNCTIONAL FORM

The found demand systems we estimate are forms of the quadratic expenditure system or the generalized translog.[1] The QES we estimate, in share form, is given by:

(1)
$$w_i = \frac{p_i b_i}{\mu} + a_i\left(1 - \sum \frac{p_k b_k}{\mu}\right)$$
$$+ \left(\frac{p_i}{\mu} c_i - a_i \sum \frac{p_k c_k}{\mu}\right) \prod \left(\frac{p_k}{\mu}\right)^{-2a_k} \left(1 - \sum \frac{p_k b_k}{\mu}\right)^2 , \quad \sum a_k = 1 ,$$

[1] We view demand theory as a model of expenditure allocation among an exhaustive set of commodity groups.

where p's denote prices, x's quantities, $\mu$ total expenditure, $w_i$ the share of the ith good in total expenditure, ($w_i = p_i x_i/\mu$), and the a's, b's, and c's parameters to be estimated.[2] It is generated by the indirect utility function

$$\text{(2)} \qquad \Psi(P,\mu) = \frac{g(P)}{\mu - f(P)} - \frac{\alpha(P)}{g(P)},$$

where:

$$(P) = \prod p_k^{a_k}, \ \sum a_k = 1$$
$$f(P) = \sum p_k b_k$$
$$\alpha(P) = \sum p_k c_k \ .$$

The QES contains 3n-1 independent parameters. Howe, Pollak, and Wales (1979) characterize the entire class of theoretically plausible demand systems quadratic in expenditure and report estimates of the QES based on U.S. per capita data.[3]

The linear expenditure system (LES) is obtained from the QES by setting $c_i = 0$ for all i, so that the third term on the right hand side of (1) vanishes. The LES contains 2n-1 independent parameters.

The generalized translog (GTL) demand system, in share form, is given by:

$$\text{(3)} \qquad w_i = b_i \frac{p_i}{\mu} + [1 - \sum p_k b_k/\mu] \left\{ \frac{\alpha_i + \sum_j \beta_{ij} \ln[p_j/(\mu - \sum p_k b_k)]}{\sum \alpha_k + \sum \sum_j \beta_{kj} \ln[p_j/(\mu - \sum p_k b_k)]} \right\}$$

$$\beta_{ij} = \beta_{ji} \text{ for all i, j and } \Sigma\alpha_k + \Sigma\Sigma_j \beta_{kj} = 1$$

where the b's, $\alpha$'s, and $\beta$'s are parameters to be estimated. It is generated by the indirect utility function:

$$\text{(4)} \qquad \psi(P,\mu) = -\Sigma a_k \log[p_k/(\mu - \Sigma_t p_t b_t)]$$

$$- \frac{1}{2} \Sigma\Sigma_j \beta_{kj} \log[p_k/(\mu - \Sigma_t p_t b_t)] \log[p_j/(\mu - \Sigma_t p_t b_t)],$$

$$\beta_{ij} = \beta_{ji} \quad \text{for all i, j and} \quad \Sigma\alpha_k + \Sigma\Sigma_j \beta_{kj} = 1 \ .$$

The GTL contains $(n^2 + 5n-2)/2$ independent parameters, and was first proposed and estimated in Pollak and Wales (1980). As its name suggests, the GTL is a generalization of the basic translog (BTL) introduced by Christensen, Jorgenson, and Lau (1975). The BTL is

---

[2] Unless otherwise indicated, all summations run from 1 to n. We use k exclusively as a running subscript; $\Sigma$ without indexes or limits of summation, means $\sum_{k=1}^{n}$.

[3] Throughout this paper we refer to (1) as the QES. Pollak and Wales (1978, 1980) and Darrough, Pollak, and Wales (1983) estimate another demand system quadratic in expenditure using U.K. and Japanese household budget data and refer to that system as the QES.

obtained from the GTL by setting $b_i = 0$ for all i and the LES is obtained from the GTL by setting $\beta_{ij} = 0$ for all i,j.

## 2.2 DYNAMIC STRUCTURE

Empirical demand analysis must either assume that demand system parameters remain constant over time or specify how they change. We estimate the usual static model in which all demand system parameters remain fixed, and two dynamic specifications which permit some demand system parameters to vary with past consumption. The two dynamic specifications, dynamic translating and dynamic scaling, are general procedures for allowing systematic parameter variation in empirical demand analysis. That is, either specification can be used in conjunction with any original demand system, not just with a restricted class of functional forms. We describe both specifications as modifications of an original class of demand systems, $\{x_i = \bar{h}^i(P,\mu),\ i=1,...,n\}$. We assume these original demand systems are "theoretically plausible," (*i.e.*, they can be derived from "well-behaved" preferences), and we denote the corresponding direct utility function by $\bar{U}(X)$ and the indirect utility function by $\bar{\Psi}(P,\mu)$.

Our dynamic translating procedure varies according to whether the original demand system contains constant terms. When it does, we assume that they depend on past consumption. In principle they may depend on any variables representing past consumption (*e.g.*, a weighted average of all past consumption or the highest level of consumption attained in the past), but we assume that they depend only on the previous period's consumption. Denoting the constant terms by d's, we write: $d_i = D^i(x_{it-1})$. Log linear dynamic translating, the specification we estimate, is given by

$$D^i(x_{it-1}) = d_i^* x_{it-1}^{\gamma_i} \tag{5}$$

and adds n parameters to the modified system.

When the original demand system does not contain constant terms, our dynamic translating procedure replaces the original system by:

$$h^i(P,\mu) = d_i + \bar{h}^i(P,\mu - \Sigma p_k d_k). \tag{6}$$

This introduces n constant terms into the demand system, and we assume they depend on past consumption, as in the preceding case.[4,5] If the original demand system is theoretically plausible, the modified system is also, at least for d's close to zero. The modified system satisfies the first order conditions corresponding to the indirect utility function

$$\Psi(P,\mu) = \bar{\Psi}(P,\mu - \textstyle\sum p_k d_k).$$

Dynamic scaling replaces the original demand system by:

---

[4] Dynamic translating was originally proposed by Stone (1954, p. 522) in conjunction with the linear expenditure system. See Pollak (1978) for references to the literature.

[5] A more general formulation of translating would replace (5) by $D^i(x_{it-1}) = c_i + d_i^* x_{it-1}^{\gamma_i}$.

Given the computational difficulties in converging our simpler models, it is unlikely that this more general specification would converge. A drawback of our specification (5) is that the resulting demand system need not contain constant terms unless all the $\gamma$'s are zero.

(7) $$h^i(P,\mu) = m_i\bar{h}^i(p_1m_1,...,p_nm_n,\mu)$$

where the m's are scaling parameters that depend on the previous period's consumption: $m_i = M_i(x_{it-1})$.[6] If the original demand system is theoretically plausible, then the modified system is also, at least for m's close to one. The modified system satisfies the first order conditions corresponding to the indirect utility function $\Psi(P,\mu) = \bar{\Psi}(p_1m_1,...,p_nm_n,\mu)$ and the direct utility function $U(X) = \bar{U}(x_1/m_1,...,x_n/m_n)$. Loosely speaking, we might interpret $x_i/m_i$ as a measure of $x_i$ in "efficiency units" rather than physical units.

Log linear dynamic scaling, the specification we estimate, is given by

(8) $$M^i(x_{it-1}) = x_{it-1}^{\gamma_i}$$

This specification guarantees that the implied value of $m_i$ will be positive, as is required on theoretical grounds. It adds n parameters to the original demand system.

Specifications allowing demand system parameters to depend on past consumption are formally analogous to those allowing them to depend on demographic variables. Thus, dynamic translating is analogous to demographic translating and dynamic scaling to demographic scaling. Although we do not consider more general dynamic specifications here, all the demographic specifications discussed in Pollak and Wales (1981) have obvious dynamic counterparts.

### 2.3 STOCHASTIC STRUCTURE

We estimate three stochastic specifications; one in which disturbances in different periods are independent, and two others that allow first order serial correlation. The "diagonal" autocorrelation specification involves only one serial correlation parameter, while the "free" specification involves $(n-1)^2$ independent serial correlation parameters.

All of our stochastic specifications postulate an additive disturbance term on the share equations. In vector form we write

(9) $$w_t = g(P_t,\mu_t) + u_t,$$

where $u_t=(u_{t1},...,u_{tn})'$, and $E(u_t) = 0$ for all t.

The free stochastic specification assumes that $u_t$ follows a general first-order autoregressive process

(10) $$u_t = R*u_{t-1} + \varepsilon_t ,$$

where $R^*$ is an n x n matrix of autoregressive parameters and $\epsilon_t$ is an n x 1 vector of disturbances with $E(\epsilon_t) = 0$ and *e)$\epsilon_t\epsilon_t'$) = $\Omega$ for all t. The diagonal specification is a special case in which $R^*$ is diagonal; the independent specification corresponds to $R^* = 0$. Although the diagonal specification might appear to allow n independent serial correlation parameters, Berndt and Savin (1975) show that it allows only one. When the covariance matrix of the u's is singular (as it might be for the budget constraint to hold as an identity) and serial

[6] A more general formulation would allow $m_i$ to depend on consumption in all previous periods.

correlation takes this simple form in which $u_{it}$ is related to $u_{it-1}$ but not to $u_{jt-1}$, then a single correlation coefficient must be used for all goods.[7]

### 3. Data, Estimation, Results

Our estimates are based on annual U.S. per capita data for the years 1948-1977. Selecting consumption categories for demand analysis involves an inescapable element of arbitrariness. We use three broad commodity groups constructed from the national product accounts: "Food," "clothing," and a "miscellaneous" category which excludes shelter, consumer durables, and non-durables which seem closely related to them.[8] Excluding shelter and durables is justified if our three included commodity groups are separable from the excluded ones. The alternative of including the flow of services of shelter and consumer durables would require time series data representing these service flows and the corresponding implicit rents, and would require that consumption of these services be in equilibrium given their implicit rates.[9] Our three included commodity groups account for about half of "personal consumption expenditure." Precise definitions of our commodity groups are given in Appendix A.

Since observed and predicted expenditure shares sum to one, we can estimate the demand systems after dropping one equation. With three goods, we can identify four independent transformations of the parameters of the $R^*$ matrix. We denote the 2 x 2 transformed $R^*$ matrix by R.[10]

There is evidence, especially strong in the single equation context, that parameter estimates and hypothesis tests can be sensitive to omission of the first observation. The literature suggests that this is especially likely to be true in small samples when the independent variables exhibit time trends.[11,12] To investigate this phenomenon in the demand system

---

[7] The only paper we know which estimates demand systems using a free $R^*$ matrix is Anderson and Blundell (1982). They estimate a general dynamic short run model, using a generalized first difference procedure (see below).

[8] The treatment of shelter is problematic. Although national product accounts purport to measure the flow of housing services, we have excluded shelter because we are skeptical about these data. Howe, Pollak, and Wales (1979) report estimates based on four commodity groups, including shelter.

[9] See, for example, Diewert (1974). It is difficult to think of assumptions that justify ignoring durability and treating reported purchases of durables as current consumption flows.

[10] R is obtained from $R^*$ by first subtracting the last column of $R^*$ from each of the other columns of $R^*$, and then deleting the last row and column. See Berndt and Savin (1975) for a detailed discussion of this procedure.

[11] In our sample, the normalized prices for food and clothing exhibit a strong time trend, falling almost monotonically over the period. For the miscellaneous category, normalized prices rise initially until about the middle of the period, and then fall.

context, we use two alternative estimation procedures: The "generalized first difference" procedure, which drops the first observation; and the "maximum likelihood" procedure, which does not. The generalized first difference procedure premultiplies the system of two equations by R, lags once, and subtracts from the original observation. This yields a system of equations with independent disturbances with mean 0 and covariance matrix **. Maximum likelihood estimates of this differenced system do not coincide with maximum likelihood estimates based on the original system and sample: the generalized first difference procedure fails to make full use of the first observation, which it uses only in differencing. When the autoregressive matrix is free, using the generalized first difference procedure offers major computational advantages: Estimation is relatively straightforward because the likelihood function corresponding to the differenced system can be concentrated and maximized in the usual way. On the other hand, maximum likelihood estimates corresponding to the original system and sample are difficult to calculate because there appears to be no way of concentrating the likelihood function.[13] Since the generalized first difference procedure is asymptotically maximum likelihood, the two procedures yield different results only in "small" samples.

We report results for thirty difference models: (i) Three dynamic structures (static, dynamic translating, dynamic scaling); (ii) four functional forms (LES, QES, BTL, GTL); and (iii) three stochastic specifications (R = 0, R diagonal, R free).[14] Table 1 shows the number of independent parameters (other than disturbance covariance parameters) in each model.

Table 2a presents log likelihood values for thirty models estimated with the generalized first difference procedure, and shows the number of sample price-expenditure situations at which each estimated demand system corresponds to well-behaved preferences.[15] Table 2b presents the corresponding values for the maximum likelihood procedure. The likelihood values reported in Tables 2a and 2b are not comparable because the estimates are based on different procedures and different samples.[16]

---

[12] See, for example, Park and Mitchell (1980) and Maeshiro (1979) for single equation estimation, and Beach and MacKinnon (1979) for systems estimation.

[13] We present the likelihood functions in Appendix B. On the problem of concentrating the likelihood function, see Beach and MacKinnon (1979).

[14] As the footnotes to Table 1 explain, this yields thirty rather than thirty-six distinct models.

[15] Since our estimates are based on aggregate rather than household data, there is no theoretical presumption that these demand functions correspond to well-behaved preferences.

[16] Indeed, it is not clear whether we should expect the likelihood values in Table 2b to be greater or smaller than those in Table 2a. As shown in Appendix B, the likelihood function for the maximum likelihood procedure contains two terms which do not appear with the generalized first difference procedure, and it is not clear *a priori* which likelihood function will be larger.

Before discussing our results, we briefly consider the effect on the standard likelihood ratio tests of a rough adjustment for sample size. In the case of linear regression, it is well known that with small samples the likelihood ratio test rejects linear hypotheses too often, and it seems likely that this is true in the nonlinear case as well. Anderson (1958, p. 208) considers zero restrictions in a system of linear equations with the same variables appearing in each question. He shows that the appropriate adjustment factor to ensure that the likelihood ratio test has the correct significance level to order $1/T$ is $[T-q-(1/2)(m-q_1+1)]/T$ where T is the number of observations, q the number of parameters in each equation, m the number of equations, and $q_1$ the number of restrictions in each equation. Although our model differs from his -- ours is nonlinear and the number of restrictions we impose is not a multiple of the number of equations due to the singularity of the covariance matrix -- it is nevertheless of interest to apply Anderson's correction factor to our tests.[17] With $q_1 = 1.5$, $m = 2$, $q = 5$, and $T = 29$ we obtain a correction factor of about .8.[18]

In the tests of nested hypotheses, we present full results for the usual likelihood ratio tests (*i.e.*, minus twice the logarithm of the likelihood ratio) and comment briefly on how the conclusions differ using Anderson's sample size correction factor.

Dynamic translating appears slightly superior to both dynamic scaling and the static model. Translating and scaling are not nested, but since they contain the same number of independent parameters we can informally compare them on the basis of their likelihood values. Translating yields a higher likelihood value than scaling in all 6 cases for QES models, and in 5 of 6 cases for the GTL models. Translating and scaling do about equally well when we compare the number of sample points at which regularity conditions are satisfied (*i.e.*, at which the Slutsky matrix is negative semi-definite). From this we conclude that dynamic translating is slightly superior to scaling.

Since the static models are nested in the dynamic ones, we compare them using standard likelihood ratio tests. We find the dynamic translating models superior to static ones: At the 5% significance level the parameters associated with lagged consumption are jointly significant in 8 or 9 comparisons using the maximum likelihood estimates (Table 2b), and in 7 of 9 for the first-difference estimates (Table 2a). Using the small sample adjustment, we find that dynamic translating is superior to the static model in 7 of 9 cases using both the maximum likelihood and the generalized first difference method. Because dynamic translating is superior to both dynamic scaling and the static model, we emphasize it in presenting our results.

We next consider stochastic structure, treating dynamic translating as a maintained hypothesis. Comparing models in which R is free with those in which R is diagonal, we find that the restriction significantly reduces the likelihood in 1 of 3 cases with the maximum

---

[17] Monte Carlo evidence in Wales (1982) suggests that Anderson's correction factor does a fairly good job of correcting the test bias for sample sizes of 20 and 40 when testing the significance of the QES estimated from data generated by the LES. Bera, Byron, and Jarque (1981) find that Anderson's correction is not appropriate when applying cross-equation restrictions, but we consider only zero restrictions within equations.

[18] We let $q_1 = 1.5$ so that $q_1 \cdot m = 3$, the number of restrictions in the system for most tests. Similarly q is set to correspond to the value used in most tests.

**TABLE 1: NUMBER OF INDEPENDENT PARAMETERS IN VARIOUS MODELS**

| | LES | QES | BTL | GTL |
|---|---|---|---|---|
| Static | | | | |
| R = 0 | 5 | 8 | 8 | 11 |
| R diagonal | 6 | 9 | 9 | 12 |
| R free | 9 | 12 | 12 | 15 |
| Dynamic Translating | | | | |
| R = 0 | 8 | 11 | + | 14 |
| R diagonal | 9 | 12 | + | 15 |
| R free | 12 | 15 | + | 18 |
| Dynamic Scaling | | | | |
| R = 0 | 8 | 11 | 11 | 14 |
| R diagonal | 9 | 12 | 12 | 15 |
| R free | 12 | 15 | 15 | 18 |

**Notes :**

We do not include the disturbance covariance parameters in this count.

For the LES, translating and scaling yield identical results.

\+ Translating can only be applied to systems containing translating parameters; when translating parameters are introduced into the BTL it becomes the GTL.

**TABLE 2A: LOG LIKELIHOOD VALUES: GENERALIZED FIRST DIFFERENCE PROCEDURE**

| | LES | QES | BTL | GTL |
|---|---|---|---|---|
| Static | | | | |
| R = 0 | 219.11(10) | 237.30(0) | 239.97(0) | 240.18(2) |
| R diagonal | 250.10(29) | 253.04(29) | 252.61(0) | 255.67(19) |
| R free | 256.20(29) | 258.78(29) | 259.29(0) | 262.60(0) |
| Dynamic Translating | | | | |
| R = 0 | 249.75(19) | 251.25(29) | + | 260.75(13) |
| R diagonal | 253.18(29) | 260.83(0) | + | 261.89(9) |
| R free | 257.61(29) | 264.44(0) | + | 268.14(0) |
| Dynamic Scaling | | | | |
| R = 0 | 249.75(19) | 251.20(10) | 254.18(17) | 258.78(12) |
| R diagonal | 253.18(29) | 258.80(0) | 258.47(13) | 263.75(14) |
| R free | 257.61(29) | 261.99(29) | 260.95(24) | 266.40(0) |

**Notes :**

1. See Table 1.

2. The numbers in parentheses indicate at how many of the 30 sample price-expenditure situations preferences are quasi-concave.

**TABLE 2B: LOG LIKELIHOOD VALUES: MAXIMUM LIKELIHOOD PROCEDURE**

| | LES | QES | BTL | GTL |
|---|---|---|---|---|
| Static | | | | |
| R = 0 | 225.11(9) | 242.58(0) | 245.34(0) | 245.42(0) |
| R diagonal | 248.81(29) | 252.92(0) | 254.14(0) | 255.55(0) |
| R free | 259.43(29) | 262.67(28) | 259.20(0) | 263.31(28) |
| Dynamic Translating | | | | |
| R = 0 | 258.45(18) | 260.39(7) | + | 265.60(20) |
| R diagonal | 258.59(20) | 264.60(0) | + | 265.65(20) |
| R free | 260.36(29) | 267.26(0) | + | 270.51(0) |
| Dynamic Scaling | | | | |
| R = 0 | 258.45(18) | 260.22(8) | 260.68(20) | 264.27(0) |
| R diagonal | 258.59(20) | 262.21(0) | 261.79(11) | 265.60(15) |
| R free | 260.36(29) | 265.85(0) | 266.65(0) | 268.78(0) |

**Notes :** See Table 2a.

likelihood estimates, and in 2 of 3 cases with the generalized first difference estimates (at the 5% level). Using the standard likelihood ratio test, the restriction that R be zero, as compared with R free, results in a significant reduction in the likelihood in all but one case; using the small sample adjustment, this is true in all but 2 cases. Thus we conclude that the models with R=0 are dominated by those with R diagonal or free.

We turn now to functional forms, basing our comparisons on dynamic models with R diagonal or free. We consider three nested comparisons: The LES-QES with dynamic translating; the LES-GTL with dynamic translating; and the BTL-GTL with dynamic scaling (we use scaling for this comparison because the BTL does not contain translating parameters). Table 3 contains the relevant calculated and the 5% critical Chi-square values. Two unambiguous conclusions emerge: First, the LES restrictions on the QES cannot be sustained; second, the LES restrictions on the GTL cannot be sustained. These conclusions hold even with the small sample adjustment. We interpret this as further evidence that the LES is an unsatisfactory functional form for empirical demand analysis using per capita time series data.[19]

The BTL-GTL comparison depends crucially on the estimation procedure. The GTL appears significantly superior under the first differencing method, but not on the basis of maximum likelihood estimates.

Since the QES and the BTL are not nested, the likelihood ratio test cannot be used to compare them. They do, however, involve the same number of independent parameters, so we can compare them informally on the basis of their likelihood values. The results of this comparison (assuming dynamic scaling) are inconclusive.

If we order these functional forms by the number of sample price-expenditure situations at which regularity conditions are satisfied, the ranking (from most to least) is: LES, BTL, QES, GTL. Although aggregate demand behavior need not satisfy regularity conditions even if the behavior of each household does, demand systems which violate regularity conditions may imply implausible responses to price or expenditure changes. To investigate this possibility we examine the five cases in which very few regularity conditions are satisfied -- namely, the QES and GTL with translating using both estimation methods; and the BTL using maximum likelihood, all with R free. In all but one of these five cases, the price elasticities are negative and marginal budget shares are between zero and one for all goods in all periods. Only the GTL with generalized first difference estimates yields unacceptable results, *e.g.*, negative marginal budget shares for food in all periods. None of the maximum likelihood estimates yield results that are *a priori* implausible in terms of own price and expenditure elasticities.

---

[19] Using U.S. per capita data for the period 1929-75 (excluding the war years), Howe, Pollak, and Wales (1979) estimate the QES with dynamic translating and diagonal first order serial correlation using the generalized first difference procedure. Using four commodity groups (the three used here and shelter), they find the QES is not significantly superior to the LES even at the 25% level.

Using household budget data, Pollak and Wales (1978, 1980) and Darrough, Pollak, and Wales (1981) estimate another demand system quadratic in expenditure that nests the LES and find the quadratic system significantly superior to the LES.

**TABLE 3: CALCULATED AND CRITICAL $X^2$ VALUES**

| | Calculated $\chi^2$ Values: Generalized First Difference Procedure | Maximum Likelihood Procedure | Critical $\chi^2$ Values (5%) |
|---|---|---|---|
| LES-QES | | | |
| R diagonal | 15.3 | 12.0 | 7.8 |
| R free | 13.7 | 13.8 | 7.8 |
| LES-GTL | | | |
| R diagonal | 19.6 | 14.1 | 12.6 |
| R free | 21.1 | 20.3 | 12.6 |
| BTL-GTL* | | | |
| R diagonal | 10.6 | 7.6 | 7.8 |
| R free | 10.9 | 4.3 | 7.8 |

**Notes :**

* The BTL-GTL comparison is based on dynamic scaling rather than translating since the BTL does not contain translating parameters. The other two comparisons are based on dynamic translating models.

We have investigated the dynamic stability of the nonstochastic models using simulations based on the estimated parameters. With prices and expenditure fixed at actual levels for the final year of the sample, all models but one converge to a steady state. The exception is the GTL with R free, estimated by the generalized first difference procedure, the only model which yielded unacceptable price elasticities and marginal budget shares.

In Table 4 we present estimated marginal budget shares and own price elasticities for three models at several data points. To compare the effects of the two estimation techniques on predicted responses to changes in prices and expenditures, we present maximum likelihood and generalized first difference estimates of the QES. To illustrate the effect of functional form, we present maximum likelihood estimates of the GTL to compare with the QES. All three models are estimated with dynamic translating and R free.

A comparison of the two QES estimates reveals that the marginal budget shares are quite similar and exhibit the same trend over time (except for clothing). For the own price elasticities, there are substantial differences in the clothing category, large but less substantial differences in food, while miscellaneous is about the same. Thus the estimation method -- whether or not the first observation is included -- has a substantial effect on some of the price elasticities but not on the predicted marginal budget shares. Turning to the GTL, we find that the marginal budget share for food and miscellaneous differ substantially from those implied by the QES. The own price elasticities implied by the maximum likelihood estimates of the GTL are closer to those of the first difference QES, and indeed, are more similar to them than the two sets of QES estimates are to each other.

One possible explanation of our finding that the treatment of the first observation has some effect on the ranking of functional forms and predicted behavior is that the roots of the R matrix may be near unity. To investigate this possibility, we have calculated the roots of the estimated R matrices for both the generalized first difference and maximum likelihood estimates. For the generalized first difference estimates with dynamic translating, the value of the largest root ranges from .23 to .99, with an average of .77; for the maximum likelihood estimates, it ranges from -.05 to .99, with an average of .42. The value of the largest root is higher in 5 of 6 cases using the generalized first difference estimates. When R is diagonal, a similar result holds. The average value of $\rho$ is .41 for the generalized first difference method and .09 for maximum likelihood. These substantial differences in the roots of the R matrix with the two estimation methods are consistent with our finding that the two methods, differing only in their treatment of the first observation, can yield different behavior predictions and different rankings of functional forms.[20]

Although the generalized first difference and maximum likelihood procedures yield different estimates and different rankings of functional forms in some cases, it is not clear which procedure is better. The maximum likelihood procedure requires strong assumptions about the stationarity of the autoregressive process and the normality of the disturbances. In particular, it assume that the autoregressive process [appendix equation (B2)] is not stationary,

[20] For the QES and BTL with dynamic scaling, the largest roots of R are .97 and .99 with the first difference method and .46 and .63 with maximum likelihood. For both models the estimation procedure dramatically affects the number of sample points at which regularity conditions are satisfied.

**TABLE 4: MARGINAL BUDGET SHARES AND OWN PRICE ELASTICITIES FOR SELECTED MODELS**

| | Marginal Budget Shares | | | Own Price Elasticities | | |
|---|---|---|---|---|---|---|
| QES (maximum likelihood) | | | | | | |
| | F | C | M | F | C | M |
| 1950 | .51(.05) | .31(.04) | .18(.03) | -.69(.08) | -.51(.07) | -.14(.06) |
| 1960 | .48(.05) | .28(.04) | .24(.04) | -.63(.07) | -.51(.08) | -.18(.05) |
| 1970 | .42(.04) | .30(.03) | .28(.04) | -.52(.05) | -.41(.06) | -.20(.05) |
| QES (first difference) | | | | | | |
| 1950 | .47(.03) | .35(.02) | .17(.02) | -.68(.05) | -.93(.09) | -.06(.08) |
| 1960 | .44(.03) | .33(.02) | .23(.02) | -.74(.06) | -.82(.08) | -.18(.07) |
| 1970 | .43(.03) | .32(.02) | .26(.02) | -.72(.05) | -.64(.06) | -.24(.06) |
| GTL (maximum likelihood) | | | | | | |
| 1950 | .48(.05) | .32(.03) | .20(.04) | -.73(.09) | -.79(.12) | -.15(.10) |
| 1960 | .50(.05) | .29(.03) | .21(.04) | -.72(.08) | -.77(.10) | -.16(.07) |
| 1970 | .52(.05) | .26(.03) | .22(.04) | -.70(.07) | -.60(.07) | -.19(.06) |

**Notes :**

1. F, C, and M refer to food, clothing, and miscellaneous categories.
2. All estimates are based on dynamic translating and a free R matrix.
3. Numbers in parentheses are standard errors.

whereas the generalized first difference procedure does not.[21] Hence, if the process generating the disturbances changed shortly before the sample period, then the maximum likelihood procedure involves a specification error while the generalized first difference procedure does not. Since our sample period (1948-1977) begins shortly after World War II, it is plausible that the process generating the disturbances changed shortly before the beginning of our sample period.[22] The maximum likelihood procedure also assumes that the disturbances have a multivariate normal distribution. Although we have described the generalized first difference procedure in terms of a normal likelihood function that excludes the first observation, it can also be interpreted as an iterative-Zellner procedure which iterates on the elements of the covariance matrix and R as well as on the structural parameters. Thus interpreted, the generalized first difference procedure does not require normality.

Since our sample size -- 30 price-expenditure situations -- is small, even if we accept stationarity and normality we need not prefer maximum likelihood to generalized first difference estimates.[23] The desirable efficiency properties of maximum likelihood only hold asymptotically. Monte Carlo evidence would be useful but we know of only one study dealing with equation systems. Maeshiro (1980) investigates the properties of various estimators for a non-singular two-equation linear system assuming that the disturbances have a diagonal serial correlation matrix, and that the contemporaneous covariance matrix is known. From his Monte Carlo analysis he concludes that with small samples and trended explanatory variables it is extremely important to use an estimator, such as maximum likelihood, that takes full account of the first observation. Further, of the estimators he studies, the one corresponding most closely to our generalized first difference procedure frequently performs worst.

Similarly, Monte Carlo evidence from single equation linear models strongly suggests that when the independent variables are trending, retaining the first observation reduces substantially the root mean square error of parameter estimates.[24] To the extent that these results apply to non-linear equation systems, maximum likelihood may be superior.

---

[21] By stationarity we mean that the process has been operating for a long time and that the characteristic roots of R [in (B2)] lie within the unit circle. Without stationarity (B4) does not hold and the first observation cannot be used separately in the estimation.

[22] Theil (1971, p. 253) and Poirier (1978) make similar arguments in the single equation case.

[23] In the single equation autoregressive case Park and Mitchell (1979) report a Monte Carlo study using data generated from a stationary normal distribution; they find the iterative Prais-Winston procedure slightly superior to maximum likelihood.

[24] See, for example, Beach and MacKinnon (1978), Harvey and McAvinchey (1978), Maeshiro (1979), and Park and Mitchell (1980). In the single equation case our generalized first difference procedure corresponds to the iterative Cochrane-Orcutt method. Although we have not presented results for the system analogue of the iterative Prais-Winston method, there is evidence [Park and Mitchell (1979)] that in the single equation case it is very similar to maximum likelihood in small samples. In our case such an estimator could be obtained by maximizing $L_1$ in (B5) after deleting the Jacobian term.

Finally, turning to the plausibility of the estimates as a guide to choosing between estimators, there is weak evidence in favor of maximum likelihood. Unlike the generalized first difference procedure, there is no case in which maximum likelihood yields both high likelihood values and unacceptable price or expenditure elasticities.

## 4. Conclusion

Our investigation of alternative estimation procedures differing in their treatment of the first observation yielded mixed results. The rankings of specifications was generally the same whether the comparisons were based on the generalized first difference procedure or on the maximum likelihood procedure. The two estimation procedures, however, sometimes yielded substantially different predictions of responses to price and expenditure changes. Our finding that rankings are not very sensitive to the estimation procedure employed is encouraging; our finding that predicted behavior often depends on the estimation procedure is not: While unambiguous predictions are desirable, there are arguments for and against each procedure and econometric theory fails to offer a basis for choosing between them.

General conclusions about functional forms, dynamic structure, and stochastic structure must blur the trees to reveal the forest. We found the LES dominated by the QES and by the GTL, but we could not unambiguously rank the BTL and the GTL. Dynamic translating, a dynamic structure allowing demand system parameters to depend on lagged consumption, was superior to both the static specification, in which demand system parameters remain fixed over the sample period; and to dynamic scaling, an alternative dynamic structure. Stochastic structures allowing first order serial correlation dominated those requiring independent disturbances in different periods, but we could not choose between the two autoregressive structures we considered. Thus, we found that in terms of functional form, dynamic structure, and stochastic structure the simplest, most restrictive specifications were dominated by more complex, general ones; in many cases, however, we were unable to discriminate among these more complex, general specifications.

## APPENDIX A

Constant (1972) dollar expenditures on the various categories of goods were obtained from Table 2.7 of *The Survey of Current Business*, July, 1978. Corresponding current dollar expenditures were obtained from Tables 2.6 of the same source. In terms of the categories reported in Table 2.7, we defined our three commodity groups as follows (numbers in parentheses correspond to those in Table 2.7):

I. Food
1. Food (17)

II. Clothing
1. Clothing and shoes (23)
2. Shoe cleaning and repair (61)
3. Cleaning, laundering, dyeing, etc. (62)

III. Miscellaneous
1. Toilet articles and preparations (31)
2. Tobacco products (30)
3. Drug preparations and sundries (34)
4. Nondurable toys and sports supplies (35)
5. Domestic service (48)
6. Barbershops, beauty parlors and baths (63)
7. Medical care services (64)
8. Admissions to specified spectator amusements (69)

Per capita consumption of each good was calculated by dividing annual expenditure in 1972 dollars by population. The population figures are "resident population" in the U.S. and are taken from Table 2 of *The Statistical Abstract of the U.S.*, 1976. Price indices were determined by dividing current dollar expenditure by constant dollar expenditure for each of the three categories.

## APPENDIX B
## LIKELIHOOD FUNCTIONS

Let the system of n-1 share equations at time t ($w_t$) be:

(B1) $$w_t = f(z_t,\delta) + u_t \qquad t = 1,\ldots,T$$

where $z_t$ is the set of explanatory variables, $\delta$ the parameters to be estimated and $u_t$ the (n-1)x1 vector of disturbances. We assume that $u_t$ follows a first-order autoregressive process:

(B2) $$u_t = Ru_{t-1} + e_t \qquad t = 2,\ldots,T$$

where the $e_t$ are normally distributed with mean zero, contemporaneous covariance matrix $\Omega$, and are serially independent. We assume that the process is stationary, hence the $u_t$ are normally distributed with mean zero and contemporaneous covariance matrix $\Theta$ which from (B2) satisfies:

$$\text{(B3)} \qquad \Theta = R\Theta R' + \Omega$$

We further assume that $u_1 = Se_1$, where S ensures the stationarity of the u process, that is:

$$\text{(B4)} \qquad \Theta = S\Omega S'$$

The log likelihood function for all T observations is then:

$$\text{(B5)} \qquad L_1 = k_1 - \frac{T}{2} \log |\theta - R\theta R'| + \frac{1}{2}\log(|\theta - R\theta R'|/|\theta|)$$

$$- \frac{1}{2}\left[u_1'\theta^{-1}u_1 + \sum_2^T (u_t - Ru_{t-1})'(\theta - R\theta R')^{-1}(u_t - Ru_{t-1})\right].$$

This likelihood can be concentrated with respect to $\Theta$ only when R is a diagonal matrix with a common element $\rho$ on the diagonal, in which case (B5) becomes:[1]

$$\text{(B6)} \quad L_2 = k_2 + \frac{(n-1)}{2}\log(1-\rho^2) - \frac{T}{2}\log|(1-\rho^2)u_1u_1' + \sum_T^2(u_t - \rho u_{t-1})(u_t - \rho ut-1)'| .$$

When the first observation is not included the log likelihood is:

$$\text{(B7)} \quad L_3 = k_3 - \frac{T-1}{2}\log|\theta - R\theta R'| - \frac{1}{2}\left[\sum_T^2(u_t - Ru_{t-1})'(\theta - R\theta R')^{-1}(u_t - Ru_{t-1})\right],$$

which can always be concentrated with respect to $\Theta$ in the usual way to give:

$$\text{(B8)} \quad L_4 = k_4 - \frac{T-1}{2}\log|\sum_2^T (u_t - Ru_{t-1})(u_t - Ru_{t-1})'|.$$

For the estimations in the text we maximized (B8) when T-1 observations were used, (B6) when T observations were used and R was diagonal, and (B5) when T observations were used and R was free. In all cases we employed a nonlinear algorithm due to Fletcher (1972) and

[1] See, for example, Beach and MacKinnon (1979) from which these formulations are taken.

relied exclusively on numeric derivatives. Maximization of (B5) requires that the elements of $\Theta$ be estimated, as well as those of R and the parameters of the demand system. We impose the restriction that $\Theta$ be positive definite by writing it as the product of a lower triangular matrix $\Theta L$ and its transpose, and estimate the elements of $\Theta L$ rather than $\Theta$. We restrict the diagonal elements of $\Theta L$ to be positive to guarantee uniqueness of the factorization.

## REFERENCES


Anderson, G.J. and R.W. Blundell (1982), "Estimation and Hypothesis Testing in Dynamic Singular Equation Systems," *Econometrica*, Vol. 50, No. 6, November 1982, 1559-1572.

Anderson, T.W. (1958), *An Introduction to Multivariate Statistical Analysis*, Wiley and Sons Inc., New York, 1958.

Beach, C.M. and J.G. MacKinnon (1978), "A Maximum Likelihood Procedure for Regression with Autocorrelated Errors," *Econometrica*, Vol. 46, No. 1, January, 1978, 51-58.

Beach, C.M. and J.G. MacKinnon (1979), "A Maximum Likelihood Estimation of Singular Equation Systems with Autoregressive Disturbances," *International Economic Review*, Vol. 20, No. 2, June 1979, 459-464.

Bera, A.K., R.P. Byron, and C.M. Jarque (1981), "Further Evidence on Asymptotic Tests for Homogeneity and Symmetry in Large Demand Systems," *Economic Letters*, 8, 1981, 101-105.

Berndt, E.R. and N.E. Savin (1975), "Estimation and Hypothesis Testing in Singular Equation Systems with Autoregressive Disturbances," *Econometrica*, 43, September-November 1975, 937-958.

Christensen, L.R., D.W. Jorgenson, and L.J. Lau (1965), "Transcendental Logarithmic Utility Functions," *American Economic Review*, 65, 1965, 367-383.

Darrough, M., R.A. Pollak, and T.J. Wales (1983), "Dynamic and Stochastic Structure: An Analysis of Three Time Series of Household Budget Studies," *Review of Economics and Statistics*, 65: 2, May 1983, 274-281.

Diewert, W.E. (1974), "Intertemporal Consumer Theory and the Demand for Durables," *Econometrica*, 42, May 1974, 497-516.

Fletcher, R. (1972), "Fortran Subroutines for Minimization by Quasi-Newton Methods," Theoretical Physics Division, Atomic Energy Research Establishment, Harwell, England, 1972.

Harvey, A.C. and I.D. McAvinchey (1978), "The Small Sample Efficiency of Two-step Estimators in Regression Models with Autoregressive Disturbances," Discussion Paper No. 78-10, Department of Economics, U.B.C., April 1978.

Howe, H., R.A. Pollak, and T.J. Wales (1979), "Theory and Time Series Estimation of the Quadratic Expenditure System," *Econometrica*, 47, September 1979, 1231-1247.

Maeshiro, A. (1979), "On the Retention of the First Observations in Serial Correlation Adjustment of Regression Models," *International Economic Review*, Vol. 20, No. 1, February 1979, 259-265.

Maeshiro, A. (1980), "New Evidence on the Small Sample Properties of Estimators of SUR Models with Auto-correlated Disturbances: Things Done Halfway May not be Done Right," *Journal of Econometrics*, Vol. 12, No. 2, February 1980, 162-176.

Park, R.E. and B.M. Mitchell (1979), "Maximum Likelihood vs. Minimum Sum of Squares Estimation of the Autocorrelated Error Model," A Rand note, November 1979.

Park, R.E. and B.M. Mitchell (1980), "Estimating the Autocorrelated Error Model with Trended Data: Further Results," *Journal of Econometrics*, 13, June 1980, 185-201.

Poirier, D.J. (1978), "The Effect of the First Observation in Regression Models with First Order Autoregressive Disturbances," *Applied Statistics*, 27 January 1978, 67-68.

Pollak, R.A. (1978), "Endogenous Tastes in Demand and Welfare Analysis," *American Economic Review*, Vol. 68, No. 2, May 1978, 374-379.

Pollak, R.A. and T.J. Wales (1969), "Estimation of the Linear Expenditure System," *Econometrica*, 37, October 1969, 611-628.

Pollak, R.A. and T.J. Wales (1980), "Comparison of the Quadratic Expenditure System and Translog Demand Systems with Alternative Specifications of Demographic Effects," *Econometrica*, 48, April 1980, 595-612.

Pollak, R.A. and T.J. Wales (1981), "Demographic Variables in Demand Analysis," *Econometrica*, 49, November 1981, 1533-1559.

Stone, J.R.N. (1954), "Linear Expenditure Systems and Demand Analysis: An Application to the Pattern of British Demand," *Economic Journal*, Vol. LXIV, 225, September 1954, 511-527.

Theil, H., *Principles of Econometrics*, John Wiley & Sons.

Wales, T.J. (1984), "A Note on Likelihood Ratio Tests of Functional Form and Structural Change in Demand Systems," *Economic Letters*, Vol. 14, Nos. 2-3, 213-220.

# REMARKS ON THE POWER OF NON-PARAMETRIC TESTS OF CONSUMER-THEORY HYPOTHESES

R. ROBERT RUSSELL
*Graduate School of Management*
*University of California, Riverside*
*Riverside, California, USA*

ABSTRACT. This paper addresses two aspects of the power of non-parametric tests of consumer-theory hypotheses. The first part discusses the tests of revealed-preference hypotheses using aggregate data, and in the process resurrects an apparently overlooked paper written by H. S. Houthakker in 1962. The second part shows that non-parametric tests for separability have no power to distinguish between strict separability and (non-strict) separability.

## 1. Introductory Remarks

Non-parametric methods of testing hypotheses about consumer behavior are typically traced back to the pioneering paper by Afriat [1967], and have been honed into a powerful tool for testing the axiomatic foundations of consumer theory as well as particular restrictions on preferences (like homotheticity and separability) by among others Afriat [1970, 1973, 1976], Diewert [1973], Diewert and Parkan [1978], and Varian [1982, 1983]. These methods were anticipated, however, in an earlier -- and apparently overlooked -- paper by Houthakker [1962].

The principal advantage of non-parametric methods of testing hypotheses about consumer behavior, as compared to the more common parametric approach, is that they do not require strong assumptions about the form of the utility function; as a result, they tend to have a lower probability of the error of rejecting the null hypothesis when, in fact, only the maintained assumptions are false.

The most popular alternative to non-parametric methods, as a way of testing consumer-theory hypotheses with relatively weak maintained hypotheses, is the use of flexible functional forms, which can provide a second-order approximation to an arbitrary twice-differentiable function. But this approach, introduced by Diewert [1971] and thoroughly mined by Diewert [1971, 1973, 1974, 1976], Christiansen, Jorgenson, and Lau [1971, 1973], Jorgenson and Lau [1975a, 1975b] and others during the 1970s, is not without its problems. If a particular flexible-form specification (like the translog or the generalized Leontief) is maintained as the "true" form, as is the case in most of this literature, then hypothesis tests remain tainted by the possibility of unknowing rejection of the maintained assumption. Moreover, at least for some types of tests, the flexibility property is lost under the null



*L. Phlips and L.D. Taylor (eds.), Aggregation, Consumption and Trade,* 121–135.

hypothesis. For example, when separability is imposed on *any* flexible functional form, neither the "macro" function nor the "micro" (or aggregator) functions in the structured representation is flexible; that is, all flexible functional forms are "separability inflexible" (see Blackorby, Primont, and Russell [1977b, 1978]).

A more ingenious use of flexible functional forms to test consumer-theory hypotheses was adopted by Jorgenson and Lau [1975a, 1975b]. They test not restrictions on the flexible form itself, but rather the *implications* of a property of the "true" underlying function for the second-order approximation at the point of approximation.[1] This approach is not fraught, for example, by the "separability inflexibility" property. The problem with this approach, however, is that a confirmation of the null hypothesis is applicable *only* at the point of approximation; the property is not confirmed in any neighborhood of the point of approximation, no matter how small the neighborhood.

Thus, the non-parametric approach forges important new ground in the testing of consumer-theory hypotheses. But these methods are not without their problems either. Most of the concern about the non-parametric approach relates to the absence of stochastic components, and hence the failure to take into account stochastic phenomena like measurement error. This drawback immeasurably enhances the probability of Type-I errors, perhaps obviating the apparent advantage over parametric methods. Ongoing research is aimed at introducing stochastic elements into non-parametric techniques and models in an attempt, with varying degrees of success, to rectify this problem. (See the appeal for such studies in the survey of frontier production functions by Schmidt [1987] and an early attempt by Banker and Maindiratta [1988].)

Another possible drawback of non-parametric methods, which in a loose sense has implications opposite to those attached to the lack of stochastic elements, has drawn little attention. This is the possibility of very low power of these tests, given the data with which economists have to work. In the remarks that follow, I consider the problem of low power in testing both the axiomatic foundations of consumer theory (Section 2) and a particular restriction (separability) on consumer preferences (Section 3).

## 2. Non-Parametric Tests of the Axiomatic Foundations of Consumer Theory

My skepticism about the power of non-parametric tests of the axiomatic foundations of consumer theory dates back to an apparently overlooked paper by Houthakker [1962] -- apparently the first such non-parametric test.[2] Houthakker used binary purchasing-power-parity indices published by the German Statistical Office to test the weak axiom of revealed preference (WARP). These indices calculate relative prices for pairs of countries using, alternatively, each of the two consumption patterns as weights -- *i.e.*, for any pair of

---

[1] Most flexible functional forms can be interpreted as Taylor's-series approximation -- *i.e.*, as numerical approximations as well as approximations in the sense of Diewert [1973] (that the values of the function, the gradient, and the Hessian of the flexible form can be equated to these values for the arbitrary twice-differentiable underlying function).

[2] By drawing attention to the overlooked paper by Houthakker, I do not mean to demean the important contributions of Afriat and others; the modern non-parametric literature not only tests for the validity of the revealed-preference axioms, but also provides algorithms to construct utility functions that rationalize the data.

countries a and b, both $p^a \cdot q^a / p^b \cdot q^a$ and $p^a \cdot q^b / p^b \cdot q^b$ (where p and q are price and quantity vectors) are calculated. Since expenditure levels were also published, Houthakker was able to recover the numerators and denominators of these indices -- the ingredients for revealed-preference tests.

These data were published for three types of workers -- steel workers, coal miners, and iron miners -- in several European countries for the year 1958. Table 1 summarizes the data availability and the number of tests of WARP in Houthakker's paper. The binary purchasing-power-parity data provide 42 opportunities for a violation of WARP. There was *not a single violation*! The absence of violations of WARP, moreover, is not attributable to an absence, or paucity, of revelations of preference: More often than not, preference was revealed. The structure of revelations is depicted by the orderings (partial for steel workers and coal miners, and total for iron miners) shown in Table 2.

Another remarkable outcome of Houthakker's tests is the uniformity of orderings across types of workers: There is only one reversal of preferences. While the Saar steelworker consumption pattern is revealed preferred to that of the Netherlands, the opposite preference is revealed for coal miners' consumption patterns. (In addition, the French steel workers' consumption pattern is revealed preferred to the corresponding Saar and Dutch consumption patterns, while no preference is revealed for these two pairs using coal miners' consumption bundles.)

Houthakker's findings are remarkable not because they confirm the consumer-consistency hypothesis, *per se*, but because they confirm it for aggregate data (as do Varian's [1983] more recent tests using aggregate U.S. data for the 1947 - 78 period). Further, Houthakker's tests confirm consistent choice for diverse collections of consumers in different countries. Loosely paraphrasing Houthakker, the tests indicate that the Italians eat more spaghetti than the Dutch not because tastes differ across countries but because spaghetti is cheaper in Italy than in the Netherlands.[3]

Given the strong conditions required for consistent aggregate choice, however, it is difficult to believe that the hypothesis is literally true. Indeed, in what may perhaps be the first non-parametric consumer-theory test of any kind, Engel [1857] long ago implicitly rejected the necessary conditions for consistent aggregation across consumers by rejecting homotheticity of preferences (explicitly by confirming "Engel's Law).[4]

These remarks suggest the possibility that the non-parametric tests of the axiomatic foundations of consumer theory lack power. Indeed, as Varian [1982] has pointed out, these tests will have low power if the variation in total expenditure over time is large relative to the

---

[3] Houthakker acknowledges the possibility that prices will adjust to tastes if there are increasing returns to scale in production, but ventures the opinion "that the Italian liking for spaghetti is the result rather than the cause of the low price."

[4] Of course, as is now well known, the necessary condition for consistent aggregation of consumer choice *if* the quantities are restricted to the strictly positive *n*-orthant is *quasi*-homotheticity (called the Gorman [1961] Polar Form by Blackorby, Primont, and Russell [1978]). Sufficiency requires, in addition, that the (linear) Engel curves of different individuals be parallel. This property has not fared well in empirical tests either (see, for example, Pollak and Wales [1979]). On the other hand, the non-parametric test of Manser and McDonald [1988] fails to reject homotheticity. I should also note that these aggregation conditions can, of course, be weakened if one is willing to make strong assumptions about income distributions (see, for example, Hildenbrand [1983] and Varian [1984]).

*Table 1.* Number of Houthakker tests.

| Type of Worker | Number of Countries | Number of WARP Tests |
|---|---|---|
| Steel Workers | 7 | 21 |
| Coal Miners | 6 | 15 |
| Iron Miners | 4 | 6 |
| TOTAL | | 42 |

*Table 2.* Orderings implied by Houthakker tests.

*Code:*

| | |
|---|---|
| B = Belgium | L = Luxemburg |
| F = France | N = the Netherlands |
| G = Germany | S = the Saar |
| I = Italy | → = "revealed preferred to" |

*Steel Workers:*

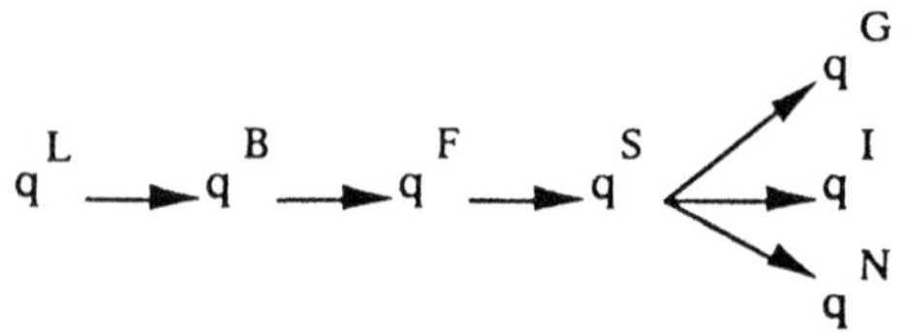


*Coal Miners:*

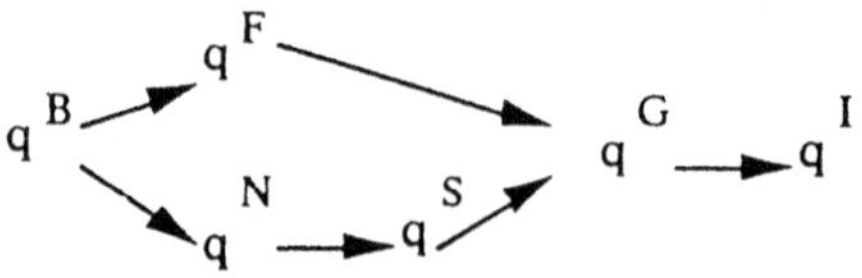


*Iron Miners:*

variation of relative prices. If, for example, the budget hyperplanes do not intersect, the tests have zero power. The same point can be made about Houthakker's tests, if the variation of total expenditure across countries is large relative to the variation of relative prices.

The only explicit test of the power of non-parametric tests of the axiomatic foundations of consumer theory of which I am aware is by Bronars [1987]. Using Varian's data on prices and total expenditures (but not quantities), he shows that the Afriat inequalities have a surprisingly high degree of power to reject the Generalized Axiom of Revealed Preference[5] when the alternative hypothesis is Becker [1962]-type irrational behavior -- *viz.*, utterly random distribution of quantities over the budget hyperplane.

I find these results unconvincing. Becker's formulation is not wholly unreasonable as an alternative to rational individual behavior (although more recent weakenings of the preference axioms, like quasi-transitivity, are perhaps more reasonable). But it is not a reasonable alternative to rational *aggregate* behavior. Skepticism about the latter has nothing to do with, and does not depend upon, individual irrationality. Rather, it derives from skepticism about the satisfaction of the necessary conditions for consistent aggregation across individual preferences.

Thus, the appropriate alternative hypothesis is not Becker-type individual "irrationality," but rather aggregation inconsistency. Far from implying random distribution of quantities across the budget hyperplane, inconsistent aggregation over consumers would impose a considerable amount of structure on aggregate data. Moreover, it would not be difficult to model inconsistent aggregation as an alternative hypothesis in Monte Carlo studies like Bronar's. That is, one could specify individual utility functions that do not satisfy the conditions for consistent aggregation and aggregate across the derived demand functions to obtain hypothetical aggregate quantities, given the actual prices and aggregate incomes. I strongly suspect that such a study would indicate very low power of non-parametric tests of the axiomatic foundations of consumer theory using aggregate data.

## 3. Non-Parametric Tests of Separability Restrictions

In a regrettably unpublished paper, Afriat [1970] suggested an application of his revealed preference methods to test separability restrictions non-parametrically. This approach has been publicized and refined by Varian [1983] and Diewert and Parkan [1985]. The above remarks on the power of non-parametric tests would apply equally to these tests for separability using aggregate data. In this section, however, I would like to draw attention to an additional problem regarding the power of non-parametric separability tests. To do so, it is useful to lay out the Afriat structure explicitly (though not rigorously).

The Afriat inequalities, where $p^t$ and $x^t$ are N-dimensional price and quantity vectors observed in situation t (*e.g.*, time period t), $t = 1,\ldots,T$, and $0^{(NT)}$ is the NT-dimensional zero vector, are[6]

(Af. $\leq$) Given $\langle p^1,\ldots,p^T\rangle > 0^{(NT)}$, and $\langle x^1,\ldots,x^T\rangle > 0^{(NT)}$, there exist $\langle u^1,\ldots,u^T\rangle$ and $\langle \lambda^1,\ldots,\lambda^T\rangle > 0^{(NT)}$ such that $u^s \leq u^t + \lambda^t p^t \cdot (x^s - x^t)\ \forall\ s,t$.

[5] The data satisfy the generalized axiom of revealed preference if $x^i R x^j$ implies $p^j \cdot x^j \leq p^j \cdot x^i$, where R is the transitive closure of the (binary) revealed-preference relation.

[6] The (strict) vector inequality, $x > y$, means $x_i > y_i$ for all i.

The utility maximization (consumer rationality) hypothesis is[7]

(U Max) There exists a concave, (weakly) monotonic function, U, such that
$x^t = \arg\max\{U(x) \mid p^t \cdot x \leq p^t \cdot x^t\} \ \forall \ t.$

The salient theorem of non-parametric tests of the axiomatic foundations of consumer theory is

**Afriat's Theorem:** (Af. ≤) ⇔ (U Max).

The Afriat inequalities hold if and only if there exists a concave, monotonic utility function that rationalizes the data. Thus, the $(u^1,\ldots,u^T)$ in (Af.≤) can be interpreted as utility levels and the $(\lambda^1,\ldots,\lambda^T)$ can be interpreted as marginal utilities of expenditure. The requisite function can be constructed as follows:

$$U\left(x^s\right) = \min_t \left\{u^t + \lambda^t p^t \cdot \left(x^s - x^t\right)\right\}. \tag{3.1}$$

The Afriat inequalities hold if and only if the generalized axiom of revealed preference is satisfied by the data (see Varian [1983]).

The extension of Afriat's equivalence condition to non-parametric tests for separability restrictions is straightforward. Letting $\langle x_1,x_2\rangle$ be a partition of the quantity vector, x, we say that the data are rationalized by a utility function in which $x_1$ is separable from $x_2$ if

(Strictly Sep. U Max)[8] There exists a monotonic function $U^1$, and a monotonic function $\hat{U}$, which is *increasing* in its first argument, such that
$x^t = \arg\max\{\hat{U}(U^1(x_1),x_2) \mid p^t \cdot x \leq p^t \cdot x^t\} \ \forall \ t.$

The Afriat inequality conditions for separable utility maximization are

(Af. Sep. ≤) Given

$\langle p^1,\ldots,p^T\rangle > 0^{(NT)}$ and $\langle x^1,\ldots,x^T\rangle > 0^{(NT)}$,

there exist

$\langle u^1,\ldots,u^T\rangle, \langle u_1^1,\ldots,u_1^T\rangle, \langle \beta^1,\ldots,\beta^T\rangle > 0^{(T)}$,

and

$\langle \lambda^1,\ldots,\lambda^T\rangle > 0^{(T)}$

such that

---

[7] A function is (weakly) monotonic if it is nondecreasing in each of its arguments. In what follows, I omit the modifier "weakly."

[8] The rationale for the modifier "Strictly" in the designation of this condition will be discussed below.

*(a)* $u_1^s \leq u_1^t + \beta^t p_1^t \cdot (x_1^s - x_1^t) \;\; \forall \; s,t,$

and

*(b)* $u^s \leq u^t + \lambda^t(\beta^t)^{-1}(u_1^s - u_1^t) + \lambda^t p_2^t \cdot (x_2^s - x_2^t) \;\; \forall \; s,t.$

The non-parametric separability test suggested by Afriat [1970], Varian [1983], and Diewert and Parkan [1985] is provided by

**Afriat's Separability Theorem:** (Af. Sep. $\leq$) $\Leftrightarrow$ (Strict. Sep. U Max).

This theorem says that the data can be rationalized by a separable utility function if and only if the Afriat separability inequalities hold. In (Af. Sep. $\leq$), the variables, $u^t$, $u_1^t$, $\lambda^t$, and $\beta^t$ can be interpreted, respectively, as the overall utility level, the subutility level (for sector 1), the marginal utility of overall expenditure, and the marginal sector-1 utility of expenditure on sector-1 commodities. The requisite functions, $\hat{U}$ and $U^1$, can be constructed analogously to the constructions of U above.

The inequalities *(a)* in (Af. Sep. $\leq$) are simply the original Afriat inequality conditions restricted to the sector-1 subspace. By the original Afriat theorem, then, the inequalities (a) in (Af. Sep. $\leq$) are equivalent to the maximization of a sector-specific (micro) utility function subject to the sector-specific expenditure constraint:

$$x^t = \arg\max\{U^1(x_1) \mid p_1^t \cdot x_1 \leq p_1^t \cdot x_1^t\} \;\; \forall \; t. \tag{3.2}$$

Similarly, the inequalities *(b)* in (Af. Sep. $\leq$) are equivalent to the existence of a concave macro utility function, strictly increasing in its first argument, that rationalizes the data:[9]

$$\langle u_1^t, x_2^t\rangle = \arg\max\{\hat{U}(u_1,x_2) | (\beta^t)^{-1}u_1 + p_2^t \cdot x_2 \leq (\beta^t)^{-1}u_1^t + p_2^t \cdot x_2^t\} \;\; \forall \; t. \tag{3.3}$$

These conditions -- particularly the first -- are the finite-data counterparts of the (global) concept of *decentralizability*: The ability to carry out sector-specific maximization, knowing only sector-specific prices and expenditure, without loss of overall utility (see Blackorby, Primont, and Russell [1978, Ch. 5]). What is at first glance surprising about Afriat's separability result is that *finite-data* decentralizability is shown to be equivalent to a separability condition that is *stronger* than the separability condition required for global decentralizability. To explicate this apparent paradox, we need to describe the two kinds of separability.

Let $L^1(x_1,x_2)$ be the collection of bundles in sector 1 that are no worse than $x_1$ (*i.e.*, the projection onto the sector-1 subspace of the upper level set corresponding to utility level

---

[9] In this construction, $(\beta^t)^{-1}$ can be interpreted as the price of the aggregate (sector 1) commodity in period t (and, of course, $u_1^t$ is the quantity of this aggregate commodity). Note, however, that $(\beta^t)^{-1}$ is not a sectoral price index, since its value depends on all prices and total expenditure. In fact, $(\beta^t)^{-1}$ is a sectoral price index if and only if $x_1$ is homothetically separable from $x_2$, in which case $U^1$ can be chosen to be positively homogeneous of degree one (and its dual unit cost function is the price index). (See Blackorby, Primont, and Russell [1978], Section 5.4.5].)

$U(x_1,x_2)$). The stronger separability notion -- and the one most people think of as separability -- is

(Strict. Sep.) $L^1(x_1,x_2)$ is independent of $x_2$.

Intuitively, indifference surfaces in the sector-1 subspace are independent of the values of variables outside of sector 1. The weaker separability notion, originally attributable to Bliss [1975], is

(Sep.) The collection of sets, $L^1(x_1,\{x_2\})$, is nested.[10]

Representations for the two types of separability are as follows:

**Gorman's Representation Theorem:**

$$\text{(Strict. Sep.)} \Leftrightarrow U(x) = \hat{U}(U^1(x_1),x_2),$$
$$\text{where } \hat{U} \text{ is increasing in } U^1(x_1).$$

**Bliss's Representation Theorem:**

$$\text{(Sep.)} \Leftrightarrow U(x) = \hat{U}(U^1(x_1),x_2).$$

Thus, the stronger of the two separability conditions is equivalent to a structure that entails a strict monotonicity condition for the macro function, $\hat{U}$.

A simple and familiar example, the Leontief function, illustrates the case of non-strict separability:

$$\begin{aligned} U(\chi_1,\chi_2,\chi_3) &= \min\{\chi_1,\chi_2,\chi_3\} \\ &\min\{\min\{\chi_1,\chi_2\},\chi_3\} \\ &= \hat{U}(U^1(\chi_1,\chi_2),\chi_3). \end{aligned}$$

Note that, in this representation, $\hat{U}$ is not increasing in its first argument. To see that the underlying ordering satisfies (Sep.) but not (Strict. Sep.), consider the following level sets in the 1-2 subspace: $L^1(1,1,1)$ and $L^1(1,1,1/2)$, illustrated in Figure 1. The two level sets are not identical, as would be the case if goods 1 and 2 were strictly separable from good 3, but they are nested.

---

[10] The relationships between the two notions are discussed in Blackorby, Primont, and Russell [1977a, 1978 (Ch.3)] and Färe and Primont [1981]. The two are equivalent if and only if the projections of the preference ordering onto the sector-1 subspace satisfy local non-satiation.

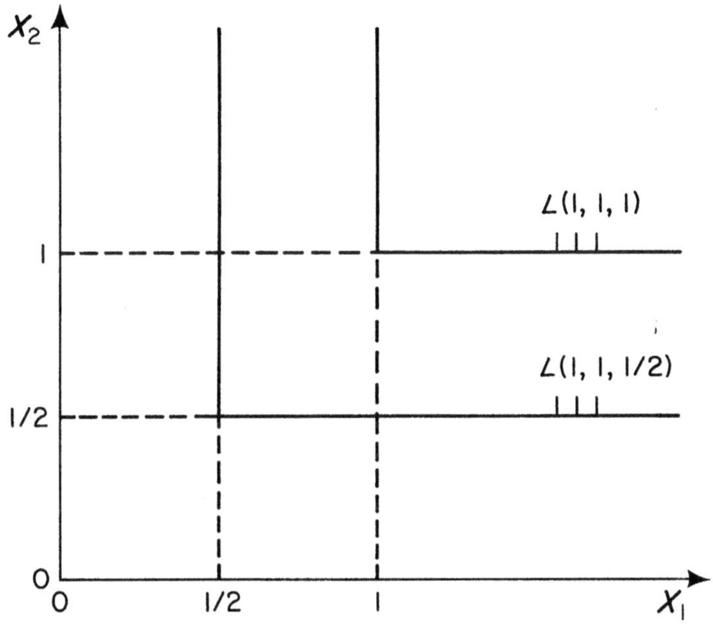


*Figure 1. Nested level sets for a Leontief function*

Decentralizability (of sector 1) is defined as follows:

(Decent.) There exist functions, $\Phi^1$ and $\Theta$, such that
$x_1^* = \Phi^1(p_1,y_1)$ and $y_1 = \Theta(p,y)$,
where $x_1^*$, $p_1$, and $y_1$ are, respectively, the optimal consumption vector, the price vector, and optimal expenditure in sector 1, and y is total expenditure.

In this definition, the functions, $\Phi^1$ and $\Theta$, are generated by maximization conditions analogous to those in (3.2) and (3.3) above.

The principal theorem on decentralizability was independently proved by Gorman [1971] and Primont [1971] (see also Blackorby, Primont, and Russell [1978, Ch. 5]):

**Gorman/Primont Decentralizability Theorem:** (Decent.) $\Leftrightarrow$ (Sep.)

This result would seem to be at odds with Afriat's separability theorem, which states that his decentralizability inequalities (Af. Sep. $\leq$) are equivalent to the existence of a *strictly* separable utility function that rationalizes the data, as reflected in the strict monotonicity condition in

(Strict. Sep. U Max). There is, however, no inconsistency between these two results. To clarify their compatibility, consider the following modification of the Afriat separability condition:

(Sep. U Max) There exist (weakly) monotonic functions, $U^1$ and $\hat{U}$, such that
$x^t = \arg\max \{\hat{U}(U^1(x_1),x_2) \mid p^t \cdot x \leq p^t \cdot x^t\} \;\forall\, t.$

Then minor modification of the proof of Afriat's separability theorem establishes the following:

**Separability Theorem:** (Af. Sep. $\leq$) $\Leftrightarrow$ (Sep. U Max).

Since (Strictly Sep. U Max) $\Rightarrow$ (Sep. U Max), sufficiency,

(Af. Sep. $\leq$) $\Rightarrow$ (Sep. U Max),

is immediate. Inspection of the proofs of necessity in Afriat's separability theorem (see Diewert and Parkan [1985]),

(Strictly Sep. U Max) $\Rightarrow$ (Af. Sep. $\leq$),

reveals that the strict montonicity condition in (Strict. Sep. U Max) is not exploited. Only weak monotonicity is needed, so that in fact

(Sep. U Max) $\Rightarrow$ (Af. Sep. $\leq$).

To summarize, the Afriat separability inequalities are equivalent to the condition that the data can be rationalized by a utility function that satisfies decentralizability. This condition, in turn, is equivalent to *both* a separable and a strictly separable utility function that rationalizes the data. The set of continuous, monotonic, quasi-concave functions that satisfy the separability condition is a strict subset of the set of such functions that satisfy *strict* separability, but the set of separable functions that can be rationalized by a finite set of data is identical to the set of strictly separable functions that can be rationalized by the data. In short, the Afriat non-parametric methods have zero power to distinguish between separability and strict separability.

An obvious question to ask is whether the distinction between strict and non-strict separability is a matter of any importance. Here are some results that go through with strict separability but do not go through, or at least have not been shown to go through, with non-strict separability:

*(1) Inheritance of differentiability and (strict) concavity.* An attractive property of the representation theorems for separability conditions is that the macro and micro (aggregator) functions tend to inherit the properties of the parent function.[11] This is important because, for example, the micro and macro functions, $U^1$ and $\hat{U}$, in the representation

$$U(x) = \hat{U}(U^1(x_1), x_2),$$

[11] See Blackorby, Primont, and Russell [1978, Ch. 3].

can themselves be interpreted as utility functions. Most of the properties of U are inherited by $U^1$ and $\hat{U}$ under the assumption of non-strict separability, but two properties that have not been shown to be inherited are differentiability and strict or non-strict concavity. Because U is assumed to be unique only up to monotonic transformations in much of consumer theory, the latter conditions often are unimportant, but they are important in the theory of decision making under uncertainty using von Neumann/Morgenstern utility (especially in the analysis of risk aversion). Inheritance of concavity conditions is also important, of course, in production theory, and the above separability results go through for production functions.

*(2) Reference-vector construction of $U^1$.* If sector 1 is strictly separable from its complement, the aggregator function, $U^1$, can be constructed straightforwardly by

$$U^1(x_1) = U(x_1,\underline{0}_2).$$

where $\underline{0}_2$ is an appropriately chosen sector-1 reference vector.[12] That this inheritance property, in fact, does not go through under non-strict separability is immediately shown by examination of the above Leontief example, where

$$U^1(x_1,x_2) = \min\{x_1,x_2\} \neq \min\{x_1,x_2,\underline{0}^{(3)}\} = U(x_1x_2,\underline{0}^{(3)})$$

for any $\underline{0}^{(3)}$.

*(3) Complete (additive) separability representation theorems.* An important and often-invoked result in separability is that, if there are m sectors, with m > 2, such that arbitrary unions of sectors are strictly separable from their complements, then the function has an additive representation:

$$U(x) = \hat{U}\left(\sum_{s=1}^{m} U^s(x_s)\right). \tag{3.4}$$

This result does not go through for non-strict separability, as evidenced by the n-variable Leontief function, which is separable in any partition but which has no additivity separable representation.

*(4) Dual structures.* Separability of a (primal) function does not necessarily imply separability of its dual(s). Under sectoral (subspace) homotheticity restrictions, however, such implications go through. Moreover, the conjunction of primal and dual separability conditions often imply homotheticity restrictions. Some of the duality results that go through for strict, but *not* non-strict, separability are as follows:

- The following conditions are equivalent to homothetic strict separability (*i.e.*, strict separability with homothetic aggregator functions):[13]
  - Strict separability of the utility (or production) function *and* the distance function;
  - strict separability of the indirect utility (or production) function *and* the cost function;

---

[12] This construction is attributable to Gorman [1968].

[13] See Blackorby, Primont, and Russell [1978, Theorem 4.5].

- strict separability of the utility (or production) function *and* the cost function; and
- strict separability of the indirect utility (or production) function *and* the cost function.

- Strict separability of the utility (or production) function *and* the distance function is equivalent to homothetic separability of the utility function. Moreover, strict separability of the indirect utility (or production) function *and* the cost function is equivalent to homothetic strict separability of the indirect utility function.[14]

- The following are equivalent:[15]
  - Homotheticity and complete (additive) strict separability of the utility (or production) function;
  - homotheticity and complete (additive) strict separability of the indirect utility (or production) function;
  - complete (additive) strict separability of the cost function (along with separability of prices from utility or output); and
  - complete (additive) strict separability of the distance function (along with separability of prices from utility or output).[16]

- With more than two sectors, homotheticity of the direct and indirect utility (production) function is implied by complete (additive) separability of
  - the utility (production) function and the distance function;
  - the utility (production) function and the cost function;
  - the indirect utility (production) function and the distance function; and
  - the indirect utility (production) function and the cost function.[17]

These examples indicate that the distinction between strict and non-strict separability is an important one.[18] That non-parametric methods have no power to distinguish between the two is therefore a matter of some concern. Moreover, the fact that it is not difficult to construct parametric tests that are capable of rejecting strict separability while accepting, or maintaining, non-strict separability suggests that there remains a role for parametric methods

---

[14] See Blackorby, Primont, and Russell [1978, Theorem 3.9].

[15] See Blackorby, Primont, and Russell [1978, Theorem 4.12].

[16] While I have interjected parenthetically the modifier "additive" as though it were synonymous with "complete," I hasten to add that the two are equivalent only if there are more than two sectors. The necessary and sufficient conditions for additivity in a binary partition of the variables are stronger than strict separability (as should be obvious from the fact that [strict] separability and complete [strict] separability are identical in the two-sector case).

[17] See Blackorby, Primont, and Russell [1978, Section 4.6].

[18] Until just a few years ago, one could have said that the most fundamental and powerful result in the theory of separability and functional structure, the Gorman [1968] overlapping theorem, was proved only for strict separability. The penetrating results of Mak [1986], however, have generalized the Gorman theorem to non-strict separability.

in the testing of consumer theory (and producer theory) hypotheses.[19] While parametric methods have their costs, they also have their benefits.

[19] Indeed, Blackorby, Boyce, and Russell [1978], maintaining separability of a Gorman Polar Form (with generalized Leontief fixed- and marginal-cost functions), decisively reject strict separability. (In particular, the macro function is Leontief.)

## REFERENCES


Afriat, S. N. 1967, "The Construction of Utility Functions from Expenditure Data," *International Economic Review*, Vol. 8, pp. 67 - 77.

Afriat, S. N. 1970, "The Construction of Separable Utility Functions from Expenditure Data," Unpublished paper, Chapel Hill, N.C.: University of North Carolina.

Afriat, S. N. 1973, "On a System of Inequalities in Demand Analysis: An Extension of the Classical Method," *International Economic Review*, Vol. 14, pp. 460 - 472.

Afriat, S. N. 1976, **Combinatorial Theory of Demand**, Input-Output Publishing Co., London.

Banker, R. D., and A. Maindiratta, 1988, "Maximum Likelihood Estimation of Monotonic and Concave Production Frontiers." Working paper: School of Urban and Public Affairs, Carnegie Mellon University (to appear in *Journal of Productivity Analysis*).

Becker, G. S. 1962, "Irrational Behavior and Economic Theory," *Journal of Political Economy*, Vol. 70, pp. 1 - 13.

Blackorby, C., R. Boyce, and R. R. Russell, 1978, "Estimation of Demand Systems Generated by the Gorman Polar Form: A Generalization of the S-Branch Utility Tree," *Econometrica*, Vol. 46, pp. 345 - 364.

Blackorby, C., D. Primont, and R. R. Russell, 1977a, "Separability vs. Functional Structure: A Characterization of Their Differences," *Journal of Economic Theory*, Vol. 15, pp. 135 - 144.

Blackorby, C., D. Primont, and R. R. Russell, 1977b, "On Testing Separability Restrictions with Flexible Functional Forms," *Journal of Econometrics*, Vol. 5, pp. 195 - 209.

Blackorby, C., D. Primont, and R. R. Russell, 1978, **Duality, Separability, and Functional Structure: Theory and Economic Applications**, North-Holland, Amsterdam.

Bronars, S. G., 1987, "The Power of Nonparametric Tests of Preference Maximization," *Econometrica*, Vol. 55, pp. 693 - 698.

Christensen, L. R., D. W. Jorgenson, and L. J. Lau, 1971, "Conjugate Duality and the Transcendental Logarithmic Production Function," *Econometrica*, Vol. 39, pp. 255 - 256.

Christensen, L. R., D. W. Jorgenson, and L. J. Lau, 1973, "Transcendental Logarithmic Production Frontier," *The Review of Economics and Statistics*, Vol. 60, pp. 28 - 45.

Diewert, W. E. 1971, "An Application of the Shephard Duality Theorem: A Generalized Leontief Production Function," *Journal of Political Economy*, Vol. 79, pp. 481 - 507.

Diewert, W. E. 1973, "Separability and a Generalization of the Cobb-Douglas Cost, Production, and Indirect Utility Function," *Technical Report No. 86*, Institute for Mathematical Studies in the Social Sciences, Stanford University.

Diewert, W. E. 1976, "Exact and Superlative Index Numbers," *Journal of Econometrics*, Vol. 4, pp. 115 - 146.

Diewert, W. E. and C. Parkan, 1985, "Tests for the Consistency of Consumer Data," *Journal of Econometrics*, Vol. 30, pp. 127 - 147.

Engel, E., 1857, "Die Produktions- und Konsumptionsverhältnisse des Königreichs Dachsen," *Zeitschrift des Statistischen Büros des Königlich Sach...*, Ministerium des Inneren.

Färe, R. and D. Primont, 1981, "Separability vs. Strict Separability: A Further Result," *Journal of Economic Theory*, Vol. 25, pp. 455 - 460.

Gorman, W. M. 1961, "On a Class of Preference Fields," *Metroeconomica*, Vol. 13, pp. 53 - 56.

Gorman, W. M. 1968, "The Structure of Utility Functions," *The Review of Economic Studies*, Vol. 35, pp. 369 - 390.

Gorman, W. M. 1971, "Two Stage Budgeting," Unpublished paper, London School of Economics and Political Science.

Hildenbrand, W. 1983, "On the Law of Demand," *Econometrica*, Vol. 51, pp. 997 - 1019.
Houthakker, H. S. 1962, "Some Problems in the International Comparison of Consumption Patterns," in **Les besoins de biens de consommation**, R. Mosse (ed.), Centre National de la Recherche Scientifique, Grenoble.
Jorgenson, D. C. and L. J. Lau, 1975a, "The Structure of Consumer Preferences," *Annals of Social and Economic Measurement*, Vol. 4, pp. 49 - 101.
Jorgenson, D. C. and L. J. Lau, 1975b, "Transcendental Logarithmic Utility Functions," *American Economic Review*, Vol. 65, pp. 367 - 383.
Mak, K-T, 1986, "On Separability: Functional Structure," *Journal of Economic Theory*, Vol. 40, pp. 250 - 282.
Manser, M.E., and R.J. McDonald, 1988, "An Analysis of Substitution Bias in Measuring Inflation, 1959-85," *Econometrica*, Vol. 56, pp. 909 - 930.
Pollak, R. A. and T. J. Wales, 1979, "Welfare Comparisons and Equivalent Scales," *American Economic Review*, Vol. 69, pp. 216 -221.
Primont, D. 1971, "Functional Structure and Economic Decision Making," Ph.D. dissertation, University of California, Santa Barbara.
Schmidt, P. 1987, "Frontier Production Functions," *Econometric Reviews*, Vol. 4 (2), pp. 289 - 328.
Varian, H. 1982, "The Nonparametric Approach to Demand Analysis," *Econometrica*, Vol. 50, pp. 945 - 973.
Varian, H. 1984, "Social Indifference Curves and Aggregate Demand," *Quarterly Journal of Economics*, Vol. 99, pp. 403 - 414.
Varian, H. 1983, "Nonparametric Tests of Consumer Behavior," *Review of Economic Studies*, Vol. 50, pp. 99 - 110.

# BRAIN STRUCTURE AND CONSUMPTION DYNAMICS

LESTER D. TAYLOR*
*Department of Economics*
*University of Arizona*
*Tucson, AZ 85721*

**ABSTRACT.** This paper approaches the dynamics of consumption behavior in terms of a vertically integrated tri-level brain structure whose third (or highest) level is viewed metaphorically of a central processor that rides herd over a series of interconnected modular centers practicing a division of labor. The individual is assumed to be motivated by a desire to maintain a satisfactory level of physiological and psychological well-being. Consumption activity is assumed to be hierarchical, with first claim going to activities associated with the maintenance of physiological and psychological comfort. These higher-order activities are assumed to be controlled primarily by the two lower levels of the brain. The lower-order (or creative) activities are assumed to be controlled by the third-level brain. The third-level brain is assumed to monitor the activities of the lower-level brains, to react to distress signals from these brains, and to have the capability of initiating actions to counteract their activities.

## 1. Introduction

It is now generally accepted in the neuro-sciences that the human brain functions modularly, that it consists of distinct but interconnected centers whose functionalities overlap (at least to some extent), but which in general practice a division of labor.[1] A related view is that the brain really consists of three brains: A "lizard" brain which is located at the top of the spinal column and controls autonomic processes such as breathing and heartbeat; a "monkey" brain which lies at the base of the skull and which (among other things) is capable of learning from experience; and a third-level brain which occupies most of the brain cavity and is what we ordinarily think of as the human brain.[2]

My motivation for writing this paper is a strong feeling that demand analysis can benefit handsomely from an approach that takes its cue from the organizational structure and functioning of the brain. I hope to show a few of these benefits by examining some of the implications for consumption behavior of the three-level modular brain structure just described. I am especially interested in the consumption dynamics that such a structure can imply. One might think that simple brain structures give rise to simple dynamics, but this is not the case, for we shall see that the dynamics generated by the lizard and monkey brains can

[1] See Ellis and Young (1988), Fodor (1983), Gazzaniga (1985, 1988), and Shallice (1988).

[2] See Fisher (1982) and Franklin (1988).



*L. Phlips and L.D. Taylor (eds.), Aggregation, Consumption and Trade,* 137–157.

be surprisingly complex. Indeed, most of the standard dynamical consumption models, including the original Houthakker-Taylor models, can be adduced from the functionalities of the lizard and monkey brains.

## 2. Assumptions and Terminology

My point of departure will be a stylized human brain that is assumed to consist of three connected levels. These three levels will be referred to as the alpha, beta, and gamma brains. The alpha brain is the lowest level, while the gamma is the highest. Assumptions concerning the functionalities of the three levels are as follows:

*1. Alpha brain*

The alpha brain is assumed to control all of the autonomic processes of the body, such as breathing, heartbeat, and the standard reflexes. This brain can be viewed as monitoring the basic physical life needs of the body in terms of minimum consumption levels of food, clothing, and shelter.

*2. Beta brain*

The beta brain, unlike the alpha brain, is capable of learning from experience and of figuring out the most efficient way of achieving a particular goal. It is capable of forming likes and dislikes and acting upon these in relationships with others and in responding to changes in environment. Many emotions arise in this brain, including love, anger, excitement, boredom, and regret. Habits can be formed and budget constraints recognized.

*3. Gamma brain*

Unlike the alpha and beta brains, the gamma brain is capable of abstract reasoning and of thinking through the implications of a particular action. It can form expectations and act upon the basis of these expectations, and it can embellish or dampen actions arising out of the alpha and beta brains. The gamma brain recognizes the passage of real time and can recognize that tastes and preferences can be real-time dependent, and is capable of initiating actions to counteract the destructive consequences of certain consumption activities. It is the overall monitor of consumption activity, searching for activities that contain sufficient novelty to relieve boredom but with enough redundancy to forestall panic.[3]

The gamma brain will be assumed to have a modular structure, consisting of a group of interconnected centers that have some functional overlap, but which in general practice a division of labor. The centers of the gamma brain are assumed to be interconnected so that information can flow in both directions among centers. Information flow in the vertical structure, however, is assumed to be one-way: The beta brain receives information from the alpha brain, the gamma brain receives information from both the alpha and the beta brain,

[3] For a discussion of novelty and redundancy in this context, see Scitovsky (1976).

but the alpha brain receives no information from either the beta or the gamma brain and the beta brain receives no information from the gamma brain.

The brain structure that is being assumed necessitates several breaks from conventional demand theory, beginning with the standard assumption that the individual optimizes with respect to a single utility indicator. While this assumption could probably be retained, it would require the existence of a "headquarters" center in the gamma brain of a type that I do not wish to postulate. Why this is the case will become clear later. I shall assume, instead, that the three brains pursue individual goals, which in most circumstances are mutually compatible. The goal at each level I shall assume to be "comfort."

Comfort at the alpha level is defined in terms of motivation to maintain the autonomic processes at proper levels. For processes, such as metabolism, which require goods as inputs, discomfort is dealt with through the sending of signals to the upper brains, and these then decide upon the inputs needed and how they are to be provided. Comfort at the beta level will be defined in the next section. Comfort at the gamma level is defined in terms of an "acceptable" filling of time. Since this will undoubtedly strike some as a peculiar motivation, let me elaborate what I mean by it. Economics has traditionally taken the view that consumption and happiness are synonymous. The view that underlies this paper is that an individual's main preoccupation is how to spend time rather than income. Unlike income, for which most of us have to work, time appears each day as a gift.[4] The amount is fixed and its receipt cannot be escaped. The physiology and psychology of the human organism is such that unless a certain number of neurons are firing at any time, the individual is uncomfortable. As psychologists say, arousal is at too low a level. In general, stimulation in some form is required in order to maintain arousal, and much of this occurs through the consumption of market goods and services. Since goods and services are scarce, some of an individual's time must be spent in acquiring the income needed for their purchase. When not asleep or at work, however, the basic question facing the individual is how to maintain arousal at an acceptable level, which amounts to deciding how to allocate time amongst consumption activities. Such decisions are assumed to be in the province of the gamma brain.

A second break with standard demand theory, at least at the level of principle, is a separation of consumption from expenditure. The view in this paper is that the individual has two roles in the theory of demand, as a consumer and as a purchasing agent. Time is the constraint on consumption behavior while income is the constraint on expenditure. The individual, acting as a consumer, decides what activities to consume, and the goods required as input are assumed to be in inventory in amounts necessary for the activities to proceed. Income becomes a constraint when the individual, acting as a purchasing agent, receives orders for the goods that are to be stocked.

An important function of the gamma brain in maintaining an acceptable level of arousal is combining novelty with redundancy. Redundancy in this context refers to the amount of familiarity in a consumption activity and can be identified with what Stigler and Becker (1978) define as consumption capital. Too much redundancy leads to boredom because everything has an aura of *déjà vu* (or "familiarity breeds contempt"), while too much novelty leads to confusion and immobility because one does not know what to expect. Some surprise is highly desirable, but too much causes discomfort because of limited capacity to process new information. Redundancy is created through exposure, and (as will be seen in a later section) arises through the internal dynamics of a consumption activity. The quest for novelty, in

---

[4] *Cf.* to classical exchange theory which assumes that individuals have an endowment of goods.

contrast, is viewed as inhering in the psyche of an individual as monitored by the gamma brain. It functions independently of exposure (although exposure to a new activity can remind one how pleasant novelty can be), and provides the motivation for seeking new activities. It is the *raison d'être* for wants being endless, and incites the continual appearance of new goods.[5]

A third break with standard demand theory relates to orderings of wants and preferences. Since Pareto, economists have been reluctant to think in terms of consumption hierarchies,[6] but that some needs are of higher order than others is a clear consequence not only of common sense but of the brain structure being assumed. The physiological needs associated with the autonomic processes controlled by the alpha brain are cases in point. Later, we will find it useful to assume that needs associated with certain psychological processes have a hierarchical structure as well.

Still another break with standard demand theory relates to rationality. Two concepts of rationality are involved, the psychologist's concept which focuses on the processes of decision-making and the economist's concept which focuses on outcomes and is usually defined in terms of transitivity of preferences. The individual in this paper is assumed to be rational in the psychologist's sense, but not necessarily in the economist's sense.

As should be evident, choice in the discussion is seen as being registered with respect to consumption activities rather than goods *per se*. Goods are viewed simply as inputs. Treating goods in this way has been a common practice since Becker (1965) and Lancaster (1966), and does not really represent a break with standard demand theory.

## 3. Motivations Associated with the Beta and Gamma Brains

We now turn to a discussion of factors that motivate consumption behavior of the beta and gamma brains. From evidence generated in experiments involving rat and pigeon "workers", it is clear that the beta brain is capable of organizing much of the static demand and labor-supply behavior predicted by the Slutsky-Hicks-Allen theory of demand. Animal workers recognize budget constraints and respond in predictable ways to changes in prices, income, and wage rates.[7] The beta brain is also clearly capable of learning from experience. The suggestion, accordingly, is that much of observed demand behavior can be viewed as arising in the beta brain -- downward sloping demand functions, negative income-compensated substitution effects, positive sloping supply curves of effort, and a potentially rich dynamics arising from experience and state- and flow-adjustment processes.

The assumption in this paper is that the consumption behavior controlled by the beta brain is in response to signaled needs. These needs are psychological in origin as well as physiological. The physiological needs arise from the autonomic processes controlled by the

[5] Keynes (1936) saw "animal spirits" as the major force for investment; the quest for novelty is the counterpart for consumption.

[6] *Cf.*, however, Georgescu-Roegen (1954) and Ironmonger (1972). When speaking of consumption hierarchies, reference must also be made to the psychologist Abraham Maslow. See in particular Maslow (1970). For a consumption model that accommodates Maslow's hierarchy of needs, see Coursey (1982).

[7] See Battalio, Kagel, and Green (1979) and Battalio and Kagel (1985).

alpha brain, while the psychological needs are assumed to arise from psychological processes that reside in the beta brain itself. In both cases, it is postulated that the needs in question are defined in terms of desired values of certain flow or state variables. As actual values of these variables depart from the values desired, the beta brain initiates actions to eliminate the discrepancies. The dynamics involved, which involve a form of a bang-bang control system, will be described in the next section.

As noted, the primary motivation for the gamma brain is assumed to be to maintain a satisfactory overall state of physiological and psychological well-being.[8] Doing this requires the processing of a great deal of information that flows not only from the external environment but also from the activities controlled by the alpha and beta brains as well as from those controlled by the gamma brain itself. The highest center in the gamma brain is viewed metaphorically as a central processor. Following Gazzaniga (1988), I shall assume that, among other things, this center functions as an "interpreter" in that it is constantly engaged in "making sense" of information that arises from both within and without.[9] In general, the central processor is viewed as keeping tabs on what is going on. It can acquire information both through interrogation (*i.e.*, by directing questions such as why is such-and-such happening) and through the receiving of distress signals. (Just what is meant by distress in this context will become clear in the next section.)

Tastes and preferences are assumed to be described in terms of a set of state variables. Included in the state variables will be concrete quantities such as stocks of durable goods and stocks of financial assets, as well as (a possibly long list of) variables of purely psychological dimensions. The state variables will also include the core beliefs and myths that in an important sense can be said to guide an individual's behavior, not just consumption behavior, but behavior in general. The set of beliefs will embody the individual's moral code, or sense of right and wrong, and among other things will reflect attitudes towards self-interest, altruism, and cooperation.

## 4. Consumption Dynamics

We now turn to a discussion of the consumption dynamics that can be adduced from the brain structure that is being postulated. The assumption, as just noted, which underlies the discussion is that at any point in time an individual's relationship to the world can be described in terms of a set of state variables. Individuals are assumed to select their consumption from a set of consumption activities. A consumption activity is taken to be a well-defined production process which [per Becker (1965) and Lancaster (1966)] has market goods and time as inputs. An activity may be simple (such as eating an apple) or complex (such as giving a dinner party) and may involve just a single good or a combination of goods.

---

[8] Comfort for the gamma brain could be equally well defined in terms of security in a broad sense -- security in emotional and economic senses as well as security in a physical sense.

[9] Experimental evidence suggests that the "interpreter" is physically located in the left hemisphere of the gamma brain and that it is associated with the so-called language facility of this hemisphere. Gazzaniga sees core beliefs as arising out of the actions of the interpreter. See Gazzaniga (1985, Chapter 11).

As noted, the consumption behavior of an individual is assumed to be motivated primarily by a desire for comfort. Comfort in the case of the alpha and beta brains will be defined in terms of state-variable equilibria, physiological in the case of the alpha brain and psychological as well as physiological in the case of the beta brain. Comfort for the gamma brain will be defined in terms of maintaining the individual in an overall physiological and psychological equilibrium and in reconciling consumption requirements of market goods with the financial resources that are available to purchase them.

## 4.1 CONSUMPTION DYNAMICS ASSOCIATED WITH THE ALPHA AND BETA BRAINS: STATE-AND FLOW-ADJUSTMENT MODELS AND OPPONENT PROCESSES

The consumption dynamics that arise from the actions of the alpha and beta brains are essentially of the state- and flow-adjustment variety. For notation, let q denote the flow (measured instantaneously) of an input into an activity and let s denote a state variable that is associated with the activity. Finally, let $S^*$ denote a desired value of the state variable.[10] Comfort, then, can be defined in terms of maintaining s equal to $S^*$ and consumption can be defined in terms of manipulating q so as to achieve this relationship.

Assume $s \neq S^*$ and consider:

$$\dot{q}(t) = \gamma\,[q(t) - \alpha - \beta s(t)] \tag{1}$$

$$\dot{s}(t) = q(t) - \delta s(t), \tag{2}$$

where $\dot{q} = dq/dt$, $\dot{s} = ds/dt$, and $\alpha, \beta, \gamma$, and $\delta$ are parameters. Expression (1) can be interpreted as the consumption action initiated by one of the lower level brains in response to a divergence between s and $S^*$. The parameters in this relationship represent both the behavioral response of the controlling brain and the production technology of the activity or process. Expression (2) represents an involuntary dynamic that describes the law-of-motion of s.

The process described by expressions (1) and (2) will be in equilibrium -- *i.e.*, "comfort" will be achieved -- when both $\dot{s}$ and $\dot{q}$ equal zero, in which case we can write:

$$q^* = \alpha + \beta S^* \tag{3}$$

$$q^* = \delta S^*. \tag{4}$$

Subtracting and adding $q^*$ to the term in the brackets in expression (1) and then using equation (3) allows (1) to be rewritten as

$$\dot{q}(t) = \gamma[q(t) - q^* - \beta\{s(t) - S^*\}], \tag{5}$$

which describes how q adjusts in response to a discrepancy between s and $S^*$.

---

[10] There is no presumption of $S^*$ being determined through an optimization process. For activities involving autonomic processes, the $S^*$s are physiologically determined. For activities involving psychological processes, they can be interpreted as representing minimum acceptable levels of comfort.

For autonomic processes controlled by the alpha brain, S* can be interpreted as a physiologically determined constant. In the case of nutrition, for example, S* can represent a desired reserve of "nutritional well-being," while $\delta$ represents the body's physiological demands on this reserve and q represents the rate at which the reserve is replenished. On the behavioral side, $\beta$ can be interpreted as representing the beta brain's desired response in q to a change in the actual value of s. This desired response, however, is tempered by the coefficient $\gamma$.

The dynamical system described by equations (1) and (2) actually embodies several well-known dynamic demand models, including both of the original Houthakker-Taylor models. The state-adjustment model is obtained as a limiting case by dividing expression (1) by $\gamma$ and then letting $\gamma$ become large. This corresponds to instantaneous adjustment in q. The flow-adjustment model, in contrast, corresponds to the state variable being absent from the behavioral equation. This could arise either because a state variable is irrelevant ($\beta$=0) or because the state variable depreciates instantaneously (s=o).

Other interpretations are also possible. As it stands, the model is identical with the generalization of the Houthakker-Taylor state-adjustment model that has recently been suggested by Bergstrom and Chambers (1989)[11], and it can also support an error-correction interpretation.[12] The error-correction interpretation is as follows: In equilibrium, q will be equal to $\alpha + \beta s$, so that $q(t) - \alpha - \beta s(t)$ represents disequilibrium error; q is then corrected in response to this error according to the adjustment parameter $\gamma$.

While it is reasonable to define comfort in autonomic processes in terms of physiological constants, this is not the case for psychological processes, for allowance needs to be made for desired values of the state variables to evolve in response to exposure to the activities involved. In two earlier papers [Taylor (1987, 1989)], I have suggested psychological opponent processes as a framework for describing the dynamics for a variety of consumption activities. I will now take a few paragraphs to describe what an opponent process entails.

The point of departure for an opponent-process model is the observation that many feelings of pleasure or pain seem to be followed by a contrary after-effect -- pain by a pleasant feeling of relief, pleasure by a feeling of let-down or emptiness. The model consists of three components, a primary process which is initiated by a stimulus, an opponent process which is aroused by the primary process, and a summator which sums the hedonic effects of the primary and opponent processes. Solomon and Corbit (1974) refer to the primary process as an a-process and the opponent process as a b-process. The magnitude of the a-process is postulated to correlate closely with the intensity, quality, and duration of the stimulus. The function of the b-process is to oppose or suppress the state generated by the a-process.[13] The b-process is postulated to be (i) of sluggish latency, (ii) inertial, or slow to build to its

---

[11] *Cf.* also Taylor and Houthakker (1990).

[12] See Sargan (1964), Hendry, Pagan and Sargan (1984), Salmon (1982), and Pagan and Wickens (1989).

[13] Opponent processes were introduced by Hurvich and Jameson (1957). The model has been most extensively developed by Richard L. Solomon and his associates at the University of Pennsylvania. See Solomon and Corbit (1974) and Solomon (1980). *Cf.* also Solomon (1989). Opponent processes were brought to the attention of economists by Tibor Scitovsky in **The Joyless Economy.** An edited version of Solomon and Corbit's paper was reprinted in the 1978 *Handbook of the American Economic Association.*

peak intensity, and (iii) slow to decay after the stimulus has terminated and the a-process has stopped. Finally, the hedonic quality of the b-process is opposite to that of the a-process.

To illustrate the role that opponent processes can play in describing consumption dynamics, let us consider a consumption activity that has associated with it a pair of opponent processes, an a-process which is initiated by the stimulus which defines the activity and a b-process which is triggered by the a-process. For convenience, it will be assumed that the a-process is hedonically positive and the b-process negative. The activity will have goods and time as inputs and the stimulus associated with it will be identified with the physical consumption of the goods. The individual is assumed to influence the a-process by controlling the timing, intensity, and duration of the stimulus. The b-process, however, is governed by its own dynamics and can be controlled only through reapplying the stimulus (or "redosing"). When redosing occurs in order to kill the effects of a painful b-process, the individual has reached a state of addiction.[14]

Following Solomon and Corbit (1974), let the hedonic function at time t that is associated with the consumption activity be given by

$$(6) \qquad \phi(t) = \phi_a(t) + \phi_b(t),$$

where $\phi_a$ ( > 0 ) and $\phi_b$ ( < 0) denote the hedonic values of the a- and b-processes, respectively. For $\phi_a$, it will be assumed that

$$(7) \qquad \phi_a(t) = \beta d(t)q(t),$$

where $\beta$ is a parameter, d(t) is a stimulus indicator variable, and q(t) represents the intensity of the stimulus. Three possible shapes for $\phi$ are given in Figure 1. The solid portions of these curves correspond to d(t) = 1, q(t) > 0, while the dashed portions correspond to d(t) = 0, q(t) = 0. Since $\phi_a = 0$ for d = 0, the dashed portions accordingly represent $\phi_b$ when d = 0.

Redosing can be taken to occur when the discomfort associated with the b-process reaches a point where it can no longer be tolerated. The timing of a redose for an addicting activity will therefore be determined by the shape of the b-process. The curve in the first panel in Figure 1 describes an activity that is nonaddicting, as the dashed curve does not reach the threshold level of discomfort. The second panel, in contrast, describes an addicting activity such as smoking, for $\phi_b$ drops below the threshold. Finally, the third panel describes a physiologically addicting activity such as (normal) eating. $\phi_b$ in this case begins slowly, eventually reaches the threshold, and then keeps on falling, reflecting the fact that endless fasting ultimately results in death. The steepness of the discomfort curves in panels b and c explains the difference in time intervals between redosing for smoking and eating. The curve is much steeper for smoking, which causes redosing to occur at much shorter intervals than for food. The extreme, of course, is chain-smoking, which corresponds to continuous redosing.

It seems reasonable to assume that each opponent process has associated with it a minimum of two state variables, one for the a-process and one for the b-process. The state variable for the a-process can be viewed as a generalized stock of consumption capital in the sense of Stigler and Becker (1978). Intangibles will be contained in this stock, and in many cases physical capital as well. Included in the intangibles will be knowledge of the activity that has

---

[14] Obvious cases in point are redosing to escape the withdrawal pains from heroin and drinking to kill a hangover.

Figure I

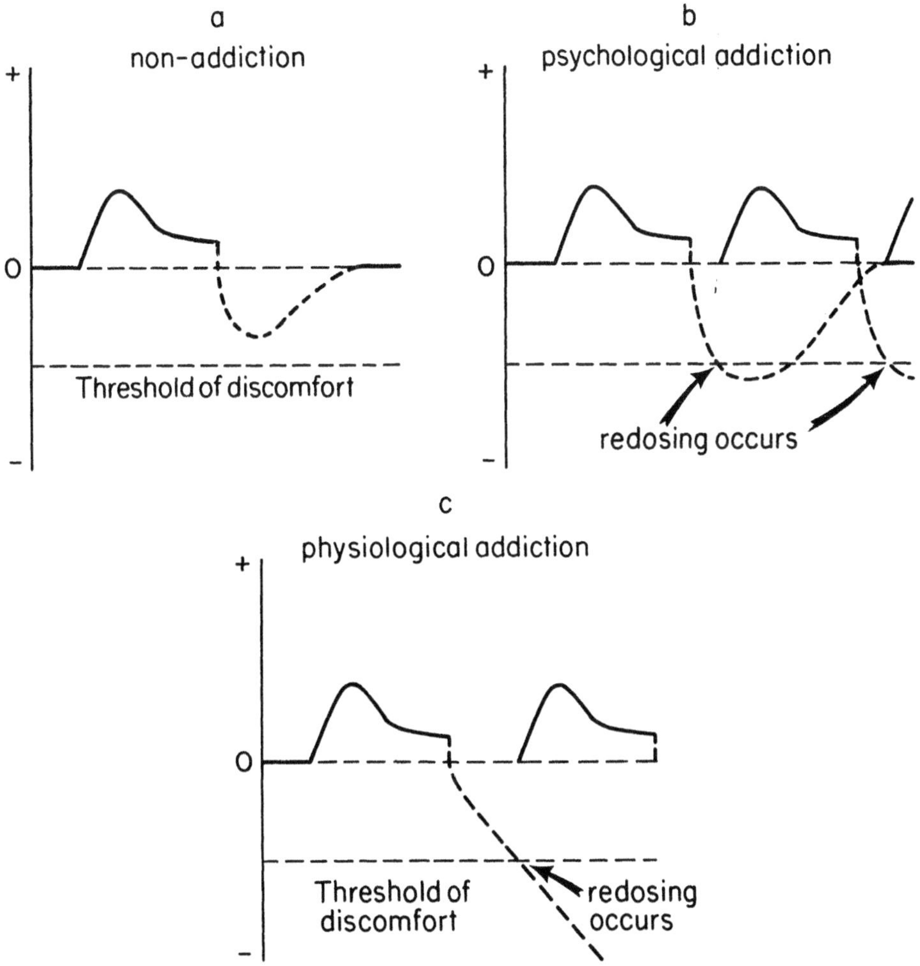
a
non-addiction
+
0
Threshold of discomfort
-
b
psychological addiction
+
0
redosing occurs
-
c
physiological addiction
+
0
Threshold of discomfort
redosing occurs
-

been acquired through previous exposure, or what was referred to earlier as redundancy. This stock of consumption capital, which will be denoted by A, can be assumed to be subject to depreciation. The law-of-motion for the state variable for the a-process can accordingly be given the same form as in expression (2),

$$\dot{A}(t) = q(t) - \delta A(t). \tag{8}$$

The law-of-motion for the state variable associated with the b-process will be more complicated than expression (8) because of a need to allow for the b-process to strengthen with repetition. Accordingly, let us define a state variable B(t) as

$$B(t) = B_0 + \sum_{i=1}^{n*} e^{-\sigma i} q[i], \ \sigma > 0, \tag{9}$$

where $B_0$ denotes the strength of the b-process at the time of the first exposure to the activity, q[i] denotes the strength of the stimulus during $i^{th}$ exposure, and n* denotes the number of distinct exposures. Finally, $\sigma$ is a parameter which allows for B(t) to reach an eventual asymptote. The hedonic function $\phi_b$ can then be defined as:

$$\begin{aligned} \phi_b(t) &= -S(t,\tau) \\ &= -e^{-\kappa(t-\tau)} B(t). \end{aligned} \tag{10}$$

Two types of time are represented in this expression, historical (or chronological) time, which refers to consumption decision points, and process (or activity) time, which refers to the time interval over which a consumption activity occurs. The former is indexed by t and the latter by $\tau$. Note that it is assumed that B(t) is independent of $\tau$, the state variable is affected only by the frequency and intensity of the stimulus associated with the activity. Finally, let B* denote a threshold level of discomfort such that $B \geq B^*$ will trigger reapplication of the stimulus (*i.e.*, redosing).

From the preceding, it is clear that actions of the beta brain in regard to opponent processes and the nature of the consumption dynamics involved will depend upon whether or not a consumption activity is addictive -- *i.e.*, whether B(t) reaches the threshold of discomfort B*. Activities for which this is the case will be retriggered automatically by the beta brain whenever $B \geq B^*$, hence the consumption dynamics for these activities should be similar to those already discussed in connection with autonomic processes. B* serves the same function as the desired value (S*) of the state variables. The situation is different for non-addicting activities, for without the automatic trigger afforded by $B \geq B^*$, the beta brain lacks the capability of initiating the activity. "Redosing" in this case is an act of choice exercised by the gamma brain.

In thinking about the dynamics associated with opponent processes, it is important not to confuse consumption dynamics with the internal dynamics of the processes themselves. Consumption dynamics are external to the processes and describe how the individual responds to signals to initiate the activities involved. Consumption dynamics operate in historical time and are indexed in terms of t. Process dynamics, in contrast, are internal to the processes, operate in process time, and are indexed in terms of $\tau$.

From the foregoing, it is clear that much of the consumption associated with activities that have negative b-processes can be viewed as being motivated by a desire to eliminate discomfort. The extreme would be an addicting activity for which $\phi$ is never positive. This would describe an activity in which $\phi_a$ is "beaten down" by exposure and repetition. The individual may receive no stimulation from the activity *per se*, but its absence causes discomfort.[15]

## 4.2 DYNAMICS ASSOCIATED WITH THE GAMMA BRAIN

We now turn to the consumption actions of the gamma brain, which in contrast with the alpha and beta brains is not constrained to be reactive. The primary motivation of the gamma brain, as has been noted, is assumed to be to maintain an acceptable level of physiological and psychological well-being. As with the alpha and beta brains, this is assumed to be accomplished through the monitoring of a set of state variables that, among other things, embodies the moral (or ethical) code of the individual. Well-being is acceptable when actual values of these state variables are in proximity of certain desired values. The gamma brain has capacity to choose among activities (when real-time permits this to be done), can initiate activities in response to distress signals from the alpha and beta brains, and in some cases can alter decisions of those two brains. In addition, the gamma brain can form expectations which become inputs into consumption plans that cover both near-and long-term horizons. The gamma brain directs the acquisition of market goods and provides for the resources for their purchase through choosing the amount of time to be spent in the pursuit of income.

One of the capabilities of the gamma brain is to monitor the addictive processes of the beta brain and to assess whether an addiction is "good" or "bad". If an addiction is deemed hostile, the gamma brain has the capability of taking corrective action, that is, of initiating activities that can overcome or break the addiction. A "bad" addiction in this context can be defined in terms of the effect that the addicting activity has on the state variables that describe the individual's *overall feeling of well-being*. Denote the desired values of these state variables by $M^*$ and their actual values by M.[16] Assume that the elements of M are functions of the threshold levels of pain that trigger redosing of the addicting activities, that is, let

$$M(t) = G[B^*(t),Z(t)], \quad (11)$$

where $B^*$ is as previously defined and Z represents all of the other factors affecting M.

An addicting activity (with a negative b-process), j, can be defined as "bad" if, for some $M_i$, $\partial M_i/\partial B_j^* < 0$. Such an activity will cause $M_i$ to depart negatively from $M_i^*$. Eventually, the shortfall can reach a value that causes the central processor of the gamma brain to begin

---

[15] *Cf.* Scitovsky (1976, Chapter 6). This type of consumption is also related to what Hawtrey once referred to as "defensive" consumption, as opposed to "creative" consumption. See Hawtrey (1925, pp. 189-192). The focus in the discussion has been on opponent processes in which the a-process has been positive and the b-process negative. There are also situations in which this is reversed, the a-process is negative and the b-process is positive. Parachuting and bungee-jumping provide examples. Soloman and Corbit (1970) discuss other examples.

[16] The elements of M* represent the core beliefs of an individual and are assumed to reflect cultural, sociological, and family influences. For present purposes, they are viewed as being in- variant to consumption activities, so that in a sense they can be viewed the preferences of conventional demand theory. The elements of M*, however, are more inclusive than the preferences of conventional theory, for *inter alia* they will embody attitudes toward love and marriage, religion, interpersonal relations, self-interest, and altruism.

searching for ways to combat the addiction. As this occurs, conflict will almost certainly emerge, for the individual is not behaving in accord with his/her moral code. The result could be ambivalence[17] or even mental pathology.

Latter possibilities aside, the central processor can be viewed as taking action to combat an addiction when $M_i^* - M_i$ reaches a particular threshold. Such action can vary from the establishment of "anti-markets" of the type discussed by Schelling (1978), participation in support groups (Alcoholics Anonymous, Weight-Watchers, *etc.*), to sheer acts of will (*i.e.*, quitting the addicting activity "cold-turkey"). Stop-and-go consumption behavior could emerge that could imply dynamics -- specifically, nonlinear dynamics[18] -- that are more complicated than any that have been discussed in connection with the alpha and beta brains.

We now turn to the gamma brain's capacity to anticipate and to form expectations. As has been noted, the gamma brain can monitor both its own activities as well as the activities of the alpha and beta brains. When combined with a capacity to anticipate, this means that the gamma brain has the capability of thinking through the consequences not only of its own actions but actions of the two lower brains. If the consequences of a particular act are judged to be harmful, the decision to act could be revised or a consumption plan could be formulated that contains or undoes the harm.[19]

In formulating consumption plans, the gamma brain is assumed to have the capacity to form expectations regarding the future course of prices and income and also to anticipate the wants and needs that relate to stages of the life cycle. Expectations in these cases are with reference to calendar time rather than process time, and are more relevant to purchase decisions than to consumption decisions. A variety of expectations mechanisms could be considered at this point, including naive, extrapolative, adaptive, Bayesian, or rational. Of these, it would seem that rational expectations is the only one that requires the capability that has been ascribed to the gamma brain. Expectations for all of the other mechanisms can be formulated on the basis of current and past information, and the capacity for doing this has been ascribed to the beta brain. Rational expectations, however, requires abstract reasoning that only the gamma brain is capable of.

## 5. From Consumption to Expenditure

The dynamics that have been considered to this point relate to the consumption side of the consumption/expenditure dichotomy that was postulated earlier. The dichotomy has been characterized in terms of the individual wearing two "hats:" One as a "consumer" whose motivation is primarily to maintain an acceptable level of physiological and psychological well-being through time through consumption activities that use time and market goods as inputs; and the other as a "purchasing agent" whose motivation is primarily to obtain the

---

[17] This would be reflective of a circumstance where "part of me wants to do this and part of me wants to do that," but where one action forecloses the other.

[18] For an analysis of such dynamics in the context of opponent processes, see Lancry and Saldanha (1991).

[19] For a model of endogenous taste change that allows for considerations such as this, see Manove (1973).

market goods required in the most efficient way possible given the resources that are available. I want now to look at the expenditure side of the dichotomy.

The bridge between consumption and expenditures occurs in the gamma brain, where one can imagine that consumption needs are transmitted to the "purchasing agent" who then goes out into markets to shop. Dynamics on the expenditure side arise from two different sources of dynamical phenomena. The first source is the consumption dynamics that we have been discussing, that is, the dynamics that inhere in the consumption activities that are undertaken in efforts to maintain physiological and psychological well-being at an acceptable level. State variables change over time as a result of exposure, experience, and depreciation, and this leads to time-dependent changes in the amounts and types of market goods that are required by consumption activities as inputs. This is the type of dynamics associated with inertia, habit-formation, and stock-adjustment.

The second type of dynamics describes how the individual, functioning as a purchasing agent, responds to changes in the external environment. The behavior reflected in these dynamics will include delays in adjusting to changes in prices and wage rates, the appearance of new goods, and changes in the type and intensity of marketing efforts. Response delays can arise from a variety of reasons, including recognition lags and other imperfections in information flows, uncertainty, and certain intrinsic characteristics of the individual. Finally, expectations will also contribute to this category of dynamics if they are formulated on the basis of present and past values of income, prices, and interest rates.

Complicated expectations aside, the dynamics represented in equations (1) and (2) are appropriate for goods that involve the holding of physical inventories. In this case, equation (1) would be augmented by price and income, so that we would have:

$$(12) \qquad q(t) = \Phi[q(t) - \alpha - \beta s(t) - \gamma x(t) - \lambda p(t)],$$

$$(13) \qquad \dot{s}(t) = q(t) - \delta s(t),$$

where x and p denote the flow-rates of income and level of price and s denotes the level of inventory. The coefficient $\delta$ in expression (13) can now be seen as representing the using-up of the good in question as input into consumption activities. $\alpha$, $\beta$, $\gamma$, and $\lambda$ in expression (12) reflect intrinsic behavioral characteristics of the individual (as purchasing agent), while $\Phi$ can be viewed as incorporating delays and adjustments resulting from imperfections in information flows.

The bridge between the consumption and expenditures sides in the gamma brain is represented in the parameter $\delta$. Strictly speaking, $\delta$ should be written as a function of time, for in substantial part it is psychologically based and thus reflective of the "endogenous" taste changes occasioned by the internal dynamics of consumption activities and the gamma brain's efforts to maintain a satisfactory level of psychological well-being. Closing the system accordingly requires the specification of a law-of-motion for $\delta$. For now, I leave this as an open question.

Expressions (12) and (13) can also be used to describe the expenditure behavior of goods, such as concerts, theater, and sporting events, that are consumed at the time of purchase. Inventories will continue to be involved for such activities, except that reference must be to psychological quantities rather than physical stocks. For concerts, one can imagine a stock of "music enjoyment" that periodically needs replenishing, and similarly for theater and sporting events. Moreover, many services, such as travel and telecommunications, are inputs into consumption activities that have conceptually well-defined state variables associated with them, and in some instances these can be identified directly with the psychological quantities in question.

The expenditure dynamics are clearly complicated by expectations. One way of bringing expectations into the picture is to rewrite equation (12) as

$$\text{(14)} \qquad \dot{q}(t) = \Phi[q(t) - \alpha - \beta s(t) - \gamma x^e(t) + \lambda p^e(t)],$$

where $x^e$ and $p^e$ denote the purchasing agent's expectations for income and price. To illustrate the complications that can be introduced, let the formation mechanisms for $x^e$ and $p^e$ be given by:

$$\text{(15)} \qquad \dot{x}^e(t) = \psi[x(t)-x^e(t)]$$

$$\text{(16)} \qquad x^e(t) = \int_{t-\Delta}^{t} w(\tau)x(\tau)d\tau$$

$$\text{(17)} \qquad \dot{p}^e(t) = \theta[p(t)-p^e(t)]$$

$$\text{(18)} \qquad p^e(t) = \int_{t-\Delta}^{t} w(\tau)p(\tau)d\tau,$$

where

$$\Delta > 0, \; w(\tau) \geq 0,$$

and

$$\int_{t-\Delta} w(\tau)d\tau = 1.$$

These expressions posit that expectations are formulated as a weighted average of past values of x and p, with a partial adjustment to new information. Differentiation of expression (14) with respect to time and then using (15) and (17) for $\dot{x}^e$ and $\dot{p}^e$ yields

$$\text{(19)} \qquad \ddot{q}(t) = \Phi\left[\dot{q}(t) - \beta\dot{s}(t) - \gamma\{\psi[x(t)-x^e(t)]\} - \lambda\{\theta[p(t)-p^e(t)]\}\right],$$

which is a second-order differential equation in q.

The point of the foregoing is to show that the capacity to form expectations has material implications for expenditure dynamics. As simple adaptive expectations lead to a second-order process, one can imagine (without getting caught up in details) the complexity that more sophisticated expectation mechanisms would imply. As has been noted, the dynamics represented in expressions (12) and (13) can be associated with decisions of the beta brain, as can also the formation of simple adaptive expectations. Dynamics arising out of more complex expectation mechanisms, however, must be attributed to the gamma brain.

As the purchasing agent's expenditure behavior at any point in time is obviously constrained by the income that is available, the final task in this section is to incorporate the budget constraint into the analysis. For notation, let y denote income, q a vector of consumption activities, and x a vector of market goods and services that (*à la* Becker and Lancaster) are inputs into these activities. Let p denote the vector of associated prices, and finally, for those goods for which physical inventories are relevant, let X and $X^*$ denote vectors of actual and desired levels of inventories.

$X^*$ is assumed to represent a "safe" level of inventories (paper towels, milk, soap, *etc.*) over some relevant consumption horizon. Specifically, let $X^*$ be defined by

$$X^*(t) \geq \int_t^{t+\Delta} x(\tau)d\tau, \tag{20}$$

where $\Delta$ represents the consumption horizon, and $x(\tau)$ is determined by the activity "production" functions,

$$q(\tau) = f[x(\tau)]. \tag{21}$$

Next, let x(t) be defined by

$$x(t) = \begin{cases} X^*(t) - X(t) \text{ for } X^* > X \\ 0 \text{ otherwise.} \end{cases} \tag{22}$$

Finally, it is assumed that the purchasing agent acquires x(t) at minimum cost subject to the income constraint:[20]

$$p'(t)x(t) \leq y(t). \tag{23}$$

## 6. Consumption/Income Relationships

Nothing has been said thus far about how the *structure* of consumption relates to the *level* of income. A clear implication of the analysis is that activities controlled by the alpha and beta brains have first claim on income. Topping the list will be the physiological needs of the autonomic processes, followed by the needs of addicting psychological processes. It is only

---

[20] Since saving is not taken into account, the budget constraint will normally be satisfied as an inequality. Because of possibilities to dissave or borrow, there is actually no necessity (depending upon the definition of income that is used) for any particular point in time that the budget constraint be satisfied. Persistent deficits, however, could not occur, not only because of the obvious threat of bankruptcy, but also because solvency for most individuals is an important part of their moral code (as defined in $M^*$ in the preceding section). Once the gamma brain recognizes that solvency is threatened, actions would be initiated to avert it.

after the needs of these two categories have been satisfied that needs associated with boredom-relieving activities can assert claims. We can accordingly conclude that goods that are primary inputs into activities controlled by the alpha and beta brains will have smaller income elasticities than goods that are primarily inputs into activities controlled by the gamma brain. In terms of the conventional grouping of goods into luxuries and necessities, goods associated with the alpha and beta brains will tend to be necessities, while goods associated with the gamma brain will tend to be luxuries.

An empirical implication of the foregoing is that we should expect to observe greater variation in consumption patterns among individuals with high income than with low income. Consumption will be proscribed the closer it is associated with activities that involve the elimination of physiological and psychological discomfort, activities which in general will be controlled by the alpha and beta brains. One would expect these activities to have greater uniformity across individuals than the activities controlled by the gamma brain, which allows for much greater expression of individual tastes. High income, in short, provides much greater scope for individual tastes to manifest themselves.[21]

Still another implication of the analysis is that, in general, consumption behavior will be asymmetrical with respect to income increases and income decreases. As has been noted, the goods that have first claims on income are those that are associated with eliminating physiological discomfort, so that for decreases in income, expenditures for these goods will probably not fall and certainly will not fall proportionately with the fall in income. For increases in income, on the other hand, novelty and new wants can be pursued, and expenditures will increase. While the increase in expenditures may again be less than proportionate to the increase in income, the increase will almost certainly be larger (in absolute value) than what any decrease in expenditures would be for a like fall in income. The likely result, accordingly, is a "ratchet" in expenditure for changes from the current level of income.[22, 23]

---

[21] I remember Professor Houthakker once commenting on this point in his office when I was a (low income!) graduate student at Harvard. Moreover, such is consistent with the heteroscedasticity that is usually observed in the residuals of Engel curves. See Prais and Houthakker (1955).

[22] This paragraph assumes that the income level from which changes are measured is one to which the individual had more or less adjusted. The effects described accordingly refer to short-run responses. Long-run responses may be more symmetrical to income increases and decreases, although it is doubtful, because of learning and other state-variable creation, that consumption behavior is ever fully reversible, as is the case in conventional demand theory. Thus, at the level of the individual, the short-run dynamics of this paper are consistent with the Relative-and Permanent-Income Hypotheses [Duesenberry (1949), Friedman (1957)] and the Life-Cycle Model [Modigliani and Brumberg (1954, 1980)]. This will not necessarily be the case for the long run, however, because of irreversibility.

[23] A few words about aggregation are also in order. Despite the concern that is often expressed (although usually in passing), aggregation is in the end not that much of a problem in traditional demand theory because of the easy appeal to a representative consumer. On the other hand, there would appear to be severe aggregation problems in the present approach, for as Louis Phlips has put it, "how do you aggregate over a smoker like me and a nonsmoker like you?"

## 7. Rationality

As noted in the introduction, a question which naturally comes up is whether the brain structure that has been postulated in this paper gives rise to consumption behavior that is rational. In dealing with this question, it is important to distinguish between rationality as this term is used by psychologists and as it is used by economists. For psychologists, the focus is on the process (or processes) that leads to a decision, whereas for economists the focus is on the outcomes of decisions.[24] In standard economic theory, rationality is essentially identified with transitivity of preferences: If A is preferred to B and B is preferred to C, then A is preferred to C.[25] In general, the brain structure that is postulated is consistent with the first concept of rationality, but not the second. In its role as the ultimate arbiter of consumption decisions, the gamma brain takes into account both current information and consequences of past activities and forms expectations concerning the effects of current acts. Its cognitive processes are many, and there is no reason to think that these are (in normal circumstances) not coordinated in a compatible fashion by the central processor to provide an acceptable level of comfort and well-being.

Rationality is the second (or economist's) sense, however, is another matter. As a way of analyzing this question, let us imagine a conceptual experiment in which from a given set of initial conditions a short segment of real time is repeated. Rationality in the second sense would require that an individual make identical consumption decisions. But, unless all consumption activity is controlled by the alpha and beta brains, there is no reason for this to be the case. This is because, for consumption activities that do not involve the elimination of discomfort, the particular consumption activities that are engaged over any interval would seem to be inherently random as a consequence of the random firing of neurons. Put another way, there is no reason to think that the moods (or dispositions) that drive the selection of activities to stave off boredom would be repeated. Rationality in the second sense would therefore seem to be an event with probability zero.

The foregoing is with reference to the individual as a consumer. A different conclusion can emerge with regard to expenditure behavior (*i.e.*, to the individual in his/her role as a purchasing agent). The conceptual experiment to be imagined here is the usual one in which income is held constant and the individual is confronted with a sequence of vectors of relative prices which at some point begins to repeat itself. The question is then whether the expenditure pattern would also begin to repeat. If this were the case, the demand functions would be integrable, or equivalently the expenditure patterns would be consistent with the strong axiom of revealed preference.[26] Either way, rationality in the second sense would be present.

Whether or not this would be the case turns on what besides income is assumed to be held constant. If everything on the consumption side were held constant, I see no reason why rationality in the second sense would not hold. The question, however, is whether everything on the consumption side can meaningfully be held constant. The problem is that the conceptual experiment envisioned implies a passage of time, and this could affect, among

---

[24] See Simon (1986).

[25] For a discussion of how the concept of rationality has evolved in economics, see Arrow (1986).

[26] See Houthakker (1950).

other things, the expectations that are formed by the gamma brain. This could lead to non-repeating expenditure patterns in the conceptual experiment and hence to apparent non-transitivities.

## 8. Summary and Final Remarks

This paper has postulated a vertically integrated tri-level brain structure whose third (or highest) level consists of a central processor that rides herd over a series of interconnected modular centers practicing a division of labor. The individual is assumed to be motivated by a desire to maintain a satisfactory level of physiological and psychological well-being. Consumption behavior accordingly consists of a mixture of activities, some of which serve to eliminate acute discomfort and others of which serve to inject novelty and reduce boredom. Preferences (as usually understood) change irreversibly through time and in general are lexicographical and non-transitive. The individual is rational in the psychologist's sense, but (because of possible intransitivities) not necessarily in the economist's sense.

Consumption activity is assumed to be hierarchical, with first claim going to activities associated with the maintenance of physiological and psychological comfort. These higher-order activities are assumed to be controlled primarily by the two lower levels of the brain. The lower-order (or creative) activities are assumed to be controlled by the third-level, or gamma, brain. The gamma brain is also assumed to monitor the activities of the lower-level brains, to react to distress signals from these brains, and to have the capability of initiating actions to counteract their activities. Finally, the individual is depicted as consisting of two entities, a consumer who uses market goods and services together with time as inputs into consumption activities to produce physiological and psychological well-being and a purchasing agent who takes orders from the consumer as to the market goods and services that are to be acquired.

In keeping with a career-long interest of Professor Houthakker, the focus in the paper has been on the consumption dynamics associated with each level of the brain, with particular emphasis on the presence and operation of psychological opponent processes. We have seen that the standard dynamical consumption models, including the original Houthakker-Taylor state- and flow-adjustment models and the Bergstrom-Chambers error-correction generalization thereof, can be adduced from the actions of the alpha and beta brains. The dynamics associated with the gamma brain are more complicated because of its capacity to reason, formulate expectations, and ponder the consequences of both its own actions and those of the two lower-level brains. The gamma brain's capability of establishing "anti-markets" for activities that are painfully addicting can lead to dynamics that are nonlinear. This is a complicating factor that has only been briefly addressed in this paper.

In his 1956 *Kyklos* paper on speciation and the division of labor, Professor Houthakker noted that a certain amount of speculation is vital in scientific discourse. Obviously, the present paper entails speculation. My purpose has been to show the possibilities for consumption analysis of approaching consumer behavior in terms of the organization of the brain. The brain structure that is postulated can accommodate all of standard neoclassical demand theory and all of the conventional dynamical consumption models, plus some (involving nonlinear dynamics) that are probably still to be devised. It can also accommodate many features of the non-traditional approaches to consumption behavior, such as Duesenberry and Veblen effects and the formation of anti-markets, as well as multiple-motivation structures of the type studied by Georgescu-Roegen (1954), Sen (1977), and Winston (1980). An approach such as the one proposed offers a framework within which economists can cooperate, rather than compete, with psychologists, sociologists, and marketers. Finally (and rather obviously), the framework provides a meaningful link between economics and the neuro-sciences.

## REFERENCES


Arrow, K.J. (1986), "Rationality and Utility from the Standpoint of Evolutionary Biology," in **Rational Choice: The Contrast Between Economics and Psychology**, University of Chicago Press.

Battalio, R.C., Kagel, J.H., and Green, L. (1979), "Labor Supply Behavior of Animal Workers: Towards an Experimental Analysis," in *Research in Experimental Economics*, Vol. 1, pp. 231-253, Jai Press.

Battalio, R.C. and Kagel, J.H. (1985), "Consumption-Leisure Tradeoffs of Animal Workers: Effects of Increasing and Decreasing Marginal Wage Rates in a Closed Economy Experiment," in *Research in Experimental Economics*, Vol. 3, pp. 1-29, Jai Press.

Becker, G.S. (1965), "A Theory of the Allocation of Time," *Economic Journal*, Vol. 75, September 1965, pp. 493-517.

Bergstrom, A.R. and Chambers, M.J. (1989), "Gaussian Estimation of a Continuous Time Model of Demand for Consumer Durable Goods With Applications to Demand in the United Kingdom, 1973-1984," University of Essex.

Coursey, D.L. (1982), *Hierarchical Preferences in Consumer Choice*, unpublished Ph.D. dissertation (economics), University of Arizona, Tucson.

Duesenberry, J.S. (1949), **Income, Saving, and the Theory of Consumer Behavior**, Harvard University Press.

Ellis, W.E. and Young, A.W. (1988), **Human Cognitive Neuro-psychology**, Lawrence Erlbaum Associates, Publishers.

Fisher, H. (1982), **The Sex Contract**, William Marrow.

Fodor, J. (1983), **The Modularity of Mind**, MIT Press.

Franklin, J. (1988), **Molecules of the Mind**, Dell Publishing Co.

Friedman, M. (1957), **A Theory of the Consumption Function**, Princeton University Press.

Gazzaniga, M. (1985), **The Social Brain**, Basic Books.

Gazzaniga, M. (1988), **Mind Matters**, Basic Books.

Georgescu-Roegen, N. (1954), "Choice, Expectations, and Measurement," *Quarterly Journal of Economics*, Vol. 68, No. 3, August 1954, pp. 503-544.

Hawtrey, R.G. (1925), **The Economic Problem**, Longmans, Green, and Company.

Hendry, D.F., Pagan, A.R., and Sargan, J.D. (1984), "Dynamic Specification," in *Handbook of Econometrics*, Vol. 3, ed. by Z. Griliches and M. Intriligator, North Holland Publishing Co.

Houthakker, H.S. (1950), "Revealed Preference and the Utility Function," *Economica*, New Series, Vol. 17, May 1950.

Houthakker, H.S. (1956), "Economics and Biology Specialization and Speciation," *Kyklos*, Vol. 9, pp. 181-189.

Houthakker, H.S. and L.D. Taylor (1970), **Consumer Demand in the United States**, Second Edition, Harvard University Press.

Hurvich, L.M. and Jameson, D. (1957), "An Opponent-Process Theory of Color Vision," *Psychological Review*, Vol. 64, pp. 384-404.

Ironmonger, D.S. (1972), **New Commodities and Consumer Behavior**, Cambridge University Press.

Keynes, J.M. (1936), **The General Theory of Employment, Interest, and Money**, MacMillan Publishing Co.

Lancaster, K. (1966), "A New Approach to Consumer Theory," *Journal of Political Economy*, Vol. 74, pp. 132-157.

Lancry, P.J. and Fernando Saldanha (1988), "A Psychological Opponent Processes Theory of Consumption," in **Applied Behavioral Economics**, ed. by Sholomo Maital, Wheatsheaf Books, Sussex.

Manove, M. (1973), "Consumer Behavior and Preference Formation," CORE, Catholic University of Louvain, August 1973.

Maslow, A.H. (1970), **Motivation and Personality**, 2nd edition, Harper and Row Publishing Co.

Modigliani, F. and Brumberg, R. (1954), "Utility Analysis and the Consumption Function," in **Post Keynesian Economics**, ed. by K.K. Kurihara, Rutgers University Press.

Modigliani, F. and Brumberg, R. (1980), "Utility Analysis and Aggregate Consumption Functions: An Attempt at Integration," in *The Collected Papers of Franco Modigliani*, Vol. 2, ed. by A. Abel, MIT Press.

Pagan, A.R. and Wickens, M.R. (1989), "A Survey of Some Recent Econometric Methods," *Economic Journal*, Vol. 99, December 1989, pp. 962-1025.

Prais, S.J. and Houthakker, H.S. (1955), **The Analysis of Family Budgets**, Cambridge University Press.

Salmon, M. (1982), "Error Correction Mechanisms," *Economic Journal*, Vol. 92, pp. 615-629.

Sargan, J.D. (1964), "Wages and Prices in the United Kingdom: A Study in Econometric Methodology," in *Econometric Analysis for National Economic Planning*, ed. by P.E. Harat, G. Mills, and J.N. Whittaker, Butterworths.

Schelling, T.C. (1978), "Economics, or the Art of Self-Management," *American Economic Review*, Vol. 68, No. 2, May 1978, pp. 290-294.

Scitovsky, T. (1976), **The Joyless Economy**, Oxford University Press.

Sen, A.K. (1977), "Rational Fools: A Critique of the Behavioral Foundations of Economic Theory," *Philosophy and Public Affairs*, Vol. 6, 1977, pp. 317-345.

Shallice, T. (1988), **From Neuropsychology to Mental Structure**, Cambridge University Press.

Simon, H.A. (1986), "Rationality in Psychology and Economics," in **Rational Choice: The Contrast Between Economics and Psychology**, University of Chicago Press.

Soloman, R.L. (1980), "The Opponent-Process Theory of Acquired Motivation: The Costs of Pleasure and the Benefits of Pain," *American Psychologist*, Vol. 35, pp. 691-712.

Soloman, R.L. (1989), "How the Opponent-Process Theory of Motivation Came Into Economics," in **Psychological Foundations of Economic Behavior**, ed. by P.J. Albanese, Praeger.

Soloman, R.L. and Corbit, J.D. (1974), "An Opponent-Process Theory of Motivation: I. Temporal Dynamics of Affect," *Psychological Review*, Vol. 81, pp. 119-145.

Stigler, G.J. and Becker, G.S. (1977), "De Gustibus Non Est Disputandum," *American Economic Review*, Vol. 67, 16.2, March 1977, pp. 76-90.

Taylor, L.D. (1987), "Opponent Processes and the Dynamics of Consumption," in **Economic Psychology: Intersections in Theory and Application**, ed. by A.J. MacFadyen and H.W. MacFadyen, North Holland Publishing Company.

Taylor, L.D. (1989), "A Model of Consumption and Demand Based Upon Psychological Opponent Processes," in **Psychological Foundations of Economic Behavior**, ed. by P.J. Albanese, Praeger.

Taylor, L.D. and Houthakker, H.S. (1990), "Co-Integration and Habit Formation: A Reformulation of the Dynamics of the Houthakker-Taylor Models, presented at the Sixth World Congress of the Econometric Society, Barcelona, Spain, August 1990, Department of Economics, University of Arizona, Tucson.

Winston, G.C. (1980), "Addiction and Backsliding: A Theory of Compulsive Consumption," *Journal of Economic Behavior and Organization*, Vol. 1, 1980, pp. 295-324.

# CORNERS IN ORGANIZED FUTURES MARKETS

L. G.TELSER*
*Department of Economics*
*University of Chicago*
*1126 East 59th Street*
*Chicago, Ill. 60637*

**ABSTRACT.** Following a concise description of organized futures markets, the traders, and some of the rules and their purposes, necessary and sufficient conditions for corners in these markets are presented. It is shown that a profitable corner depends on what happens in the cash markets from its start to its termination. Activities in the futures market are ancillary. If the supply schedules in these spot markets remain constant then corners are usually not profitable.

## 1. Introduction

While the gap between theory and fact about organized futures markets is still present, it is narrower on many important topics than it once was. Theories about speculation and hedging, their effects on prices, output and inventories now rest on a solid empirical base. Economists at the Federal Trade Commission and the US Department of Agriculture deserve much praise for their pioneering studies that illuminate the theory and practise of organized futures markets. The FTC studies (1920) are a monumental source of information about the history and details of these markets. Duvel and Hoffman (1927 and 1928) and Hoffman (1930) contain sophisticated studies of the effects of the trades of large speculators on wheat and corn futures prices. Moreover, these are perhaps the first to study the relation between the velocity of trading and price volatility. Mehl (1930) examines hedging in detail and is still valuable. Until Hartzmark (1991), the only study of profits and losses of speculators based on their actual trades was that of Stewart (1949). This evidence shows that profits from futures trading are highly concentrated among relatively few accounts and that the commercial interests do far better than the noncommercial traders on their futures trading (see below p. 10 for the distinction between commercial and noncommercial traders). The view that hedgers pay for price insurance they buy from speculators, questioned by Hoffman (1941, p. 39) as well as by others, does not square with this evidence. Because commercials get a positive return on their futures positions, to the extent they are hedging, this hedging is costless.

* I am grateful to Frank Easterbrook and Virginia France for their helpful comments on an earlier draft. Responsibility for all remaining errors is mine.



*L. Phlips and L.D. Taylor (eds.), Aggregation, Consumption and Trade,* 159–167.

Many scholars in the field accept the close relation between the theory of money and the theory of futures markets.[1] We recognize that the standardized contracts traded on organized futures markets perform many quasi-monetary functions. They allow handlers of the commodity underlying the futures contracts to use them as temporary abodes of purchasing power. Active liquid markets can serve this function and thrive to the extent they do so. However, the gap between theory and fact about corners seems as wide as ever. Judging from some recent contributions in Anderson (1984) with the notable exception of Kilcollin's (1984) comments, this gap may even be wider than it was when Hoffman (1932 and 1941) analyzed corners and delivery problems on organized futures exchanges. Easterbrook (1984) is a notable contribution that emphasizes how fraud and deception are crucial elements behind attempts to corner. This essay is in the spirit of Easterbrook's contribution.

## 2. When Can a Corner Occur?

To describe the conditions that are necessary for a corner to take place on an organized futures market requires at the outset a statement of the assumptions about the rules governing trade in that market, the nature of the traders, and the properties of the commodity traded in that market. It must be understood that the survival of an organized exchange depends on the nature and enforcement of its rules as well as on the extent to which the customary practices of the exchange are guided by ethical and moral principles. Rules and the law cannot apply in every conceivable situation that occurs in these markets. New circumstances can arise that no written code can forsee so that the participants must act with discretion. Notions of what is fair and honorable may fill the gap between the letter of the law and the real situation. Therefore, the survival of an exchange depends on what is formally prescribed as well as on what is informally understood. The great principle of an organized exchange lies in this: To arrange matters so that the traders can focus their attention on price and quantity alone. The terms of the contract, all the rules and practices of the exchange aim toward this goal. The particulars of the commodity underlying the contract traded, the integrity of the traders, whether a seller has legal title to what he sells, whether a buyer will satisfy his obligations, all the details about the actual commodity, its location, how it will be shipped and when -- it is the purpose of the organized exchanges to subsume all of these factors by an appropriately designed futures contract. A well enough designed standardized contract can secure the benefits of specialization. Those who trade such contracts for others require only relatively simple instructions in terms of prices and quantities from those on whose behalf they trade. As agents, the traders are spared the task of learning all the details of the objects underlying the thing that they trade. These details are the proper domain of the principals upon whose instructions the traders act. Consequently, by directing their activities more narrowly, each becomes more proficient in his own business.

The leading exchanges in the US, the Chicago Board of Trade and the Chicago Mercantile Exchange, are among the survivors of a competitive industry with a long history. This history contains numerous instances of many kinds of fraud and sharp practices as well as attempts

---

[1] These theories are advanced in Houthakker (1959), Telser and Higinbotham (1977), Telser (1981), and especially Telser (1986).

to manipulate prices. Because many of the members of an exchange have a considerable financial stake in its survival, this furnishes them with an incentive to avoid and prevent actions that will threaten the survival of the exchange and, as a consequence, the survival of their own businesses as members of that exchange. Long experience demonstrates that survival of an exchange depends on the maintenance of a competitive market in which bona fide trades occur at valid prices. Moreover, because the trade on these exchanges comes from two sources, from the members of the exchange acting on their own behalf and from the members acting under instructions as agents for principals who are not themselves members of the exchange, there are additional temptations that members have, acting as agents, for enriching themselves at the expense of their customers. The history affords numerous ingenious examples of the various ways in which some of these agents have succumbed to temptation. The exchanges have reacted to many of these events by adding rules and by modifying existing rules with effects that may not be immediately clear to the public. For instance, since at least 1928, a customer of a broker trading on the Chicago Board of Trade has the right to know the identity of the other party to a transaction. One purpose of this rule is to prevent the broker from bucketing the order. Bucketing an order means that the broker takes the other side of the customer's order so that it is not filled by an actual trade on the exchange floor. An order filled by a transaction on the exchange floor is at a competitive, bona fide and public price. An example of another rule with a similar purpose prohibits wash trades. These are prearranged trades between pairs of colluding traders.

Organized exchanges define standard contracts of a given size. Trades in these contracts are the obligation of its clearing house and are fungible among its members without regard to the identity of the parties to the transaction. This means that the clearing house guarantees the integrity of the contract, and that all the contracts of the same maturity in a commodity are perfect substitutes for each other. The current price of a contract is determined in a bilateral auction by open outcry among the traders on the floor of the exchange. These prices may change from one trade to the next. A bid or offer by a trader on the floor is valid only at the instant when it is made and can then be accepted by any other trader. Selling a contract is referred to as going short, and buying as going long. A contract matures or expires at a prescribed time. Two different procedures are now used to settle futures contracts at maturity -- one is by delivery and the other is by cash settlement.

A short who still has an open position in the maturing month of the futures contract may close his obligation by buying a quantity of futures equal to his position in the futures market at any time up to the expiration date. The typical exchange rules allow 15 trading days for this purpose. Except for certain financial futures contracts in which there is cash settlement, in most other cases a short has the alternative of actual delivery of the commodity in order to settle his liability to the clearinghouse. This means presenting a warehouse receipt for that commodity of a deliverable grade (quality) in an approved warehouse to the clearing house. Because in many cases there are different qualities of the commodity, the rules of the exchange state which are deliverable and at what premiums or discounts with respect to a standard type. These premiums or discounts may be fixed or they may vary with prevailing prices for these qualities in cash markets. In the former case, Gresham's law determines which grade will be used to make actual delivery. This means that among an array of commodities that can be delivered at the same price, it is the cheapest that actually will be delivered. Because the commodity may be produced and stored over a wide area, there is an additional complication. The rules of the exchange must stipulate which are the acceptable locations and the discounts and premiums, depending on location, from a standard location. Here too depending on how these premiums and discounts are determined, Gresham's Law may explain where delivery is likely to occur. The clearing house in turn presents this warehouse receipt to the still outstanding long positions starting with the oldest one. A long who does not want to obtain actual possession of the commodity could sell the warehouse receipt on the cash market. There are two other important points about this procedure. First, a long with an open position during the delivery month cannot refuse delivery of a deliverable grade at a deliverable location for any reason when it is tendered by the clearing house. Second, such a long cannot be certain of exactly what, where or when his open long position will be settled by delivery if more than one grade or location is allowed by the rules of the exchange. The warehouse receipt represents an actual physical commodity available for use by the processors or merchants. It may be a quantity of wheat, corn, live cattle, live hogs, gold, silver, frozen pork bellies or US Treasury bonds. However, it does not follow that there is necessarily a one-to-one correspondence between the transaction in the warehouse receipt and the physical stock of the deliverable commodity. It is most important to recognize that the relation between the two is the same as the relation between the flow of money transactions and the stock of money, which is velocity. Unless the act of buying the warehouse receipt results in actual consumption -- that is, disappearance of the physical commodity -- a given receipt, corresponding to a given stock, can circulate more than once during a given time interval so that the velocity of warehouse receipts exceeds one just as the velocity of money exceeds one. It follows that even if the quantity of the stock of the commodity of deliverable grades in deliverable positions at the maturity month is below the open short interest, it may still be possible to settle all the open short positions by delivery provided the warehouse receipts circulate rapidly enough during the period allowed for delivery by the exchange.

Delivery as a means of settling open futures contracts in the maturity month was the universal practise in the US until the introduction of the Eurodollar futures contract on the Chicago Mercantile Exchange for which cash settlement is used in place of delivery. Cash settlement means that open positions at the maturity date of the futures contract are closed at a price based on spot prices in prescribed markets on that date. Exchange officials collect spot prices at prescribed times and locations in designated cash markets and compute the settlement price by formula using these spot prices. At first blush, cash settlement may seem less costly than delivery to close positions of maturing futures contracts; however, it would not be acceptable to the traders unless the spot prices come from liquid and competitive markets. The alternative of physical delivery dominates cash settlement when there are many diverse qualities of the commodity, it is costly to ship them, the cash markets are widely scattered, and trade in particular grades at these markets is relatively inactive compared with the activity at the organized exchange where futures are traded. The very conditions that explain why physical delivery dominates cash settlement can breed attempts to corner. The cash markets must be almost as well-organized and active as the futures market itself before they can be a reliable source of spot prices for use in cash settlement of maturing futures contracts. It is this organization and activity that would seem to explain the successful use of cash settlement for the Standard and Poor 500 futures contract and the Eurodollar futures contract, both traded on the Chicago Mercantile Exchange. The Eurodollar market in London and the New York Stock Exchange are both examples of liquid and competitive markets.

Although not entirely accurate, it suffices for present purposes to say that only exchange members can trade on the floor of an organized futures market in the US.[2] These traders are either principals or agents. As principals they trade on their own account, and as agents they trade under the instructions given them by their customers. It is also useful to distinguish between commercial and noncommercial traders. The former are directly involved in the commodity so that they may be processors, merchants, operators of mutual or pension funds, banks, farmers, ranchers, mining companies, refiners, shipping firms and so on, depending on the thing underlying the futures contract. Only commercial traders are hedgers, but not necessarily all commercial positions in futures are hedging positions. Presumably the commercial traders have more information about the factors affecting the prices of the thing traded on the futures market. The noncommercial traders are not directly involved in the business. Surveys of who trades on organized futures markets obtained by questioning brokers to find out who their customers are turn up members of the clergy, teachers, physicians, dentists, housewives, lawyers, retired persons, businessmen in lines unrelated to their futures trading, and others. Brokerage firms have been placed under increasingly stringent restrictions with respect to the qualifications of the customers they are allowed to accept. These regulations aim at ensuring that customers have a large enough net worth and some degree of awareness of the risks of trading futures contracts. Because brokers advance their self-interest by having customers who get profits from their trades, it is not apparent that these regulations would change the composition of the noncommercial clientele of the brokers.

Something more must be said about what happens on the floor of the exchange. The floor traders can see the bids and offers and they can see the accepted prices. People who are not on the floor can only see the accepted prices and quantities as recorded on the tape. Therefore, the floor traders have more information about what is going on during a trading session than does anyone who is not present on the floor. However, pertinent information about the more fundamental factors affecting prices is more readily accesible to those who are not engaged in the hurley burley of actual trading. Indeed, unless there were some benefits to being off the floor, the trade coming from the outside would be incomprehensible.

A definition of a corner is necessary at this point. A corner is a situation in which the holders of open positions on one side of the futures markets, either the longs or the shorts (typically the latter), are unable to close their positions at a competitive price. This begs the question of what is a competitive price. For now, take it to be a price that is not imposed by any individual or group of individuals.

Consider those organized futures markets where short futures positions still open during the maturing month can be settled by delivery. If the holders of each such position have an equal quantity of a deliverable grade at a deliverable location then there can be no corner. Hence a *necessary* but not a sufficient condition for a corner is that the open short positions in the maturing month exceed their supplies. Also, because a warehouse receipt for these supplies can circulate among the traders even if the short positions exceed the deliverable stock, it is still possible to close the short positions by tendering warehouse receipts. In the

---

[2] On some exchanges it is possible for someone to rent a seat from a member and execute his own trades on the floor of the exchange. Also some exchanges have special categories of members who are allowed to trade only certain contracts.

latter case, it may be that the velocity of the stock will be high enough at some high enough spot price to settle all the open positions. Because the rules of the exchange allow time for delivery, an attempt to corner has a better prospect of success, the larger the fraction of deliverable supplies it can control. If the corner controls all the deliverable supplies then the shorts cannot deliver except at the prices set by the holders of these stocks. Hence a *sufficient* condition for a successful corner is control over *all* of the deliverable supplies. However, this assertion is subject to some qualifications. First, stocks of deliverable qualities may be available that can be moved to deliverable locations. Hence the supply of deliverable stocks may not be perfectly inelastic even if some group does have control over all the currently available deliverable supplies at deliverable locations. Second, it should be pointed out that the rules of many exchanges would apply under these circumstances. Under these rules an exchange can stop trading in the contract and can force the longs to settle at a prescribed price.

Suppose there is a group that does control all the deliverable supplies in the final month of some futures contract. Suppose also that the corner is successful and forces the spot price up above the competitive level. Any attempt by the cornering group to sell their inventory of the deliverable supplies by hypothesis must be at a lower price than the one that the shorts were forced to accept in order to close their positions. Nor is this all. While the corner was being built up, the cornering group was buying both deliverable supplies and futures contracts. They were buying more futures contracts than deliverable supplies because otherwise the size of the short position could not have exceeded the stock of deliverable supplies and the corner would have no chance of success. Because these purchases by the cornering group constitute an increase in the demand for both the futures and the spot commodity, it must raise both the spot and the futures prices -- even if the shorts in futures and the sellers of the spot supplies suspect nothing -- so that the supply schedules that are their response to shifts of the demand schedule do not change and are not infinitely elastic.[3] The *futures* prices at which the cornering longs will take delivery are determined when these longs opened their long positions in futures, which is well before the maturity of the futures contracts. The profit of the corner depends entirely on what happens to the spot price, not only when the corner is under construction and when the shorts are forced to pay unduly high spot prices to the corner in order to close their positions, but also on the spot prices at which the corner eventually sells its spot positions. The latter spot prices must be lower than the spot prices at which the corner settled with the shorts and they must also be lower than the prices at which the corner acquired these supplies when the corner was starting. That is, given no change in the underlying supply and demand conditions for the actual commodity and reckoning the profit at the spot prices when the cornerers acquired and disposed of deliverable supplies, the cornerers have a loss. They have only one possible source of gain. It stems from the higher spot price extorted from the shorts with an open position in the

---

[3] If the supply schedule is infinitely elastic then shifts in the demand schedule would not affect the market clearing price. Hence the increase in demand would not change the current market clearing price. If the supply schedule remained constant then the longs would close their positions at the same price at which they opened them and would break even, ignoring transaction costs.

maturing month of the futures contract who are without deliverable supplies. It does not follow from this argument that the corner gets a net profit even if it is successful in pushing up the spot price during the maturity month. It must subtract from this gain the loss it will bear when it sells the cornered deliverable supplies. In the parlance of futures markets, this is known as 'disposing of the corpse.'[4] This is not to say that a profitable corner is impossible. It depends on how high a price the longs can extract from those shorts who have an open position and no chance of satisfying their obligations by tendering a warehouse receipt in the final days of the maturing futures contract.

An instructive situation pertinent to this analysis occurred in 1930 and 1931. There were very large supplies of wheat in the US relative to the demand. It was the onset of the Great Depression. The Hoover administration embarked on a program to raise grain prices by means of a price support program in which the Federal Farm Board, a new Federal agency, purchased wheat on the open market. It not only financed the purchase of actual wheat, but also bought wheat futures and especially the 1931 May wheat contract. As a result and despite the large supply of wheat, in May, the price of this May contract surged to a 20 cent per bushel premium over the July contract. This is a very big premium. Although the Federal Farm Board cornered the 1931 May contract, presumably by inadvertence, it could hardly sell its wheat inventory at a profit. The result was not a profitable corner (Hoffman, 1941, pp. 62 - 7).

Consider the situation facing those who contemplate taking a short position. These people do not know that others plan an attempt to corner. Let the construction of the corner begin. The futures and the spot prices must rise for the reasons given above. What would a speculator observe in this situation? He may have thought that supplies were in line with prevailing demand conditions but now he sees prices are higher in both the futures market and in the spot markets. A speculator suspecting a corner would avoid going short. Less sophisticated traders, especially a naive chart reader, would be more inclined to float with the tide and go long than go short. By selling futures, a short commences a struggle with the longs that must terminate when the futures contract expires. Models of this situation that allow only two or three trading periods omit crucial aspects. It is better to think of a continuous interval from the opening to the expiration of the futures contract. During this interval, anyone with an open position can enter the futures market and attempt to take an offsetting position. Who will blink first -- the longs or the shorts?

Because all futures contracts are mortal, all must terminate and, unlike death, everyone knows the termination date. Therefore, all open positions must close by a certain date. If there is an increase on the demand side and no change of supply, then the futures price must be higher unless the supply is infinitely elastic. If the supply schedule does not change and is not infinitely elastic, then the longs will discover that they have closed their positions at a lower price on average than the prices they paid when they bought futures. Therefore, their futures trading will have resulted in losses. However, if the longs more or less correctly anticipate that the excess supply schedule of the commodity will be smaller later than it is now, then they will be able to sell their long positions later at a higher price than they paid

---

[4] For analysis of this aspect of the difficulties encountered by those who plan corners, see Hieronymus (1971, pp. 309-10).

at the time when they bought the contracts. If so, the longs will have obtained a profit. Moreover, it will also follow that stocks of the commodity will be lower than the shorts had expected. Indeed were this not so, the shorts would have asked higher prices at the time they sold futures. An outside observer would see that prices are higher than they were when trading in the futures contract had begun. This is no corner. On the contrary it shows how a market responds to an unanticipated reduction of the excess supply. Some traders (the longs) may have anticipated, and others (the shorts) may not have anticipated these new conditions. The former gets profits and the latter, losses.[5]

The central point of this analysis directs attention to the state of competition in the cash markets, and not the organized futures markets, as the source of conditions that may encourage attempts to corner. Diverse qualities of the actual commodity traded in scattered locations in cash markets without the elaborate structure and rules of the organized exchanges may lack enough publicity and liquidity to stifle incipient corners. The organized exchanges, aware of these problems in cash markets, choose deliverable grades and locations that will discourage the use of futures markets as a means of obtaining the actual commodity. Owing to these rules and to the inherent obstacles of profits from corners, they are a minor offset to the net benefit the public derives from organized futures markets.

---

[5] While the silver episode in 1979 and 1980 is instructive, it is not a corner judging from the evidence given by the Commodity Futures Trading Commission to Congress (CFTC, 1981). It represents a struggle between the longs -- the Hunts and their associates -- and the shorts to see which was the better predictor of silver prices. Owing to a steady increase in the industrial demand for silver, the US Treasury inventory of silver fell steadily, forcing the Treasury in 1963 to abandon its policy of selling silver at a fixed price. (The $1.29 per ounce of silver had been set by the first Secretary of the Treasury, Alexander Hamilton.)

Starting at the end of August, 1979, weekly average silver prices were below $10 per ounce. By the end of January, 1980, the price touched nearly $50 per ounce. Four months later it had fallen to a level not far above the August, 1979 price. During this period, while there was little change in the quantity of silver refined from primary sources, the quantity of silver refined from scrap rose by about 75 per cent to a level above the primary output (CFTC Report, 1981, Fig. V-7). The Hunts and their associates held large long positions in silver futures on both Comex and the Chicago Board of Trade. The reporting positions in these markets were either hedging or spreading, and only a small proportion were short speculations (CFTC Report, 1981, pp. 19, 25). Nothing is known about the composition of the nonreporting positions. The reporting short hedgers had little difficulty in meeting their futures obligations. Indeed, they sold large quantities of silver to the Hunts at prices ranging up to $35 per ounce. After the price broke in January, 1980, the Hunts were in great financial distress. They had accumulated large debts with silver as collateral now selling at prices far below what they had paid. In this case the laurels (and profits) went to the shorts.

## REFERENCES


Anderson, Ronald W., ed. (1984), *The industrial organization of futures markets*, Lexington, MA, Lexington Books.

Commodity Futures Trading Commission (1981), *Report to the Congress in response to Section 21 of the Commodity Exchange Act*, P.L. No. 96-276, 96th Congress, 2d Session, Section 7,94 Stat. 542 (June 1, 1980), May 29, 1981.

Duvel, J.W.T. and G. Wright Hoffman (1927), *Speculative transactions in the 1926 May wheat futures*, US Dept of Agriculture Bulletin 1479, Washington, D.C.: US Government Printing Office.

Duvel, J.W.T. (1928). *Major transactions in the 1926 December wheat future.* US Dept of Agriculture Technical Bulletin No. 79, Washington,D.C.: US Government Printing Office.

Easterbrook, Frank H. (1986), "Monopoly, manipulation and the regulation of futures markets," *Journal of Business*, 59:S103-S127.

Federal Trade Commission (1920), *Report on the grain trade*, Washington, D.C.: US Government Printing Office.

Hartzmark, Michael L. (1991), "Luck versus forecast ability: determinants of trader performance in futures markets," *Journal of Business*, 64:49-74 (January).

Hieronymous, Thomas A. (1971), *Economics of futures trading for commercial and personal profit*, New York: Commodity Research Bureau, Inc.

Hoffman, G. Wright (1932), *Futures trading upon organized commodity markets in the United States*, Philadelphia: University of Pennsylvania Press.

Hoffman, G. Wright (1941), *Grain prices and the futures market: a 15-year survey, 1923-1938*. US Department of Agriculture Technical Bulletin No. 747, Washington, D.C.: US Government Printing Office.

Houthakker, H.S. (1959), "The scope and limits of futures trading," *The allocation of economic resources*, Abromovits *et al*, pp. 134-59, Stanford: Stanford University Press.

Kilcollin, Thomas E. (1984), "Comment [on Kyle]," Anderson, Ronald W., ed., *The industrial organization of futures markets*, pp. 189-91, Lexington, MA, Lexington Books.

Kyle, Albert S. (1984), A theory of futures market manipulations, Anderson, Ronald W., ed., *The industrial organization of futures markets*, pp. 141-88, Lexington, MA, Lexington Books.

Mehl, J.M. (1931), *Hedging in grain futures*, US Department of Agriculture Circular No. 151, Washington, D.C.: US Government Printing Office.

Stewart, Blair (1949), *An analysis of speculative trading in grain futures*. US Department of Agriculture Technical Bulletin No. 1001, Washington, D.C.: US Government Printing Office.

Telser, Lester G. and Harlow N. Higinbotham (1977), "Organized futures markets: costs and benefits," *Journal of Political Economy*, 85:969-1000 (October).

Telser, Lester G. (1981), "Why there are organized futures markets," *Journal of Law and Economics*, 24:1-22 (April).

Telser, Lester G. (1986), "Futures and actual markets: how they are related," *Journal of Business*, 59:S5-S20 (April).

# OIL FUTURES AND STRATEGIC STOCKS AT SEA

PETER MØLLGAARD and LOUIS PHLIPS*
*Department of Economics*
*European University Institute*
*Badia Fiesolana*
*I-50016 S. Domenico di Fiesole (FI)*
*Italy*

ABSTRACT. A theoretical model explaining the determination of prices in the markets for North Sea crude oil is set up. Three markets are analysed in a three-stage game in which market concentration increases by each stage: In the first stage, the International Petroleum Exchange is modeled as a thick futures market. This market is also used to hedge against the uncertain outcome of the 15-Day forward market, modeled in the second stage. There, a small club of traders enter futures contracts knowing that this will affect the storage decision and thereby the spot price profile. The third stage models the spot market as a two-period duopoly with inventories. The strategic effect of, and interaction between, inventories and futures positions is investigated.

## 1. Introduction

In his *The World Price of Oil* (1976), Henk Houthakker wondered why there existed no futures market for oil. Oil is a relatively standardised commodity that is stored under the ground or the sea by Mother Nature and storable above the ground and at sea. A standardised futures contract is easy to design. Let us quote (p. 2):

* Many thanks to Robert Waldmann for lucid comments. The usual disclaimer applies.



*L. Phlips and L.D. Taylor (eds.), Aggregation, Consumption and Trade*, 169–196.

"For oil, there has been nothing like the Chicago wheat market or the London copper market, where prices are set daily by the offers of producers and the bids of consumers, with considerable participation by merchants and speculators.

Why does petroleum lack such a central market? In common with most commodities that are traded on futures markets, petroleum is storable. While not as homogeneous as copper, it is not more heterogeneous than wheat, and a serviceable standard contract would not be hard to design. Although transportation costs are relatively more important than for most centrally traded commodities, this would not seem an insuperable obstacle either. Perhaps the main reason for the failure of a central market to develop is that for many years the industry has been dominated by integrated companies that handle oil from the well to the gasoline pump. Merchants, brokers, and other intermediaries are relatively unimportant; as a result, arm's-length transactions have traditionally been less prevalent in petroleum than in many other raw materials. The significance of this point is that the integrated companies appear to be losing much of their control over crude oil, so that arm's-length transactions will become more common. In due course, a central market may emerge."

In the eighties, Houthakker's forecast became a reality. In the US, the Nymex crude oil contract for West Texas Intermediate (WTI) was successfully launched in 1983, as a result of the increased volatility of the price of oil after the Iranian revolution. In the meantime, North Sea oil was discovered. The need for "forward" trading of Brent oil was felt for the same reason and led (around 1986) to a standardised Contract for Brent crude oil, on what began to be called the "Brent 15-Day market". Initially, the pairwise contracts were "forward" in the strict sense of the word, that is, the particular seller had to deliver to his particular trading partner. Gradually, this market developed into a futures market, that is, a market where a large proportion of the trade was for hedging and speculation purposes only. On top of it, the International Petroleum Exchange (IPE) launched -- with mixed success -- a classic crude oil futures contract,[1] copied from the Nymex contract, in 1983. Today, two futures markets for Brent crude exist on top of each other: The 15-Day and the IPE. The latter has a centralised open outcry exchange, a clearing house and a growing number of participants, including the majors, oil traders and locals. The Brent 15-Day market, to the contrary, is in the hands of a club of producers and traders.

The emergence of these markets motivates the present paper, which tries to simultaneously model the oligopolistic interplay of the majors who produce North Sea oil, for whom stocks at sea have a strategic role, and the presence of two futures markets for Brent crude on which these majors are also in a strategic situation, given their size and small number. To put it simply, this paper is an attempt to combine the modeling of strategic stocks, as pioneered by Allaz (1991) and further developed by Møllgaard (1990), with an effort to give a

---

[1] Its modifications are described in Phlips (1991).

game-theoretic explanation of how two futures markets for the same natural resource work when the corresponding spot market is controlled by a few producers. The basic approach is the one developed by Phlips and Harstad (1990 and 1991).

We shall confine the analysis to the minimum oligopoly model that allows for strategic interaction between supplies, that is, a duopoly. The game proceeds in three stages. In the first stage, the producers meet with an anonymous futures market, which is supposed to mimic the characteristics of the IPE. Having determined the futures price and positions, we model the 15-Day market as the second-stage subgame, where the oil companies trade bilateral futures contracts among themselves and with a speculator. These 15-Day contracts will depend on the positions already taken on the IPE. In the third stage, the companies then play a two-period extraction game. They each have a known total to extract over the two periods, but can use stocks of crude oil at sea and the extraction profile to manipulate prices so as to render their IPE and 15-Day positions more profitable. This comes about because the maturity futures price is taken to be the second-period spot price.

Time only plays a role in the two periods, 1 and 2, of the extraction game of the third stage. The two previous stages modelling the two futures markets allow the producers to precommit themselves to certain sales (or purchases) in the second period of the third stage. One can imagine that the IPE (in the first stage) opens and closes in period -0 leaving enough time for the producers to sell or buy IPE futures as they wish. When the IPE has closed, in period +0 the three market participants agree on their 15-Day contracts (in the second stage). When the 15-Day market closes, the extraction game of the third stage takes place. At this stage, the two producers decide on the optimal extraction, sales and storage profiles over the two periods. Only after this third stage will the stochastic demand be revealed and it is in this sense that time does not play a role in stages one and two modelling the futures markets: No relevant information is revealed during or between these two stages. This assumption allows us to focus on the strategic and speculative motives of futures market trading. We shall return to the interpretation of time in relation to the real world markets in Section 7.

The rest of the article is organized as follows: *Section 2* introduces the necessary notation for the spot market, which is described as a fairly traditional duopoly extracting an exhaustible resource. Everything is kept nicely linear or quadratic but the results carry through if these assumptions are substituted by appropriate convexity conditions. The following four sections then unravel the game backwards. *Section 3* solves the Cournot duopoly for the extraction game. The production schedule is unaffected by the futures markets while the sales depend on the net position taken by the producers on the two futures markets. To close this gap inventories must necessarily depend on these same net positions. *Section 4* analyses the strategic use of stocks by changing the basic model of the spot market slightly so as to highlight the strategic effect of holding inventories. These strategic inventories are also found to depend on the futures positions as well as on the producers' beliefs regarding the future spot price. *Section 5* then recedes to the second stage, modelling the 15-Day market. The set of contracts that are mutually beneficial to the market participants (*i.e.*, the core) is characterized. This will be a large set depending on price expectations and the futures positions taken on the IPE. *Section 6* takes us back to the first stage, where the producers' optimal positions on the IPE are modelled. Given the potential multiplicity of outcomes of the imperfectly organized 15-Day market, the IPE serves as a vehicle for the producers to speculate and hedge not only against the uncertainty of the spot market, but also against the non-uniqueness of the 15-Day market.

## 2. Setting the Stage: Duopoly, Storage and Futures

Since the play of all three stages focuses on the cash market, we shall begin our story here. Two companies, A and B, supply a homogeneous product, crude oil, to a spot market. Extraction takes place in two periods, 1 and 2, but each extractor $(i = A, B)$ has a known maximum $\bar{x}_i$ to be extracted over the two periods. We shall generally assume that cost conditions are such that it pays to pump all of $\bar{x}_i$. First-period production can however be stored in tankers rather than being sold immediately.

Let the first (alphabetical) subscript refer to the companies and the second (numeric) to the period. $q$ denotes sales and $x$ production. We impose the constraints

(1) $$q_{i1} + q_{i2} = x_{i1} + x_{i2} = \bar{x}_i, \qquad i = A,B$$

on total production and sales. Stocks at sea $s_i$ are produced but not sold in the first period, that is,

(2.1) $$s_i \equiv x_{i1} - q_{i1}$$

(2.2) $$q_{i2} = x_{i2} + s_i, \qquad (i = A,B)$$

so that the tankers have to be delivered in the second period.

Production and storage are not costless activities. We assume that production costs, C, are convex, and for simplicity, that they are quadratic in the number of barrels pumped:

(3) $$C_{it} = \tfrac{1}{2}\, c_t\, x_{it}^2 \qquad (i = A,B; \quad t = 1,2).$$

The cost of storage, I, is taken to be linear in the number of barrels stored,

(4) $$I_i = j\, s_i \qquad (i = A,B; \quad j \geq 0),$$

and the profit of company $i$ thus becomes

(5) $$\Pi_i = p_1\, q_{i1} + p_2\, q_{i2} - (C_{i1} + C_{i2} + I_i) + (p^F - p_2)\, N_i,$$

where $p_1$ and $p_2$ are the spot prices in the two periods and $p^F$ and $N_i$ are the futures price and the net position resulting from the two first stages of the game.

To complete the description of the spot market, we propose linear inverse demand functions[2] to determine the spot prices:

(6.1) $$p_t = \alpha - b\, q_t\,, \qquad \text{where} \qquad q_t = q_{At} + q_{Bt}, \qquad t = 1,2$$

and where the strength of demand, $\alpha$ , is a stochastic variable which is perceived by the agents as being distributed normally with unknown mean $\hat{\alpha}$ and known variance $Var(\alpha) = 1$:

(6.2) $$\alpha \sim N(\hat{\alpha},1)\ .$$

The participants on the futures markets hold different beliefs $E_i(\alpha)$ on $\hat{\alpha}$; they assign probability one to their own belief (their subjective probability distribution) and (thus) probability zero to the beliefs of the other players. We are thus in a situation of inconsistent prior beliefs in the sense of Selten (1982).[3]

The risk-averse producers' ex-ante payoffs are modelled according to the mean-variance model:

(7) $$W_i = E_i(\Pi_i) - \frac{K_i}{2} Var(\Pi_i)\ ,$$

---

[2] In earlier papers [Brianza, Phlips and Richard (1990); Phlips and Harstad (1991 and 1990)] the specification $q_t = \alpha' - \beta\, p_t$, leading to the inverse demand curve

$$p_t = \frac{\alpha'}{\beta} - \frac{1}{\beta} q_t\ ,$$

was chosen. While this gives us a natural interpretation of $\alpha'$ as the level of demand, the notational simpler version with $\alpha = \alpha'/\beta$ and $b = 1/\beta$ has been chosen here. The 'strength' of demand $\alpha$ and the 'level' of demand $\alpha'$ are thus related through $\alpha = a'b$.

[3] It will take us too far from the main argument to discuss the origin of the differences in beliefs. We take it for an empirical fact that traders act on differences in subjective probability distributions (agreeing to disagree) even if they hold the same information (which they thus interpret differently), optimism and pessimism being inexplicable motivations for trading. Everyday futures and financial markets are crowded with busily trading agents that share the same information, thereby rejecting any zero-trade theorem. On optimistic and conservative standards of behaviour, see Greenberg (1990). On rejecting the rational expectations, hypothesis, see Lovell (1986). On informational differences leading to different positions, see Stein (1987) and p. 27.

where $K_i$ measures constant absolute risk aversion.[4] The expected profit is readily found by taking i's expectation of (5). The variance of the profit can be shown to be

$$\text{(8)} \qquad Var(\Pi_i) = (\bar{x}_i - N_i)^2.$$

We shall leave the description of the modelling of the 15-Day market and the IPE for Sections 5 and 6. Here we follow many a good theatre play, and first offer the solution to the final stage, in which the strategic effects of stocks are highlighted.

## 3. Stage Three: Cournot Duopoly and the Extraction Game

First note that the variability of profits arises from the unhedged part $(\bar{x}_i - N_i)$ of total extraction [see (8)) and $Var(\alpha)(=1)$]. It is unaffected by the time profile of sales or production. In order to decide on these time profiles, the companies maximize $W_i$ with respect to $x_{i1}$, $q_{i1}$, $x_{i2}$, $q_{i2}$, and $s_i$, which amounts to maximizing expected profits subject to the constraints (1) and (2).

Manipulation of the first-order conditions leads to the following extraction schedule:

$$\text{(9.1)} \qquad x_{i1} = \frac{c_2}{c_1+c_2}\bar{x}_i - \frac{2j}{c_1+c_2} = \delta_1\bar{x}_i - \frac{2j}{c_1+c_2}, \qquad i = A,B$$

$$\text{(9.2)} \qquad x_{i2} = \frac{c_1}{c_1+c_2}\bar{x}_i + \frac{2j}{c_1+c_2} = \delta_2\bar{x}_i + \frac{2j}{c_1+c_2}, \qquad i = A,B,$$

where the first term represents cost smoothing:

$$\text{(9.3)} \qquad \delta_1 = \frac{c_2}{c_1+c_2} = \frac{c_2x}{c_1x + c_2x} = \frac{\frac{1}{2}c_2x^2}{\frac{1}{2}c_1x^2 + \frac{1}{2}c_2x^2}$$

$$\text{(9.4)} \qquad \delta_2 = \frac{c_1}{c_1+c_2} = \frac{c_1x}{c_1x+c_2x} = \frac{\frac{1}{2}c_1x^2}{\frac{1}{2}c_1x^2 + \frac{1}{2}c_2x^2}.$$

The chosen quadratic form of the cost function implies that comparing the total cost of producing a given quantity, $x$, in one period with the total cost of producing the same amount in both periods is equivalent to comparing the marginal cost, $c_tx$, in this period with the sum of marginal costs and is equivalent as well to just comparing increments, $c_t$, in the

[4] This follows automatically if the underlying preferences are represented by a utility function that is exponential in profits and if profits follow the normal distribution. See Newbery and Stiglitz (1981), pp. 74-75.

marginal cost. At any rate, (9.1) has the natural interpretation that the higher the cost of production in the second period (the higher $\delta_1$), the more that should be produced in advance in period 1. Vice-versa for second-period production: The higher the cost of first-period production, relatively speaking, the more of it that should be postponed to the cheaper second period. The second term of (9.1) and of (9.2) compares the costliness of storage with that of production. Not surprisingly, we find that the higher the cost of storage, the less that should be produced in advance and the more that should be postponed to the second period. Note that the optimal extraction policy does not depend on the futures positions taken.

The sales schedule for company A, say, is found to be

(10.1) $$q_{A1} = \frac{1}{2}\bar{x}_A - \frac{1}{3}N_A + \frac{1}{6}N_B + \frac{1}{6}\left(\frac{j}{b}\right) \quad \text{and}$$

(10.2) $$q_{A2} = \frac{1}{2}\bar{x}_A + \frac{1}{3}N_A - \frac{1}{6}\left(\frac{j}{b}\right)$$

and its stocks of crude oil can therefore be expressed as[5]

(11.1) $$s_A = \frac{1}{2}\,\Delta\,\delta\,\bar{x}_A + \frac{1}{3}N_A - \frac{1}{6}N_B - \frac{1}{6}\gamma j\,, \quad \text{where}$$

(11.2) $$\Delta\delta = \delta_1 - \delta_2 \quad \text{and}$$

(11.3) $$\gamma = \frac{12b + c_1 + c_2}{b(c_1 + c_2)}\,.$$

That sales depend on the net short futures positions in the manner shown in equations (10) is in perfect concordance with the findings in Phlips and Harstad (1991) (see equations (6) there). In addition, we find that sales depend on the term $j/b$ which relates the marginal cost of storage to the slope of the inverse demand curve, and thus to the marginal revenue of the operation. We see that the higher the marginal cost of storage, the lower will be stocks and thus the lower will be second-period sales. First-period sales will be correspondingly higher.

The size of inventory holdings is given by (11.1). The first term shows the cost-smoothing purpose of stocks. If $c_2 > c_1$ so that $\Delta\delta > 0$, a part of second-period sales should be produced in the first, less costly period and stored. This operation should take the cost of storage into account, as indicated by the fourth term, from which it is seen that higher cost of storage lowers the optimal level of stocks, as indeed should be the case. The second term of (11.1) shows that if producer A has precommitted herself by taking a short position on the futures markets $(N_A > 0)$, then part of this quantity will optimally be met by sales from stocks. If the rival takes a similar position $(N_B > 0)$, this lowers the profitability of the operation, thereby also lowering the optimal level of stocks for company A. Aggregate stocks $(s_A + s_B)$ depend positively on the aggregate net position $(N_A + N_B)$.

---

5 Using (2), (9.1) and (10.1).

Before discussing the strategic use of stocks, let us examine the expected spot prices:

$$(12.1) \qquad E(p_1) = \hat{p} + \frac{1}{6}b(N_A + N_B) - \frac{1}{3}j$$

$$(12.2) \qquad E(p_2) = \hat{p} - \frac{1}{6}b(N_A + N_B) + \frac{1}{3}j$$

$$(12.3) \qquad \hat{p} = \hat{\alpha} - \frac{1}{2}b(\bar{x}_A + \bar{x}_B) .$$

$\hat{p}$ is the price that would be obtained in both periods if the futures markets and the storage facility did not exist. Net short futures positions $(N_i > 0)$ represent a binding commitment to furnish the second-period cash market with a certain amount of crude, and to the extent that this amount is already sold at the price $p^F$, the companies have a common interest to manipulate prices by lowering $p_2$ (and therefore raising $p_1$).

## 4. The Strategic Use of Stocks

The strategic use of stocks is in many ways similar to that of futures positions. Indeed, by undertaking a larger production in the first period and storing some of it for sale in the second period, the companies incur the extra cost of production and the cost of storage in the first period. In the second period these costs are sunk and the supply from stocks is costless. Stocks therefore represent a credible commitment to raise second-period sales, thereby offering a potential position as a Stackelberg leader.

In a more general model, the strategic effect of inventories would imply that total production was increased and that the average price was lower than if storage were impossible.[6] The producers are trapped in a suboptimal Nash equilibrium because both are trying to position themselves as leaders. Most of this strategic effect is so far lost in our model since the oil companies are required to produce and sell a given total (see (1)). What is left is the direct effect of storage costs on prices, whereby higher cost of storage discourages holding inventories and leads to higher immediate sales.

To illustrate this point, we change the model slightly for the sake of this subsection. It is crucial that the companies be allowed to determine the size of total production. We therefore abandon the second equality of constraint (1) and only require total production to be sold by the end of period 2. To keep things simple, we also assume that demand only materializes in the second period, which implies that everything that is produced in the first period is stored:

$$(13.1) \qquad x_{i1} = s_i$$

[6] See Allaz (1991) and Møllgaard (1990).

(13.2) $$q_{i2} = x_{i1} + x_{i2}.$$

The situation is more complicated than before since uncertainty now not only pertains to the average price that results from a known total production, but involves the determination of this total itself.

Maximization of $w_i$ with respect to $x_{i2}$ results in the following sales for company A:

(14) $$q_{A2} = s_A + \frac{1}{D}\{b[\Delta(\alpha) + b(s_B - s_A) - b(N_B - N_A) + K_B(s_B - N_B) - K_A(s_B - N_B)]$$

$$+ (b + c_2 + K_B)[E_A(\alpha) - b(s_A + s_B) + (b+K_A)(N_A - s_A)]\} ,$$

where $D = (2b + c_2 + K_A)(2b + c_2 + K_B - b^2 \geq 0$, $\Delta(\alpha)$ is the difference in opinion $(E_A(\alpha) - E_B(\alpha))$ on $\hat{\alpha}$, $(s_B - s_A)$ is the difference in stock levels and $(N_B - N_A)$ is similarly the difference in futures positions. $(s_i - N_i)$ represents the unhedged part of stocks, so that the two last terms in the first square brackets represent the different risk valuation of unhedged stocks.

The effect of an increase in the stocks of company A is seen to increase its own sales by

(15) $$\frac{dq_{A2}}{ds_A} = \frac{1}{D}c_2 (2b + c_2 + K_B) > 0 ,$$

whereas it will decrease company B's sales by

(16) $$\frac{dq_{B2}}{ds_A} = -\frac{1}{D}c_2 b < 0 ,$$

so that total production and thus total sales are increased

(17) $$\frac{dq}{ds_A} = \frac{1}{D}c_2(b + c_2 + K_B) > 0 ,$$

while the spot price at maturity is lower,

(18) $$\frac{dp_2}{ds_A} = -\frac{1}{D}bc_2(b + c_2 + K_B) < 0 ,$$

than would otherwise be the case.

The expressions for the sales quantities (14) can be substituted back into the payoff functions (7) which then can be maximized to find the subgame-perfect first-period production (or, equivalently, stocks). These will depend on the beliefs about the strength of demand and on the futures positions taken at an earlier stage:

(19.1) $$s_A = \nu_A E_A(\alpha) + \phi_A E_B(\alpha) + \psi_A N_A + \omega_A N_B$$

$$(19.2) \qquad s_B = \phi_B E_A(\alpha) + \nu_B E_B(\alpha) + w_B N_A + \psi_B N_B \ ,$$

where the coefficients $\nu_i$, $\phi_i$, $\psi_i$ and $w_i$ depend on the original parameters of the model, b, $c_1$, $c_2$, $K_A$, $K_B$ as reported in the appendix.[7]

The main difference in comparison with the solution to the model where total production is given [see (9-11)] is that the beliefs regarding the strength of demand enter the production/storage/sales decisions explicitly [see (14) and (19)]. Intuition suggests that production depends positively on the agent's own expectations regarding the strength of demand (*i.e.*, $\nu_i > 0$) and negatively on the rival's (*i.e.*, $\phi_i < 0$), but this may not be true for all parameter constellations. Another difference is that risk aversion affects decision making at the production level. This was not the case when total production was given, because in that case uncertainty regarding the strength of demand only affected profits through the average price $\hat{p}$ that pertained to the given quantity [see (12)], whereas here the total quantity can also be chosen freely. This renders the decision process much more complex. In a sense, the effect of changing the model to allow for strategic stocks has been to replace $\bar{x}_A$ and $\bar{x}_B$ in (9) and (10) by $E_A(\alpha)$ and $E_B(\alpha)$ in (14) and (19), and to render the corresponding coefficients more complex.

Summarizing, we have found that the production, sales and storage decisions of the two rivals of the duopoly cash market depend on the futures positions taken in advance. If there *is* a constraint on total production, then this enters the decisions, and storage mainly serves as a cost-smoothing device. If the restriction is *not* present (or not effective), then the agents' beliefs regarding the strength of demand are important, and the inventories serve a strategic purpose (in addition to the cost smoothing). The two companies are trapped in the non-cooperative Nash equilibrium of the prisoner's dilemma type: The effect of simultaneously positive stocks of crude oil will raise total production (19) and lower the spot price at maturity (18). The cooperative outcome that is obtained if both agree not to store would yield higher profits, but then each company would have an incentive to defect (15), thereby making the other firm worse off (16). Since both firms simultaneously try to act as (Stackelberg-) leaders by precommitting themselves to higher sales through inventories, a sub-optimal Nash equilibrium results.[8]

We now move on to describe the futures markets and find the futures positions that are so crucial for the sales, storage and production schedules.

---

[7] We subsume the cost of storage in the cost of production of the first period. Since first-period production is not sold, the storage and the production decisions are essentially one and the same.

[8] The incentive to try to act as a leader depends crucially on the convexity of the cost functions (*i.e.*, on $c_1$ and $c_2$) as also noted by Arvan (1985). The more convex the cost function (the higher $c_1$ and $c_2$ are), the higher are the strategic inventories. For this reason it is difficult to separate the cost smoothing and the strategic motive for holding stocks.

**5. Stage Two: The 15-Day Market**

As mentioned above there are two futures markets for North Sea crude oil: The IPE and the 15-Day market. The 15-Day market, which is the subject of the present subsection, is characterised by there being only few big participants in the market. The functioning of the market is described in Mabro et al. (1986, ch. 12), and in Phlips (1991). It is "an informal, self-regulating club of North Sea producers, oil traders, refiners and brokers, each of which is in the market for a variety of reasons" [Mabro et al. (1986, p. 169)]. These market participants bargain about standardised forward contracts via telephone and the agreed-upon contracts are then telexed. This bargaining can only be realistically modelled at the cost of a considerable increase in complexity.[9] We shall refrain from this here and simplify the model to highlight the role played by our two producers, A and B.

To be specific we assume that only three agents take part in the 15-Day market: A, B and an oil trader, S, who is not interested in the crude oil *per se* but only in buying (selling) crude oil on the 15-Day market with the expectation of being able to sell (buy) it on the spot market at a higher (lower) price. Such agents are referred to as arbitrageurs or speculators in the literature and we shall not deviate from this habit.

So far the two futures markets have been described crudely by an aggregate futures price $p^F$ and the quantity, $N_i$, by which a producer $i (i = A,B)$ is net short. We now have to be more specific. Let $F_i$ denote the net position of player $i$ on the IPE and $f_i$ the net position on the 15-Day market, i.e.

$$N_i = F_i + f_i \qquad i = A,B,S. \tag{20}$$

We concentrate on the 15-Day positions in this subsection. Each of these $f_i$'s results from potentially four different contracts

$$f_i = f_{ij}' - f_{ji}' + f_{ik}' - f_{ki}', \quad \text{where } i = A,B,S, \quad i \neq j,\ j \neq k,\ i \neq k \quad \text{and all } f' \geq 0, \tag{21.1}$$

where $f'_{ik}$ signifies that $i$ is selling to $k$. In our model, what is making agents trade is differences in beliefs regarding the future spot price. This being the case, it will never happen that two contracts are set up where an agent $i$ both sells to and buys from another agent at different futures prices. If the futures price is equal in the two contracts it will only be the net position that matters anyway. We shall therefore let the signed quantity

$$f_{ij} = f_{ij}' - f_{ji}' \tag{22}$$

[9] This is the topic of our ongoing research.

denote the net position of i vis-à-vis j. $f_{ij} > 0$ implies that i takes a short position (sells futures) in the contract with j. We shall take this to mean that $f'_{ij} = f_{ij}$ and $f_{ji} = 0$. Then note that $f_{ji} = - f'_{ij} = - f_{ij}$, so that net positions on the 15-Day market can be written:

(21.2) $$f_A = f_{AB} + f_{AS}$$

(21.3) $$f_B = -f_{AB} + f_{BS}$$

(21.4) $$f_S = (f_{AS} + f_{BS}),$$

where $f_i > 0$ if the player is net short in total on the market. Nọte that $f_A + f_B + f_S = 0$.

The three agents, A, B, and S, trade on the expected spot price in period 2 and they all know that the spot price is formed according to (12.2 - 3). That is to say, they know that the producers' net positions on the two futures markets will influence the spot price or, to put it more polemically, that the producers will manipulate the time profile of spot prices, raising the first-period price where all sales are cash and lowering the second-period price where part of the sales have been made in advance (assuming that they are net short, *i.e.*, that $N_A + N_B > 0$). All this is common knowledge for the market participants and it will not discourage the speculator from trading on the market. What the market participants do not agree upon is the mean value of $\alpha$. Each has his firm opinion $E_i(\alpha)$ on this. They thus expect three different mean spot prices $E_i(p_2) = p_2^i$ according to their different beliefs on $\hat{\alpha}$ and according to (12.2-3). It follows from (6.2) that they perceive $p_2$ as being normally distributed with mean $p_2^i$ and unit variances.

## 5.1 THE SPECULATOR'S PAYOFF

We assume that the speculator is risk-neutral[10] and thus maximizes expected profit:

(23.1) $$E_S(\Pi_S) = \left(p_2^S - p_{AS}^{15}\right) f_{AS} + \left(p_2^S - p_{BS}^{15}\right) f_{BS} \ ,$$

where $p_{is}^{15}$ is the price of the contract that s agrees upon with i. (Such a contract is fully described by the pair $\left(p_{ij}^{15} \ , \ f_{ij}\right)$. The expected profit can be rewritten using (12.2 - 3):

(23.2) $$-E_S(\Pi_S) = \left[\hat{p}_S - \frac{1}{6}bF + \frac{1}{3}j\right] f_s + p_{AS}^{15} f_{AS} + p_{BS}^{15} f_{BS} \ ,$$

---

[10] To assume that he is risk averse does not change the analysis substantially.

where

$$\hat{p}_S = E_S(\hat{\alpha}) - \frac{1}{2}b(\bar{x}_A + \bar{x}_B)$$

and $F = F_A + F_B$ is the producers' joint net position on the IPE.

## 5.2 THE TWO PRODUCERS' PAYOFFS

The producers' payoffs from trading on the futures markets are found by substituting (10) and (12) into (7) and subtracting the profit that would have been made on the spot market in the absence of the futures markets. This leaves us with the following expressions

$$(24.1)\qquad W_A^{FUT} = (p^F - \hat{p}_A)N_A + \frac{1}{18}\left[b(N_A + N_B)^2 - j\,(7N_A - 2N_B)\right] - \frac{K_A}{2}(\bar{x}_A - N_A)^2$$

$$(24.2)\qquad W_B^{FUT} = (p^F - \hat{p}_B)N_B + \frac{1}{18}\left[b(N_A + N_B)^2 + j(2N_S - 7N_B)\right] - \frac{K_B}{2}(\bar{x}_B - N_b)^2 .$$

The first term on the r.h.s. of these expressions illustrates the immediate gain from having a futures market: $p^F$ is the average futures price and $\hat{p}_i$ is the spot price that i would expect in the absence of futures markets. If $p^F > \hat{p}_A$ then A should, *ceteris paribus* , take a net short position $N_A > 0$. The third term indicates the advantage of hedging the uncertain profit. In the case of complete hedging $\bar{x}_A = N_A$ and the term is effectively optimized. The second term shows the strategic effect on the spot market profits of having a futures market. This term occurs because taking futures positions provides a credible vehicle for precommitment of spot sales or purchases. Note that, for example, A's payoff varies proportionally with

$$(24.3)\qquad (N_A + N_D)^2 - \frac{j}{b}\,(7N_A - 2N_D)$$

and that the futures markets affect A's output even if he does not participate, namely via the rival's net position on these markets. Indeed, if $N_A = 0$, $W_A^{FUT}$ varies in proportion to

$$(24.4)\qquad N_B^2 + 2\frac{j}{b}N_B.$$

B's net position will always affect A's payoff positively in the absence of costly storage (j=0). This comes about because a producer with a zero position responds to the rival's position by shifting sales to the period with a higher price. If storage is possible at a cost this is no longer true for all values of $N_B$, as illustrated by Figure 1.

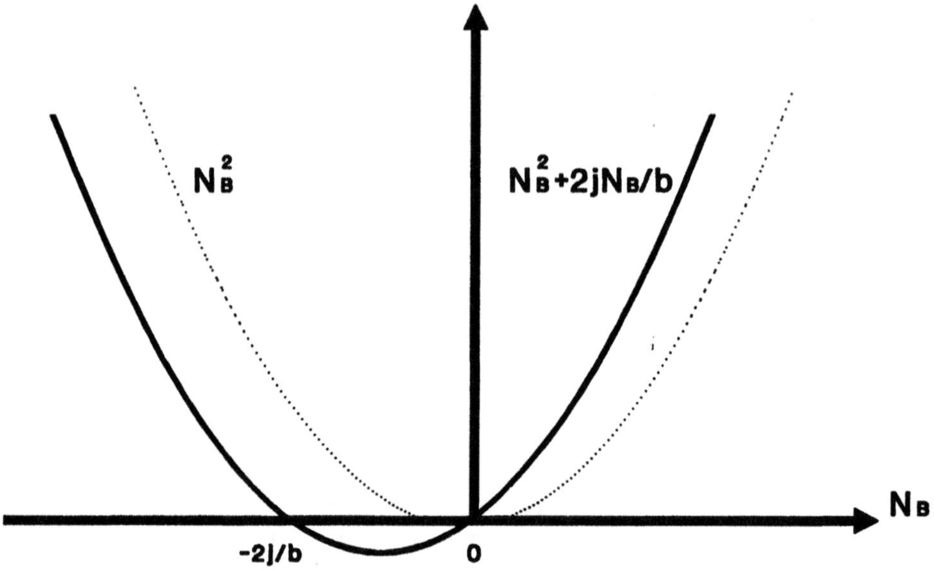


*Figure 1:* The effect of a unilateral futures position on the rival's profit

If B is long in the range

$$(24.5) \qquad 0 > N_B > -2\frac{j}{b} \qquad (N_A = 0) ,$$

then A's optimal response on the spot market is to shift sales [see (10)] with $N_B/b$ from period 1 where the price is then low [see (12.1)], to period 2 where the price is higher (12.2). Since the optimal extraction is independent of the futures positions (9), this operation can only be done via increased inventories (11.1). But increasing stocks has a cost, and so for small, long positions, B forces A to incur a loss since the cost of increasing the stocks dominates the extra expected revenue.[11]

The producers of course realize the strategic interdependence of their futures positions, an interdependence that stems from the effect of these positions on the equilibrium spot

[11] Note, however, that this result may hinge crucially on the assumptions of the model. In particular the uniflexibility of total production (1) seems important.

prices and quantities. Indeed, when taking positions on the futures markets, the producers weigh the speculative, the strategic and the hedging motives according to (24).

The payoffs of the two futures markets can be split up according to the market that gives rise to them, or, put differently, we find the subgame perfect equilibria by maximising the payoff of the second stage, the 15-Day market, for given positions on the IPE, before solving the first stage.

The ex-ante payoff stemming from the 15-Day market (including this market's effects on the spot market payoff) can be written:

$$(25.1) \qquad W_A^{15} = (p_{AB}^{15} - \hat{p}_A)\, f_{AB} + (p_{AS}^{15} - \hat{p}_A)\, f_{AS} + \tau_1\,(f_{AS} + f_{BS}) + \tau_{2A}\, f_{AS} + \tau_3\, f_{BS} + \tau_{4A}\, f_{AB} - \frac{K_A}{2}(f_{AB} + f_{AS})^2 ,$$

$$(25.2) \qquad W_B^{15} = (\hat{p}_B - p_{AB}^{15}\, f_{AB} + (p_{BS}^{15} - \hat{p}_B)\, f_{BS} + \tau_1(f_{AS} + f_{BS}) + \tau_3\, f_{AS} + \tau_{2B}\, f_{BS} - \tau_{4B}\, f_{AB} - \frac{K_B}{2}(f_{BS} - f_{AB})^2 ,$$

where

$$(25.3) \qquad \tau_1 = \frac{1}{18}b > 0$$

$$(25.4) \qquad \tau_{2i} = \frac{1}{9}bF - \frac{7}{18}j + K_i(\bar{x}_i - F_i) , \qquad i = A,B$$

$$(25.5) \qquad \tau_3 = \frac{1}{9}(bF + j)$$

$$(25.6) \qquad \tau_{4i} = -\frac{1}{2}j - K_i(\bar{x}_i - F_i) , \qquad i = A,B.$$

## 5.3 THE CONTRACT CURVES

Now, what can we say about the solutions to the 15-Day stage, without imposing further structure on the game? We require that any contract

$$(p_{ij}^{15} , f_{ij})$$

belongs to the contract curve between i and j, *i.e.*, it must be true that

$$MRS_i\left(p_{ij}^{15} ,f_{ij}\right) = MRS_j\left(p_{ij}^{15} ,f_{ij}\right),$$

where the marginal rates of substitution are given implicitly by (25) for the producers and (23) for the speculator. For example, the contract between the two producers should obey

$$(26) \qquad MRS_A^{AB} = \frac{\dfrac{\partial W_A^{15}}{\partial p_{AB}^{15}}}{\dfrac{\partial W_A^{15}}{\partial f_{AB}}} = \frac{\partial f_{AB}}{\partial p_{AB}^{15}} = \frac{\dfrac{\partial W_B^{15}}{\partial p_{AB}^{15}}}{\dfrac{\partial W_B^{15}}{\partial f_{AB}}} = MRS_B^{AB} .$$

These requirements are fulfilled if $f_{ij} = 0$, that is, if the two participants do not enter a contract. Less trivially, if $f_{ij} \neq 0$, (26) leads to

$$(27.1) \qquad (K_A + K_B)\, f_{AB} + K_A f_{AS} - K_B f_{BS} = (\hat{p}_B - \hat{p}_A) + K_A(\bar{x}_A - F_A) - K_B(\bar{x}_B - F_B)$$

$$(27.2) \qquad - K_A\, f_{AB} - (K_A + \frac{2}{9}b)\, f_{AS} - \frac{2}{9}b\, f_{BS} = (\hat{p}_A - \hat{p}_S) - K_A(\bar{x}_A - F_A) - \frac{1}{18}(bF + j)$$

$$(27.3) \qquad -K_B f_{AB} + \frac{2}{9}b\, f_{AS} + (K_B + \frac{2}{9}b) f_{BS} = (\hat{p}_S - \hat{p}_B) - K_B(\bar{x}_B - F_B) - \frac{1}{18}(bF + j) ,$$

which apply to the contracts $\left(p_{AB}^{15}, f_{AB}\right)$, $\left(p_{AS}^{15}, f_{AS}\right)$ and $\left(p_{BS}^{15}, f_{BS}\right)$, respectively.

Phlips and Harstad (1991) use an equivalent approach and find a similar system of equations.[12] The main differences are that the producers' positions on the IPE, $F_A$ and $F_B$ enter on the r.h.s. because they too can be used for hedging purposes; that their joint position on the IPE (F) enters because of the strategic effect of futures on the spot market (a feature which the two markets share); and that the cost of storage shows up since taking a futures position (on either market) changes optimal inventories (11.1).

The equational system (27) cannot be solved to obtain a unique set of three 15-Day contracts. There are two reasons for this. The first reason has to do with the fact that individual rationality points to a range of possible prices depending on the quantities. The second reason arises because (27) only determines the net positions $f_A$, and $f_B$ and $f_S$ uniquely, not the decomposition on the three quantities $f_{AB}$, $f_{AS}$ and $f_{BS}$. We discuss each point in turn.

## 5.4 INDIVIDUAL RATIONALITY

First, note that the futures prices, $p_{ij}^{15}$ do not appear in (27). All we can say about these prices is that they should be individually rational according to (23) and (25). Individual rationality simply states that any contract should contribute a non-negative amount to each player's payoff since a zero contribution can always be achieved by **not** entering the contract. This requirement puts the following bounds on the prices:

For the contract $\left(p_{AB}^{15}, f_{AB}\right)$:

[12] See their equations (13).

$$\text{(28.1)}\quad \hat{p}_A - K_A\left(\bar{x}_A - F_A - f_{AS} - \frac{1}{2}f_{AB}\right) + \frac{1}{2}j \le p_{AB}^{15}$$

$$\le \hat{p}_B - K_B\left(\bar{x}_B - F_B - f_{BS} + \frac{1}{2}f_{AB}\right) + \frac{1}{2}j \qquad \text{for } f_{AB} > 0\,;$$

for the contract $\left(p_{AS}^{15},\, f_{AS}\right)$:

$$\text{(28.2)}\quad \hat{p}_A + \left(\frac{K_A}{2} - \frac{1}{18}b\right)f_{AS} - \frac{1}{9}b(F + f_{BS}) - K_A(\bar{x}_A - F_A - f_{AB}) + \frac{7}{18}j \le p_{AS}^{15}$$

$$\le \hat{p}_S - \frac{1}{6}b(F + 2f_{AS} + f_{BS}) + \frac{1}{3}j \qquad \text{for } f_{AS} > 0;$$

and finally for the contract $\left(p_{BS}^{15},\, f_{BS}\right)$:

$$\text{(28.3)}\quad \hat{p}_B - \frac{1}{9}b(F + f_{AS}) + \left(\frac{K_B}{2} - \frac{1}{18}b\right)f_{BS} - K_B(\bar{x}_B - F_B + f_{AB}) + \frac{7}{18}j \le p_{BS}^{15}$$

$$\le \hat{p}_S - \frac{1}{6}b(F + f_{AS} + 2f_{BS}) + \frac{1}{3}j \qquad \text{for } f_{BS} > 0.$$

Note that the above three inequalities are true under the condition that $f_{AB}$, $f_{AS}$ and $f_{BS}$ be strictly positive. For each of them the inequality is reversed if the sign of the quantity is reversed. Observe also the following: The range of futures prices that are acceptable for the two players involved in a contract depends on the futures positions taken by the producers on the IPE, on the quantities of the other 15-Day contracts, on the expected spot price and on the cost of storage. This range may or may not be empty, depending on the values of these variables. In case the range is empty, this corresponds to the players agreeing on the contract

$$\left(p_{ij}^{15}, f_{ij}\right) = (0,0)$$

which is always a possibility. This just means that these two players do not find it profitable to enter a contract.

(28.1) says that if A is selling to B ($f_{AB} > 0$) then A will require a higher minimal sales price:

(1) The more she has already hedged on the IPE ($F_A$),
(2) the more she has already hedged in a contract with the speculator ($f_{AS}$),
(3) the higher is her spot price expectation ($\hat{p}_A$), and
(4) the higher is the cost of storage ($j$).

Buyer B will accept a higher maximal buying price

(1) The more he went short on the IPE ($F_B$),
(2) the more he went short in a contract with S ($f_{BS}$),
(3) the higher is his expected spot price ($\hat{p}_B$), and
(4) the higher is the cost of storage (j).

Note that the cost of storage raises the minimal selling price and the maximal buying price by the same amount, thus preserving the spread. Further, observe that the minimal selling price is increasing and the maximal buying price is decreasing in the quantity $f_{AB}$ of the contract. This ensures that the individually rational contract must have finite quantity. Indeed, it can be shown that the contract must satisfy *either*

$$(28.1a) \qquad 0 < f_{AB} < \frac{2}{K_A + K_B}\left(\hat{p}_B - \hat{p}_A + K_A(\bar{x}_A - F_A - f_{AS}) - K_B(\bar{x}_B - F_B - f_{BS})\right)$$

in the case of A selling to B, *or*

$$(28.1b) \qquad 0 > f_{AB} > \frac{2}{K_A + K_B}\left(\hat{p}_A - \hat{p}_B - K_A(x_A - F_A - f_{AS}) + K_B(\bar{x}_B - F_B - f_{BS})\right)$$

when B is selling to A.

The analysis of the contracts where the producers are selling to the speculator (28.2-3) follows the discussion above with the following two qualifications: Firstly, increased storage costs increase the producers' minimal selling price a bit more than the speculator's maximal buying price. Secondly, if $K_i/2 < \tau_1$, the minimal selling price will be falling in the size of the contract. However, the speculator's maximal buying price will decrease at a much faster rate in $f_{iS}$, thus still ensuring finite positions. The equivalents of (28.1a-b) are

(28.2a-b)

$$0 < | f_{AS} | < \left[\hat{p}_S - \hat{p}_A - \tau_1(F + f_{BS}) + K_A(\bar{x}_A - F_A - f_{AB}) - \frac{1}{18}j\right] \Big/ \left(\frac{K_A}{2} + \frac{5}{18}b\right),$$

(28.3a-b)

$$0 < | f_{BS} | < \left[\hat{p}_S - \hat{p}_B - \tau_1 (F + f_{AS}) + K_B (\bar{x}_B - F_B + f_{AB}) - \frac{1}{18}j\right] \Big/ \left(\frac{K_B}{2} + \frac{5}{18}b\right).$$

Equations (28) all imply individual rationality by securing that each contract adds positively to the payoffs. Each player can, however, secure himself a minimum payoff without participating in the 15-Day market at all. Individual rationality then implies that payoffs should satisfy:

$$(29.1) \qquad W_A \geq \tau_1 f_{BS}^2 + \tau_3 f_{BS}$$

(29.2) $$W_B \geq \tau_1 f_{AS}^2 + \tau_3 f_{AS}^2$$

(29.3) $$E_S(\Pi_S) \geq 0 .$$

Note, though, that the minimal payoff of producer i may become negative if the rival k takes a position $f_{kS} \in ]\,0, -2\,(F + j/b)\,[$.

## 5.5 NET 15-DAY POSITIONS

The second observation on the system (27) is that it exhibits linear dependence in $f_{AB}$, $f_{AS}$ and $f_{BS}$ implying that the quantities of the contracts are indeterminate. This can be remedied partly by manipulating the system (27) using the identities (21) to find the net positions:

(30.1) $$f_A^* = \Theta\,[\,K_B(\hat{p}_S - \hat{p}_A) + \frac{2}{9}b(\hat{p}_B - \hat{p}_A) + (K_A K_B + \frac{2}{9}bK_A)(\bar{x}_A - F_A) - \frac{2}{9}bK_B(\bar{x}_B - F_B) - \frac{1}{18}K_B(bF + j)\,]$$

(30.2) $$f_B^* = \Theta\,[\,K_A(\hat{p}_S - \hat{p}_B) - \frac{2}{9}b(\hat{p}_B - \hat{p}_A) + (K_A K_B + \frac{2}{9}bK_B)(\bar{x}_B - F_B) - \frac{2}{9}bK_A(\bar{x}_A - F_A) - \frac{1}{18}K_A(bF + j)\,]$$

(30.3) $$f_S^* = -\Theta\,[\,K_A(\hat{p}_S - \hat{p}_B) + K_B(\hat{p}_S - \hat{p}_A) + K_A K_B(\bar{x}_A + \bar{x}_B - F) - \frac{1}{18}(K_A + K_B)(bF + J)\,]$$

(30.4) $$\Theta^{-1} = K_A K_B + 2b(K_A + K_B)/9.$$

The net positions are thus uniquely determined by the parameters of the spot market, the speculations about the spot price and the positions already taken on the IPE during the first stage, but the distribution on individual contracts cannot be found.

## 5.6 THE CORE

The set of contracts described by equations (27) - (30) consists of those contracts that are individually and coalitionally rational at the same time and is thus basically the core. By substituting (30) into (27) the core can be described as the set of contracts,

$$\left\{ \left(p_{AB}^{15}, f_{AB}\right), \left(p_{AS}^{15}, f_{AS}\right), \left(p_{BS}^{15}\right) \right\},$$

that satisfy the following equations simultaneously:

(31.1) $$f_{AB} + f_{AS} = f^*_A$$

(31.2) $$-f_{AB} + f_{BS} = f^*_B$$

(31.3) $$-(f_{AS} + f_{BS}) = f^*_S$$

(31.4) $$g - \frac{1}{2}K_A f_{AB} < p^{15}_{AB} < g + \frac{1}{2}K_B fAB \quad \text{if } f_{AB} > 0$$

(31.5) $$g' - \frac{1}{2}(K_A - \frac{1}{9}b)f_{AS} < p^{15}_{AS} < g'' + \frac{1}{6}bf_{AS} \quad \text{if } f_{AS} > 0$$

(31.6) $$g' - \frac{1}{2}(K_B - \frac{1}{9}b)f_{BS} < p^{15}_{BS} < g'' + \frac{1}{6}bf_{BS} \quad \text{if } f_{BS} > 0 ,$$

where:

(31.7) $$g = \Theta \left[\frac{2}{9}b ( K_B \hat{p}_A + K_A\hat{p}_B ) + K_AK_B\hat{p}_S \right] - \frac{2}{9} \Theta bK_AK_B (\bar{x}_A + \bar{x}_B - F ) + \frac{1}{18} \Theta K_AK_B (bF + j ) + \frac{1}{2}j$$

(31.8) $$g' = \Theta \left[\frac{1}{9}b ( K_B\hat{p}_A + K_A\hat{p}_B ) + ( K_AK_B + \frac{1}{9} ( K_A + K_B ) ) \hat{p}_S \right] - \frac{1}{9} \Theta bK_AK_B ( \bar{x}_A + \bar{x}_B - F ) + \frac{1}{18} \Theta (K_AK_B - \frac{1}{9} (K_A + K_B) ) ( bF + j) - \frac{1}{9}bF$$

(31.9) $$g'' = \Theta \left[\frac{1}{3}b ( K_B \hat{p}_A + K_A \hat{p}_B ) + \left\{K_AK_B - \frac{1}{9} ( K_A + K_B ) \right\}\hat{p}_S \right] - \frac{1}{3} \Theta b K_AK_B ( \bar{x}_A + \bar{x}_B - F ) + \frac{1}{54} \Theta b( K_A + K_B ) ( bF + j ) - \frac{1}{6}bF .$$

The linear system for the quantities (31.1-3) has one degree of freedom implying that the quantities will be uniquely determined once one quantity is known. [Fix for example $f_{AB}$. Then (31.1) uniquely determines $f_{AS}$, whilst (31.2) uniquely determines $f_{BS}$. These quantities will be consistent with (31.1).]

Once the quantities are known, (31.4-6) determine the ranges of prices acceptable. Note that each of the inequalities is reversed if the corresponding quantity becomes negative. Also note that the lower bound appears to be decreasing and the upper bound increasing in the quantity. This somewhat surprising result has to be interpreted in the light of the constraints on quantities: If a contract becomes larger (say $f_{AB}$) and the price "spread" therefore increases then the other contracts become correspondingly smaller ($f_{AS}$ decreases and $f_{BS}$

increases one-to-one with $f_{AB}$ positive but $f_{AB}$ and $f_{BS}$ have opposite signs in B's payoff function).

The three ranges that bound prices are determined by the g's given in equations (31.7-9). The first term in each of these consists of a weighted average of the three agents' expected price, $\hat{p}_A$, $\hat{p}_B$ and $\hat{p}_S$, the weights being functions of $K_A$, $K_B$ and b. The second term depends on the degree to which the producers have hedged their production on the IPE. In case they hedged fully on the IPE $(\bar{x}_A + \bar{x}_B = F)$, the term drops out. In case they hedged less on the IPE, the bounds on prices will be lower, implying that it will be more costly for the producers to hedge on the 15-Day market. The last two terms of the g's depend on the producers' IPE position and on storage costs and basically incorporate the strategic effects of futures and storage on spot prices.

This core is never empty and always non-unique (in fact, infinitely large). We will not elaborate on the solution to the 15-Day stage here, but simply note that, *a priori*, there is no means to pointing out a subset of the core as being more likely as a solution.

## 6. Stage One: The International Petroleum Exchange

The IPE, as described in the introduction, is a formal futures market with an open outcry exchange and a clearing house. We therefore assume that a single price, $p^{IPE}$, will be determined on this market. The question then is what positions $F_A$ and $F_B$ the producers should take on this market.

The payoffs arising from the IPE are [13]

(32.1)
$$W_A^{IPE} = \left(p^{IPE} - \hat{p}_A\right) F_A + \tau_1 F - \frac{1}{18}\left(7F_A - 2F_B\right) - \frac{1}{2}K_A\left(\bar{x}_A - F_A\right)^2 + E_A\left[W_A^{15}\left(F_A, F_B\right)\right]$$

(32.2)
$$W_B^{IPE} = \left(p^{IPE} - \hat{p}_A\right) F_B + \tau_1 F + \frac{1}{18}j(2F_A - 7F_B) - \frac{1}{2}K_B(\bar{x}_B - F_B)^2 + E_B\left[W_B^{15}(F_A, F_B)\right],$$

where

$$E_A\left[W_A^{15}(F_A, F_B)\right] \text{ and } E_B\left[W_B^{15}(F_A, F_B)\right]$$

[13] Using (24), (20) and (7).

are the payoffs that A and B expect to gain from the 15-Day market depending on what solution they expect to prevail. This could be formalized by claiming that they hold one subjective possibility distribution, $h_i$, on what the size of, say, $f_{AB}$ will be and other subjective distributions, $h_i^{AB}$, $h_i^{AS}$, $h_i^{BS}$ on what the price will be, conditional on the quantities. These probability distributions could be thought of as representing the way in which the agents think the 15-Day market works.

A's expected value of $f_{AB}$ will then be

$$(33.1) \qquad E_A(f_{AB}) = \int_{-\infty}^{\infty} f_{AB} h_A df_{AB}$$

and the expectations with respect to the two other 15-Day quantities will therefore be

$$(33.2) \qquad E_A(f_{AS}) = \int_{-\infty}^{\infty} \left[ f_A^*(F_A,F_B) - f_{AB} \right] h_A df_{AB}$$

and

$$(33.3) \qquad E_A(f_{BS}) = \int_{-\infty}^{\infty} \left[ f_B^*(F_A,F_B) + f_{AB} \right] h_A df_{AB}.$$

The expected prices will be:

$$(33.4) \qquad E_A \left[ p_{AB}^{15} \mid f_{AB} \right] = \int_{g-K_A f_{AB}/2}^{g+K_A f_{AS}/2} p_{AB}^{15} h_A^{AB} dp_{AB}^{15} ,$$

$$(33.5) \qquad E_A(p_{AS}^{15} \mid f_{AB}) = \int_{g' -(K_A-\frac{1}{9}b)(f_A^*-f_{AB})/2}^{g'' + b(f_A^*-f_{AB})/6} p_{AS}^{15} h_A^{AS} dp_{AS}^{15} ,$$

and

$$(33.6) \qquad E_A(p_{BS}^{15} \mid f_{AB}) = \int_{g' -(K_B-\frac{1}{9}b)(f_B^* + f_{AB})/2}^{g'' + b(f_B^*+f_{AB})/6} p_{BS}^{15} h_A^{BS} dp_{BS}^{15} .$$

Note that the net positions on the 15-Day market $f_i^*$ depend on the position taken on the IPE, so that the limits of the integrals in (33.4-6) depend on $F_A$ and $F_B$.

The expected value to A of the 15-Day transactions can be found by taking the expectation of (25.1) using (33) and (30). This will give the payoff $E_A\,(W_A^{15}(F_A,F_B))$ which occurs in (32.1). A similar exercise can be done for B by substituting ($h_A$, $h_A^{AB}$, $H_A^{AS}$, $h_A^{BS}$)) by ($h_B$, $h_B^{AB}$, $h_B^{AS}$, $h_B^{BS}$) in (33) and taking the expectation of (25.2). This will identify ($W_A^{IPE}$, $W_B^{IPE}$) in (32.1). If the two sets of subjective probability distributions are common knowledge (to be precise: if A knows B's and B knows A's probability distributions) and if the two players take the IPE positions simultaneously, a subgame-perfect Nash equilibrium will result where A maximizes $W_A^{IPE}$ with respect to $F_A$ and B $W_B^{IPE}$ with respect to $F_B$.

Note that when the two producers take positions on the IPE they do this for the same three motives as applies to the 15-Day market: A speculative, a strategic, and a hedging motive are at play; (32) captures exactly these effects. But in the fifth term, the producers will realize that the position they take will have an effect on the unknown solution to the 15-Day game. So, in a sense, this adds another speculative motive: Speculation with respect to the non-unique outcomes of the 15-Day game.

## 7. The Model and the Oil Markets

The model that was put forth above is based on several abstractions compared with the real world. One important abstraction is connected to the treatment of time. The model can be seen as a snapshot in a sense that will soon be made precise. The real world is rather a continuous series of rolling and overlapping snapshots. This section discusses how the model could be interpreted and what would be necessary to create a moving picture.

The interpretation of our game in terms of real world actions starts with the observation that the organization of the 15-Day market requires the producers to give the purchasers a 15-day notice before delivery. This notice specifies a three-day range within which delivery will take place. The oil traded thereby transits from being undated to being dated: From being traded forward to being traded spot. These fifteen days correspond to our period 1 of the extraction game since the futures markets for oil to be delivered in this period are closed. Cargoes that are lifted but not sold during this period represent an increase in stocks that can be sold in period 2.

In order to make period 2 of the extraction game correspond to the real world, we adopt a strong abstraction: Assume that all cargoes of a given month are lifted within a given delivery range. In other words, the delivery month is collapsed into this range. Assume for concreteness that all September oil is to be delivered between the first and the third of September for a given year. Period 2 of the production game could be interpreted as this period (September 1-3). This then would correspond to the maturity of the 15-Day contract. The fifteen days prior to September 1st (*i.e.*, August 16th-31st) would constitute period 1.

The two futures markets are collapsed into points in time. We can interpret this by assuming that on the 15th of August the 15-Day market opens. This is technically the last day that forward oil can be traded for delivery on September 1-3. So the market closes before August 16, and will not reopen until period 2 where, by definition, the maturity price is identical to the spot price.

The IPE closes the trading of paper barrels, referring to a given delivery month in the middle of the previous month -- that is to say, well before the 15-Day market stops trading this delivery month. In fact, what is the first forward month on the IPE is normally the second forward month of the 15-Day market, and the maturity price of the IPE is the 15-Day price on the closing day. The latter fact is ignored in the model and the maturity price on both futures markets is chosen to be the spot price of the second period of the extraction game. The first feature is however modelled by letting the IPE precede the 15-Day game. In other words, we assume that the IPE opens and closes only once prior to maturity, on the 14th of August.

In reality, of course, the oil markets are much more dynamic than our model allows for. First, a sequence of extraction games are played and stocks are increased or decreased between them. Stocks therefore serve as a state variable in a dynamic game. This may change the strategic effect of inventories since it is no longer true that everything that was produced but not sold in one period has to be sold in the next. Rotemberg and Saloner (1985), for example, see inventories as a means to sustain high collusive prices by threatening to float the market if a rival deviates.

The two futures markets are treated as one-shot situations in our model. In the real world, these markets are open every day and trade different contracts (up to six months ahead) simultaneously. This implies that there may be much more dynamic interaction going on than here presented. For example, informational intricacies have been ignored by assuming that the subjective probability distributions and all strategic features are common knowledge. This leaves the difference in subjective probability distributions unexplained. A natural explanation of this involves differences in information (asymmetric information or incomplete knowledge) or optimistic/pessimistic behaviour as noted in footnote 3. A model of a futures market for a storable good explaining the reasons for the existence as well as the effects of asymmetric information is found in Stein (1987). This model, however, does not analyze the strategic aspects of inventories and of futures but concentrates on risk sharing and informational externalities.

Lastly, it should be noted that the structure of the three markets has been simplified in the model. An obvious example of this is the quasi omission of refineries from the analysis. They are solely represented by the downward sloping demand curves (6), which is inadequate. Similarly the problem of integrated oil companies has been ignored. These problems are at the core of our current research.

## APPENDIX TO SECTION 4: STRATEGIC STOCKS

This appendix is offered as a help to the reader who wants to obtain a full understanding of the model demonstrating the strategic use of stocks.

Recall that we made the following assumptions:

(A.1) There is no exogenous upper bound to production, i.e., no $\bar{x}_i$, $i = A,B$.

(A.2) There is no demand in the first period, implying that the production of the first period has to be stored, and that sales (in the second period) equal total production over the two periods [cf. expression (13)].

The profit functions are then given by

$$\text{(A.3.1)} \qquad \Pi_A = (s_A + x_{A2} - N_A)p_2 - \frac{c_1}{2} s_A^2 - \frac{c_2}{2} x_{A2}^2 + p^F N_A ,$$

$$\text{(A.3.2)} \qquad \Pi_B = (s_B = (s_B + x_{B2} - N_B)p_2 - \frac{c_1}{2} s_B^2 - \frac{c_2}{2} x_{B2}^2 + p^F N_B .$$

Note that the cost of storage is subsumed in the period 1 cost function: The decision to produce in period one is essentially the same as the decision to store, and we do not need two cost variables to describe the decision. All other assumption remain unchanged, i.e., the demand curve is stochastic, linear and downward sloping (6) and the producers' utilities from profits follow the mean-variance model (7).

The last decision the producers take regards second-period production: They take this decision by simultaneously maximizing their payoffs (7) with respect to their respective decision variables ($x_{A2}$, $x_{B2}$) taking the stocks ($S_A$, $S_B$) and the net futures positions ($N_A$, $N_B$) as given. This results in the following second-period production for A (the expression for B is similar):

(A.4.1)

$$x_{A2} = \frac{1}{D} b \left[ \Delta(\alpha) + b ( s_B - b ( N_B - N_A ) + K_B ( S_B - N_B ) - K_A ( S_A - N_A ) \right]$$

$$+ \frac{1}{D} ( b + c_2 + K_B ) \left[ E_A(\alpha) - b ( s_A + s_B ) + ( b + K_A ) ( N_A - s_A ) \right],$$

which is comparable to (14) and where

$$\text{(A.4.2)} \qquad D = ( 2b + c_2 + K_A ) ( 2b + c_2 + K_B ) - b^2 , \qquad \text{and}$$

$$\text{(A.4.3)} \qquad \Delta(\alpha) = E_A(\alpha) - E_B(\alpha) .$$

The multipliers (15)-(17) follow directly from (A.4.1) and (18) follows with the additional use of (6.1). The second-to-last decision the producers take regards how much to produce in the first period or, equivalently, how much to store. Substituting the optimized second-period productions into the payoff functions and performing a simultaneous maximization of these with respect to the stocks (taking net futures positions as given), we obtain

(19.1) $$s_A = \nu_A E_A(\alpha) + \phi_A E_B(\alpha) + \psi_{AS} N_A + \omega_A N_B$$

(19.2) $$s_B = \phi_B E_A(\alpha) + \nu_B E_B(\alpha) = \omega_B N_A + \psi_B N_B \; ,$$

where:

(A.5.1) $$\nu_A = ( \rho_{B1}\delta_{A\alpha} - \delta_{B1}\rho_{A\alpha} ) / H \; ; \; \nu_B = ( \delta_{A1}\rho_{B\alpha} ) / H$$

(A.5.2) $$\phi_A = ( \rho_{B1}\delta_{B}\alpha - \delta_{B1}\rho_{B}\alpha ) / H \; ; \; \phi_B = ( \delta_{A1}\rho_{A}\alpha - \rho_{A1}\delta_{A}\alpha ) / H$$

(A.5.3) $$\psi_A = ( \rho_{B1}\delta N_A - \delta_{B1}\rho N_A ) / H \; ; \; \psi_B = ( \delta_{A1} \, \rho N_B - \rho_{A1}\delta N_B ) / H$$

(A.5.4) $$\omega_A = ( \rho_{B1}\delta N_B - \delta_{B1}\rho N_B ) / H \; ; \; \omega_B = ( \delta_{A1}\rho N_A - \rho_{A1}\delta N_A ) / H$$

(A.5.5) $$H = \rho_{A1}\delta_{B1} - \rho_{B1}\delta_{A1}$$

(A.6.1) $$\rho_{A1} = - ( c_1 + c_2 ) D + c_2^2 ( 2b + c_2 + K_B ) ( 1 + b^2/D )$$

(A.6.2) $$\rho_{B1} = ( 2b + K_B - c_2 b^2/D ) \, b \, c_2$$

(A.6.3) $$\rho_{A\alpha} = c_2 ( 2b + c_2 + K_B ) ( 1 + b^2/D ) > 0$$

(A.6.4) $$\rho_{B\alpha} = -b \, c_2 ( 1 + b^2 / D ) < 0$$

(A.6.5) $$\rho N_A = c_2 ( 2b + c_2 + K_B ) (b + K_A ) ( 1+b^2/D ) - c_2 b^2 > 0$$

(A.6.6) $$\rho N_B = - b \, c_2 ( b + K_B ) ( 1 + b^2/D ) < 0$$

(A.7.1) $\delta_{A1} = b\ c_2\ (\ 2b + K_A - c_2 b^2/D\ )$

(A.7.2) $\delta_{B1} = -\ (\ c_1 + c_2\ )\ D + c_2^2\ (\ 2b + c_2 + K_B\ )\ (\ 1 + b^2/D\ )$

(A.7.3) $\delta_{A\alpha} = \rho_{B\alpha} < 0$

(A.7.4) $\delta_{B\alpha} = c_2\ (\ 2b + c_2 + K_A\ )\ (\ 1 + b^2/D) > 0$

(A.7.5) $\delta N_A = -b\ c_2\ (\ b + K_A\ )\ (\ 1 + b^2/D\ ) < 0$

(A.7.6) $\delta N_B = c_2\ (\ 2b + c_2 + K_B\ )\ (\ b + K_B\ )\ (\ 1 + b^2\ /\ D\ ) - c_2\ b^2 > 0$ .

The signs of the parameters are indicated where possible. The sign of the most important determinant, *D*, is however undermined but will generally be positive. Sufficient, but not necessary, conditions for non-negativity of *D* are, for example, that simultaneously $c_2 > 1$ and $(c_1 + c_2)^2D > b^2c_2(1 + b^2/D)$. But these requirements are not easily interpreted.

## REFERENCES

Allaz, B. (1991), "Duopoly, Inventories and Futures Markets," in L. Phlips (ed.), **Commodity Futures and Financial Markets**, Kluwer Academic Publishers, Dordrecht, 249-271.

Arvan, L. (1985), "Some Examples of Dynamic Cournot Duopoly with Inventory," *Rand Journal of Economics*, 16(4), 569-578.

Brianza, T., Phlips, L. and J.F. Richard (1990), "Futures Markets, Speculation and Monopoly Pricing," *EUI Working Paper ECO Nº 90/8*, European University Institute, Florence.

Greenberg, J. (1990), **The Theory of Social Situations -- An Alternative Game-Theoretic Approach**, Cambridge University Press, Cambridge, U.K.

Lovell, M.C. (1986), "Tests of the Rational Expectations Hypothesis," *American Economic Review*, 76, 110-124.

Mabro, R., et al. (1986), *The Market for North Sea Crude Oil*, Oxford Institute for Energy Studies, Oxford University Press, Oxford.

Møllgaard, H.P. (1990), "Strategic Aspects of Inventories in Two Period Duopoly: What Are Conjectural Variations Trying to Accomplish," *Mimeo*, presented at the Students' Workshop, October 9, 1990, European University Institute, Florence.

Newbery, D.M.G., and J.E. Stiglitz (1981), **The Theory of Commodity Price Stabilization -- A Study in the Economics of Risk**, Clarenden Press, Oxford.

Phlips, L. (1991), "Manipulation of Crude Oil Futures," *EUI Working Paper ECO Nº 91/36*, European University Institute, Florence.

Phlips, L. and R.M. Harstad (1990), "Oligopolistic Manipulation of Spot Markets and the Timing of Futures Market Speculation," *EUI Working Paper ECO Nº 90/20*, European University Institute, Florence.

Phlips, L. and R.M. Harstad (1991), "Interaction Between Resource Extraction and Futures Markets: A Game-Theoretic Analysis," in R. Selten (ed.), **Game Equilibrium Models II**, Springer-Verlag, Heidelberg, 289-307.

Rotemberg, J.J. and Saloner, G. (1985), "Strategic Inventories and the Excess Volatility of Production," *Sloan School of Management Working Paper No. 1685-65*, MIT, Cambridge, MA.

Selten, R. (1982), "Einführung in die Theorie der Spiele mit unvollständiger Information," in *Information in der Wirtschaft*, Schriften des Vereins für Sozialpolitik, Gesellschaft für Wirtschafts- und Sozialwissenschaften, N.F. Band 126, Duncker & Humboldt, Berlin, 81-147.

Stein, J.C. (1987), "Informational Externalities and Welfare-Reducing Speculation," *Journal of Political Economy*, 95(6), 1124-1145.

# THE EFFECT OF INCOME AND PRICES ON PROTECTION AND RENT SEEKING IN THE U.S., 1950-1986

STEPHEN P. MAGEE
*Visiting Professor of Business*
*University of Chicago and*
*Fred H. Moore Professor of Finance and Economics*
*Department of Finance*
*University of Texas*
*Austin, TX 78712*

ABSTRACT. Houthakker and Magee (1969) explored the effects of income and prices on trade. This paper explores the effects of income and prices on U.S. tariffs and rent seeking. Houthakker and Magee predicted secular declines in the U.S. trade balance with income growth. Would the secular increase in imports relative to exports generate growing U.S. protectionism through time? Not necessarily: Protection can go either up or down in response to income growth, depending on the cause of the growth in income. This paper shows that if labor, the factor benefitting from protection, grows relatively faster than capital, then protection would increase. However, we find that capital grew faster than labor from 1950 to 1986 so that U.S. protection declined because of income growth.

This paper employs a political-economic general equilibrium model of endogenous protection developed by Young and Magee (1986) to predict changes in U.S tariffs, export subsidies and simulated levels of lobbying over trade policy between two years, 1950 and 1986. The model predicts that protection also declined because factor intensities of production got closer together, making protection a more potent redistributive tool. After the changes, a smaller amount of protection emerges in the new political equilibrium. Labor suffered declining wages according to the model because of increased capital intensities. Labor compensates for its declining economic fortunes by devoting a larger fraction of its resources to protectionist lobbying; capital devotes less. For the economy as a whole, there was a decline in resources devoted to rent seeking over trade policy.

What are the effects of prices on protection? Econometric estimates from earlier work indicate there should have been about a 6 percentage point increase between 1950 and 1986 in the *ad valorem* equivalent level of U.S. protection caused by the decline in U.S. import prices relative to export prices on world markets.

## 1. Introduction

What are the effects of income and prices on protectionism and rent seeking over trade policy? Mancur Olson (1982) suggests economic sclerosis might cause protectionism and rent seeking to increase as income rises. My own interest in the effects of income and prices on



*L. Phlips and L.D. Taylor (eds.), Aggregation, Consumption and Trade*, 197–216.

trade were stimulated by H.S. Houthakker, my mentor and coauthor in the first academic paper that I published.

Henk Houthakker has contributed importantly to both research and policy on U.S. international trade. I first met him in 1968-69 when I was a Junior Economist and he was a Member of the Council of Economic Advisers. Even though I was still a lowly graduate student, he invited me to work with him on the demand for U.S. exports and imports. He was a kind mentor and became a good friend. We wrote a series of memoranda predicting a decline in the U.S. trade balance which were later published as Houthakker and Magee (1969). In that paper, we found an asymmetry in the income elasticities of demand for U.S. trade: The domestic income elasticity of demand for U.S. imports was significantly higher than the foreign income elasticity of demand for U.S. exports. The paper is routinely used in Washington to explain secular declines in the U.S. trade balance. We also estimated income and price elasticities for the exports and imports of 15 countries over the period 1951 through 1966. This paper explores the effect of income and prices on U.S. protection and simulated U.S. rent seeking over trade policy for two points in time, 1950 and 1986.

It would appear that the Houthakker-Magee income elasticity asymmetry might generate a secular push for increased protection in the U.S. As imports grow faster than exports, import-competing forces should increase their political pressure relative to free-trade forces. But protection in the U.S. has, in fact, declined between 1950 and 1986. This paper attempts to resolve this puzzle.

It turns out that whether pressure for protection increases or decreases depends on the cause of the increase in income. Data from 1900-1984 indicates that protection in the U.S. favors labor and freer trade favors physical and human capital (Magee and Young (1987). Thus, if the income growth is caused by labor growth, protection will rise because labor has more political clout; if the income growth is caused by capital growth, protection will decline because the proexport lobby has more resources at its disposal. Since capital depending has more than doubled the U.S. capital/labor endowment ratio between 1950 and 1986, the level of U.S. protection has fallen because of the declining importance of labor. Economic clout means political clout. Country factor endowments determine protection: expansion of the scarce factor in an economy increases the level of protection.

There is a second reason why U.S. protection has declined since 1950. There was a rise in the capital intensity of production, which lowers wages relative to capital returns. Labor follows the compensation effect of endogenous policy theory: With lower wages, the opportunity cost of political activity falls, so that labor engages in more lobbying for protection and capital engages in less. The partial equilibrium consequence of this is greater protection. But this effect was more than offset by another: The factor intensities of production in exportables and importables also got closer together. The consequence is an increase in magnification: The elasticities of both factor rewards increase with respect to relative product price changes. With greater magnification, labor will be willing to lobby even more for a tariff but ironically, a smaller tariff emerges because it is now so much more effective as a redistributive tool.

The bottom line is that labor lobbies more but gets a lower tariff. But the lower tariff now increases wages much more than before. When the medicine gets stronger, less is needed and it does more. These results come from Magee, Brock and Young's (1989, chp. 14) endogenous policy model in which all of the economic and political actors demonstrate maximizing behavior. Thus, lobbying (by capital and labor), the trade policies (the tariff and export subsidy), and the electoral outcomes (the probabilities of election of the parties) are fully endogenous. The simulations reported below use data from the United States in 1950 and 1986 to calibrate the model. The simulations are necessary because resources devoted to lobbying are largely unobservable.

Between 1950 and 1986, the model suggests six specific changes in the United States. All six are driven by an increase in the U.S. capital intensity of production for both exportables and importables. This paper uses tariff data in measuring U.S. protection.

(1) Resources devoted to lobbying on trade policy declined from 3.2 percent of value added to 2.4 percent, assuming an effectiveness parameter of .10 for the lobbies.

(2) There is a dramatic decrease in the fraction of capital devoted to lobbying and an increase in the fraction of labor devoted to lobbying.

(3) The probability of election of the procapital party (presumably the Republicans) increases from .42 in 1950 to .92 in 1986.

(4) The equilibrium U.S. tariff and export subsidy decline.

(5) In 1986, the model hits a production specialization boundary, suggesting that the United States produces importables but not exportables.

(6) The model implies a decline in U.S. labor welfare relative to capital. The cause is the increased capital intensity of production, the increasing fraction of labor devoted to lobbying, and decreased protection.

The theoretical effect of relative prices on tariffs depends on the functional form of the model employed. Magee, Brock and Young (1989) show that in a model with Leontief production, relative prices have the expected effect: When the price of importables falls, the intensive factor in the import-competing industry substitutes into political activity and tariffs rise. However, with Cobb-Douglas production, utility and logit probability of election functions, a curious thing happens. The equilibrium tariff rate is independent of relative prices (*i.e.*, the country's terms of trade). For the simulations in this paper, which are based on the Cobb-Douglas model, we conclude that any relative price changes would have no effect on the equilibrium tariffs. While the Leontief model has not been estimated structurally, reduced-form estimates are available in Magee and Young (1987) and Magee, Brock and Young (1989, ch. 13). The 30 percent fall in the price of U.S. manufactured imports relative to the price of U.S. manufactured exports suggests that U.S. tariffs should have risen over 6 percentage points from 1950 to 1986. Indeed, the rise of VERs and other nontariff restrictions on U.S. imports in the 1970s and 1980s are the political consequences of these economic changes.

One contribution of this paper is its implicit estimates of the amount of rent seeking by capital and labor over U.S. trade policy. What does the literature have to say on the subject of rent seeking? Positive views of rent seeking are held by Becker (1983), who views it in a Coasian light. The negative school on lobbying started with Tullock (1967), who noted that perhaps the entire area of producers' surplus in the Corden (1957) diagram might be wasted through lobbying to get the tariff. Krueger (1974) coined the term "rent seeking" to describe these resources wasted in redistributive competition. She found that 7% of Indian GNP was absorbed in rent-seeking while 15% of Turkish GNP was lost to rent-seeking over import licenses alone.

Mohammed and Whalley (1984) get higher numbers than Krueger, indicating that redistributive activity might consume as much as 25-40% of Indian GNP. Hamilton, Mohammad, and Whalley (1984) have world-wide measurements of the rent-seeking costs of trade restrictions across countries. Ross (1984) finds that rent seeking is approximately 38% of gross domestic product in Kenya. The most extreme theoretical position by the negative school is provided by Magee, Brock and Young's (1989, chp. 15) economic "black hole," into which an economy can plunge with sufficiently high magnification in production and degrees of relative risk aversion approaching 1.0.

In general, the work in this paper extends the foundations laid by Buchanan, Tollison and Tullock (1980), Lindbeck (1985) and Stigler (1974). Contributions in the area of public choice include Aranson and Ordeshook (1981), Austin-Smith (1981, 1984), Hinich (1981) and Tollison (1982). Contributors in the area of lobbying, both domestic and international, include Baron (1986), Bernholz (1977), Conybeare (1982), Olson (1965), Varian (1987) and Wellisz and Wilson (1986). Contributors to the development of tariff and international commercial policy theory include Baldwin (1984, 1986), Becker (1983), Brander and Spencer (1985), Hillman (1987), Stern (1987), Stolper and Samuelson (1941), Whalley (1985). Contributions to endogenous tariff theory include Brock and Magee (1978, 1980), Findlay and Wellisz (1982), Hillman (1982), Mayer (1984), Young and Magee (1986) and Magee, Brock and Young (1989).

## 2. A Review of the Model

The model described below has been discussed at length elsewhere: See Young and Magee (1986) and Magee, Brock, and Young (1989, chp. 14). It is a general equilibrium 2x2x2x2 endogenous policy model with 2 goods, 2 factors, 2 lobbies and 2 political parties.We review the essential features here. The numeraire is good 1, the more capital intensive good. The country is small and faces an international price P for good 2, which is exported. However, politically motivated trade distortions can lead to a domestic price Q which differs from P. Let W and R be the wage and rental rates. If Q does not induce specialization in production then, by the factor price equalization, the equilibrium wage and rental rates depend only on Q and are independent of factor endowments. Since good 2 is relatively labor intensive, the Stolper-Samuelson Theorem implies that $\partial W/\partial Q > 0$ and $\partial R/\partial Q < 0$.

The impact of Q on the returns to capital and labor motivates their owners to form lobbies which contribute resources to politics. For simplicity, we assume that the capital and labor lobbies make direct contributions K and L of the factor that they own to the party proposing the policy more favorable to themselves. We assume that there are procapital and prolabor parties, each using its policies to bid for votes and for political contributions. The procapital party's policy is to set a domestic price of P/S, *e.g.*, by a subsidy on exports of good 1, which is more capital intensive, while the prolabor party's policy is to set a domestic price of PT, *e.g.*, by a tariff on imports of good 2.

We assume that the probability of victory by the procapital party is $\pi = \pi$ (K,L,S,T) where $\pi$ is increasing in K and T and decreasing in L and S. We suppose that each lobby chooses its political contributions in order to maximize the expected utility of a representative owner of the corresponding factor, while each party chooses its policy in order to maximize its probability of election. We assume that the capital lobby's choices are as if made by a representative individual who owns $K_0$ units of capital and has an indirect utility function, VR = VR(Q, IR) where IR is his income. K is chosen to maximize expected utility, *i.e.*, the lobby maximizes its expected utility. The capital owner takes account of the impact of the election on his cost of living because Q appears independently in his indirect utility function. The representative labor owner owns L units of labor and has an indirect utility function, VW = VW (Q, IW ), where IW is his income. L is chosen to maximize his expected utility. Let $K^*$(L,S,T) and $L^*$(K,S,T) be the optimal policies of the two lobbies. We shall assume that $KS^* > 0$ and $LT^* > 0$, *i.e.*, if a party proposes a domestic price more favorable to the lobby that it leads, then it attracts more resources from that lobby.

Since the procapital party is a Stackelberg leader with respect to the capital lobby and adopts Nash behavior toward the other players, it maximizes its probability of victory by maximizing $\pi(K^*(L,S,T),L,S,T)$ with respect to S. Similarly, the prolabor party maximizes its probability of victory by minimizing $\pi(K,L^* (K,S,T),S,T)$ with respect to T. Let the optimal policies of the two parties be $S^*(L,T)$ and $T^*(K,S)$ respectively. The action of each player in the political game depends on the actions of two or three of the other players, as expressed by the reaction functions $K^*(L,S,T)$, $L^*(K,S,T)$, $S^*(L,T)$ and $T^*(K,S)$. An equilibrium is a set of mutually consistent actions (Ke,Le,Se,Te) satisfying:

$$(1) \qquad K_e = K^*(L_e, S_e, T_e), \quad Le = L^*(K_e, S_e, T_e)$$
$$S_e = S^*(L_e, T_e), \quad Te = T^*(K_e, S_e)$$

For the special case of Cobb-Douglas utility and production functions and a logit probability of election function, Young and Magee (1986) found closed-form solutions for the equilibrium actions of the four players. Since these solutions are expressed in terms of the model parameters alone, the general equilibrium effects of comparative static changes are particularly transparent.

Henceforth, we shall suppose that the production functions for goods 1 and 2 are Cobb-Douglas. With a suitable choice of units, the unit cost functions of the two industries can then also be written in the Cobb-Douglas form, C1(R,W) = RaW1-a and C2(R,W) = $R^{\beta}W1\text{-}^{\beta}$, where $\alpha$, $\beta$ are constant such that $0<\beta<\alpha<1$. The numeraire is the more capital-intensive good 1. If the domestic price of good 2 is Q then, in a nonspecialized equilibrium, the wage and rental rates are determined by the conditions for equilibrium in the two industries, $1 = R^{\alpha}W^{1-\alpha}$ and $Q = R^{\beta}W^{1-\beta}$. The equilibrium factor prices are:

$$(2) \qquad W = QN \text{ and } R = Q\text{-}M,$$

where $N \equiv \alpha/(\alpha-\beta)$ and $M \equiv (1-\alpha)/(\alpha-\beta)$. Suppose that the representative owners of capital and labor are risk neutral and have Cobb-Douglas utility functions. Hence, their indirect utility functions have the form:

$$(3) \qquad VR(IR,Q) = IRQ\text{-}g, \quad VW(IW,Q) = IWQ\text{-}d$$

where IR, IR are the incomes of the respective factor owners and $0\leq\gamma,\delta\leq 1$. By (2), $I_R$ = (KO - K)Q-M. Therefore, the utility of the capital lobby when the domestic price is Q is VR = (KO - K)Q-m, where $m \equiv M+\gamma$. Similarly the utility of the labor lobby is VW = (LO - L)Qn, where $n \equiv N - \delta$. Since $1 > \alpha > \beta > 0$ we have $m > 0$. Moreover, $N \equiv \alpha/(\alpha-\beta) > 1 \geq d$ so $n > 0$. Thus, an increase in Q harms the capital lobby and benefits the labor lobby, as implied by the Stolper-Samuelson Theorem.

By (3), combinations of income IR and commodity price Q such that IRQ-gis fixed will yield the same utility for the capital owner. Hence, Qg is an index of his cost of living. Q-m = Q-M/Qg can be interpreted as the "real" return to capital: The return Q-M in terms of the numeraire, deflated by the cost of living index Qg. Similarly, Qn is the real return to labor. m and n are respectively the elasticities of the real returns to capital and labor with respect to the commodity price Q. They measure the sensitivity of the lobbies to the political outcome.

In the political sector, we shall suppose that the function $\pi(K,L,S,T)$ giving the procapital party's probability of election has the logit form, which is widely used to model dichotomous choices. Under the most general logit model, the procapital party's odds of victory would be a loglinear function of the explanatory variables:

$$\log [\pi/(1-\pi)] = e + k \log K - l \log L - s \log S + t \log T$$

where e, k, l, s, t are positive constants. To simplify the exposition, we begin by assuming that the elasticities k, l, s, t of the electoral odds with respect to K, L, S, T are all unity. We also assume that e = 0.

This ensures that $\pi = 1/2$ when K = L and S = T and yields the probability of election function, $\pi(K,L,S,T) = 1/(1+LS/K) = KT/(KT+LS)$. Thus, the capital lobby solves:

(4) $\max_{0<K<K_0} e(K) = (K_0-K)f(KT(P/S)-m + LS(PT)-m, K\% + LS),$

while the labor lobby solves:

(5) $\max_{0<L<L_0} f(L) = (L_0-L)f(KT(P/S)n + LS(PT)n, KT + LS)$ .

The reaction functions of the four players are given by the following results. Let:

(6) $K(L,S,T) = (LS/T)[\{(1 - (ST)-m)(1+K_0T/LS)\}1/2 - 1]$

The optimal policy of the capital lobby is: $K^*(L,S,T) = \max\{0,K(L,S,T)\}$. Let:

(7) $L(K,S,T) = (KT/S)[\{(1 - (ST)-n)(1 + L_0S/T)\}1/2 - 1]$

The optimal policy of the labor lobby is: $L^*(K,S,T) = \max\{0,L(K,S,T)\}$

**(A)** The first order condition determining the optimal procapital policy S* is:

(8) $1 + m + mSL/K_0T - (ST)m = 0.$

**(B)** If:

(9) $m > 1$

or:

(10) $m = 1$ and $L < K_0T2$,

then (8) is satisfied by a unique positive value of S which also satisfies the second order condition.

If:

(11) $m < 1$ and $L < K_oT2m(1 - m)(1-m)/m$,

then (8) can have two solutions but only the one in the interval $0 < S < (K_0T1+m/L)1/(1-m)$ satisfies the second order condition.

**(C)** If, in addition:

(12) $(Tm - 1 - m)TK_0/m < L$,

then the solution S to (8) defined in (B) is greater than 1 and is the optimal procapital policy S*. However, if neither (9), (10), nor (11) holds or if (12) is violated, then the optimal procapital policy is free trade, *i.e.*, S*=1.

The optimal prolabor policy T* can be obtained from (8) through (12) by replacing m with n, interchanging K and L and interchanging S and T.

The set of interior solutions in the model can be characterized in terms of the solution to the following equation. For m > 0, n > 0 the following equation in r:

(13) $1 = f(\{1-(1+m)r-m\}1/2, 1-r-m) + f(\{1-(1+n)r-n\}1/2, 1-r-n)$

has a unique solution re(m,n) > 1. Let

(14) $a(m,n) \equiv -1 + (1-re-m)\{1 - (1+m)re-m\}1/2$
(15) $b(m,n) \equiv -1 + (1-re-n)\{1 - (1+n)re-n\}1/2$
(16) $c(m,n) \equiv m/rem- m - 1)$
(17) $d(m,n) \equiv n/ren - n - 1)$.

Suppose that:

(18) $1/r_e < (d/bc)K_0/L_0 < r_e$.
Then the game has a unique interior equilibrium ($K_e$, $L_e$, $S_e$, $T_e$,) given by:

(19) $K_e = K_0\, a/c$
(20) $L_e = L_o\, b/d$
(21) $S_e = \{K_0 r_e d/L_0 bc\}1/2$
(22) $T_e = \{L_o r_e c/K_0 ad\}1/2$

If (18) is violated, then the game has no interior equilibrium. Notice that:

(23) $a = K_e T_e/L_e S_e = 1/b$

(24) $r_e = S_e T_e$

Thus, a and b are respectively the odds of victory for the procapital and the prolabor parties, while re is the product of the distortions that they propose. Since re > 1, condition (18) for an interior equilibrium will certainly be satisfied for a range of values of $K_0/L_0$.

The parameters of the model are the world price P, the endowments Ko, Lo and the elasticities m and n. P does not influence the equilibrium political choices of the players, a result special to the Cobb-Douglas model. If production functions are Leontief then P does affect these choices. See Magee, Brock and Young (1989, chp. 10) for a detailed discussion of the Leontief model.

What is the relationship between income growth and a country's tariff rate? If the country were in steady state growth such that capital and labor were growing at the same rate, tariffs, export subsidies and the fractions of capital and labor devoted to lobbying would not change. However, if the cause of income growth is different rates of growth of capital and labor, then tariffs will change. We will see shortly that there has been capital deepening in the U.S. from 1950 to 1986 so that the labor/capital ratio has fallen. This reduction in the economic importance of labor translates into less political clout as well so that tariffs fall.

Notice in Figure 1 the relationship between T, which equals 1 plus the country proportional tariff rate, and the country's labor/capital endowment ratio. From 1950 until the present, the U.S. labor/capital ratio has been falling so that we are moving southwest along the curve toward the origin. Notive from equation (22) that the elasticity of (1+t) with respect to $L_0/K_0$ is .5. Thus, a doubling of the labor/capital endowment ratio would cause (1+t) to increase by only 50 percent.

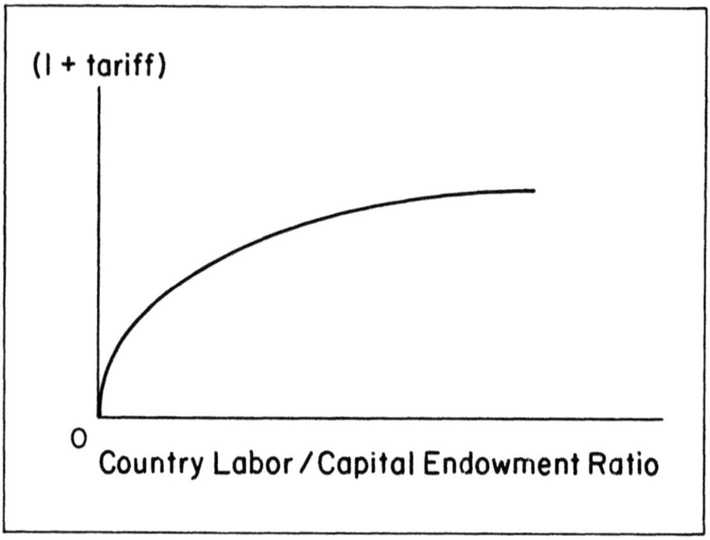


*Figure 1.* *The effect of income growth on protection depends on the cause of the growth. If the growth in income was accompanied by a rise (fall) in the country's labor/capital endowment ratio, then protection increases (decreases).*

**Table 1. The Parameters and the Results for the United States**

| **Predicted Endogenous Variables** | **1950** | **1986** | |
|---|---|---|---|
| Capital devoted to lobbying = .1*($K_e/K_0$) | 3.6% | 0.8% | |
| Labor devoted to lobbying = .1($L_e/L_0$) | 2.9% | 4.8% | |
| Probability of Election of the Procapital Party Republicans) = p | 42% | 92% | |
| Tariff Rate t = | .060* | .050** | |
| Export Subsidy s = | .021 | .000** | s = .021 |
| **Parameters** | | | |
| *Actual values* | | | |
| a (share of capital inexportables) | .488 | .598 | |
| b (share of capital inimportables) | .479 | .594 | |
| capital/labor endowment in the US | $5,711 | $12,367 | |
| the tariff rate (proportional) | .060 | .036 | |
| *Assumed values* | | | |
| g (share of good 2 in comsumption by K) | .50 | .50 | |
| d (share of good 2 in consumption by L) | .50 | .50 | |
| *Calculated values using the parameters above* | | | |
| Implied elasticities of factor returns with respect to relative prices: | | | |
| capital returns m = | 57 | 101 | |
| wages n = | 54 | 149 | |

Notes

* The predicted tariff was set equal to the actual tariff in 1950.

** The policy values for 1986 were determined by the production boundary condition in the model.

## 3. A Reader's Guide to the Model and the Results

The parameters and the simulation results are shown in Table 1; Table A1 in the Appendix shows the results in more detail. Tables A2 and A3 provide the U.S. production data by 2-digit SIC on which the exportable and importable factor intensities are based, and Table A4 shows the detail underlying the lobbying calculations.The parameters were chosen by taking the actual values of a and $\beta$ for 1950 and 1986 and assume the value g=d=.5 throughout. The parameters $\alpha$ and $\beta$ are the shares of capital income in value added in exportables and importables, respectively. The results were sensitive to changes in $\alpha$ and $\beta$ but not to changes in g and d. Data was not available for the consumption parameters so that g and d were both set equal to .5 throughout. Also, a simulation was performed which found that the 1986 equilibrium was quite insensitive to g and d. When values of .4 were used for g and d in 1986, the value of r was unchanged to the fourth decimal place and none of the endogenous was affected, except that the solution for the fraction of capital lobbying fell from .077 to .075. In addition, the model assumes throughout that the elasticity of the odds of election by the parties are unit elastic with respect to the ratio of lobbying resources that they receive and (minus) unit elastic with respect to the policies which they support.

### 3.1 THE INDEPENDENCE OF ECONOMICS AND POLITICS

The independence results in the model are illustrated in Table 2. The four Level 1 parameters, a, b, d and g, completely determine the fractions of lobbying done by the two factors, the probabilities of election of the political parties, and the policy product, r=(1+s)(1+t). The result that electoral outcomes are independent of the country's factor endowment is surprising. For example, even if the capital/labor endowment ratio of the U.S. doubled overnight, the electoral fortunes of the procapital party (presumably the Republicans) would not increase. I conjecture that this result is driven by the assumption of certain key functional forms: The logit probability of election function is unit elastic in the resources going to each party, and negatively unit elastic with respect to the policy of each party and the Cobb-Douglas production and utility functions embody unitary elasticities of substitution.

### 3.2. THE CONSTANT-SUM POLICY GAME

The model behaves as follows. Once the production parameters, consumption parameters (*i.e.*, a,b, d and g) and electoral elasticities are selected, the Level 1 variables are determined: The lobbying ratios for capital and labor, the probabilities of election of the two parties, and the policy product r = (1+t)(1+s), where t is the proportional tariff and s is the proportional export subsidy. The actual values of the policies are then determined by these parameters plus the country's factor endowment ratio. To illustrate this, observe the 1950 equilibrium shown in Appendix Table A1. The equilibrium value of r is 1.081, which equals (1+t)(1+s). Toward the bottom of the table are given minimum and maximum values of the country's capital/labor endowment ratio which are required for nonspecialized production (.526 to .614). If the country had a low capital endowment ratio (.526), capital would have little clout politically so that the political system would provide a zero export subsidy (s=0) and the maximum possible tariff (t=.081). If the country had the highest possible endowment ratio consistent with nonspecialized production, the reverse would be true: The export subsidy would beat the maximum value of s=.081 and the tariff would be t=0 because labor would be less powerful. Thus, the battle between protection and export promotion is a constant-sumgame: The constant is determined by the production, consumption, and electoral parameters while

**Table 2. Two Independence Results**

1. Lobbying Ratios and Party Success are Independent of Country Factor Endowments and World Prices

2. The Policies are Independent of World Prices

**Level 1 Parameters Only Determine Level 1 Endogenous Variables**

*Level 1 Parameters*

| | |
|---|---|
| Factor intensities of production: | a,b |
| Consumption preferences: | d,g |
| Elasticities of votes with respect to resources: | 1 |
| Elasticities of votes with respect to policies: | -1 |

*Level 1 Endogenous Variables*

| | |
|---|---|
| The lobbying ratios: | $K_e/K_0, L_e/L_0$ |
| The "policy product": | $r=(1+s)(1+t)$ |
| The probability of election of the parties: | $\pi,(1-\pi)$ |
| The cone of diversification within which the country's factor endowment ratio must fall for both goods to be produced: | $(K_e/K_0)$min and $(K_e/K_0)$ max |

**Level 1 plus Level 2 Parameters Completely Determine the Policies**

*Level 2 Parameter:* The country's capital/labor endowment ratio Ko/Lo

*Level 2 Endogenous Variables:* The policies

| | |
|---|---|
| The tariff | t |
| The export subsidy | s |

if $K_e/K_0<(K_e/K_0)$ min, then s=0 and t=r-1 from the policy product equation r above
if $K_e/K_0>(K_e/K_0)$ max, then t=0 and s=r-1 from the policy product equation r above

**Level 1, 2 and 3 Parameters Determine the Domestic Economic Variables**

*Level 3 Parameter:* The world product price ratio

*Level 3 Endogenous Variables:*

| | |
|---|---|
| The domestic product price ratio | Q |
| The domestic factor returns labor | W |
| Capital | R |

the specific values of the two policies are then determined by the country's factor endowment ratio.

The increase in capital intensities has an interesting effect on the probabilities of election. In 1950, the model predicts that the probability of election of the procapital party is .42. However, by 1986, this probability has increased to .92. This observation is roughly consistent with the approximately 50-50 electoral outcomes for president in United States from the 1940s through the 1960s and the increase in Republican electoral success since 1968 (Republicans have won 5 out of the last 6 presidential elections). While the model's predictions are in accord with the facts, this result is probably coincidental because we are focussing here only on lobbying over trade policy.

### 3.3. THE RESEARCH STRATEGY

The strategy was to select the parameters for both 1950 and 1986, calibrate the model so that it exactly predicts the tariff in 1950 (because we are free to choose one of the two factor units), and then see how the model does in predicting the 1986 tariff. The bottom line is that the policy part of the model goes off track but the reasons are instructive. The actual production data shows that both exportables and importables became significantly more capital intensive over the past half century. Notice in Table 1 that the capital intensity of production for both U.S. exportables and importables increased from about .5 to .6. This raises capital returns relative to labor returns in both sectors. According to the model, such increases lower capital's participation rate in politics relative to labor's: The grass is greener in production for capital while labor compensates for its declining relative economic position by lobbying more.

The upshot is that increased capital intensities increase the U.S. capital/labor endowment required to keep the capital-intensive export industry in production. But the actual U.S. endowment of capital per laborer just more than doubled between 1950 and 1986 where as the increase in the capital/labor ratio required to avoid production specialization in the import good much more than doubled (notice that it gives a whopping minimum value of 64.858 in TableA 1). At this particular spot, the model is just off track. To compensate for this, I assume that the policy prediction of the model for 1986 is at the lower bound allowable for the country's capital/labor endowment ratio.

Given these assumptions, the model gives a predicted tariff of t=.05 and a predicted export subsidy of s=.00 in 1986. We have nothing to compare the export subsidy within either period. However, we know that in 1986, the *ad valorem* equivalent of all U.S. tariffs was .036 and the similar equivalent for U.S. quantitative restrictions was approximately the same (Magee, Brock and Young, 1989, p. 262 and p. 328). Thus, the total level of protection increased slightly from .06 in 1950 to just over .07 by 1986, while the model predicts a slight decrease.

### 3.4. LOBBYING

The surprising result of the model was its prediction of a decline in the proportion of redistributive activity and the change in its composition over the last half century. The compositional changes are dramatic. The model assumes that there is no free riding within lobbies. First, I describe how the calculations were made. We know from work of Tullock and others that the amounts spent on lobbying are only a fraction of the value received by the lobbies. For purposes of this paper, I assume an arbitrary appropriability parameter on lobbying success of .10 for both factors. Thus the amounts reported below are only 1/10 of the equilibrium amounts predicted by the model. However, this does not affect the political equilibrium since only the ratio of capital and labor resources devoted to lobbying matter in the policy equations and the probabilities of election. All it does is override the two lobbying first-order conditions.

Recall that the only thing that affects the fractions of capital and labor devoted to lobbying are the Cobb-Douglas parameters for capital in production (a inexportables and b inimportables) and the fractions of the importable good in the expenditures by capital and labor (g and d). Decreases in the difference between a and b generate greater magnification. Notice that the capital intensity of importables approaches that of exportables by 1986: The difference between a and b narrows from .009 in 1950 to .004 in 1986. This and the other parameter changes cause m, the elasticity of rentals with respect to relative prices, to about double, from 57 to 101. However, n, the elasticity of wages with respect to relative prices, nearly triples from 53 to 149. Our intuition predicts that such a move will induce labor to devote more resources to politics. In the final general equilibrium, this view is supported: Labor devotes a lot more to politics while capital devotes a lot less.

Capital lobbying drops to 20% of its 1950 value while labor lobbying rises over 60% above its 1950 level. The intuition behind these changes is that the rise in rental rates relative to wages induced substitution effects toward economic activity by capital but toward politics by labor.

When we combine lobbying by both factors, lobbying activity as a percent of value added in manufacturing declined from 3.2 percent to 2.4 percent, or by about 25%. The fraction of capital lobbying declined from 3.6% of capital to .8%; the fraction of labor lobbying rose from 2.9% to 4.8% (Table1). When we apply these numbers to the levels of income in Tables A2 and A3, we get the calculations shown in Table A4.

The bottom line: The model predicts an increase in the absolute level of lobbying by both factors but a decrease in lobbying as a fraction of value added. News accounts have suggested that the absolute level of lobbying is up. The model suggests that we should not confuse this with an increase in the relative importance of rent seeking.

## 4. The Effects of Prices on Protection

Using the Cobb-Douglas production, utility and logit probability of election functions, the equilibrium tariff rate is independent of relative prices (*i.e.*, the country's terms of trade). For the simulations in this paper based on the Cobb-Douglas model, we would conclude that any world relative price changes would have no effect on the equilibrium tariffs. However, with Leontief production, when the price of importables falls, labor increases its political activity and tariffs rise. The calculations here and those underlying Figure 2 use reduced-form estimates with Leontief production from Magee, Brock and Young (1989, chp. 13). Notice in Figure 2 that exogenous decreases in the world prices of a country's imports induce increased protectionist lobbying and ultimately higher tariffs.

Between 1950 and 1986, there was a 30 percent rise in the U.S. terms of manufacturing trade (the index rose .244 from .803 to 1.047). This implies a fall in the price of manufactured imports relative to manufactured exports, which stirs up U.S. protectionists. The .244 rise in the terms of trade times the tariff equation coefficient of .256 yields a predicted change in equilibrium protection of .062 (the estimates are from an endogenous tariff equation estimated over the period 1905-1980). U.S. tariffs should have risen 6.2 percentage points because of the increased import price pressure. The rise of VERs and other nontariff restrictions on U.S. imports in the 1970s and 1980s are a political consequences of these economic changes.

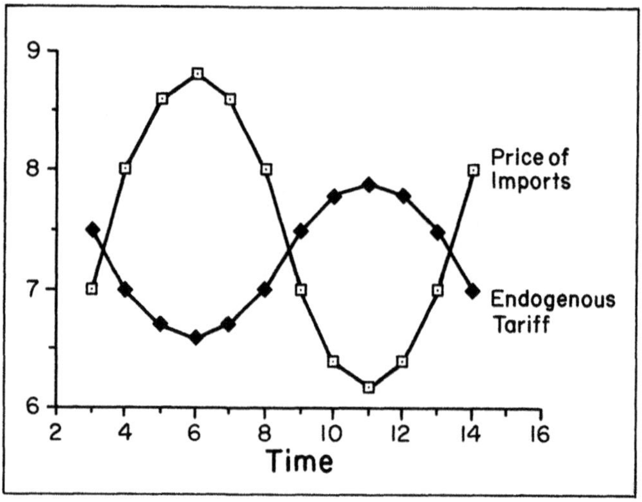


*Figure 2. Illustration of the effects of changes in the world price of imports relative to exports on the equilibrium tariff. Notice that there is less variability in the tariff line, so that that endogenous tariffs do not fully offset the effects of world prices on domestic prices. Thus, with endogenous politics, domestic prices will vary less than international prices.*

Table A1

Details of the Simulations

| | 1950 | 1986 |
|---|---|---|
| r= | 1.08104 | 1.046928 |
| alpha | 0.488 | 0.598 |
| beta | 0.479 | 0.594 |
| gamma | 0.5 | 0.5 |
| delta | 0.5 | 0.5 |
| m= | 57.4 | 101 |
| n= | 53.7 | 149.0 |
| a= | 0.713 | 10.939 |
| b= | 1.402 | 0.091 |
| c= | 1.970 | 142.939 |
| d= | 4.861 | 0.191 |
| r equation | 0.000 | 0.000 |
| (rc/ad)= | 0.784 | 8.452 |
| (rd/bc)= | 1.379 | 0.124 |
| $K_e/K_o$= | 0.362 | 0.077 |
| $L_e/L_o$= | 0.289 | 0.475 |
| $K_o/L_o$ max=rbc/d | 0.614 | 71.089 |
| T= | 1.000 | 1.002 |
| S= | 1.081 | 1.047 |
| $K_o/L_o$ min=bc/rd | 0.526 | 64.858 |
| T= | 1.081 | 1.050 |
| S= | 1.000 | 1.000 |
| pi=1/b= | 0.416 | 0.917 |

Table A2

Basic Data for 1950

| A | B | C | D | E | F | G | H | I | J |
|---|---|---|---|---|---|---|---|---|---|
| SIC | All Employees Salaries | Production Workers Wage: Total | Value Added | Wages/ Value Added | Prod Wages/ Val Added | Exports 1970 (in millions) | Imports 1970 | All wage shr exports G*E | All wage shr imports H*E |
| 20 | 4,411,245 | 2,854,851 | 10,094,708 | 0.44 | 0.28 | 2,520 | 3,562 | 1101.20 | 1556.54 |
| 21 | 212,536 | 177,313 | 806,118 | 0.26 | 0.22 | 191 | 17 | 50.36 | 4.48 |
| 22 | 3,354,821 | 2,853,294 | 5,624,030 | 0.60 | 0.51 | 461 | 1,059 | 274.99 | 631.71 |
| 23 | 2,764,024 | 2,169,240 | 4,174,430 | 0.66 | 0.52 | 251 | 1,287 | 166.20 | 852.16 |
| 24 | 1,748,234 | 1,509,888 | 3,165,760 | 0.55 | 0.48 | 687 | 989 | 379.38 | 546.16 |
| 25 | 1,012,877 | 774,085 | 1,666,898 | 0.61 | 0.46 | 48 | 217 | 29.17 | 131.86 |
| 26 | 1,604,172 | 1,237,443 | 3,432,115 | 0.47 | 0.36 | 1,106 | 1,548 | 516.94 | 723.54 |
| 27 | 2,906,083 | 1,699,948 | 4,902,972 | 0.59 | 0.35 | 333 | 176 | 197.38 | 104.32 |
| 28 | 2,341,957 | 1,470,795 | 7,236,618 | 0.32 | 0.20 | 3,997 | 1,256 | 1293.53 | 406.47 |
| 29 | 850,261 | 623,752 | 2,138,570 | 0.40 | 0.29 | 575 | 1,560 | 228.61 | 620.23 |
| 30 | 831,103 | 639,271 | 1,609,586 | 0.52 | 0.40 | 341 | 661 | 176.07 | 341.30 |
| 31 | 949,271 | 773,381 | 1,498,811 | 0.63 | 0.52 | 64 | 702 | 40.53 | 444.61 |
| 32 | 1,529,473 | 1,220,126 | 3,138,263 | 0.49 | 0.39 | 445 | 542 | 216.88 | 264.15 |
| 33 | 4,157,451 | 3,400,055 | 7,950,990 | 0.52 | 0.43 | 2,323 | 3,916 | 1214.66 | 2047.62 |
| 34 | 3,404,061 | 2,523,638 | 6,210,759 | 0.55 | 0.41 | 1,361 | 799 | 745.95 | 437.92 |
| 35 | 5,063,008 | 3,609,065 | 8,764,652 | 0.58 | 0.41 | 7,880 | 2,339 | 4551.98 | 1351.15 |
| 36 | 2,517,870 | 1,789,460 | 4,793,948 | 0.53 | 0.37 | 2,972 | 2,717 | 1560.95 | 1427.02 |
| 37 | 4,679,459 | 3,656,460 | 8,546,828 | 0.55 | 0.43 | 6,486 | 6,362 | 3551.14 | 3483.25 |
| 38 | 828,204 | 539,891 | 1,418,291 | 0.58 | 0.38 | 1,294 | 659 | 755.62 | 384.82 |
| 39 | 1,432,901 | 1,043,742 | 2,501,432 | 0.57 | 0.42 | 507 | 1,196 | 290.43 | 685.11 |
| | 46,599,011 | 34,565,698 | 89,675,779 | | | 33,842 | 31,564 | 17,342 | 16,444.43 |
| | | | | | | wage share for X,M | | .512 | .521 |
| | | | | | | alpha,beta | | .488 | .479 |

Table A3

Basic Data for 1986

| A<br>SIC | B<br>All Employees Salaries | C<br>Production Workers Wage: Total | D<br>Value Added | E<br>Wages/ Value Added | F<br>Prod Wages/ Val Added | G<br>Exports 1970 (in millions) | H<br>Imports 1970 | I<br>All wage shr exports G*E | J<br>All wage shr imports H*E |
|---|---|---|---|---|---|---|---|---|---|
| 20 | 28,567,300 | 17,788,700 | 112,190,500 | 0.25 | 0.16 | 2,520 | 3,562 | 641.67 | 907.00 |
| 21 | 1,360,400 | 912,400 | 12,724,600 | 0.11 | 0.07 | 191 | 17 | 20.42 | 1.82 |
| 22 | 10,305,800 | 7,897,900 | 22,232,300 | 0.46 | 0.36 | 461 | 1,059 | 213.70 | 490.90 |
| 23 | 12,471,200 | 8,948,900 | 28,451,300 | 0.44 | 0.31 | 251 | 1,287 | 110.02 | 564.14 |
| 24 | 10,819,700 | 8,135,200 | 23,238,600 | 0.47 | 0.35 | 687 | 989 | 319.86 | 460.47 |
| 25 | 8,030,400 | 5,556,400 | 17,659,400 | 0.45 | 0.31 | 48 | 217 | 21.83 | 98.68 |
| 26 | 16,112,800 | 11,296,900 | 43,924,500 | 0.37 | 0.26 | 1,106 | 1,548 | 405.71 | 567.85 |
| 27 | 29,890,400 | 14,099,300 | 78,150,400 | 0.38 | 0.18 | 333 | 176 | 127.36 | 67.32 |
| 28 | 23,710,900 | 11,755,600 | 100,013,200 | 0.24 | 0.12 | 3,997 | 1,256 | 947.60 | 297.77 |
| 29 | 4,214,700 | 2,598,200 | 17,495,800 | 0.24 | 0.15 | 575 | 1,560 | 138.52 | 375.80 |
| 30 | 15,273,300 | 10,123,600 | 37,236,400 | 0.41 | 0.27 | 341 | 661 | 139.87 | 271.12 |
| 31 | 1,690,300 | 1,213,400 | 3,611,400 | 0.47 | 0.34 | 64 | 702 | 29.95 | 328.57 |
| 32 | 11,745,200 | 8,351,800 | 30,676,700 | 0.38 | 0.27 | 445 | 542 | 170.38 | 207.52 |
| 33 | 18,881,600 | 13,471,700 | 38,092,300 | 0.50 | 0.35 | 2,323 | 3,916 | 1151.47 | 1941.08 |
| 34 | 33,115,800 | 21,816,700 | 68,620,600 | 0.48 | 0.32 | 1,361 | 799 | 656.81 | 385.59 |
| 35 | 49,645,200 | 25,421,900 | 108,365,000 | 0.46 | 0.23 | 7,880 | 2,339 | 3610.06 | 1071.56 |
| 36 | 49,213,600 | 23,360,900 | 112,421,500 | 0.44 | 0.21 | 2,972 | 2,717 | 1301.02 | 1189.39 |
| 37 | 56,707,600 | 33,625,500 | 125,705,600 | 0.45 | 0.27 | 6,486 | 6,362 | 2925.93 | 2869.99 |
| 38 | 14,818,200 | 6,704,000 | 40,005,300 | 0.37 | 0.17 | 1,294 | 659 | 479.31 | 244.10 |
| 39 | 5,892,300 | 3,520,400 | 14,622,000 | 0.40 | 0.24 | 507 | 1,196 | 204.31 | 481.96 |
| | 46,599,011 | 236,599,400 | 1,035,437,400 | | | 33,842 | 31,564 | 13,616 | 12,823 |
| | | | | | | wage share for X,M | | .402 | .406 |
| | | | | | | alpha,beta | | .488 | .594 |

**TABLE A4**
**LOBBYING CALCULATIONS**

| | | 1950 | 1986 |
|---|---|---|---|
| | LOBBYING FRACTIONS | | |
| Share of Capital | | 0.36 | 0.08 |
| | 0.1 | 0.036 | 0.008 |
| Share of Labor | | 0.29 | 0.48 |
| | 0.1 | 0.029 | 0.048 |
| | ACTUAL WAGE AND VALUE ADDED DATA | | |
| Total Wages | | 46.6 | 402.5 |
| Total Capital | | 43.1 | 632.9 |
| Value added<br>(Source: Tables A2 and A3) | | 89.7 | 1035.4 |
| | LOBBYING ($ BILLIONS) | | |
| Value of Capital | | $15.5 | $50.6 |
| | 0.1 | $1.6 | $5.1 |
| Value of Labor | | $13.5 | $193.2 |
| | 0.1 | $1.4 | $19.3 |
| Total | | $29.0 | $243.8 |
| | 0.1 | $2.9 | $24.4 |
| Total Lobbying | | $32.4 | $23.5 |
| As % Value Added | | 3.2 | 2.4 |

# REFERENCES


Aranson, Peter H. and Peter C. Ordeshook, 1981, "Regulation, Redistribution and Public Choice," *Public Choice*, Vol. 37, 69-100.

Austen-Smith, D., 1981, "Voluntary Pressure Groups," *Economica*, Vol. 48, 143-153.

Austen-Smith, D., 1984, "Interest Groups, Campaign Contributions and Spatial Voting," presented to the Allied Social Science Association Annual Meeting, Dallas, Texas.

Baldwin, Robert E., 1984, "Trade Policies in Developed Countries," in Ronald W. Jones and Peter B. Kenen (eds.), **Handbook of International Economics**, Amsterdam: North Holland, 571-619.

Baldwin, Robert E., 1986, **The Political Economy of U.S. Import Policy**, Cambridge: MIT Press.

Baron, David P., 1986, "Service-Induced Campaign Contributions and the Electoral Equilibrium," Paper presented at the Conference on Political Information and Political Theory, University of Texas, February.

Becker, Gary S., 1983,"A Theory of Competition Among Pressure Groups for Political Influence," *Quarterly Journal of Economics*, Vol. 98, 371-400.

Bernholz, Peter, 1977, "Dominant Interest Groups and Powerless Parties," *Kyklos*, Vol. 30, 411-420.

Brander, James A. and Barbara J. Spencer, 1985, "Export Subsidies and International Market Share Rivalry," *Journal of International Economics*, Vol. 18, 83-100.

Brock, William A. and Stephen P. Magee, 1978,"The Economics of Special-Interest Politics: The Case of the Tariff," *American Economic Review*, Vol. 68, 246-50.

Brock, William A. and Stephen P. Magee, 1980, "Tariff Formation in a Democracy," in John Black and Brian Hindley (eds.), **Current Issues in Commercial Policy and Diplomacy**, New York: St. Martins Press, 1-9.

Buchanan, James M., Robert D. Tollison and Gordon Tullock , 1980, **Toward a Theory of the Rent-Seeking Society**, College Station, Texas A&M University Press.

Conybeare, John A. C., 1982, "The Rent-Seeking State and Revenue Diversification," *World Politics*, Vol. 35, 1, 25-42.

Findlay, Ronald J. and Stanislaw Wellisz, 1982, "Endogenous Tariffs, the Political Economy of Trade Restrictions and Welfare," in Jagdish N. Bhagwati (ed.), **Import Competition and Response**, Chicago: University of Chicago Press, 223-238.

Hillman, Arye L., 1982, "Declining Industries and Political-Support Protectionist Motives," *American Economic Review*, Vol. 72, 1180-7.

Hillman, Arye L. and Doy Samet, 1987, "Dissipation of Contestable Rents by Small Numbers of Contenders," *Public Choice*, Vol. 54, 63-82.

Hinich, Melvin J., 1981, "Voting as an Act of Contribution," *Public Choice*, Vol. 36, 135-140.

Houthakker, H.S. and Stephen P. Magee, 1969, "Income and Price Elasticities in World Trade," *Review of Economics and Statistics*, Vol. 51 (May), 111-125.

Krueger, Anne O., 1974, "The Political Economy ofthe Rent-Seeking Society," *American Economic Review*, Vol. 64, 291-303.

Lindbeck, Assar, 1985, "Redistribution policy and Expansion of the Public Sector," *Journal of Public Economics*, Vol. 28, 309-328.

Magee, Stephen P., William A.Brock and Leslie Young, 1989, **Black Hole Tariffs and Endogenous Policy Theory: Political Economy in General Equilibrium**, New York: Cambridge University Press.

Magee, Stephen P. and Leslie Young, 1987, "Endogenous Protection in the U.S., 1900 - 1984," in Robert M. Stern (ed.), **U.S. Trade Policies in a Changing World Economy**, Cambridge: MIT Press, 145-195.

Mayer, Wolfgang, 1984, "Endogenous Tariff Formation," *American Economic Review*, Vol. 74, 970-985.

Mohammad, Sharif and John Whalley, 1984, "Rent Seeking in India: Its Costs and Policy Significance," *Kyklos*, Vol. 37, 387-413.

Olson, Mancur, 1965, **The Logic of Collective Action: Public Goods and the Theory of Groups**, Cambridge: Harvard University Press.

Stern, Robert M. (ed.), 1987, **U.S. Trade Policies in a Changing World Economy**, Cambridge: MIT Press.

Stigler, George J., 1974, "Free Riders and Collective Action: An Appendix to Theories of Economic Regulation," *Bell Journal of Economicss and Management Science*, Vol. 5, 359-365.

Stolper, Wolfgang and Paul A. Samuelson, 1941, "Protection and Real Wages," *Review of Economic Studies*, Vol. 9, 58-73.

Tollison, Robert D., 1982, "Rent Seeking: A Survey," *Kyklos*, Vol. 35, 28-47.

Tullock, Gordon, 1967, "The Welfare Cost of Tariffs, Monopolies and Theft," *Western Economic Journal*, Vol. 5, 224-232

Varian, Hal R. 1987, "Measuring the Deadweight Costs of DUP and Rent Seeking Activities," Conference on Political Economy, The World Bank, Washington, D.C., June.

Wellisz, Stanislaw and Wilson, John D., 1986, "Lobbying and Tariff Formation: A Deadweight Loss Consideration," *Journal of International Economics*, Vol. 20, 367-375.

Whalley, John, 1985, **Trade Liberalization Among Major World Trading Areas**, Cambridge: MIT Press.

Young, Leslie and Stephen P. Magee, 1986, "Endogenous Protection, Factor Returns and Resource Allocation" *Review of Economic Studies*, Vol. 53, 407-419.

## FOUR UNPUBLISHED PAPERS AND NOTES OF H.S. HOUTHAKKER

*Editors' introduction*

This section includes four papers that were written by Henk in the 1960s which have never been published. Three of the papers relate to Houthakker and Taylor -- indeed, two of these relate to the very origins of the basic Houthakker-Taylor model -- while the fourth was Henk's presidential address to the Econometric Society in 1967. The first paper, "On a Class of Dynamic Demand Functions," was given at the U.S. winter meetings of the Econometric Society in New York City in December 1961.[1] In that paper, Henk presented for the first time the basic ideas underlying the dynamics of state and stock adjustment and habit formation and showed how such dynamics can be integrated into utility maximization. The quadratic utility function discussed by Henk was subsequently applied to data for the U.S. and Canada in Chapter 5 of the 1970 edition of H & T. The second paper, "A Technique for Estimating Demand Functions from Time Series," is a short note describing the procedure for eliminating the unobservable state variables from the empirical demand functions. With minor modifications this procedure underlay estimation of all of the state-and flow-adjustment models in both editions of H & T.

Shortly after the first edition of H & T was completed (in early 1965), the Office of Business Economics (now the Bureau of Economic Analysis of the Department of Commerce) published a major revision in the National Income Accounts, including all of the PCE data which had been used in the empirical analyses. The third paper in this section, "The Dynamics of Total Consumption and Saving," was motivated by a desire to see what effect these revisions had on the results for total consumption and saving. The research was undertaken by Henk in collaboration with Suresh Tendulkar, then a gifted young economics graduate student at Harvard, now a Professor of Economics at the Delhi School of Economics. Most, although not all, of the results were subsequently published in Chapter 7 of the 1970 edition of H & T. The results that were not published related to a reformulation of the aggregate consumption and saving functions with disposable income disaggregated into its NIA components of wages and salaries, income from property, transfer payments, social insurance taxes, and personal taxes. The models allowed for different types of income (or subtractions from income, in case of taxes) to have different marginal propensities to consume or save. This model was subsequently used by Taylor (1972) to analyze saving out of different types of income and by Juster and Taylor (1975) to investigate how saving reacts to uncertainty and changing price expectations.

As noted in the Introduction to this volume, one of Henk's many honors is that he is a past president of the Econometric Society. The fourth paper, "Are There Laws of Consumption?," was his presidential address presented at the 1967 winter meetings of the Society in Washington, D.C. Henk delivered his address mid-way through an academic-year stay at the Council of Economic Advisers. His intent was clearly to publish the address, complete with

---

[1] An abstract of this paper was published in *Econometrica*, Vol. 30, No. 3, July 1962, pp. 588 - 9.



*L. Phlips and L.D. Taylor (eds.), Aggregation, Consumption and Trade*, 217–218.

tables and charts, but this never materialized (which is hardly surprising to anyone who has ever spent time at the Council of Economic Advisers). The paper that is published here is just as he delivered it -- complete with the standard CEA disclaimer!

## REFERENCES


Juster, F.T. and Taylor, L.D. (1975), "Towards a Theory of Saving Behavior," *American Economic Review*, Vol. 65, No. 2, May 1975, pp. 203-209.

Taylor, L.D. (1972), "Saving Out of Different Types of Income," *Brookings Papers on Economic Activity*, 1971, No. 2, pp. 383-407.

# ARE THERE LAWS OF CONSUMPTION?

H. S. HOUTHAKKER*
*Henry Lee Professor of Economics*
*Department of Economics*
*Harvard University*
*Littauer Center*
*Cambridge, MA 02138*

As most of you will recognize, the title of this address is second-hand. It is a variation of one used nearly two decades ago by one of the leaders of our profession, whom the Econometric Society is proud to count among its earliest Fellows. When Paul Douglas gave his Presidential Address to the American Economic Association, he was able to point to a large body of evidence in support of the production function that has made his name a household word among us. And twenty years later it appears that subsequent experience with this function has amply justified the faith of its originatiors in the possibility of establishing simple quantitative laws in economics.

But production is not my subject this afternoon. What matters in the the title for the present purpose is the question, "Are there laws?" This question is of fundamental importance not only to economics, but all empirical sciences; it is in fact *the* question with which these sciences are concerned. Laws are in the first instance empirical regularities, which may originally have been observed without much theoretical basis. This is what happened, for instance, with two of the most important economic laws discovered in the Nineteenth Century, Engel's law of food consumption and Pareto's law of the distribution of income; it was not until much later that these empirical regularities could be incorporated into a theoretical framework. A large part of the business of the empirical sciences is to develop theories within which already discovered laws have their place and new regularities can be explored. By linking these laws to other phenomena the theories give meaning to the laws, for a mere empirical regularity conveys only limited credibility and cannot be extrapolated with much confidence. In their turn, the laws give significance to the theories that can account for them. In particular, the establishment of empirical laws enables us to avoid the *ceteris paribus* assumption that has long been the bane of economic theory. The propositions of economic theory are always conditional, but empirical research tells us which of the conditions have to be formulated explicitly and which can be swept under the rug in the form of an error term.

---

* [Presidential Address to the Econometric Society, Washington, D.C., December 1967.] The views expressed in this paper are not necessarily those of the Council of Economic Advisers. The published version will contain supporting tables and charts.
[The address was never published; an abstract appeared in *Econometrica*, July 1968.]



*L. Phlips and L.D. Taylor (eds.), Aggregation, Consumption and Trade,* 219–223.

That laws of consumption are possible is by no means obvious. It is, in fact, denied by two widespread opinions, which I shall descibe as the naive and the vulgar views. The naive view is that consumers are inherently unpredictable creatures full of arbitrary whims and fashions, rather like the normal male view of women. There is no lack of substance in this observation, and I shall return to it later on. What the naive view overlooks, however, is that aggregate behavior is often more predictable than individual behavior, and it is the aggregate behavior that matters for most of the purposes of economics. A life insurance company does not normally seek to determine when one of its policy-holders will die; it knows that aggregate mortality is much more predictable than indicidual mortality, and its whole business is based on this fact.

The vulgar view holds that consumers' purchases are largely the result of advertising pressure. It has long been fashionable at Madison Avenue cocktail parties and it has now also cropped up in the works of J. K. Galbraith. It implies that advertising agencies can deliver the demand just as old-fashioned machine politicians could deliver the vote.

Now it cannot be denied that advertising has some influence on the pattern of comsumer demand, especially when we descend to a very detailed breakdown of expenditures. It may well be true that the comsumption of different brands of soap has something to do with the advertising expenditures of soap manufacturers. In fact, some years ago I participated in an evaluation of an advertising campaign conducted by a group of California lettuce growers and demonstrated that their campaign had indeed shifted the damand curve for lettuce to the right. But when it comes to broader items of expenditure than soap or lettuce, it becomes very hard to detect any effect at all. A clear case in point is cigarettes, where we have the phenomenon of two opposite kinds of advertising -- the tobacco companies want us to smoke, the Government wants us not to smoke. The net effect appears to be a standoff; so far it does not seem that tobacco consumption has deviated appreciably from its normal pattern. The cigarette situation is typical of the contempt with which consumers are often viewed. Galbraith may be right in saying that only a gravely retarded citizen needs to be told that the American Tobacco Company has cigarettes for sale, but it is equally true that only a greatly retarded citizen needs to be told that there appears to be some causal connection between cigarettes and cancer. What the citizen has not been told is whether cigarette smoking is any more hazardous to health than, say, drinking whisky or driving a car. Perhaps consumers are not as gravely retarded as the advertising profession (not to mention the Federal Trade Commission) would have us believe.

And this is where ecomomics comes in. Neither the arbitrary-whims-and-fashions school nor the Madison Avenue school can carry us far in explaining consumption, despite the element of truth contained in both of them. To explain consumption we have to recognize the advantages of attributing a considerable degree of rationality to consumers, at least in the aggregate. The assumption of rationality is a good one, not only because there is much direct and indirect evidence that consumers are basically rational, but also because it is a powerful assumption, by which I mean that it has a great many testable implications. It is not by accident, therefore, that the leading investigators of consumer demand have all sought to link their empirical work to the pure theory of consumers' choice. However, we should not go too far in this either. The pure throry of consumers' choice is a useful first step towards the establishment of a realistic conception of consumer behavior, but it is not adequate by itself. For one thing, it is too general and needs to be specialized, in particular by postulating particular types of preference orderings. It also needs to generalized, particularly in a dynamic direction so as to recognize that rationality is a process of adaptation. In our book Taylor and I have tried to show the power of a dynamic approach to the study of consumer demand. The model used there lets current consumption depend on past determinants, but in a very specific manner which keeps the analysis reasonably simple. Not only does such an approach give good fits and reasonably accurate forecasts, it also enables us to deal more directly with the statistical problem of autocorrelation, which has long plagued time-series analysis.

The approach used in the first edition of our book, however, is not fully integrated into the pure theory of consumers' choice. This is so because the linear demand fuctions used do not satisfy the budget equation identically if prices change. It is, however, possible to make a relatively minor modification in these functions which presents them as derivations from a dynamic quadratic utility function in which the arguments are stocks as well as flows. In a paper presented at last year's Econometric Society meetings Taylor and I reported on some first work along those lines and since then we have gained much more experience. The main feature of this dynamic utility function is that it requires estimation of the marginal utility of income of total expenditure. This may at first seem like a relapse into cardinalism, but it really is nothing of the sort. We do not measure the marginal utility of income as such, but only that particular measure which corresponds to a quadratic utility function. Since the data do not identify the cardinal form of [the] utility function, there is nothing which enables us to say that the particular measure used is the "true" measure, if indeed there is such a thing.

Experience with this dynamic quadratic preference ordering has been fairly encouraging. The estimates of the income and price elasticities are mostly plausible, and the predictions made from the model do not compare too badly with actual data. Nevertheless, it appears the restriction to a quadratic utility function is a rather severe one. Quadratic utility functions have the unpleasant property that saturation can reached rather easily, because the marginal utility of income is a linear declining function of income. Since there is no evidence that in our society we are anywhere near saturation, it would be better if other dynamic preference orderings could be developed, but here we run into a technical difficulty. The success of the linear dynamic demand functions, and of the quasi-linear dynamic functions derived from a quadratic preference ordering, depend on a trick due to Koyck and Nerlove, who first showed how it is possible to eliminate stock variables from a flow equation. Unfortunately, this trick does not work for nonlinear equations. What we really need is a dynamic logarithmic preference ordering, because there is other evidence of the suitability of double-logarithmic functions for demand analysis. So far I have not been successful in finding such a preference ordering that can be estimated without too much difficulty.

Mention of the double logarithmic function brings us almost inevitably to household budget data, the study of which was the main occupation of the early period of consumption analysis and which was also my own starting point 25 years ago. In those days time series existed only for a few commodities and they were often unsatisfactory as regards quality and length. Budget surveys, on the other hand, have been available for many countries and for many years. It is only recently that time series of consumption have become good enough and long enough to become the main raw material of demand analysis. The development of national income accounting has revolutionized this area, as it has many others in economics. Budget surveys, on the other hand, have lost ground, partly as a result of unavoidable and avoidable technical weaknesses. The information obtained in budget surveys is of very variable quality. If answers are collected by interview methods relying on the memory of respondents, gross errors can easily be introduced, especially on the income side. A more accurate method appears to be the keeping of account books by participating households, but this cuts into the response rate and therefore may easily make the sample unrepresentative. As yet it does not appear that a good course has been found between the Scylla of meaningless answers and the Charybdis of biased samples. In this area there is certainly no safety in numbers. The only difference between a poorly designed survey of 3000 households and a poorly designed survey of 10,000 households is that the latter will probably cost three times as much. Detailed comparisons between the aggregates obtained by blowing up surveys with national accounts reveal many inconsistencies, even in items such as rent paid where recall is presumably not a problem. The question must be raised whether household surveys of the kind traditional in the United States are really worth their very considerable cost, and whether the money could not be better spent on smaller but more accurate surveys. Merely providing a basis for the consumer price index is certainly not adequate justification; the national accounts would probably provide more accurate weights at a small fraction of the cost.

Another common failing of budget surveys is that they under-represent high-income households. From the aggregate point of view a household survey shoud be so designed that every dollar spent has an equal chance of being represented in the survey, whereas present surveys more often aim at equal representation of all households, irrespective of their income level.

There are nevertheless important purposes for which cross-section data are inevitable. I have already mentioned the problem of the shape of demand functions, which can best be studied from cross-section data because the range of income or total expenditure is much wider than in time series. Another problem of interest, which brings us back to the naive view I mentioned earlier, is the variablility of consumption patterns among households. If we run regressions on individual households in a survey, the multiple correlation coefficients are generally very low, indicating that the explanatory variables have little power at the individual level. Explanation of individual behavior would almost certainly carry us far outside economics, but it is not really necessary to go in that direction., From many points of view it would already be interesting if we could say something about the disperison of households around the Engel curve. The studies which have been made of this problem suggest that for a given family size the coefficient of variation of expenditures is roughly constant throughout the income range, but much work remains to be done. An intriguing application of the study of variability would be to the estimates of effects of household size. It can be argued that a household's well-being depends on the discretion it enjoys in choosing its consumption pattern. We expect to find more variation in small households than in large households at the same income level because in large households "needs" in some sense are more important in determining what can be bought. It is conceivable, therefore, that by taking household groups with equal variability we can construct an indifference curve between income and household size, which would provide us with a new answer to an old and practically important question.

A question which is of importance both in cross-section and in time-series analysis is the choice of the the explanatory variable, in particular whether we should use income or total expenditure. In time series there does not seem to be much to choose between these two, but in household surveys there is clear evidence that total expenditure is a much more useful variable, and that in fact income is useful only to the extent that it is correlated with total expenditure. These conclusions follow from a principal components analysis of individual households' expenditures, and it may be due to the poor quality of the income data obtained in cross sections. But it is also likely to reflect some kind of permanent income effect. In this connection, it is worth mentioning that income change, which is an important variable in time-series analysis, does not appear to be useful in cross-section analysis. This may again be due to problems of data quality.

If the dynamic theory used in time-series analysis is indeed valid, then it is clear that single-period cross sections are not sufficient for consumption analysis. The model requires data not only on past income (or on income change) but also on past consumption. This means that we need panel surveys, in which the same household appears in more than one period. It was in fact the analysis of a panel survey that first led me to this dynamic model when I generalized the already accepted idea that the demand for cars depends, among other things, on the pre-existing inventory of cars. Panel data are not only expensive but they also raise troublesome statistical problems; however, there can be little doubt that this is the direction which household survey analysis has to take.

I have talked so far about time-series and cross-section analysis. There is another type of material that has already been shown to be useful to demand research, namely, geographical comparison. I do not have the time to go into this area now.

Returning the question raised in the title of my address, I believe that the accumulated experience justifies us in saying,"Yes, Virginia, there are laws of consumption." We now have good equations for most categories of consumption, and what is even more important, the results obtained by different investigators tend to agree. Consumer behavior is certainly no less predictable than most other economic behavior. This being said, however, I should also admit that the nature of the laws of consumption is still rather obscure. Why, for instance, is it that the income elasticity of demand for food is less than 1, although certainly much greater than zero? This has traditionally been attributed to physiological considerations, but I doubt whether these provide the answer. After a relatively modest level, increased expenditures on food do not consist in buying larger quantities but in buying better qualities. There is nothing in physiology which tells us that the available range of qualities is so limited the the income elasticity has to be less than 1. If people were to buy more and more luxury foods at higher income levels, they could spend an increasing proportion of their income [on food] if they wanted to, but somehow this is not what happens. Much the same applies to other items of expenditure. Perhaps to understand the nature of the laws of consumption we have to know more about the supply side.

This brings me to the final point, namely, the role of general equilibrium analysis in the study of demand. In the past we have had to rely perhaps excessively on ordinary least squares techniques because an adequate theory of supply has not been available. Recent work on price equations suggests that the situation may be changing. It now appears that the simple proposition that prices are largely determined by production costs may serve as a crude theory of supply, and this will in turn enable us to formulate demand analysis with greater regard to the endogenous nature of prices. I believe it is an area where much progress can be expected in the not-too-distant future.

# THE DYNAMICS OF TOTAL CONSUMPTION AND SAVING*

**H. S. HOUTHAKKER**
*Henry Lee Professor of Economics*
*Department of Economics*
*Harvard University*
*Littauer Center*
*Cambridge, MA 02138*

**SURESH D. TENDULKAR**
*Delhi School of Economics*
*University Avenue*
*Delhi 110007*
*India*

In Houthakker and Taylor [3], certain variants of the dynamic stock-flow model developed for forecasting individual items of consumption expenditure were applied also to total consumption and saving. After the results had gone to press, a drastic revision of the basic data was published by the United States Department of Commerce in the August 1965 *Survey of Current Business*. According to the revised data, the personal savings ratio is much lower than it appeared to be and has had a downward trend in recent years. Since the earlier research gave a good explanation of the old data, the question arises whether the equations used can also account for the rather surprising new picture of savings. This paper reports on new calculations to assess the changes in the estimates of the structural parameters as a result of the revision. It also seeks to examine the population effect (the aggregate model as compared to the per capita model) and the effect of disposable income components on savings (in particular different saving propensities of labor and non-labor income-earners). The analysis proceeds both on the annual and the quarterly level. The basic demand function is formulated in continuous time and theoretically implies certain relations between the annual and the quarterly estimates; if these relations are satisfied, the underlying theory receives support.

Some general observations about the data used are in order. The series of aggregate personal expenditure and aggregate saving are those given by the Office of Business Economics in the framework of its national income calculations. In particular, saving is obtained as a residual between personal income on the one hand and the sum of personal consumption outlays and personal tax and non-tax payments on the other. Because of its derivation, this difference cannot be broken down either by forms of saving or by groups of savers. Moreover, relatively small changes in the personal income and expenditure aggregates

---

*Research supported by a grant from the National Science Foundation. We are grateful to Lester D. Taylor for his comments.



*L. Phlips and L.D. Taylor (eds.), Aggregation, Consumption and Trade*, 225–245.

may lead to disproportionately large changes in the estimated personal saving. We are warned accordingly ([7] p. 99) to interpret quarterly estimates "more as broad indicators of general tendency than as precise measures of the quarter-to-quarter movements." Another notable feature relates to the seasonal adjustment procedure. The quarterly saving estimates are not directly corrected for seasonal patterns but result from the seasonal corrections applied separately to the various components of the aggregate personal income and expenditures. Hence it is difficult to judge what sort of seasonally adjusted annual savings rates for each quarter are obtained. (It would have been desirable to get unadjusted estimates and work out the equations with seasonal dummies.) This factor may assume importance in assessing the theoretically given relations between the annual and quarterly estimates. Although no specific reference is made to the revision of the seasonal procedures in the August 1965 issue of the *Survey*, one gets the impression from [7] that the revised and improved seasonal corrections were applied in most cases from the beginning of 1951, thereby implying that the adjustments for the quarterly data from 1946 to 1950 were either of doubtful value or that the data were too crude for adjustment. This may be seen from the very wide swings in the quarterly estimates of saving from 1947 to 1951.

The effects of the latest revision on the variables of interest may now be noted. The definitional changes, much smaller in magnitude than the statistical change, scale down personal saving to the extent that the profits of life insurance and all mutual institutions (savings banks, savings and loan associations, credit unions and insurance companies) are credited not to the policy holders but to the institutions themselves. Disposable income underwent upward statistical revision as a result of upward corrections in the rental value of owner-occupied housing and the employers' contributions to employee group insurance programs. The overall result of the revision is that the ratio of saving to disposable income has gone down, especially in the post-1952 period, as compared with the previously available estimates (*cf.* [8] p. 19).

## 1. Theoretical Model

The underlying theoretical model (See [3], pp. 8-21) is of the dynamic stock-flow variety formulated in continuous time and linear in the basic variables. It may be written as:

$$(1) \quad q(t) = \alpha + \beta s(t) + \gamma x(t)$$

$$(2) \quad \dot{s}(t) = q(t) - \delta s(t),$$

where q(t) and x(t) are instantaneous flows of consumption per capita at time t and s(t) is the level of the state variable per capita at t. The second equation makes the time rate of change in the state variable equal to the flow at that time reduced by depreciation, which is assumed to be proportional to the level of the state variable. This fact can be used to eliminate the state variable from (1).

If in this model the state variable is held constant, the short-run marginal propensity to consume (MPC) may be seen to be $\gamma$. When the state variable is fully adjusted (with $\dot{s}(t) = 0$) the long run MPC comes out to be

$$(3) \quad \gamma' = \frac{\gamma\delta}{\delta - \beta} \, .$$

As could be intuitively expected, the short-run MPC exceeds its long-run counterpart for durable goods ($\beta < 0$) and falls short of it for nondurable habit-forming commodities ($\beta > 0$). In the case of steady linear growth, which implies the constancy of the time-derivatives of q, s, and x over time, we obtain (3) as the proportionality factor between the time-rates of change of consumption and disposable income.

Using the finite approximation to continuous time (for further details see again [3]), (1) and (2) can be reduced to the following estimation equation:

$$(4)\quad q_t = \frac{\alpha\delta\tau^2}{1-\frac{\tau}{2}(\beta-\delta)} + \frac{1+\frac{\tau}{2}(\beta-\delta)}{1-\frac{\tau}{2}(\beta-\delta)}\, q_{t-\tau} + \frac{\gamma(1+\frac{\tau\delta}{2})}{1-\frac{\tau}{2}(\beta-\delta)}\, \Delta x_t + \frac{\gamma\delta\tau}{1-\frac{\tau}{2}(\beta-\delta)}\, x_{t-\tau}$$

where $\tau$ is the finite time-period chosen.[1] The structural parameters can be uniquely determined from this reduced form. Observe that $\alpha$, $\beta$ and $\delta$ always appear in combination with $\tau$ whereas $\gamma$ is independent of $\tau$, the period of observation. If $\tau = 1$ corresponds to a year, it follows that the quarterly estimates of $\beta$ and $\delta$ must be one-fourth of the annual estimates and the MPC must be the same in both cases. However, since the quarterly data are expressed in annual rates, quarterly and annual estimates of $\alpha$ should be the same. The long-run MPC $\gamma'$ is, of course, independent of the time units.

Coming now to saving, in the national accounting framework it is equivalent to the net accumulation of *financial* assets and liabilities such as money, bonds, shares, equities in unincorporated enterprises (including owner-occupied dwellings), and various forms of nonbusiness debt. Hence it may be postulated that the assets acquired through saving are durable and indeed have a zero depreciation rate. Denoting y(t) as the instantaneous flow of saving per capita at time t, (1) and (2) become

$$(1')\quad y(t) = \alpha + \beta s(t) + \gamma x(t)$$

$$(2')\quad \dot{s}(t) = y(t).$$

The assumption $\delta = 0$ leads to a zero static long-run MPS and APS because there is no necessity of accumulating non-depreciating assets in such a situation. In the case of steady linear growth, the saving-ratio can be shown to be proportional to the rate of increase in income, the factor of proportionality being $-\gamma/\beta$. The proportionality factor can also be interpreted as the long-run marginal saving-income ratio. Similarly, for exponential growth in income (at the rate $\rho$) the saving ratio may be seen to be equal to $\frac{\gamma\rho}{\rho-\beta}$ provided the structural equation (1′) is made homogeneous by putting $\alpha = 0$. Because (1′) emphasizes the growth rather than the level of income as a determinant of savings, it is closely related to

---

[1] We take the opportunity to correct three misprints occurring at this point in [3]. On page 14 the sign of the last term in equations (34) and (35) should be negative. Also the numerator of the penultimate term in (35) should have $\delta$ instead of $\beta$. These corrections do not affect anything that follows.

Modigliani's theory of savings, as was pointed out in [3]. For the same reason it is promising in explaining the downward tendency of the savings-income ratio revealed by the revised data; on the static Keynesian view of savings such a tendency in the face of rising income levels would be hard to understand.

The reduced form estimation equation of (1′), using again the finite approximation, assumes the following simple form:

$$(5)\quad y_t = \frac{1 + \frac{1}{2}\beta}{1 - \frac{1}{2}\beta} y_{t-1} + \frac{\gamma}{1 - \frac{1}{2}\beta} \Delta x_t \ .$$

$\beta$ and $\gamma$ can be easily seen to be uniquely identified. It may be noted, however, that $\alpha$ cannot be estimated for this model. As will be shown below, (5) is capable of simple extension to the components of disposable income, but the non-zero depreciation model (1) - (2) cannot be easily extended in this manner.

Finally, a few brief comments may be added on the population effect. In the basic model (1) and (2), the identity (2) is affected by the rate of population growth. Using capital letters for the aggregates and $\Pi$ for population,

$$(6)\ S = \Pi s.$$

Differentiating (6) with respect to time, we get

$$(7)\ \dot{S} = \Pi\dot{s} + s\dot{\Pi} \equiv Q - \delta S.$$

Hence,

$$(8)\ \Pi\dot{s} = Q - \delta S - \dot{\Pi}s$$

or

$$(9)\ \dot{s} = q - (\delta + \psi)s,$$

where $\psi = \dot{\Pi}/\Pi$.

Thus, the introduction of exponential population growth rate biases only the estimate of $\delta$. For practical purposes, however, the difference between $\delta$ and $(\delta + \psi)$ is found to be quite small. Working on similar lines for the zero-depreciation theory of saving, the expressions for the population bias at per-capita level could be easily checked to be

$$(10)\quad \hat{\beta} = \beta^* + \psi$$

$$(11)\quad \hat{\gamma} = \gamma^* + \left(\frac{2}{2+\psi}\right) \ ,$$

where $\psi$ is the exogenously given rate of population growth, $\hat{\beta}$ and $\hat{\gamma}$ are the unbiased estimates, and $\beta^*$ and $\gamma^*$ are the estimates from (5).

For estimation purposes, the Three-Pass-Least-Squares method as developed by Taylor and Wilson [6], was used whenever it was found to correct strong autocorrelation in the residuals.

## 2. Effects of Revision on Structural Estimates

In this section, a comparison is made between the estimates of the structural parameters with the revised data and those given in Chapter 6 of [3]. The results regarding total consumption based on equation (4) are summarized in Table 1.[2] Most of the results show relatively minor change. The theoretically expected relationships between the annual and the quarterly estimates are not realized in the new estimates either. The main difference in the annual estimates is the increase in the long-run MPC after the revision. The coefficient of the dummy variable (unit for the post-war years 1947-1961, zero otherwise) with the revised data turned out to be insignificant. Its omission further increased the long-run MPC to a more plausible figure of 0.91. The quarterly estimates are distorted as a result of the erratic behavior of savings during the period 1947 to 1952, the Korean War being seemingly responsible for the latter part of the period. All the same, an increase in the long-run MPC may be noted here, too. It is interesting that the defects of the annual and quarterly equations noted in Chapter 6 of [3] also hold in the revised equations, *viz.* poor fit of the annual equation in the post-war period and the failure of the Durbin-Watson coefficient in the quarterly equation to bring out a distinct tendency for predicted consumption to be lower than actual consumption in the upswing of the cycles and to exceed it in the downswing with predicted value lagging by one quarter behind the actual one. On the other hand, the long-run MPC's agree better with *a priori* expectations than they did in [3].

The statistical difficulties with this consumption function led us to explore the possibilities of approaching the problem from the savings side. The zero-depreciation hypothesis about savings was found to be empirically plausible and simpler to work with. Table 2 presents the relevant comparison of the results with the unrevised and revised data. The exclusion of the period prior to 1953 can be seen to bring about a distinct improvement in the quarterly estimates. Its inclusion, on the other hand, leads to an enormous increase in the short-run MPS and a very low short-run MPC if we compare the corresponding equation from Table 1. A satisfactory feature of the revised savings function is that the quarterly $\beta$ (for 1953-1962) comes out to be even closer to one-fourth of the annual estimate. The agreement between the exponential growth savings ratios, as given by the annual and the quarterly relations, is less close in the revised equations. The drop in the quarterly savings ratio for 1953-1962 seems to be due to the downward statistical revision for the post-1952 period noted already, which has had less impact on the annual estimates which cover the whole period 1929-1961 (excluding the war years).

[2] Everywhere in this paper "consumption" is identical with "personal outlays" as defined in the August 1965 *Survey of Current Business* and with the concept used in Chapter 6 of [3].

## TABLE 1
## Per-Capita Consumption Function

| | Annual Per-Capita | | | Quarterly Per-Capita | |
|---|---|---|---|---|---|
| | 1929 - 1941 and 1947 - 1961 | | | 1947 - 1962 | |
| | OLD | REVISED | | OLD | REVISED |
| | [3] Ch. 6 eqn. (2) | (a)*(I.4) | (b)*(I.3) | [3] Ch. 6 eqn. (4) | (I.7) |
| $\hat{\alpha}$ | 124.8400 | 86.6432 | 42.6621 | 20.7700 | nss |
| $\hat{\beta}$ | 0.3500 | 0.3016 | 0.4973 | 1.8170 | 1.0615 |
| $\hat{\gamma}$ | 0.5120 | 0.5414 | 0.5252 | 0.1490 | 0.2830 |
| $\hat{\gamma}/$ | 0.7910 | 0.8452 | 0.9050 | 0.8660 | 0.9698 |
| $\hat{\delta}$ | 1.2660 | 0.8392 | 0.9464 | 2.1950 | 1.5060 |

Notes:

nss: Not statistically significant

(a)*: With post-war dummy variable

(b)*: Without post-war dummy variable

Sources: Old estimates from Houthakker and Taylor [3], Ch. 6
Revised estimates from Appendix Table I.

## TABLE 2
## Per Capita Savings Function

| | Annual Per-Capita | | | | Quarterly Per-Capita | |
|---|---|---|---|---|---|---|
| | 1929 - 1941 and 1947 - 1961 | | 1947 - 1962 | | 1953 - 1962 | |
| | OLD | REVISED | OLD | REVISED | OLD | REVISED |
| | (38) | (II.2) | (39) | (II.5) | (40) | (II.6) |
| $\hat{\beta}$ | -0.0926 | -0.1197 | -0.0580 | -0.0550 | -0.0202 | -0.0283 |
| $\hat{\gamma}$ | 0.3670 | 0.4262 | 0.8970 | 0.7427 | 0.3600 | 0.3585 |
| $-\hat{\gamma}/\hat{\beta}$ | 3.9600 | 3.5606 | 15.4500 | 13.5036 | 18.9000 | 12.6678 |
| $\frac{\rho\hat{\gamma}}{\rho-\hat{\beta}}$ | 0.0780 | 0.0736 | 0.0730 | 0.0731 | 0.0780 | 0.0627 |

Notes:

$-\hat{\gamma}/\hat{\beta}$ = Linear growth long-run marginal saving-income ratio

$\frac{\rho\hat{\gamma}}{\rho-\hat{\beta}}$ = exponential growth saving rate with $\rho = 0.025$ for annual and $\rho = 0.006$ for quarterly equations

Sources: Old estimates from Houthakker & Taylor [3], Ch. 6.
Revised estimates from Appendix Table I.

Finally, the models with aggregate savings and income instead of per capita figures were worked out to trace the effect of population. The summary of results is given in Table 3. The revised annual and quarterly estimates do not conform as well to the theoretical ratios as they did with the unrevised data for the annual 1929-1961 and quarterly 1953-1962 equations, although $\hat{\beta}$ is still about four times as large in the annual equation as in the 1953-62 equation, the $\gamma$'s are rather different. Nor are the expectations expressed by (8) and (9) regarding the relations between the per capita and aggregate model borne out with respect to the estimates of the structural parameters. Perhaps the only satisfactory feature is the close agreement between the corresponding exponential growth savings ratios given by the annual 1929-1961 and quarterly 1953-1962 models at both the per capita and the aggregate levels.

### 3. The Population Effect

In this section, an attempt is made to examine the population effect in more detail with reference to both the consumption and savings functions. It has been shown that the growth rate of population affects only the estimate of the depreciation parameter $\delta$ in the basic per capita dynamic model of consumption. In the zero-depreciation theory of per capita savings, the stock -- coefficient is an underestimate and the short-run MPS is an overestimate of the corresponding true estimates without population bias [see (8) and (9)]. For aggregate equations, the growth rate of population gets added to the exponential growth rate of income used in computing the corresponding savings ratio for the aggregate model. The time period has been brought up to 1964 in all following equations. A summary of the structural estimates is presented in Tables 4 and 5.

**TABLE 3**
**Aggregate Savings Function**

| | Annual Aggregate | | | | Quarterly Aggregate | | | |
|---|---|---|---|---|---|---|---|---|
| | 1929-41 & 1947-61 | | 1947-1962 | | 1947-1962 | | 1953-1962 | |
| | Old (48) | Revised (II.8) | Old (50) | Revised (II.9) | Old (49) | Revised (II.12) | Old (51) | Revised (II.13) |
| $\hat{\beta}$ | -0.1680 | -0.1889 | -0.2110 | -0.2416 | -0.1060 | -0.0994 | -0.0406 | -0.0447 |
| $\hat{\gamma}$ | 0.4420 | 0.3839 | 0.4980 | 0.4911 | 0.8720 | 0.6795 | 0.3880 | 0.2962 |
| $-\hat{\gamma}/\hat{\beta}$ | 2.6300 | 2.0323 | 2.3500 | 2.0327 | 8.2500 | 6.8360 | 9.5600 | 6.6264 |
| $\frac{\rho\hat{\gamma}}{\rho-\hat{\beta}}$ | 0.0870 | 0.0829 | 0.0810 | 0.0712 | 0.0750 | 0.0677 | 0.0770 | 0.0648 |

Notes:

$-\hat{\gamma}/\hat{\beta}$ = linear growth long=run marginal saving-income ratio

$\frac{\rho\hat{\gamma}}{\rho-\hat{\beta}}$ = exponential growth savings rate with $\rho = 0.041$ for annual and

$\rho$ = 0.001 for quarterly equations.

Sources: Old estimates from Houthakker & Taylor [3] Ch. 6.
Revised estimates from Appendix Table II.

Examination of Tables 4 and 5 shows that the theoretically consistent relationships at all the four levels *viz.* aggregate and per-capita, annual and quarterly, are hard to realize, especially for the consumption functions. The sources of deviation from the expected pattern may lie in the possibly inadequate specification of the model, or the differences in the time periods considered,[3] or the stochastic variations, or the seasonality and other adjustments that have been carried out in the basic series, or all of these things put together. In the case of total consumption, the quarterly per-capita model gave explosive long-run MPC estimates exceeding unity whereas the corresponding aggregate estimates were all non-explosive. Apart from this, there was little evidence to discriminate between the per-capita and aggregate models.

The results appear rather better for the savings relations. There is close agreement between the short-run MPS estimates given by the equations for corresponding time periods at the per capita and aggregate levels. The annual estimates of $\beta$ are roughly four times the quarterly ones for the period 1953-1964. However, the annual estimates of the short-run MPS are somewhat larger than the quarterly estimates for 1953-1964. The exponential growth savings ratios come out between 6 and 7 per cent in all the cases and are in the empirically observed range. Here again there is not much to choose between the aggregate and per-capita equations.

## 4. The Savings Function With Disposable Income Components

As noted already, the simplified dynamic savings function given by (5) can be easily extended to take into account differences in savings propensities by different income earners. The extension can be achieved only by assuming that $\beta$ is the same for all types of incomes. This is likely to prove quite restrictive but it is not possible to get around it because of the unavailability of disaggregated time series on savings. Ideally, savings figures should have been disaggregated according to the source of income earned and each of them made a function of the corresponding income. However, the residual character of savings in the national accounting framework precludes any such classification. As an alternative, we made total savings as a function of the components of the disposable income as given by the definition:

| | | |
|---|---|---|
| Disposable Income | *equals* | Labor Income |
| | *plus* | Non-labor Income |
| | *minus* | Personal Contributions to Social Insurance |
| | *minus* | Personal Tax and non-tax Payments. |

Labor Income is defined as the sum of (i) Wages and Salary Disbursements, (ii) Other Labor Income, and (iii) Transfer Payments. Non-labor Income consists of (i) Proprietors' Income, (ii) Rental Income, of Persons, (iii) Dividends, and (iv) Personal Interest Income.

[3] Identical time periods were available for the quarterly and annual equations for 1947-1964. The annual equations (given in the Appendix Tables I and II) yielded structural estimates closely similar to those given by the annual equations 1929-1964 and did not conform to the implausible structural estimates of the quarterly equation for the same period. This strengthens our already mentioned belief about the unreliability of the quarterly data for the period 1947-1951. Had there been any structural changes during the period 1947-1964 as given by the quarterly estimates, they would also have been brought out by the annual equations for the same period.

**TABLE 4**
**Consumption Function ($\delta \neq 0$)**

| | Annual | | Quarterly | | | |
|---|---|---|---|---|---|---|
| | 1929-1941 & 1947-1964 | | 1947-1964 | | 1953-1964 | |
| | per capita (I.1) | aggr. (I.8) | per capita (I.5) | aggr. (I.9) | per capita (I.6) | aggr. (I.10) |
| $\hat{\alpha}$ | -- | -- | -28.7176 | -2.9770 | -68.2418 | -7.6230 |
| $\hat{\beta}$ | 0.2595 | 0.4422 | 0.8958 | 0.7098 | 0.2826 | 0.2267 |
| $\hat{\gamma}$ | 0.5473 | 0.5028 | -0.3241 | 0.4139 | 0.5960 | 0.7001 |
| $\hat{\gamma}'$ | 0.9413 | 0.9726 | 0.9944 | 0.9686 | 1.0146 | 0.9742 |
| $\hat{\delta}$ | 0.6193 | 0.9154 | 1.3288 | 1.2624 | 0.6848 | 0.8059 |

ource: Appendix Table I.

**TABLE 5**
**Savings Function ($\delta = 0$)**

| | Annual | | Quarterly | | | |
|---|---|---|---|---|---|---|
| | 1929-1941 & 1947-1964 | | 1947-1964 | | 1953-1964 | |
| | per capita (II.1) | aggr. (II.7) | per capita (II.3) | aggr. (II.10) | per capita (II.4) | aggr. (II.11) |
| $\hat{\beta}$ | -0.1285 | -0.1960 | -0.0571 | -0.0996 | -0.0258 | -0.0452 |
| $\hat{\gamma}$ | 0.4194 | 0.3700 | 0.7027 | 0.6600 | 0.3335 | 0.3234 |
| $-\hat{\gamma}/\hat{\beta}$ | 3.2638 | 1.8878 | 12.3065 | 6.6265 | 12.9264 | 7.1549 |
| $\frac{\rho\hat{\gamma}}{\rho - \hat{\beta}}$ | 0.0683 | 0.0770 | 0.0668 | 0.0656 | 0.0629 | 0.0700 |

ource: Appendix Table II.
$\rho = 0.025$ for annual per capita equations
$\rho = 0.006$ for quarterly per capita equations
$\rho = 0.041$ for annual aggregate equations
$\rho = 0.010$ for quarterly aggregate equations.

It is important to observe that each of the income categories includes certain parts whose *a priori* marginal propensity to save assumes the extreme values of zero or unity. In other words, these parts of income are not the objects of explicit choice between saving and consumption. In the case of labor income, for example, the component of employers' contributions under pension, health and welfare programs and group insurance protection (included in "Other Labor Income") has an MPS of unity, whereas most of the transfer payments have a very low MPS. However, since Wages and Salaries form the largest component of Labor Income the weight of these other items is not likely to be very significant in affecting the estimate of the corresponding MPS. On the other hand, Non-labor Income contains many components with a very high MPS. Income from unincorporated enterprises (*cf.* Klein & Margolis [5]) may be cited as an example. Numerical estimates of the weight given to these items are difficult to obtain but their qualitative significance has to be borne in mind in judging the estimates of MPS.[4] Personal Contributions to Social Insurance are deducted from the personal income, like taxes, but there is a definite difference between the two. The tax deduction is final and not recoverable whereas the contributions to social insurance are recoverable in the future. It is conceivable that they may enter into consideration in deciding the magnitude of personal savings. If individuals regard social security contributions as a perfect substitute for voluntary saving, then the coefficient of "employees' contributions to social insurance" in the savings equation should be about minus two since the employees' contributions are normally matched by employers.[5] The contributions by employers are included in "Other Labor Income." Personal Tax and non-tax payments[6] ought to have a negative sign if they have a significant influence on savings.

The basic structural equations are given by

$$(12)\quad y(t) = \alpha + \beta s(t) + \gamma_1 L(t) + \gamma_2 P(t) + \gamma_3 F(t) + \gamma_4 T(t)$$

$$(13)\quad \dot{s}(t) \equiv y(t).$$

The corresponding reduced-form estimation is

---

[4] For some evidence from international comparison see [1] and [2].

[5] In a recent cross-section study [4] Katona claims to have shown that pension plan stimulate voluntary saving. It would not be the first time that cross-section and time-serie analyses of savings lead to an apparent paradox, but in this instance the matter is obscured b Katona's unusual definition of savings (his page 44). He defines savings as the change i liquid assets, thus disregarding nonliquid assets (such as houses and equities in life insuranc and pension funds) and liabilities. In recent years the aggregate change in househol liabilities alone has been about as large as aggregate net household savings. In Katona' regressions, moreover, the actual amount of saving (even on his definition) is apparently neve used as a dependent variable; only certain dummy variables, loosely related to the amount o saving, are so used.

[6] It is incidentally far from clear that the National Accounts practice of lumping tax an nontax payments together makes much sense. Nontax payments, of which tuition paid to stat universities or fees paid to public hospitals are typical examples, should really be treated a consumers' expenditures.

$$(14)\quad y_t = \frac{1+\frac{1}{2}\beta}{1-\frac{1}{2}\beta}\, y_{t-1} + \frac{\gamma_1}{1-\frac{1}{2}\beta}\,\Delta L_t + \frac{\gamma_2}{1-\frac{1}{2}\beta}\,\Delta P_t + \frac{\gamma_3}{1-\frac{1}{2}\beta}\,\Delta F_t + \frac{\gamma_4}{1-\frac{1}{2}\beta}\,\Delta T_t$$

whereas:

- $y_t$ = saving in \$ per capita in 1958 prices
- $L_t$ = labor-income in \$ per capita in 1958 prices
- $P_t$ = non-labor income in \$ per capita in 1958 prices
- $F_t$ = personal social insurance contributions in \$ per capita in 1958 prices
- $T_t$ = personal tax and non-tax payments in \$ per capita in 1958 prices
- $\Delta$ = 1st difference operator
- $z_t$ = 3rd pass additional variable representing the lagged effect of the error term whenever three-pass least squares was used
- $\beta$ = stock coefficient
- $\gamma_1$ = MPS out of labor-income
- $\gamma_2$ = MPS out of non-labor-income
- $\gamma_3$ = short-run effect on saving of personal social insurance contributions
- $\gamma_4$ = short-run effect on saving of personal tax and non-tax payments.

**Annual Per-Capita Saving 1929-41 & 1947-64**

$$(15)\quad y_t = \underset{(0.0650)}{0.9810 y_{t-1}} + \underset{(0.1288)}{0.2074\,\Delta L_t} + \underset{(0.2110)}{0.8048\,\Delta P_t} - \underset{(1.7917)}{3.0435\,\Delta F_t} - \underset{(0.2850)}{0.1208\,\Delta T_t}$$

$R^2 = 0.8797$ $\quad \hat{\sigma}_e = 18.2806$ $\quad \hat{\beta} = -0.0192$ $\quad \hat{\gamma}_1 = 0.2094$ $\quad \gamma_3 = -3.0727$

$\bar{R}^2 = 0.8547$ $\quad DW = 2.2048$ $\quad \hat{\gamma}_2 = 0.8125.$

$$16)\quad y_t = \underset{(0.0615)}{0.9886 y_{t-1}} + \underset{(0.1097)}{0.1801\,\Delta L_t} + \underset{(0.1956)}{0.8347\,\Delta P_t} - \underset{(1.6447)}{3.3160\,\Delta F_t}$$

$R^2 = 0.8800$ $\quad \hat{\sigma}_e = 17.9782$ $\quad \hat{\beta} = -0.155$ $\quad \hat{\gamma}_1 = 0.1811$ $\quad \hat{\gamma}_3 = -3.3350$

$\bar{R}^2 = 0.861$ $\quad DW = 2.21$ $\quad \gamma_2 = 0.8395.$

**Quarterly Per-Capita Savings**

*a) 1947-64*

$$17)\quad y_t = \underset{(0.0204)}{0.9459\, y_{t-1}} + \underset{(0.1264)}{0.7076\,\Delta L_t} + \underset{(0.2663)}{0.6470\,\Delta Pt} - \underset{(1.4556)}{1.6499\,\Delta F_t} - \underset{(0.3239)}{0.5252\,\Delta T_t}$$

$R^2 = 0.4987$ $\quad \hat{\sigma}_e = 16.9874$ $\quad \hat{\beta} = -0.0565$ $\quad \hat{\gamma}_1 = 0.7273$ $\quad \hat{\gamma}_3 = -1.6958$

$\bar{R}^2 = 0.460$ $\quad DW = 2.36$ $\quad \gamma_2 = 0.6650$ $\quad \gamma_4 = -0.5398.$

*(b) 1953-64*

$$(18)\quad y_t = \underset{(0.0155)}{0.9843\, y_{t-1}} + \underset{(0.1112)}{0.3266\, \Delta L_t} + \underset{(0.3805)}{0.5607\, \Delta P_t} - \underset{(0.9679)}{2.0338\, \Delta F_t} - \underset{(0.2901)}{0.5852\, \Delta T_t}$$

$$R^2 = 0.6296 \quad \hat{\sigma}_e = 9.8431 \quad \hat{\beta} = -0.0158 \quad \hat{\gamma}_1 = 0.3292 \quad \hat{\gamma}_3 = -2.0499$$

$$\bar{R}^2 = 0.5865 \quad DW = 2.3260 \quad \gamma_2 = 0.5651 \quad \gamma_4 = -0.5898.$$

The consistent relationships between the annual and the quarterly estimates fail to hold in this case, too. In particular, from equations (14) to (18), changes in non-labor income may be seen to exert a stronger influence on savings at the annual than at the quarterly level. An opposite tendency is found for the effect of changes in labor-income. Part of the explanation may perhaps be found in differential intensities of response as measured by $\beta$. Since we do not have separate data for savings out of labor and out of nonlabor income, we are unable to introduce different $\beta$'s for different types of income.[7] One factor may be that income payments are fewer and less regular for the non-labor sources. Another may be that non-labor income is relatively more important in high-income brackets. There may also be simultaneous-equations complications in that non-labor income may be closely correlated with investment.

However this may be, it seems hard to justify a very high short-run MPS at the annual level (between 0.81 and 0.85) out of non-labor income, although the short-run MPS between 0.18 and 0.21 appears plausible for labor income. At the quarterly level, the inclusion of the Korean War in the earlier period makes the two short-run marginal propensities statistically indistinguishable and empirically implausible. But the exclusion of that period gives more meaningful estimates of short-run MPS of 0.33 out of labor-income and 0.57 out of non-labor income. The coefficient of the personal social insurance contributions has the expected direction and magnitude. The personal tax and non-tax payments also exercise an influence in the theoretically desired direction with a plausible magnitude. However, the differences between coefficients of $\Delta L_t$, $\Delta P_t$, and $\Delta T_t$ are not statistically significant. Hence it was decided to pool the corresponding variables to define a new variable

$$X_t = L_t + P_t - T_t$$

which may be called "gross" disposable income because we have not allowed for the personal social insurance contribution which was put in as an explicit explanatory variable along with $X_t$. This experiment yielded the following results:

[7] It was suggested to us that the introduction of the income-distribution variable (defined in [3] pp. 33-34) in the annual model might overcome in some sense the limitations of a uniform $\beta$-coefficient for both types of income. This introduction did lead to the reduction of non-labor-income coefficient, leaving the labor-income coefficient unchanged. However the coefficient of the income distribution variable came out to be statistically significant with a negative sign. This result, which would make the MPS lower at high incomes than at low levels, is hard to explain and requires more detailed investigation.

**Annual Per-Capita Saving 1929-64**

$$(19)\quad y_t = \underset{(0.0481)}{0.9270}\, y_{t-1} + \underset{(0.0509)}{0.3906}\, \Delta X_t - \underset{(1.6514)}{2.4498}\, \Delta F_t - \underset{(0.2083)}{0.4860}\, z_t$$

$R^2 = 0.8834$ $\quad \hat{\sigma}_e = 17.2590$ $\quad \hat{\beta} = -0.0758$ $\quad \hat{\gamma}_1 = 0.4054$ $\quad \hat{\gamma}_3 = -2.5426$

$\overline{R}^2 = 0.864$ $\quad DW = 2.03.$

**Quarterly Per-Capita Saving**

*(a) 1947-64*

$$(20)\quad y_t = \underset{(0.0199)}{0.9480}\, y_{t-1} + \underset{(0.0987)}{0.6943}\, \Delta X_t - \underset{(1.3636)}{0.1274}\, \Delta F_t$$

$R^2 = 0.4955$ $\quad \hat{\sigma}_e = 16.7773$ $\quad \hat{\beta} = -0.0534$ $\quad \hat{\gamma}_1 = 0.7128$

$\overline{R}^2 = 0.473$ $\quad DW = 2.40.$

*(b) 1953-64*

$$(21)\quad y_t = \underset{(0.0152)}{0.9860}\, y_{t-1} + \underset{(0.0892)}{0.3377}\, \Delta X_t - \underset{(0.9272)}{1.5469}\, \Delta F_t$$

$R^2 = 0.6186$ $\quad \hat{\sigma}_e = 9.7607$ $\quad \hat{\beta} = -0.0141$ $\quad \hat{\gamma}_1 = 0.3401$

$\overline{R}^2 = 0.593$ $\quad DW = 2.40.$

It may be noted to start with that the results with "gross" disposable income along with personal social insurance contributions are not very different from those obtained with disposable income proper. [Compare short-run MPS estimates given by (19) with (II.1), (20) with (II.3), and (21) with (II.4)]. This was only to be expected in view of the small proportion occupied by the personal social insurance contributions in the total disposable income. The coefficient of $\Delta F_t$, and the corresponding $\gamma_3$, are again near minus two as expected, but the standard error is large.

Secondly, it may be interesting to compare the estimates and their standard errors computed from equations (15) and (18) with those obtained directly from equations (19) and (21) as coefficients of $\Delta X_t$:

| | **Computed coefficient of $\Delta X_t$** | **Direct estimate of coefficient of $\Delta X_t$** |
|---|---|---|
| Annual savings 1929 - 64 | 0.9914 | 0.3906 |
| | (0.3191) | (0.0509) |
| Quarterly savings 1953 - 64 | 0.3021 | 0.3377 |
| | (0.4224) | (0.0892) |

The predominant influence at the annual level exerted by changes in non-labor income when introduced as a separate explanatory factor seems to vanish when it is pooled with the labor-income and the personal tax and non-tax payments. This has caused a wide divergence between the two estimates. There is fair agreement between the direct and computed estimates for the quarterly equations for 1953-64, although the latter is statistically insignificant. This seems to point towards multicollinearity among the different disposable income components in equation (18) which is overcome when the corresponding variables are pooled, thereby yielding a significant direct estimate of the coefficient of $\Delta X_t$. Another possible reason for the lack of conformity of direct and indirect estimates at the annual level and their agreement at the quarterly level may be found in the statistically significant quarterly tax coefficient and its absence in the annual equation.

## 5. Forecasting Performance of Alternative Models

In this section we wish to find how the alternative models we have obtained so far stand in relation to each other in forecasting for the year 1965. The relevant data are now available in the *Survey of Current Business*, April 1966. The saving ratio implied or given by several variants of the consumption or savings function is taken as a convenient basis of comparison. In the case of the third pass equations, following [3] p. 50, we used the value of the z variable computed from the last observation of the historical period for the first forecast and its historical mean thereafter. This procedure was found best in the Taylor-Wilson Monte Carlo Experiments. It may also be noted that since lagged savings enter into forecasting equations, two sets of predictors are possible: (a) With lagged actual savings; (b) with lagged predicted savings. The latter forecasts (from the quarterly models) are given in brackets below those for (a) in Table 7.

It appears from Table 6 that all the annual equations invariably have a tendency to overestimate the saving ratio. Post-war relations for 1947-64 seem to perform better than those for 1929-64. Moreover, predictions with aggregate models are consistently less inaccurate than their per capita counterparts. These conclusions, it may be noted, are identical to those reached in [3], p. 191. In addition, consumption function proves distinctly inferior to the savings function given by the zero depreciation theory also in forecasting at least in the annual equations.

A glance through Table 7 reveals that the equations for the post-Korean War period are consistently superior to those for 1947-64 which also exhibit a tendency to overshoot the saving ratio. Of the 1947-64 equations, the aggregate equations are slightly better than their per capita counterparts. No such basis of discrimination seems to exist for the 1953-64 equations. The Per Capita Disposable Income Components Savings Function for 1953-64 comes out to be best in forecasting followed rather surprisingly by the Aggregate Total Disposable Income Consumption Function for the same period. Finally, forecasts with lagged predicted savings as predictors are inferior to those given by lagged actual savings as predictors, contrary to what was found in [3].[8]

## 6. Conclusion

We have examined the consumption and savings functions from the point of view of plausibility of structural estimates (Sections 2 to 4) as well as on the basis of their forecasting performance

[8] In [3], p. 193, the equation references (53) and (54) in the top two lines should be interchanged.

(Section 5). It appears that in the empirical aggregate economic analysis, the zero-depreciation dynamic theory of savings provides a better approach than the non-zero depreciation theory of consumption. The major conclusions of chapter 6 of [3] remain unchanged with the revised data. In the overall analysis the aggregate model seems to possess an edge over the per-capita model. The extension of the savings model to the disposable income components does provide insights into the differential behavior of labor and non-labor income: Its forecasting performance appears moderately encouraging. However, the success of this model for structural estimation is limited by the assumption of a uniform adjustment coefficient for all types of incomes.

*Harvard University* *1967*

**TABLE 6**
Actual and Predicted Saving Ratios for 1965 Annual Equations

| MODEL: | | | | Predicted Saving Ratio (%) |
|---|---|---|---|---|
| SAVINGS FUNCTION: | | | | |
| **Per Capita** | (II.1) | Total Disp. Income | 1929-64 | 7.73 |
| | (II.2a) | Total Disp. Income | 1947-64 | 7.53 |
| | (11) | Disp. Income Components | 1929-64 | 7.84 |
| | (12) | Disp. Income Components (excl. Tax) | 1929-64 | 7.94 |
| | (15) | Gross Disp. Income | 1929-64 | 7.89 |
| **Aggregate** | (I.8) | Total Disp. Income | 1929-64 | 7.53 |
| | (I.9a) | Total Disp. Income | 1947-64 | 7.36 |
| CONSUMPTION FUNCTION: | | | | |
| **Per Capita** | (I.1) | Total Disp. Income | 1929-64 | 10.89 |
| **Aggregate** | (I.8) | Total Disp. Income | 1929-64 | 10.52 |
| | (I.9) | Total Disp. Income | 1947-64 | 10.45 |
| **Actual Saving Ratio in 1965** | | | | 6.06 |

# TABLE 7
Actual and Predicted Saving Ratios for 1965: Quarterly Equations

| MODEL : | | | | QUARTER : I | II | III | IV |
|---|---|---|---|---|---|---|---|
| SAVINGS FUNCTION: | | | | | | | |
| Per Capita | (II.3) | Total Disp. Income | 1947-64 | 6.31 | 5.35 | 5.37 | 5.92 |
| | | | | | (7.45) | (7.22) | (7.34) |
| | (II.4) | Total Disp. Income | 1953-64 | 6.41 | 5.25 | 5.37 | 5.78 |
| | | | | | (6.45) | (6.86) | (6.90) |
| | (13) | Disp. Income Components | 1947-64 | 6.41 | 5.39 | 5.91 | 6.23 |
| | | | | | (6.54) | (7.44) | (7.87) |
| | (14) | Disp. Income Components | 1953-64 | 5.34 | 5.39 | 5.50 | 5.96 |
| | | | | | (5.58) | (6.31) | (6.36) |
| | (16) | "Gross" Disp. Income | 1947-64 | 6.36 | 5.39 | 6.00 | 5.92 |
| | | | | | (6.54) | (7.53) | (7.65) |
| | (17) | "Gross" Disp. Income | 1953-64 | 6.41 | 5.30 | 5.37 | 5.78 |
| | | | | | (6.54) | (6.99) | (7.07) |
| Aggregate | (II.10) | Total Disp. Income | 1947-64 | 6.26 | 5.29 | 5.83 | 6.11 |
| | | | | | (6.28) | (7.06) | (7.35) |
| | (II.11) | Total Disp. Income | 1953-64 | 6.38 | 5.22 | 5.32 | 5.87 |
| | | | | | (6.38) | (6.71) | (6.83) |
| CONSUMPTION FUNCTION: | | | | | | | |
| Per Capita | (I.5) | Total Disp. Income | 1947-64 | 6.02 | 5.43 | 5.88 | 6.17 |
| | | | | | (5.94) | (6.62) | (6.66) |
| | (I.6) | Total Disp. Income | 1953-64 | 6.02 | 5.34 | 5.48 | 6.04 |
| | | | | | (5.85) | (6.06) | (6.26) |
| Aggregate | (I.9) | Total Disp. Income | 1947-64 | 6.05 | 5.46 | 5.85 | 5.97 |
| | | | | | (5.95) | (6.44) | (6.39) |
| | (I.10) | Total Disp. Income | 1953-64 | 6.01 | 5.34 | 5.44 | 5.70 |
| | | | | | (5.81) | (5.93) | (5.83) |
| **Actual Saving Ratio in 1965** | | | | 5.16 | 4.89 | 5.69 | 5.64 |

APPENDIX: TABLE I: BASIC DYNAMIC MODEL APPLIED TO TOTAL CONSUMPTION: per capita & aggregate; annual & quarterly

| Eqn # | | Period | Pass # ** | Const | $q_{t-1}$ | $\Delta x_t$ | $x_{t-1}$ | $d_t/z_t$ | $R^2$ | $\bar{R}^2$ | $\sigma_e$ | F | D-W |
|---|---|---|---|---|---|---|---|---|---|---|---|---|---|
| 1 | Annual per capita | 1929-64 | 1 | 9.8711<br>(21.3850) | 0.6950<br>(0.1768) | 0.6072<br>(0.0571) | 0.2871<br>(0.1572) | | 0.9971 | 0.9966 | 18.0960 | 2866.15 | 2.3905 |
| 2 | " | 1947-62 | 1 | -34.1720<br>(62.3610) | 0.0969<br>(0.2918) | 0.7946<br>(0.1308) | 0.8684<br>(0.2812) | | 0.9856 | 0.9808 | 17.8401 | 274.379 | 1.5518 |
| 2a† | " | 1947-64 | 1 | -57.6560<br>(51.2290) | 0.1243<br>(0.2774) | 0.7950<br>(0.1194) | 0.8569<br>(0.2676) | | 0.9965 | 0.9880 | 17.0827 | 494.776 | 1.5514 |
| 3 | " | 1929-61 | 1 | 31.7030<br>(25.5340) | 0.5704<br>(0.1951) | 0.6052<br>(0.0579) | 0.3888<br>(0.1712) | | 0.9966 | 0.9959 | 19.0219 | 2129.26 | 2.3461 |
| 4 | " | 1929-61 | 1 | 57.4090<br>(39.4410) | 0.5763<br>(0.1964) | 0.6058<br>(0.0582) | 0.3581<br>(0.1759) | 18.3710*<br>(21.4690) | 0.9967 | 0.9959 | 19.1388 | 1577.54 | 2.2220 |
| 5 | Quarterly per capita | 1947-64 | 1 | -31.3670<br>(21.7640) | 0.6440<br>(0.0945) | 0.4434<br>(0.1016) | 0.3540<br>(0.0909) | | 0.9900 | 0.9894 | 15.8075 | 2185.94 | 2.0905 |
| 6 | " | 1953-64 | 3 | -39.9070<br>(31.4040) | 0.6651<br>(0.1311) | 0.6661<br>(0.1065) | 0.3398<br>(0.1320) | 0.1950‡<br>(0.1867) | 0.9914 | 0.9904 | 10.8595 | 1216.93 | 1.9235 |
| 7 | " | 1947-62 | 1 | -17.2110<br>(28.2780) | 0.6396<br>(0.1008) | 0.4068<br>(0.1091) | 0.3495<br>(0.0959) | | 0.9841 | 0.9830 | 16.1584 | 1179.11 | 2.0097 |
| 8 | Annual aggregate | 1929-64 | 1 | 0.4380<br>(2.4313) | 0.6173<br>(0.1781) | 0.5927<br>(0.0819 | 0.3722<br>(0.1624) | | 0.9983 | 0.9980 | 3.6532 | 4850.78 | 2.3086 |
| 8a† | " | 1947-64 | 1 | 1.1414<br>(6.5874) | 0.4962<br>(0.2625) | 0.6464<br>(0.1888) | 0.4821<br>(0.2441) | | 0.9943 | 0.9926 | 4.3379 | 809.136 | 2.1200 |
| 9 | Quarterly aggregate | 1947-64 | 1 | -3.0166<br>(1.8384) | 0.5670<br>(0.0873) | 0.5341<br>(0.1058) | 0.4194<br>(0.0833) | | 0.9976 | 0.9975 | 2.5367 | 9181.48 | 1.9176 |
| 10 | " | 1953-64 | 1 | -4.7637<br>(2.6920) | 0.5509<br>(0.0961) | 0.7617<br>(0.1128) | 20.4375<br>(0.0940) | | 0.9978 | 0.9976 | 1.8609 | 6612.97 | 1.5763 |

See Notes on after Table II.

APPENDIX. TABLE II: SAVING AS NON-DEPRECIATING ASSETS: per capita & aggregate; annual & quarterly

| Eqn # | | Period | Pass # | $Y_{t-1}$ | $\Delta x_t$ | $z_t$ | $R^2$ | $R^2$ | $\sigma_e$ | F | D-W |
|---|---|---|---|---|---|---|---|---|---|---|---|
| 1 | Annual per capita | 1929-64 | 3 | 0.8793 (0.0375) | 0.3941 (0.0520) | -0.3642 (0.1976) | 0.8706 | 0.8551 | 17.1795 | 57.0778 | 2.0683 |
| 2 | " | 1929-61 | 3 | (0.08871) (0.0407) | 0.4021 (0.0558) | -0.3861 (0.2092) | 0.8718 | 0.8543 | 18.3828 | 49.8587 | 2.0535 |
| 2a† | " | 1947-64 | 1 | 0.8657 (0.0454) | 0.4302 (0.0940) | | 0.1708 | 0.0672 | 19.7902 | 1.6481 | 2.5396 |
| 3 | Quarterly per capita | 1947-64 | 1 | 0.9445 (0.0190) | 0.6832 (0.0962) | | 0.4937 | 0.4788 | 16.7055 | 33.1575 | 2.3947 |
| 4 | " | 1953-64 | 1 | 0.9745 (0.0145) | 0.3292 (0.0921) | | 0.5829 | 0.5648 | 10.0876 | 32.1413 | 2.3968 |
| 5 | " | 1947-62 | 1 | 0.9465 (0.0141) | 0.7228 (0.1022 | | 0.5020 | 0.4854 | 16.9520 | 30.2399 | 2.2957 |
| 6 | " | 1953-62 | 1 | 0.9721 (0.0141) | 0.3535 (0.0625) | | 0.6091 | 0.5885 | 2.5031 | 29.6032 | 2.0102 |
| 7 | Annual aggregate | 1929-64 | 3 | 0.8215 (0.0454) | 0.3370 (0.0574) | -0.3109 (0.1975) | 0.8800 | 0.8657 | 2.9853 | 61.1621 | 1.9683 |
| 8 | " | 1929-61 | 3 | 0.8274 (0.0477) | 0.3505 (0.0625) | -0.3313 (0.2089) | 0.8719 | 0.8544 | 3.0699 | 49.8994 | 1.9343 |
| 9a | " | 1947-62 | 1 | 0.7844 (0.0681) | 0.4382 (0.1211) | | 0.3663 | 0.2757 | 3.3712 | 40.4568 | 2.4101 |
| 9a† | " | 1947-64 | 1 | 0.7880 (0.0629) | 0.4009 (0.0982) | | 0.4454 | 0.3760 | 3.2283 | 6.4240 | 2.2901 |
| 10 | Quarterly aggregate | 1947-64 | 1 | 0.9051 (0.0229) | 0.6287 (0.1003) | | 0.5879 | 0.5758 | 2.7590 | 48.5028 | 2.5249 |
| 11 | " | 1953-64 | 1 | 0.9558 (0.0206) | 0.3163 (0.1011) | | 0.5744 | 0.5559 | 1.8532 | 31.0380 | 2.3426 |
| 12 | " | 1947-62 | 1 | 0.9053 (0.0237) | 0.6473 (0.1075) | | 0.5534 | 0.5385 | 2.8154 | 37.1686 | 2.4635 |
| 13 | " | 1953-62 | 1 | 0.9563 (0.0200) | 0.2897 (0.1071) | | 0.5315 | 0.5069 | 1.7590 | 21.5574 | 2.0855 |

## NOTES TO APPENDIX TABLES

TABLE I

* coefficient of the post-war dummy variable
$d_t$ = 1 for t = 1947 onwards
= 0 otherwise

‡ coefficient of the third pass variable $z_t$ representing lagged effects.

† The structural estimates of these equations are not included in the text, and hence they are given below.

**Equation** **(2a)** No structural estimates could be obtained because of the statistically non-significant coefficient of $\Delta q_t$ which enters in the estimation of all the parameters.

**(8a)**

$\hat{\alpha}$ = not statistically significant

$\hat{\beta} = 0.5148$

$\hat{\gamma} = 0.5418$

$\hat{\gamma}' = 0.9569$

$\hat{\delta} = 1.0830.$

** Third pass version of the equation is given only when (a) the coefficient of the third pass variable $z_t$ was greater than its standard error, and (b) it yielded meaningful structural estimates, and (c) it reduced the autocorrelation in the residuals significantly.

TABLE II

† The structural estimates of these equations are not included in the text and they are given below:

**Equation** **(2a)**

$$\hat{\beta} = -0.1440$$

$$\hat{\gamma} = 0.4612$$

$$-\frac{\hat{\gamma}}{\hat{\beta}} = 3.2028$$

$$\frac{\rho\hat{\gamma}}{\rho-\hat{\beta}} = 0.0682 \text{ with } \rho = 0.025$$

**(9a)**

$$\hat{\beta} = -0.2371$$

$$\hat{\gamma} = 0.4484$$

$$-\frac{\hat{\gamma}}{\hat{\beta}} = 1.8912$$

$$\frac{\rho\hat{\gamma}}{\rho-\hat{\beta}} = 0.0661 \text{ with } \rho = 0.041.$$

## REFERENCES

[1] Houthakker, H.S. (1961), "An International Comparison of Personal Savings," *Bulletin of the International Statistical Institute*, Vol. 38, pp. 56-69.

[2] Houthakker, H.S. (1965), "On Some Determinants of Saving in Developed and Underdeveloped Countries," in E.A.G. Robinson, Ed., **Problems of Economic Development**, pp. 212-227.

[3] Houthakker, H.S. & Taylor, L.D. (1966), **Consumer Demand in the United States 1929-70**, Harvard University Press.

[4] Katona, G. (1965), **Private Pensions and Individual Savings**, Michigan University Press, Ann Arbor, Michigan.

[5] Klein, L.R. & Margolis, J. (1954), "Statistical Studies of Unincorporated Business," *Review of Economics and Statistics*, Vol. 36, February 1954, pp. 33-46.

[6] Taylor, L.D. & Wilson, T.A. (1964), "Three Pass Least Squares: A Method for Estimating Models with a Lagged Dependent Variable," *Review of Economics and Statistics*, Vol. 46, November 1964, pp. 329-346.

[7] U.S. Department of Commerce (1958), "U.S. Income and Output 1958 edition," Supplement to *Survey of Current Business*.

[8] U.S. Department of Commerce (1965), *Survey of Current Business*, August 1965.

# ON A CLASS OF DYNAMIC DEMAND FUNCTIONS

**H.S. HOUTHAKKER**
*Henry Lee Professor of Economics*
*Department of Economics*
*Harvard University*
*Littauer Center*
*Cambridge, MA 02138*

The idea that demand functions may involve time (or, more precisely, the notion of "earlier and later") goes back a long time. It was elaborated in the theoretical work of Roos (1925) and Evans (1930), and its implications for empirical research were perhaps first brought out in studies of the demand for cars [De Wolff (1938); for other references see Houthakker and Haldi (1960)]. Recently the same idea has been applied more generally by Stone and Rowe (1957) and Nerlove (1959). While the general approach followed in these empirical studies has considerable intuitive appeal, the underlying theory has never been spelled out in any detail. The basic notion is that of a desired stock, actual demand during a time interval being related to the gap between the desired and the actual stock. Thus it is often assumed (partly by analogy with certain models of expectations) that the rate of demand is proportional to this gap, which leads to an exponential adjustment of actual to desired stock.

The theoretical weakness of this formulation is that it does not pay explicit attention to the budget constraint, even though income is usually introduced as an explanatory variable. Indeed the stock adjustment approach has not so far been fully integrated with the general theory of consumer's choice.[1]

## 1. General Characteristics of the Theory

The following theory differs from the classical (static) theory of consumer's choice principally in that preferences for (flow) quantities $q_i(\tau)$ depend not only on the $q_i(\tau)$ themselves but also on certain "state variables" $s_j(\tau)$. The $q_i(\tau)$ are to be interpreted as rates of purchase of the m commodities ($i = 1, 2, \ldots, m$) at time $\tau$, while the $s_j(\tau)$ ($j = 1, \ldots, n$) may provisionally be thought of as inventories, though later a more general interpretation will be given. The dependence of preferences for the $q_i(\tau)$ on the $s_j(\tau)$ expresses the possibility, among others, that the marginal utility of purchasing a shirt is smaller the more shirts one already possesses. The emphasis on this type of phenomenon puts the theory into the field of short-term dynamics.

The utility function may be written

---

[1] Attempts in this direction have been made by Bushaw and Clower (1954) and Cramer (1957).



*L. Phlips and L.D. Taylor (eds.), Aggregation, Consumption and Trade,* 247–254.

(1) $$\psi\{q_i(\tau),\ldots, q_m(\tau); s_i(\tau),\ldots, s_n(\tau)\}$$

and the budget constraint is assumed to be

(2) $$\sum_{i=1}^{m} p_i(\tau)\, q_i(\tau) = \mu(\tau) \ ,$$

where $p_i(\tau)$ is the unit price of the i-th commodity at time $\tau$ and $\mu(\tau)$ is the rate at which money income is received at time $\tau$. The state variables do not enter into the budget constraint; this is perhaps the most distinctive feature of the present theory compared with other conceivable stock-flow theories. The present theory is not (or at least not directly) concerned with the allocation of wealth among assets but only with the allocation of income among purchases. Although in principle the $q_i(\tau)$ may be negative (thus allowing sales as well as purchases), in practice consumers can rarely buy and sell at the same price. If sales were to be admitted, therefore, the budget constraint would have to be more complicated, along linear programming lines.[2] Since the methods used here are those of conventional calculus rather than of programming, and the signs of maximizing quantities can consequently not be taken into account, it seems prudent to interpret the theory as referring only to positive purchases.

The state variables $s_j(\tau)$ represent the influence of the past on the present. They appear in three kinds of relations, which describe respectively:

(a) How the $s_j$ are determined by the $q_i$;
(b) How the $s_j$ in turn affect the marginal utilities of the $q_i$;
(c) How the $s_j$ are affected by the mere passage of time.

Under the provisional interpretation of the state variables as stocks the first kind of relation will say that if the i-th commodity is durable

(3) $$\frac{\partial s_i(\tau)}{\partial q_i(\tau)} = 1,$$

no time lags being admitted. The second kind (with the same assumptions) will give an explicit expression for

(4) $$\frac{\partial^2 \psi}{\partial q_i(\tau)\partial s_i(\tau)} < 0 \ ,$$

representing the inhibiting effect of stocks on further purchases, and the third will do the same for

(5) $$\frac{\partial s_i(\tau)}{\partial \tau} < 0 \ ,$$

representing the wearing out of stocks.

To generalize this interpretation we note in the first place that the state variables need not be thought of as directly observable, since they enter into the utility function only indirectly

---

[2] The neglect of this consideration was one of the defects of the otherwise instructive analysis of Theil (1951).

and into the constraint not at all. We may therefore associate a state variable defined by equation (3) for every commodity, durable or not. This $s_i(\tau)$ will stand for (discounted) accumulated purchases of the i-th item of expenditure. There appears to be no advantage in associating an $s_j(\tau)$ with more than one $q_i(\tau)$, hence we postulate

$$\frac{\partial s_j(\tau)}{\partial q_i(\tau)} = \begin{cases} 0 \text{ if } i \neq j \\ 1 \text{ if } i = j \end{cases} . \tag{6}$$

As far as the relations of type (4) is concerned, however, intercommodity relationships are of interest. Thus the size of a person's "stock" of cars may influence the marginal utility of purchases of gasoline, motorcycles, etc. There will accordingly be cross-derivatives of the form

$$\frac{\partial^2 \psi}{\partial q_i(\tau)\, \partial s_j(\tau)} \qquad (i, j = 1,\ldots, n) , \tag{7}$$

whose sign need not be fixed *a priori*. Indeed now that state variables are defined for non-durables the inequality (4) for the case i = j is too restrictive. The fact that a person's "stock" of theater visits is large (in the sense that he has often visited the theater in the past) may increase rather than decrease the marginal utility of further theater visits. The influence of habits on marginal utility is the negative of the influence of stocks, so that a dynamic theory should deal with habits and stocks symmetrically.

The depreciation relations (5) also need to be generalized. According to the sign of $\partial s_i(\tau)/\partial\tau$ we can then distinguish three types of state variables, corresponding to wasting, perennial, and growing assets. It should be noted that the derivatives in (5) are partial; the total derivatives of the state variables with respect to time are given by

$$\dot{s}_i(\tau) = \frac{ds_i(\tau)}{d\tau} = \dot{q}_i(\tau) + \frac{\partial s_i(\tau)}{\partial \tau} . \tag{8}$$

The partial derivative $\partial s_i(\tau)/\partial\tau$ will be assumed to depend only on the $s_i$, although here again generalizations can easily be imagined.

## 2. The Linear Case

The preceding section contains the elements from which a number of general theorems could be derived with the aid of the theory of differential equations. Since this theory, at least on an elementary level, is largely confined to equations that are linear with constant or nearly-constant coefficients, it seems preferable to postpone the search for complete generality until the essentials of the present approach are set out. For this purpose the development of a special case, in which explicit solutions are available, is particularly suitable.

The case chosen is the one of a utility function quadratic in the $q_i$ and linear in the $s_i$; it will be described as the "linear" case because the quadratic aspect is not relevant to most of the results, the interesting equations being linear.

Matrix notation will be used in what follows: Capital letters denote n x n-matrices; lower case Roman letters denote n-vectors (columns unless primed); small Greek letters denote scalars. The partial derivative of a column vector with respect to a scalar (such as $\partial s/\partial\tau$) is itself a column vector, but the partial derivative of a scalar with respect to a column vector (such as $\partial\psi/\partial q$) is a row-vector.

The utility function is

$$\psi(q,s) = a'q + 1/2q'Aq + q'Bs \,, \tag{9}$$

where the matrix A is negative definite. Depreciation (or appreciation) is described by

$$\frac{\partial s}{\partial \tau} = Ws + w \,, \tag{10}$$

where W will normally be diagonal (although this is not important for the argument). If depreciation were linear, W would be zero; if it were exponential, w would be zero. As we shall see, it is necessary for the present theory that W does not vanish, but w need not be present.

We can now proceed to some manipulation. The first order conditions for a maximum of (9) under the constraint

$$p'q = \mu \tag{11}$$

are (11) itself and

$$\frac{\partial\psi}{\partial q} = a + Aq + Bs = \lambda p \,, \tag{12}$$

where $\lambda$ is the marginal utility of income. It follows that:

$$q = A^{-1}(\lambda p - a - Bs) \tag{13}$$

$$\lambda = \frac{\mu + p'A^{-1}a + p'A^{-1}Bs}{p'A^{-1}p} \,, \tag{14}$$

so that the flows are linear functions of income and of all the state variables. (The relation of the flows to the prices is more complicated.) We can write

$$q = k + Ks, \tag{15}$$

where

$$k = \frac{\mu + p'A^{-1}a}{p'A^{-1}p} A^{-1}p - A^{-1}a \tag{16}$$

and

$$K = (p'A^{-1}p)^{-1}\{A^{-1}pp'A^{-1} - (p'A^{-1}p)A^{-1}\}B. \tag{17}$$

The expression (16) is equal to the value of q in the static case, *i.e.*, when (9) lacks its final term. It can also be shown that (17) agrees with the formulae given by Basmann (1957) for the effect of changes in tastes on quantities bought; the state variables, in fact, in a static interpretation are merely parameters describing states.

Using (8) and (12) we obtain from (15), if income and prices do not vary,

$$\dot{s} = k + Ks + w + Ws = (k + w) + (K + W)s, \tag{18}$$

which is the principal result for the linear case. It is a first-order linear differential equation with constant coefficients for the vector s, whose solution is in general given by a weighted sum of exponential functions of time and by certain initial values $s(\tau_o) = s_o$. We now assume that there exists a matrix T such that

$$V = T^{-1}(K + W)T \tag{19}$$

is diagonal, and we put

$$s = Tu + \hat{s}, \tag{20}$$

where

$$\hat{s} = -(K + W)^{-1}(k + w). \tag{21}$$

Then (18) reduces to

$$\dot{u} = Vu, \tag{22}$$

and hence

$$u = e^{V(\tau-\tau_o)}u_o\ , \tag{23}$$

where

$$u_o = T^{-1}(s_o - \hat{s}). \tag{24}$$

Going back to the state variables themselves, this means

$$s-\hat{s} = Te^{V(\tau-\tau_o)}T^{-1}(s_o - \hat{s}). \tag{25}$$

The $\hat{s}$, of course, are the long-run optimum levels of the state variables; their values as given in (21) can also be obtained from (10) and (15) by putting $\dot{s} = 0$. The $(s - s_o)$ appearing in (25) may be interpreted as the gaps between actual and desired "stocks" of each commodity. As in (15) it is important to note that all commodities are normally involved in each of the equations; in empirical work a one-to-one relationship between stocks and flows has usually been assumed [see, however, Watts and Tobin (1960)].

With the aid of (21) we can rewrite (15) in the more illuminating form

$$q = (K + W)(s - \hat{s}) - (Ws + w), \tag{21}$$

from which it appears that "net investment" (which is a possible interpretation of q) is equal to the negative of depreciation plus an expression linearly related to all the gaps between actual and desired "stocks." The equation also shows -- as is obvious upon reflection -- that in long-run equilibrium

(27) $$\hat{q} = -(W\hat{s} + w) ,$$

and hence

(28) $$q-\hat{q} = K(s-\hat{s}) .$$

In the short run s is fixed, and (26) consequently implies that the influence of prices and income on the flows is exercised through $\hat{s}$. Let us therefore consider $\hat{s}$ as a function of prices and income. Taking the case of income first, we note that K does not depend on $\mu$; consequently from expression (21),

(29) $$\frac{\partial \hat{s}}{\partial \mu} = -(K + W)^{-1} \frac{\partial k}{\partial \mu} .$$

It follows from (15) and (16) that $\partial k/\partial \mu = \partial q/\partial \mu$, so that

(30) $$\frac{\partial \hat{s}}{\partial \mu} = -(K + W)^{-1} \frac{\partial q}{\partial \mu} .$$

Using (27) we also find

(32) $$\frac{\partial \hat{q}}{\partial \mu} = W(K + W)^{-1} \frac{\partial q}{\partial \mu} .$$

The vector of derivatives on the left in expression (32) may be interpreted as the effect of income on the flows in the long run (*i.e.*, after the state variables have been adjusted), while the vector of derivatives on the right gives the short-term effect of income on the flows. The importance of this distinction has long been recognized by demand analysts, but it has not so far been incorporated in a formal theory of consumer's choice. If [by virtue of (28) and (29) and the fact that $\partial s/\partial \mu$ is zero] we write (32) in the form

(33) $$\frac{\partial \hat{q}}{\partial \mu} - \frac{\partial q}{\partial \mu} = \frac{\partial q}{\partial s} \frac{\partial \hat{s}}{\partial \mu},$$

we observe a close correspondence with some relations occurring in the theory of rationing [Tobin and Houthakker (1951), especially their equation (6.1)]. In fact the change over time in the state variables is analogous not only with a change in tastes (as pointed out above), but also with a change in rations, since in short-run maximization "stocks" are regarded as constant.

In the case of price changes (compensated or not), formulae similar to the preceding ones can be derived. The analogy with rationing suggests that the Le Chatelier principle [Samuelson (1947)] applies; if so, the compensated own-price elasticity of the flows would always be smaller (in absolute value) in the short run than in the long run. I have not yet succeeded in showing this in detail.

A crucial question has so far been left out of the discussion, namely the qualitative nature of the solutions derived formally. Thus it is evidently essential to know if the differential equation (18) describes a convergent process; if it did not, $\hat{s}$ and $\hat{q}$ would be meaningless. As is well-known, convergence requires that all the latent roots of (K + W) have negative real parts. In particular, if (K + W) is symmetric, it must be negative definite. The matrix K, as defined in (17) will be symmetric if B is symmetric, for the other factor is necessarily symmetric. Symmetry of B means that the effect of $s_i$ on the marginal utility of $q_j$ is the same as the effect of $s_j$ on the marginal utility of $q_i$, a condition that seems plausible enough; it is, of course, satisfied if B is diagonal. However, B will not be negative definite if we allow habits as well as stocks. In that case the negative definiteness of K evidently puts bounds on the strength of habit formation. It has been pointed out already that W is normally diagonal, but again it need not be negative definite if "growing" as well as "wasting assets" are included; not all rates of growth are admissible if K + W is to be negative definite. The relation between short-term and long-term income effects described by (32) similarly depends on W and K.

## 3. Concluding Remarks

A discussion of non-linear cases must be left to another occasion. It would seem that these cases will turn out to be either essentially similar to the linear, or else fairly intractable, since not much is known about systems of non-linear differential equations. I also have to defer a discussion of possible empirical applications of the present approach. Under this heading appear the following questions (among others): How important is the fact that K in expression (17) is not diagonal? Is it possible to obtain a good approximation of the differential equations by difference equations? What happens if income is regarded as a random variable? Can financial assets (especially money) be treated in the same way as other consumer goods? The aim of the present paper has been merely to provide a theoretical foundation for a stock-adjustment model of consumer demand, and to work out some implications of such a model.

*Harvard University* *December 1961*

## REFERENCES


Basmann, R.L. (1957), "A Theory of Demand with Consumer's Preferences Variable," *Econometrica*, Vol. 24: 47-58.

Bushaw, D.W., and R.W. Clower (1957), *Introduction to Mathematical Economics*, Homewood, Illinois.

Cramer, J.S. (1957), "A Dynamic Approach to the Theory of Consumer Demand," *Review of Economic Studies*, Vol. 24, pp. 73-86.

DeWolff, P. (1938), "Demand for Passenger Cars in the United States," *Econometrica*, Vol. 6, pp. 113-29.

Evans, G.C. (1930), **Mathematical Introduction to Economics**, New York.

Houthakker, H.S., and J. Haldi (1960), "Household Investment in Automobiles," in **Consumption and Savings** (ed. by Friend and Jones), Vol. 1, pp. 175-224.

Nerlove, M., and W. Addison (1958), "Statistical Estimation of Long-run Elasticities of Supply and Demand," *Journal of Farm Economics*, Vol. 60, pp. 861-80.

Roos, C.F. (1925): "A Mathematical Theory of Competition," *American Journal of Mathematics*, Vol. 47, pp. 163-75.

Samuelson, P.A. (1947), **Foundations of Economic Analysis**, Harvard University Press.

Stone, R., and D.A. Rowe (1957), "The Market Demand for Durable Goods," *Econometrica*, Vol. 25, pp. 423-43.

Theil, H. (1951) **De Invloed van de Voorraden op het Consumentengedrag**, Amsterdam, Poortpers.

Tobin, J., and H.S. Houthakker (1951), "The Effects of Rationing on Demand Elasticities," *Review of Economic Studies*, Vol. 18, pp. 140-53.

Watts, H.W., and J. Tobin (1960), "Consumer Expenditures and the Capital Account," in *Consumption and Savings* (ed. by Friend and Jones), Vol. 2, pp. 1-48.

# PROPOSED TECHNIQUE FOR ESTIMATING DEMAND FUNCTIONS FROM TIME SERIES

H.S. HOUTHAKKER
*Henry Lee Professor of Economics*
*Department of Economics*
*Harvard University*
*Littauer Center*
*Cambridge, MA 02138*

The estimating technique is based on a simplified version of the theory in my paper "Dynamic Demand Functions," presented at the Christmas 1961 meetings of the Econometric Society (an abstract will appear in *Econometrica*, July 1962); it resembles the method introduced by Stone and Rowe and later modified by Nerlove.

The basic equations of this simplified version are

$$q_t = \alpha + \beta s_t + \gamma y_t , \tag{1}$$

where $q_t$ is the quantity bought in period t, $s_t$ is a "state variable" measured at the beginning of period t, and $y_t$ is income during period t; and

$$s_t = (1-\delta)s_{t-1} + (1-\delta/2)q_{t-1} , \tag{2}$$

where $\delta$ is the depreciation rate (in percent). The "state variable" $s_t$ may be interpreted as an inventory if the commodity is durable (in which case $\beta$ will be negative) or as the accumulated force of habit if it is not.

Since the $s_t$ are in general not observable and $\delta$ is usually unknown, it is necessary to obtain an equation expressed only in terms of q and y. By combining (1) and (2) we obtain

$$q_t = \alpha\delta + \{1+\beta(1-{}^{\delta}/2)-\delta\}\, q_{t-1} + \gamma(1-\delta)y_{t-1} + \gamma y_t . \tag{3}$$

This new equation contains four new parameters, from which the original four parameters $\alpha$, $\beta$, $\gamma$ and $\delta$ can be derived. By putting $s_t = s_{t-1}$, it can easily be shown that the long-term derivative of q with respect to y is $\gamma/\beta-\delta$; the short-term derivative, of course, is $\delta$. The long-term derivative will be used for projection.

In (1) there are no price terms. These were left out for simplicity of exposition, but they can easily be put in without changing (3) in any essential way. The same applies to any other variables that may affect the commodity concerned.

The estimating equation (3) will in general have autocorrelated residuals; it also contains the lagged value of q as an explanatory variable. A three-stage estimating procedure for obtaining consistent estimates of the parameters in such an equation has recently been suggested by Lester Taylor and Thomas Wilson of Harvard; it will be tried out for the present purpose.



*L. Phlips and L.D. Taylor (eds.), Aggregation, Consumption and Trade,* 255–256.

The above applies only to time series, which will be the principal class of data for deriving demand functions. Cross-section data will also be explored, both as a check on the time series results and as a supplement to them whenever the NID breakdown is too crude compared with the S-P [*i.e.*, Inter-Agency Growth Study] breakdown.

*Harvard University* *May 18, 1962*

# PUBLICATIONS OF HENDRIK S. HOUTHAKKER

## BOOKS

**The Analysis of Family Budgets** (with S.J. Prais), Cambridge University Press, 1955, reprinted 1971.

**Consumer Demand in the United States** (with Lester D. Taylor), Harvard University Press, 1st edition 1966, 2nd & enlarged edition 1970.

**Economic Policy for the Farm Sector**, American Enterprise Institute, Washington, D.C., 1967.

## PAPERS AND CHAPTERS IN BOOKS

"Afzet en Prijsvorming van Electriciteit voor Woningen," *De Economist*, Vol. 97, June 1949. ("Sales and Pricing of Residential Electricity.")

"Revealed Preference and the Utility Function," *Economica*, New Series, Vol. 17, May 1950.

"The Effects of Rationing on Demand Elasticities," (with James Tobin), *Review of Economic Studies*, Vol. 18, 1950-51.

"Electricity Tariffs in Theory and Practice," *Economic Journal*, Vol. 61, March 1951.

"Some Calculations on Electricity Consumption in Great Britain," *Journal of the Royal Statistical Society*, Series A. Vol. 114, 1951.

"Estimates of the Free Demand for Rationed Foodstuffs," (with James Tobin), *Economic Journal*, Vol. 57, March 1952.

"The Econometrics of Family Budgets," *Journal of the Royal Statistical Society*, Series A, Vol. 115, 1952.

"Les variations de qualité dans les budgets de famille," (with S.J. Prais), *Economie Appliquée*, Vol. 5, 1952.

"Compensated Changes in Quantities and Qualities Consumed," *Review of Economic Studies*, Vol. 19, 1952-53.

"La forme des courbes d'Engel," *Cahiers du Séminaire d'Econométrie*, Vol. 2, 1953.



*L. Phlips and L.D. Taylor (eds.), Aggregation, Consumption and Trade*, 257–261.

"Electronic Computation in Economic Statistics," (with J.A.C. Brown and S.J. Prais), *Journal of the American Statistical Association*, Vol. 48, 1953.

"The Pareto Distribution and the Cobb-Douglas Production Function in Activity Analysis," *Review of Economic Studies*, Vol. 23, 1955-56.

"On the Numerical Solution of the Transportation Problem," *Journal of the Operations Research Society of America*, Vol. 3, 1955.

"Economics and Biology: Specialization and Speciation," *Kyklos*, Vol. 9, 1956.

"Can Speculators Forecast Prices?" *Review of Economics & Statistics*, Vol. 39, 1957.

"An International Comparison of Household Expenditure Patterns, Commemorating the Centenary of Engel's Law," *Econometrica*, Vol. 25, 1957.

"How to Provide the Roads for Which Users Are Willing to Pay," *Federal Expenditure Policy for Economic Growth and Stability*, U.S. Joint Economic Committee, Washington, D.C. 1957.

"Education and Income," *Review of Economics and Statistics*, Vol. 41, 1959.

"The Scope and Limits of Futures Trading," in **The Allocation of Economic Resources**, by M. Abramovitz and others, Stanford University Press, 1959.

"Protection Against Inflation," *Study of Employment, Growth and Price Levels*, U.S. Joint Economic Committee, Washington, D.C., 1959.

"The Capacity Method of Quadratic Programming," *Econometrica*, Vol. 28, January 1960.

"Additive Preferences," *Econometrica*, Vol. 28, April 1960.

"The Influence of Prices and Incomes on Household Expenditures," *Bulletin de l'Institut International de Statistique*, Tome XXXVII, 1960.

"Household Investment in Automobiles: An Intertemporal Cross-Section Analysis," (with John Haldi), **Consumption and Saving**, Vol. I, Friend and Jones (eds.), University of Pennsylvania, 1960.

"An International Comparison of Personal Savings," *Bulletin de l'Institut International de Statistique*, Tome XXXVIII, 1961.

"Systematic and Random Elements in Short-term Price Movements," *American Economic Review*, Vol. LI, May 1961.

"An Economist's Approach to the Study of Spending," **Household Decision-Making**, Nelson N. Foote, New York University Press, 1961.

"The Present State of Consumption Theory," *Econometrica*, Vol. 29, October 1961.

"Toward a Solution of the Farm Problem," *The Review of Economics and Statistics*, Vol. XLIII, February 1961.

"Exchange Rate Adjustment," *Factors Affecting the United States Balance of Payments*, U.S. Joint Economic Committee, Washington, D.C., 1962.

"Some Problems in the International Comparison of Consumption Patterns," *Les Besoins de Biens de Consommation*, Colloques Internationaux du Centre National de la Recherche Scientifique, (Grenoble, 11-15 Sept. 1961,) Paris, 1963.

"New Evidence on Demand Elasticities," *Econometrica*, Vol. 33, April 1965.

"A Note on Self-Dual Preferences," *Econometrica*, Vol. 33, October 1965.

"On Some Determinants of Saving in Developed and Under-Developed Countries," in **Problems in Economic Development**, E.A.G. Robinson (ed.), International Economic Association, 1965.

"On the Logic of Preference and Choice," in **Contributions to Logic and Methodology in Honor of J.M. Bochenski**, A.T. Tymieniecka & C. Parsons (eds.), North-Holland Publishing Company, Amsterdam, 1965.

"Formation d'habitude et ajustement de stock dans l'analyse de la demande," (with Lester D. Taylor), *Economie Appliquée*, 1966.

"Future of the International Monetary System," *Economic Quarterly Review*, December 1968.

"Normal Backwardation," in **Value Capital and Growth**, N. Wolfe (ed.), Edinburgh University Press, 1968.

"The Statistical Foundation of an Incomes Policy," *American Statistical Association Proceedings*, 1968.

"Income and Price Elasticities in World Trade," (with Stephen Magee) *Review of Economics and Statistics*, Vol. LI, May 1969.

"Dynamic Demand Analyses for Gasoline and Residential Electricity," (with Philip K. Verleger, Jr. and Dennis P. Sheehan) *American Journal of Agricultural Economics*, Vol. 56, May 1974.

"The Size Distribution of Labour Incomes Derived from the Distribution of Aptitudes," **Econometrics and Economic Theory**, W. Sellekaerts (ed.), Macmillan, London, 1974.

"Incomes Policies as a Supplementary Tool," in **Answers to Inflation and Recession: Economic Policies for a Modern Society**, A.T. Sommers (ed.), The Conference Board, Inc., New York, 1975.

"Do We Need A National Food Policy?" *Proceedings of the AAEA*, December 1975.

"The Calculation of Bilateral Trade Patterns in a Ricardian Model with Intermediate Products and Barriers to Trade," *Journal of International Economics*, 6, 1976.

*The World Price of Oil: A Medium_Term Analysis*, American Enterprise Institute for Public Policy Research, Washington, 1976.

"The Economics of Nonrenewable Resources," *Die Versorgung der Weltwirtschaft mit Rohstoffen*, Beihefte der Konjunkturpolitik, Heft 23, October 1976.

"The Breakdown of Bretton Woods," **Economic Advice and Executive Policy**, Werner Sichel, (ed.), Praeger, New York, 1978.

"International Aspects of U.S. Energy Policy," *Materials and Society*, Vol. 2, Nos. 1/2, 1978.

"Purchasing Power Parity as an Approximation to the Equilibrium Exchange Ratio," *Economics Letters*, Vol. 1, No. 1, 1978.

"Long-Range Energy Prospects," (with Michael Kennedy), *Journal of Energy and Development*, Vol. IV, Autumn 1978.

"Growth and Inflation: Analysis by Industry," *Brookings Papers on Economic Activity*, 1, 1979.

"Residential Electricity Revisited," *The Energy Journal*, Vol. 1, No. 1, January 1980.

"World Energy Sources," **The United States in the 1980's**, Peter Duignan & Alvin Rabushka (eds.), Hoover Institution, Stanford University, 1980.

"A Long-run Model of World Energy Demands, Supplies and Prices," (with Michael Kennedy), **Directions in Energy Policy: A Comprehensive Approach to Energy Resource Decision-Marking**, Kursunoglu & Perlmutter (eds.), Ballinger Publishing Company, Cambridge, Mass., 1980.

"The Use and Management of North Sea Oil," **Britain's Economic Performance**, Richard E. Caves & Lawrence B. Krause (eds.), Brookings Institution, Washington, D.C., 1980.

"Competition, Regulation, and Efficiency," **Regulation and Deregulation**, Jules Backman (ed.), Bobbs-Merrill Educational Publishing Co., Indianapolis, Ind., 1981.

"Relationships between Energy Growth and Economic Growth," *World Economic Yearbook 1981*, International Chamber of Commerce Services, Paris, 1981.

"Interregional Transportation of Fossil Fuels," in *Shipping and Ships for the 1990's*, in the Proceedings of the International Conference on Supply and Demand of Water Transport, Stockholm School of Economics, Stockholm, 1981.

"The Extension of Futures Trading to the Financial Sector," *Journal of Banking and Finance*, Vol. 6, 1982, pp. 37-47.

"On Consumption Theory," **Paul Samuelson and Modern Economic Theory**, E. Cary Brown (ed.), Robert M. Solow, McGraw Hill, Inc. New York, 1983.

"The Regulation of Financial and Other Futures Markets," *The Journal of Finance*, Vol. XXXVII, No. 2, May 1982.

"Relative Prices and Floating Exchange Rates -- An Empirical Exploration," **The Economics of Relative Prices**, Bela Csikos-Nagy, Douglas Hague and Graham Hall (eds.), Proceedings of IEA Conference in Athens, MacMillan, 1984.

"The International Agenda," *Eastern Economic Journal*, Vol. XI, No. 1, Mar. 1985.

Review of Franklin M. Fisher *et al.* Folded, "Spindled, and Mutilated: Economic Analysis and U.S. v. IBM," *Journal of Political Economy*, Vol. 93, No. 3, June 1985.

"The Ups and Downs of Oil," in **Deficits, Taxes, and Economic Adjustments**, Philip Cagan (ed.), American Enterprise Institute, 1987.

## Advanced Studies in Theoretical and Applied Econometrics

1. J.H.P. Paelinck (ed.): *Qualitative and Quantitative Mathematical Economics.* 1982 ISBN 90-247-2623-9
2. J.P. Ancot (ed.): *Analysing the Structure of Econometric Models.* 1984 ISBN 90-247-2894-0
3. A.J. Hughes Hallet (ed.): *Applied Decision Analysis and Economic Behaviour.* 1984 ISBN 90-247-2968-8
4. J.K. Sengupta: *Information and Efficiency in Economic Decision.* 1985 ISBN 90-247-3072-4
5. P. Artus and O. Guvenen (eds.), in collaboration with F. Gagey: *International Macroeconomic Modelling for Policy Decisions.* 1986 ISBN 90-247-3201-8
6. M.J. Vilares: *Structural Change in Macroeconomic Models.* Theory and Estimation. 1986 ISBN 90-247-3277-8
7. C. Carraro and D. Sartore (eds.): *Development of Control Theory for Economic Analysis.* 1987 ISBN 90-247-3345-6
8. D.P. Broer: *Neoclassical Theory and Empirical Models of Aggregate Firm Behaviour.* 1987 ISBN 90-247-3412-6
9. A. Italianer: *Theory and Practice of International Trade Linkage Models.* 1986 ISBN 90-247-3407-X
10. D.A. Kendrick: *Feedback.* A New Framework for Macroeconomic Policy. 1988 ISBN 90-247-3593-9; Pb: 90-247-3650-1
11. J.K. Sengupta and G.K. Kadekodi (eds.): *Econometrics of Planning and Efficiency.* 1988 ISBN 90-247-3602-1
12. D.A. Griffith: *Advanced Spatial Statistics.* Special Topics in the Exploration of Quantitative Spatial Data Series. 1988 ISBN 90-247-3627-7
13. O. Guvenen (ed.): *International Commodity Market Models and Policy Analysis.* 1988 ISBN 90-247-3768-0
14. G. Arbia: *Spatial Data Configuration in Statistical Analysis of Regional Economic and Related Problems.* 1989 ISBN 0-7923-0284-2
15. B. Raj (ed.): *Advances in Econometrics and Modelling.* 1989 ISBN 0-7923-0299-0
16. A. Aznar Grasa: *Econometric Model Selection.* A New Approach. 1989 ISBN 0-7923-0321-0
17. L.R. Klein and J. Marquez (eds.): *Economics in Theory and Practice.* An Eclectic Approach. Essays in Honor of F. G. Adams. 1989 ISBN 0-7923-0410-1
18. D.A. Kendrick: *Models for Analyzing Comparative Advantage.* 1990 ISBN 0-7923-0528-0
19. P. Artus and Y. Barroux (eds.): *Monetary Policy.* A Theoretical and Econometric Approach. 1990 ISBN 0-7923-0626-0

## Advanced Studies in Theoretical and Applied Econometrics

20. G. Duru and J.H.P. Paelinck (eds.): *Econometrics of Health Care.* 1990 ISBN 0-7923-0766-6
21. L. Phlips (ed.): *Commodity, Futures and Financial Markets.* 1991 ISBN 0-7923-1043-8
22. H.M. Amman, D.A. Belsley and L.F. Pau (eds.): *Computational Economics and Econometrics.* 1992 ISBN 0-7923-1287-2
23. B. Raj and J. Koerts (eds.): *Henri Theil's Contributions to Economics and Econometrics.* Vol. I: Econometric Theory and Methodology. 1992 ISBN 0-7923-1548-0
24. B. Raj and J. Koerts (eds.): *Henri Theil's Contributions to Economics and Econometrics.* Vol. II: Consumer Demand Analysis and Information Theory. 1992 ISBN 0-7923-1664-9
25. B. Raj and J. Koerts (eds.): *Henri Theil's Contributions to Economics and Econometrics.* Vol. III: Economic Policy and Forecasts, and Management Science. 1992 ISBN 0-7923-1665-7
    Set (23-25) ISBN 0-7923-1666-5
26. P. Fisher: *Rational Expectations in Macroeconomic Models.* 1992 ISBN 0-7923-1903-6
27. L. Phlips and L.D. Taylor (eds.): *Aggregation, Consumption and Trade.* Essays in Honor of H.S. Houthakker. 1992. ISBN 0-7923-2001-8

**Kluwer Academic Publishers – Dordrecht / Boston / London**